LUNACY IN INDIA

LUNACY IN INDIA

A. W. OVERBECK-WRIGHT

GYAN

Published by

GYAN

Gyan Publishing House
5, Ansari Road
Daryaganj, New Delhi-110002
Phone: 011-47034999, 9811692060
E-mail: books@gyanbooks.com

Distribution Network
gyanbooks.com
India, USA, Canada, UK, Australia, France

ISBN: 978-81-212-8472-1 (PB)
First Published, 1921

2nd Impression 2023

Printed at: Gyan Press, Delhi.

LUNACY IN INDIA
Author: A. W. OVERBECK-WRIGHT

LUNACY IN INDIA

LUNACY IN INDIA

BY

A. W. OVERBECK-WRIGHT

M.D. (Pysch.Med.), M.B., Ch.B., M.P.C., D.P.H.

MEMBER OF THE MEDICO-PSYCHOLOGICAL ASSOCIATION OF GREAT BRITAIN AND IRELAND
MAJOR I.M.S.
AUTHOR OF "MENTAL DERANGEMENTS IN INDIA"
SUPERINTENDENT, LUNATIC ASYLUM, AGRA; LECTURER ON MENTAL DISEASES TO
KING GEORGE'S MEDICAL COLLEGE, LUCKNOW; AND TO AGRA
MEDICAL SCHOOL, AGRA

MENS SANA IN CORPORE SANO

LONDON
BAILLIÈRE, TINDALL AND COX
8, HENRIETTA STREET, COVENT GARDEN
1921

PREFACE

THE objects of this book are threefold: to summarise the condition of lunatics in India and the means available for treating them; to emphasise the importance of toxæmias as ætiological factors in the production of a very large proportion of such cases, and the immense aid a proper recognition of this fact is in our treatment of these conditions; and, lastly, to place on record views which a wide and varied experience of the East, spread over some nineteen years, has given rise to, and which may perhaps be of interest to the psychiatrical world.

The fulfilment of these objects has entailed dealing with insanity from many and varied aspects. Throughout my work, however, I have tried to keep the needs of the medical and legal professions in India before me, and to supply their requirements, while placing the true condition of the mentally affected in this country before my readers and indicating means for its amelioration.

A. W. OVERBECK-WRIGHT.

AGRA, U.P.
November, 1920.

CONTENTS

APPENDICES

LIST OF CASES

CORRIGENDUM

On page 20, line 28; page 29, line 1; and page 30, line 7, *insert* "original" *before* "jurisdiction."

LUNACY IN INDIA

CHAPTER I

STATISTICAL

STATISTICS of asylums and the insane for all India are practically non-existent. Those forming the basis of this chapter have been compiled from the Returns of Asylums in India for 1913 and the Census Reports of 1901 and 1911.

In the Census Report for 1911 the proportion of insane to the general population is noted as 26 or 27 per 100,000. These figures, however, "are intended to include only those who suffer from the more active forms of mental derangement," and admittedly only a very small percentage of weakminded persons are included in this category. In England and Wales the proportion is 364 per 100,000, but this includes the weakminded as well. If such were included in Indian returns, and the methods of registration were as reliable as is the case in England, I think that all who are conversant with district life, or the mohallas of any large Indian city, will agree that the latter proportion would be very much nearer the figures that would be obtained. Undoubtedly much weakmindedness remains undiscovered, owing to the simpler life prevalent among Indians calling for a much lower standard of average intelligence. Again, owing to the feeble resistance of the weakminded to disease, many such cases probably die at an early age, instead of being fostered by a kindly jurisdiction as is the case in England. Notwithstanding these two factors, however, if the returns for India were compiled as they are in England I am sure it would be found that the proportion of insane per 100,000 would increase enormously.

The effect of the spread of civilisation on the production of insanity is still an open question. As pointed out by Tredgold, where civilisation has progressed gradually the mental faculties probably have developed *pari passu*, and the wear and tear of nerve-tissue nowadays is no greater than it was some 500 years ago. The matter is totally different, however, when one comes to deal with a nation which has vegetated for some hundreds of years and then suddenly wakes to its position and strives to reach at one bound an acme of culture and learning attained, after gradual progress through centuries, by other nations of the same period. In such a case the average brain is not sufficiently developed to meet the calls upon it arising from the altered environment, and such a nation must be prepared to pay a heavy bill in nervous and mental breakdowns if it is to attain the object of its ambitions.

Asylum Accommodation.—A consideration of the Asylum Reports for 1913 shows that, out of a population of 259,716,307 (I am dealing here only with Presidencies and Provinces; the figures if Native States were included would be still more noteworthy), we have 67,836 insanes, and for the care and treatment of these asylum accommodation exists for 7,243, or, in other words roughly one out of every nine insane can receive treatment in the institutions most suited for the care and treatment of such cases.

Many factors contribute to this state of affairs. The views held by the Indian himself on the subjects of asylums and insanity, the bearing of Government on the subject until recent years, and the fact that Indian asylums are all supported practically wholly by the State, instead of by local bodies, such as municipalities, etc., have all contributed to keep such institutions antiquated and out of date. Of recent years, however, marked progress has been made towards the amelioration of the situation, and it is to be hoped that a knowledge of the true nature of insanity and its importance as an agent in the prosperity of a nation may be among the firstfruits of the progress of the Indian races, and lead to local sects and bodies forming institutions of their own for the proper care and treatment on modern lines of such cases, as well as combining in a prophylactic campaign against their common enemy.

Prior to entering upon the consideration of the figures at my disposal, it is necessary to note that the closing of Colaba and Poona Asylums in the Bombay Presidency, and the opening of the Yeravda Asylum, involving the transfer of some 287 insane, introduces an element of danger into the calculation of percentage rates from, and the basing of deductions on, these figures.

Types of Insanity most commonly met with in Indian Asylums.—The Asylum Returns for 1913 show that *mania* in all its forms comprised some 44 per cent. of the total treated in asylums during the year, of which some 13·14 per cent. recovered.

Melancholia was the cause of 15·9 per cent. of cases, of which 5·9 per cent. recovered.

Insanity due to *Cannabis indica* accounted for 6·6 per cent. of the cases treated, with a recovery rate of 18·27 per cent.

Delusional insanity produced 4·8 per cent. of cases, of which 5·03 per cent. recovered.

Idiocy was responsible for some 5·2 per cent. of cases, and *dementia* in its various forms accounted for 5·7 per cent.

Unfortunately, dementia præcox has not yet been included as a separate entity in these returns, but in my experience hebephrenia and katatonia account for a much larger proportion of cases than melancholia, though their incidence is not so great as that of mania.

The entries under *General Paralysis of the Insane* are well worth a little attention. For many years practitioners in India had it drilled into them that G.P.I. was unknown among Indians who had never left their mother-country. During the last few years prior to 1913 this had been modified to "extremely rare," but the result was the same, and many medical men in India would never dream that a case could possibly be G.P.I., even though all the cardinal symptoms were obviously present, and would pooh-pooh the very suggestion of such a possibility as absurd. These returns show that some, at least, of the Presidencies and Provinces are unbiased in their diagnosis, while others seem to be waking to a broader view of the matter.

In the light of present-day knowledge, if the general view be correct, then there must be some secondary ætiological factor, as yet unknown to us, in the production of this disease, for syphilis is as rife in India as anywhere. This being so, a double course of action seems to be necessary. Firstly, although G.P.I. is said to be extremely rare, let us, even if we accept this dictum, at least keep our eyes open for it, and not be afraid to diagnose it. In doubtful cases, or if our diagnosis be questioned, we have valuable corroborative testimony at hand. A lumbar puncture and an examination of the resulting cerebro-spinal fluid by Wassermann's reaction, the test for globulin, and a lymphocytic count will soon prove whether the diagnosis be correct or not.

Unfortunately, the state of our patients and various other factors contra-indicate this as a routine method of examination in asylum practice, unless some doubt as to the diagnosis renders it necessary in the interests of the patient and his relatives. Still, it is there to support us, and in case of any question being raised as to the accuracy of our diagnosis we have strong evidence available to support our statements.

Secondly, let those who so dogmatically lay down the absence of G.P.I. in India seek for some evidence in support of their statements, and, further, let them seek still more carefully for some reason to account for its absence with syphilis as rife as it undoubtedly is. My own views on this point are that G.P.I., though undoubtedly not seen so frequently in India as in England, is very much more prevalent than is generally believed. This smaller incidence I consider to be due to a species of partial immunity which exists among Indians and Persians to syphilis. This I believe to be due to the fact that syphilis having been widespread among these races for centuries the people have acquired a certain amount of resistive power against the *Spirochœta pallida*, which is shown by the extreme mildness manifested in the symptoms, and the comparative rarity of the severer, more distressing lesions so common in European countries.

In my experience, cases of G.P.I. are generally admitted into asylums during an exacerbation of excitement, in the second stage of the malady, and in such circumstances they are very liable to be diagnosed as " chronic mania," and to be lost sight of among the chronic insane who constitute such a large proportion of the asylum population in India.

The returns under *Insanity due to Cocaine* are interesting in view of all that has been said and written on this subject. Though its effects on the physical, mental, and moral conditions of its devotees are undoubted, and very much the same as that of opium or morphia, its direct power as a factor in the ætiology of insanity would seem to be very slight indeed, less so apparently even than that of opium, though, in the absence of any figures bearing upon the extent to which the drugs are resorted to, we can but surmise on this point.

Cases of insanity due to *epilepsy* (" Epileptic Mania " and " Dementia ") account for only 1·5 per cent. of the cases treated during the year, while among admissions it is noted as a causative factor in 107 cases, or 4·13 per cent.

The discrepancy is undoubtedly due to many cases of idiocy originating from or being complicated by this disease. On this account it is probable that the real proportion of epileptics in Indian asylums is considerably over the percentage shown among admissions, as such cases of idiocy, when once admitted, drag out their lives in the asylum, and hence there tends to be an accumulation of these cases in all such institutions.

Proportion of Females to Males in Asylums.—The proportion of females to males in asylums in India is a little under 1 in 4—*i.e.*, 1,747 females to 6,716 males—while in the general population it is a little over 1 in 2. Probably the ideas still largely prevalent among Indians regarding the nature of insanity and the true character and object of asylums have a good deal to do with these proportions, as well as their reticence about their women-folk and their unwillingness to send them from home even for medical care.

These factors also probably explain to a very great extent the very large percentage of cases of mania met with in Indian asylums. Such cases are naturally noisy and troublesome, a source of annoyance, perhaps even danger, not only to relatives and neighbours, but even to the public, and hence are much more likely to find their way to such institutions than cases of an apparently easily managed type, such as melancholia.

Recovery Rate.—The recovery rate amounts to 8·8 per cent. on the total treated, and on the admissions (taking the total recoveries, as is done in the majority of asylums), to 33·4 per cent. The recovery rate is highest among cases of insanity due to *Cannabis indica*, while cases of *Mania, Other Forms* come next.

Death-Rate.—The death-rate per cent. on the total treated amounts to 7·9 per cent., and on the admissions (calculated as for the recovery rate) to 28·6 per cent. The chief incidence here falls on cases of mania, dementia and melancholia coming next in order.

Total Treated.—The total treated during 1913 amounted to 8,463, of whom 6,716 were males and 1,747 females. Of these 2,348 were admitted during the year, among whom 1,872 were males and 476 females.

Total recoveries during the year amounted to 752, of whom 640 were males and 112 females.

Total deaths came to 677, comprising 552 males and 125 females.

Ætiological Factors.—I propose to begin the consideration of ætiological factors by a brief résumé of the results obtained from the compilation of the average annual monthly curve of admissions into Agra Asylum during the six years 1908-1913. These charts were drawn up to see if by them an explanation could be found for the falling off of the admissions during 1913 as compared with 1912. The result fully repaid the labour expended on it, and, besides giving a satisfactory explanation of the deficiency, supplies most interesting information as well. The figures worked with were small, but comprised all those available, and a consideration of the result shows that the reliability of deductions made from them is well authenticated by experience.

The curve thus obtained revealed one large wave, rising from a minimum in January to a maximum in July, and then falling again to the minimum in December. On this main wave are superimposed two secondary waves, one with its maximum in April, the other in October. The main large wave can be due to but one cause—viz., the effects of the hot weather; the corresponding fall, to the relief ensuing with the rains. The secondary wave in September and October is presumably due to malarial fever, and the secondary rise in April probably to the effects of pneumonia, chills, and malaria. A study of the six individual curves for these years goes far to substantiate these deductions. In 1913, for instance, we have a break in the primary wave due to the extremely mild, hot weather; fever undoubtedly does not account for the secondary rise in October, for the incidence of malaria in 1913 was unusually small owing to failure in the rains. Its presence, however, is explained, I think, by the unusually hot and trying weather during August, September, and October, while a further rise in November and December is probably due to distress and poverty arising from famine due to the failure in the rains. Similarly, a study of the five other individual curves, along with the climatic and epidemic records during the same years, gives us in each case a common-sense physical or climatic explanation of the variations from the average curve.

This, I submit, demonstrates clearly the tremendous part played by physical factors in the ætiology of mental derangements, a fact which is discarded too often as of small moment.

In considering the returns of ætiological factors one is at once struck by the large number of cases shown as admitted with defective histories. Such cases are not all due to faulty enquiry by any means. Pilgrims, faquirs, sadhus, jogis, beggars get their identities lost beyond hope of recovery, and if such people lose their senses it is impossible to expect any information to be available regarding them.

A *tainted heredity* figures very prominently among ætiological factors. If we include cases with a tainted family history along with those with a personal history or signs of degeneracy, then some 440 of the 2,346 admissions are afflicted from this cause, setting aside the numbers due to this cause which may be included among cases shown as "cause unknown" or "history defective."

Toxic causes come next in importance, accounting for 416 cases, of which *Cannabis indica* alone accounts for 273 or some 11·64 per cent. (These figures, however, are largely affected by the Bombay transfers, and cannot be accepted as reliable.) The small influence of opium as an ætiological factor is remarkable at first when it is considered how widespread is the consumption of this drug among Indians. It is due to the fact that opium is invariably taken in pilular form by the natives of India, and this seems a far less noxious habit than that of smoking it. Indians continue for years taking 3 to 4 grains, even up to 10 grains or more daily, without showing any tendency to increase the amount of their "dope," or to develop the general mental, physical, and moral deterioration which is invariably found among those who smoke the drug, as is the custom in Persia. Among *physical toxæmias, fever* stands pre-eminent, accounting for 81 cases, though, if any stress can be laid upon the curves already noted, it probably has figured in a good many more cases, and has been unobserved or forgotten about by the relatives.

Mental Stress accounts for 277 cases, of which 93 are due to sudden shock, and 184 to prolonged strain.

Physiological defects and errors produce 136 cases, privation and starvation accounting for 107 of these, over-exertion for 16, and sexual excesses 9.

Diseases of the nervous system were present in 128 of the cases admitted, epilepsy accounting for 107 of these.

The so-called *critical periods of life* account for 76 cases, puberty accounting for 37 and senility for 28 of these.

CHAPTER II

MEDICO-LEGAL

Definition of Insanity.—To define insanity satisfactorily is an almost impossible task. The border-line between sanity and insanity is so ill-defined, the symptoms constituting insanity vary so widely in different communities, and even in different classes of the same community, that a hard-and-fast definition cannot be satisfactorily made.

Bucknill defines insanity as "*a condition of mind in which a false action of conception or judgment, a defective power of will, or an uncontrollable violence of the emotion and instincts, have separately or conjointly been produced by disease.*"

Maudsley lays down that "*by insanity of mind is meant such derangement of the leading functions of thought, feeling, and will, together or separately, as disables the person from thinking the thoughts, feeling the feelings, and doing the duties of the social body in, for, and by which he lives.*"

Savage tells us that "*insanity is such a disorder or disease of the nervous system as prevents the individual from reacting normally as a member of the society to which by birth and education he belongs. Conduct or behaviour in relationship to society is the gauge. It is not all insanity which requires outside control.*"

Speaking in general terms, therefore, we may say that *persons are insane when, from disease or disorder of the nervous system, their beliefs and conduct become markedly changed from those of their own nation, caste, or race; when they become incapable of looking after themselves or their affairs according to the recognised methods and laws of their country, and when they become out of harmony with the community to which they belong.*

A consideration of the above shows us that there are of necessity wide differences in what would be considered insanity in different races. Thus, if a Hindu turns faquir and, leaving his family, his home, his all, wanders forth alone and unknown over the country, we think nothing of it, and it would certainly never enter into anyone's head to say he was insane. If a

European, however, donned a langote, plastered himself with mud and ashes, and wandered about in a similar manner to the faquir, he would certainly, before many hours had elapsed, be brought before a doctor for treatment as a lunatic.

This is, of course, an extreme instance; but there are many other examples which could be cited of actions which in one class and race would be considered undoubted insanity, while in another they are matters of everyday occurrence.

Legal Terms and Definitions.—The law recognises technically two states of mental disorder:

1. *Dementia naturalis*, which comprises idiocy and imbecility.
2. *Dementia adventitia*, or *accidentalis*, under which the various types of non-congenital insanity are included, and which is commonly spoken of as "lunacy."

From a legal point of view the most satisfactory proof of insanity is the existence of **delusions**—*i.e.*, a belief in the existence of something which to persons of the same race, caste, and religion would seem absurd and preposterous, and which belief influences the patient's actions and behaviour.

Many delusions may exist without unfitting their victims for the performance of their social duties, and such delusions are not considered sufficient to warrant legal interference. It is only when delusions render persons liable to injure themselves or others, in person or property, that legal interference is warranted.

Another term frequently used in medico-legal cases is, *of unsound mind* (*non compos mentis*), and its definition is by no means an easy one. According to Winslow, this phrase was first used by Lord Eldon to define a condition of mind, neither idiotic nor lunatic with delusions, but intermediary between the two, and unfitting the person for the due care and control of himself and his affairs (*Lancet*, 1872, I., p. 108). According to Amos, it would appear from various legal decisions in England that the test for *unsoundness of mind* in law has no immediate reference to the presence of delusions in the mind of a person, but rests more on his incapacity, from some morbid nervous disorder, to manage his affairs with due care and propriety. There are two conditions essential here, a morbid condition of the intellect, and an incapacity to manage himself and his affairs. Either may exist singly and yet not constitute insanity; thus there may be a morbid state of intellect without any incapacity to carry on business, and an incapacity to carry on one's duties may be due to deficient education or to physical disease. In neither of which events could the condition be said to be one of "unsoundness of mind."

Though distinctions have been attempted between the terms "insanity" and "unsoundness of mind," most authorities are, I think, agreed that the difference, if any, is purely an arbitrary one, due to "unsoundness of mind" being more a legal than a medical phrase, and implying more an inability to manage affairs, a condition which "insanity," in its wider applications, does not always imply. As regards the certification of patients, the responsibility of the medical man is by no means affected by an alternative use of these terms. According to Chitty, however, the law does recognise some sort of distinction, as it is an indictable act to maliciously publish that anyone is insane, as it imputes to him a malady rendering him liable to be shunned by mankind, while to say a man is of unsound mind is not libellous, as no human being can be said to be of absolutely sound mind.

If, however, on an examination under Chapters IV. or V. of Act IV., 1912, a medical man should use the term "unsoundness of mind," he should always have valid and convincing grounds ready to bring forward in support of his statement, and be prepared to define correctly what he means by the phrase, as questions are always liable to be put on these points if the application be defended.

Incipient Symptoms of Insanity.—In many cases in the Civil Courts a medical man is called upon to express an opinion as to the sanity or responsibility of a person at the time when a certain act was committed, perhaps some months before the medical man had any knowledge of the case. In some of such cases the person whose sanity is under investigation may even be dead (as in cases of disputed wills), and all the medical witness has then to help him frame his opinion are the statements (and often very partial and one-sided statements) of one or other party in the case.

In the Criminal Courts, too, when called upon for an opinion as to the sanity of some "under-trial" prisoner at the time when a certain crime was committed, a knowledge of the incipient symptoms of insanity is an invaluable aid. A man may have been for some time showing symptoms which, if brought to the notice of an expert, would have led to his being put under proper care and treatment, but, being misunderstood by his relatives, were neglected or disregarded until the commission of some crime led to the sufferer's arrest, and even then perhaps the true condition of affairs was not realised until some further lapse of time.

For such reasons, therefore, a knowledge of the most common incipient symptoms of insanity is very necessary to enable a medical witness to come to some valid and reasonable opinion.

Before considering generally the conditions as a whole, it would be advisable to define certain terms commonly used in detailing symptoms of mental cases to avoid interrupting the continuity of the text.

1. **Delusion.**—This has already been defined as a *belief in the existence of something which, to persons of the same race, caste, and religion would seem absurd and preposterous: this belief persisting in spite of all proofs and arguments brought against it and influencing the patient's whole life and behaviour.* Thus, at the present moment, in Agra Asylum there is a patient suffering from the delusions that her husband (who was really a farrier in a British cavalry regiment) was a most influential and important personage, knighted by King Edward's own hands; that he was rich and well-to-do, but foully murdered in South Africa shortly after the war. (He really went out there with the Imperial Yeomanry, and stayed there after peace was declared, deserting his wife.) Since then, she states, the Roman Catholics have formed a conspiracy to "obtain possession of her accumulations and children," and prevent her marrying "her sole guardian and protector, to whom she became legally engaged in the Magistrate's Court on a certain date" (her "sole legal guardian and protector," as a matter of fact, being the superintendent of the gaol where she was kept as an under-trial prisoner, and already married). Delusions may be transitory and of but little import, as in practically every case of mania. It is only when permanent or fixed that they have any vital bearing on the case.

2. **Hallucination.**—This may be best defined as a *false sense impression occurring in the absence of any external stimulus.* Thus, a person may in the silence of the night hear voices abusing him or threatening him, when there is really not a sound to be heard; or he may imagine he sees some friend, who may be dead or miles away from him, seated by his chair when no one is really present.

Hallucinations may be due to either central or peripheral causes, and are commonly associated with conditions of nervous exhaustion or toxæmias.

Patients frequently deny the presence of hallucinations, even when questioned with the utmost tact. Close watching, however, generally reveals them, the patient perhaps suddenly breaking off in the middle of a conversation to shout a reply to some question he alone has heard; or, when alone, he may be heard carrying on a conversation of which the patient's remarks alone are existent, the rest of the one-sided harangue being confined to the disordered brain of the patient, to whom alone it is audible.

Aural hallucinations are undoubtedly the most common, and, like all hallucinations, tend to be most pronounced at night. They vary from simple rustlings, creakings, and ringing of bells, up to complete sentences. Persons suffering from these may be seen sitting in a position of strained attention, with eyes fixed in the direction whence the sound is apparently coming, or may be heard carrying on conversations with, or pouring forth volleys of abuse on, some invisible being.

Visual hallucinations are frequently associated with those of hearing. They are especially characteristic of alcoholic insanity or acute insanity complicated by alcoholic excess.

Hallucinations of taste and smell are commonly associated, and generally are due to disordered alimentation. They are most typically seen in alcoholic cases. Hallucinations of smell, however, are met with in women suffering from uterine or ovarian disease, and in men addicted to the habit of self-abuse.

Hallucinations of sensation are most generally seen in delusional insanity and cases due to over-indulgence in drugs, such as morphia and cocaine. They vary from mere tingling sensations to systematised hallucinations of persecution by electricity, from feelings of being run over by innumerable insects to undergoing all sorts of elaborate tortures.

In every case where delusions or hallucinations are present, careful watching is necessary, as every such patient is a potential homicide or suicide—the motive being revenge in the former case, and, in the latter, escape from imaginary enemies.

3. **Illusions.**—These are *sense impressions where the normal external stimulus exists, but its impression is wrongly interpreted by the patient.* Thus a patient may mistake the doctor for the king, or a dog for a tiger. They are most commonly seen in delirium tremens, and are of but little import.

4. **Impulse.**—An impulse may be defined as *a sudden and irresistible force compelling a person to the conscious performance*

of some action, without motive or forethought. As a rule, persons thus affected tell us afterwards that some dark vision or cloud came over them and forced them to the commission of the deed; or that they heard a voice, generally the voice of God, telling them to do it, and that they felt they could not disobey the order. At the present moment there is a lady in Agra Asylum who suffers from the delusion that the devil, at times as a "snake" and at others as a "hawk," comes and gets into her body and puts her to excruciating torture by eating up her "vitals." She has also auditory hallucinations, by which, strange to say, she believes God converses with her and gives her orders which she must obey. She is most impulsive and unreliable, and always after a sudden assault or act of destruction, of which we never have any warning, tells us: "We are sorry. We want to harm and trouble no one, but Father" (by whom she means God) "told us to do it." The abnormal self-conceit so prevalent among the insane is evidenced here by the use of the first person plural whenever she speaks of herself.

5. **Obsession.**—This is a term applied to *an imperative idea constantly obtruding itself upon the consciousness in spite of all efforts of the sufferer to drive it from his mind.*

Very commonly such ideas merely annoy those afflicted by them through their very persistence and the inability to get rid of them. We all experience this in a minor degree when we are haunted by some tune which we cannot drive from our mind. At other times the obsession may be repugnant to the patient, whose whole being revolts at and loathes it, or it may take the form of an urgent desire for the performance of some deed against which his very soul is antagonistic.

At the present moment in Agra Asylum there is a woman who murdered her child under such conditions. She had been well-to-do, but her husband died, and adversity came her way. She was living with some distant relatives, along with her daughter. At night the mother and child occupied one room. She was worried about money and her daughter's future, and gradually felt the desire come upon her to kill the child, the only being in the world she had to love and to love her. Again and again she implored those with whom she was living to separate them, to keep them apart, and gave them her reasons. They simply scoffed, and to emphasise their incredulity took to locking in the mother and child at night, and the thing the woman dreaded and fought against came to pass. She was tried and sent to the asylum under Section 471, C.P.C.

Here the permanent and underlying wish of the person was the safety and welfare of her child, as evidenced by her efforts to remove it from danger and keep temptation out of her way. The immediate desire, *the obsession,* under certain conditions—her being left alone with her child—impelled her to the deed from which her whole being revolted, and her every action, when removed from these conditions, was antagonistic.

The **first and most common incipient signs of insanity** are, as a rule, derangements of the digestive system—dyspepsia, anorexia, constipation, etc. The patient then becomes moody and irritable, or at times apathetic and listless. His habits and temperament seem to change. He loses interest in his surroundings. He complains of headache and a feeling of fatigue without due cause. His affection for his family seems to become diminished or altered. Sleeplessness is practically an invariable symptom, and one of the earliest. A tendency to shun society is seen in many cases, and is, as a rule, the precursor of hallucinations and delusions. Delusions, however, need not necessarily exist in incipient cases of insanity, but may develop later. In some cases, although a knowledge of identity is retained, there may be a great increase in self-conceit, a patient imagining himself more talented, richer, and stronger than he really is. In other cases, again, the patient may become intensely suspicious or misanthropic from the altered state of his affections.

These symptoms gradually increase in intensity, delusions and hallucinations spring up, and suddenly the relatives and friends of the patient realise the true state of affairs, but only perhaps too late to prevent the perpetration of some crime or outrage.

Lucid Interval.—This, in a legal sense, implies either a temporary cessation of the insanity, or a perfect restoration of the senses and the mind. It thus is wholly different from a *remission,* which implies merely a temporary abatement of the severity of the symptoms.

It has been said by many that a lucid interval is only a more perfect remission, that, though the person behaves rationally and talks coherently and sensibly, yet there remains an excitable condition of the brain and a greater disposition to a fresh attack of insanity than exists in a person whose mind has never been affected. This, though undoubtedly true, is still carrying the argument a little too far, for, after all, if taken literally, it means that insanity is never cured, for the tendency to an attack is undoubtedly greater where an attack has already existed and been recovered from. Still cases undoubtedly do recover—it may be for a longer or shorter period of time—but they do undoubtedly recover to such an extent as to behave rationally and be perfectly conscious of and responsible for their actions. This is all the law implies by the term *lucid interval*, and any statement as to the probable length of the interval, the permanency of the cure, would not only be superfluous in most cases but a most foolish thing to attempt.

In some cases it is occasionally essential to prove that a lucid interval exists, or has existed at some definite period, in order to determine the validity of, or responsibility for, certain acts.

In such cases the mental powers have to be tested in the same way as when a person is being examined for insanity. Memory, reason, judgment, self-control, the affections, instincts, etc., have all to be tested, and, if it is known that any delusions existed formerly, the subject of these should be brought up casually in conversation, and the patient's manner and bearing carefully observed and his replies and remarks noted, to ascertain if these still exist. In this connection it must be remembered that many cases of *delusional insanity* get excessively clever and cunning at concealing their delusions, and only after much time and care can they be elicited. Such cases, however, can generally be got to give themselves away if they are provided with paper and pencil. They, in practically all cases, give themselves away sooner or later in their voluminous epistles, though they can often pull themselves together and write what appear absolutely sane and sensible letters to relatives and friends. Legally, it has been said, a person is responsible by law for acts committed during a lucid interval whether the acts be of a civil or a criminal nature. As a rule, however, no matter how rational the performance of a crime may appear, conviction seldom follows if it be clearly proved that the perpetrator was insane within a short period of the time of its occurrence.

Lunacy and the State.

The medico-legal responsibilities of the medical profession in connection with its dealings with insanity are heavy and varied.

In addition to our statutory duties, judges, lawyers, etc.,

constantly call for medical aid in the solution of various questions. Thus an extra responsibility is thrown on our shoulders besides those relating to the liberty of the subject, civil capacity, and control of property.

Still, again, in private practice the medical practitioner is constantly met by most delicate questions of a medico-social character, owing to the impossibility of finding elsewhere so qualified an adviser as the medical attendant.

All these duties undoubtedly call for much care, searching enquiry into facts, and, above all, grave consideration, not only of these facts, but also of the probable results of any advice given or action taken.

Disposal of the Patient.

Several trying questions arise here. Can we undertake the responsibility of treating the case at his own home ?

Should he be prevented from transacting business ?

Must he be placed under the care of attendants and a certain amount of restraint ?

Are we justified in taking the gravest action of all and sending the patient to an asylum ?

In doubtful cases, or in the early stages of the disease, these are undoubtedly serious steps to take, and involve a heavy responsibility. The patient says he is quite well, resents greatly the slightest attempt to curtail his liberty, and threatens all and sundry with the most dire consequences.

Under these circumstances the doctor should make it clearly understood that he is simply and solely an adviser, and will take no legal responsibility whatsoever for any action taken to control the patient. It is on the relatives, who have a legal right and moral duty as regards the patient, that this responsibility falls, not on the doctor, whose sole legal power is to grant certificates.

In fact, all steps taken in the treatment of the case—such as curtailment of liberty, removal to homes or asylums, etc.—should, in every case, be authorised by a relative, not necessarily the nearest relative, but any relative, whether by blood, marriage, or adoption. I would strongly advise family councils being held, whenever possible, under these circumstances, and if husband or wife be the patient, an endeavour made to have representatives of both families present at the discussion.

It must be remembered also that, in treating cases in private houses, any attendants are technically and legally the servants of the relatives and under their orders, however much, in fact, they may be under the doctor's deputed authority.

In India a patient can be treated in his own home without certification as long as his friends desire, and so long as he is under proper control and not badly treated. Ill-treatment of an insane, besides being a reason for his confinement in an asylum, also renders those responsible for it liable to heavy punishment (Section 15 (2), Act IV. of 1912).

Admission into Asylums.

1. **On a Petition from the Patient himself.**—Any person in charge of an asylum, with the consent of two of the visitors of the asylum, on a written application from the intending boarder, may receive and lodge as a boarder in such asylum any person who is desirous of submitting himself to treatment (Section 4 (1), Act IV., 1912).

2. **Reception Orders on Petition of Relatives or Others.**—The husband or wife, or any other relative of the patient, may submit an application for a reception order to the magistrate within whose jurisdiction the lunatic ordinarily resides. If such petition be presented by anyone else it must contain a statement as to why it is not submitted by a relative, of the connection of the petitioner with the alleged lunatic, and of the circumstances under which he presents the petition. No person can present a petition who has not attained the age of majority, as determined by the law to which he is subject, or who has not seen the patient personally within fourteen days before the presentation of the petition.

The *petition* must be in the prescribed form (App. I., Form I., *q.v.*), and must be signed and verified by the petitioner, and the statement of prescribed particulars (App. I., Form I.) must be signed and verified by the person making such statement. It must be supported by two *medical certificates*, in due order (App. I., Form III.), on separate forms. One of these must be from a gazetted medical officer, or a medical practitioner declared by general or special order of the Local Government a medical officer for the purposes of this Act. If either certificate be signed by any relative, partner, or assistant of the lunatic or the petitioner, this fact should be noted in the petition, and where the person signing is a relative the exact degree of relationship should also be given. If any previous application has been made in any Court for an enquiry into the mental capacity of the alleged lunatic, this must also be noted, and a certified copy of the order made thereon should be attached to the petition.

On receipt of the petition, the magistrate, if he considers there are grounds for proceeding further, must personally examine the alleged lunatic, unless for reasons, which he records in writing, he considers this inadvisable or inexpedient.

If satisfied, he may at once grant a reception order (App. I., Form II.). Failing this, he must fix a date (notification of which must be sent to the petitioner and to any others to whom notice should be given in the opinion of the magistrate) for the consideration of the petition. The magistrate may also pass such orders as he thinks fit for the suitable custody of the alleged lunatic pending the conclusion of the enquiry.

On considering the petition the magistrate may make a reception order (App. I., Form II.), or dismiss the petition, or adjourn the same for further evidence or enquiry. He may also make such orders as to payment of costs as he thinks fit.

If the petition be dismissed the magistrate must record his reasons in writing, and the petitioner must be furnished with a copy of the order.

No reception order can be made under petition, except in the case of a lunatic who is dangerous and unfit to be at large, unless the magistrate is satisfied that the person in charge of an asylum is willing to receive the lunatic, or the petitioner or some other person gives an undertaking to pay for the maintenance of the lunatic (Sections 5 to 11, Act IV., 1912).

This section is only applicable to those Presidencies and Provinces where the Local Government has passed orders for its adoption.

3. **Reception Orders otherwise than by Petition.**—*Any European subject to the terms of the Army Act,* and declared a lunatic, under the military regulations in force at the time, may be removed to an asylum which has been duly authorised for the purpose by the Governor-General in Council, on a reception order (App. I., Form IV.), signed by any administrative medical officer to whom such removal may seem necessary (Section 12, Act IV., 1912).

The question as to whom Section 12 of Act IV. of 1912 extends has given rise to much discussion, but Army Regulations and Orders are clear on that point.

Prisoners of war, being under military control and discipline, naturally come under it whether European or Asiatic. British soldiers domiciled in the United Kingdom or the Colonies also come under its terms.

British soldiers domiciled in India are not included in its category, however. King's Regulations, para. 392, sub-para. xvi., amended by Army Order (Home) No. 150 of 1918, lays down that, after being boarded once, the O.C. of the Military Hospital in which the case is being treated has the power to discharge the patient from the Army, and it is his duty to issue the necessary discharge certificate and communicate with the headquarters of the corps to which the patient belongs regarding the winding up of his accounts, etc. Such cases, therefore, should be discharged from the Army before being sent to an asylum, and should be sent in as civilian and not as military patients.

Indian soldiers also do not come under this section. Para. 358, A.R.I., vol. ii., lays down that when an Indian soldier has been pronounced insane by a medical board he shall thereupon be discharged from the Army and handed over to his relatives, or, if these be not at hand, or the patient be dangerous to himself or others, to the civil authorities for disposal as a civilian.

Every police officer in charge of a police-station may arrest or cause to be arrested all *wandering or dangerous lunatics*. Such persons must be forthwith taken before a magistrate. If the magistrate thinks fit, he shall cause such persons to be examined by a medical officer, and make any further enquiries as seem necessary. If satisfied that such a person is a lunatic, and on receipt of a proper medical certificate, the magistrate then passes a reception order (App. I., Forms V. and VI.) for the admission of such lunatic into an asylum, or licensed asylum, at the wish of the relatives of the insane. If any friend or relative of the lunatic enters into a bond for the due care of the lunatic, and the prevention of his injuring himself or others, the magistrate may, if he thinks fit, make him over to the care of such friend or relative without passing a reception order (Section 13 (1), Act IV., 1912, *et seq.*).

Every officer in charge of a police-station must immediately report to the magistrate all cases of *lunatics not properly cared for and controlled*, or who he has reason to believe are *cruelly treated*. The magistrate then causes the lunatic to be brought before him and summons such relative or other person who ought to have charge of him. An order is then passed for the proper care and treatment of the lunatic, wilful neglect of which renders the transgressor liable to imprisonment for not more than one month. If, however, the magistrate deems it advisable, he may act as in the preceding paragraph, obtain a medical certificate, and pass an order for the lunatic's reception in an asylum (Section 13 (2), Act IV., 1912, *et seq.*).

4. **Detention under Observation.**—A magistrate may, by order in writing, authorise the detention of an alleged lunatic in suitable custody under medical observation for such period, not exceeding ten days, as may seem to him necessary to determine the state of the person's mind. Such period may be extended from time to time by further orders for periods not exceeding ten days, if such extensions seem necessary to the magistrate. In any case no person can be detained for any period longer than thirty days (Section 16, Act IV., 1912).

In Presidency towns and Rangoon the Commissioner of Police has magisterial powers in the above respects, and any officer of the police force not below the rank of an inspector has the powers of an officer in charge of a police-station (Section 17, Act IV., 1912).

5. **Detention pending Removal to an Asylum.**—When a reception order has been passed, the magistrate, for reasons which he must record in writing, may direct that the lunatic may be detained in suitable custody pending his removal to an asylum (Section 23, Act IV., 1912).

Reception after Inquisition.

A lunatic, so found by inquisition, may, in the case of those subject to the jurisdiction of the High Courts of Fort William, Madras, and Bombay, be admitted into an asylum on an order made by, or under, the High Courts (Chapter IV., Act IV., 1912). In the case of those subject to the jurisdiction of a District Court, a similar order from the District Court is sufficient (Chapter V., Act IV., 1912). In such cases the Court passing the order must, on the application of the person in charge of the asylum, make an order for the payment of the cost of maintenance of the lunatic in the asylum, and direct the recovery of such sums from the estate of the lunatic or of any person legally bound to maintain him. Where no adequate means of support exists, the Court certifies to the fact in lieu of passing the above order (Sections 25 and 26, Act IV., 1912).

Medical Certificates, etc.

Every certificate under this Act (Act IV., 1912) must be signed by a medical officer or practitioner, as the case may be, and must be in the prescribed form. It must contain a concise statement of the facts observed by the person certifying which led him to the conclusion of insanity, and these facts should be clearly differentiated from those communicated to him by others. All such certificates are of the character of evidence, and have the same weight as if verified on oath (Section 18, Act IV., 1912).

No reception order can be passed unless the person, or each person, certifying to insanity, has examined the alleged lunatic not more than seven clear days before the presentation of the petition, or, in all other cases, not more than seven clear days before the passing of the order. Where two certificates are required, those signing the certificates must examine the alleged lunatic separately from each other (Section 19, Act IV., 1912).

No magistrate can make a reception order for the admission of any lunatic into any Government asylum outside the province in which he holds jurisdiction, unless by any general or special order of the Governor-General in Council (Section 22, Act IV., 1912).

Certification of Patient.

The grounds for certifying a patient and sending him to an asylum are not solely danger accruing to the patient or the public by his remaining at large, but, firstly and mainly, the due care and treatment of the case. This being so, the medical man's first duty is to decide on the definite reasons for such a course. Having done this, he must then convince the patient's relatives of the necessity for certification. In doing this, avoid pressing them if they seem disinclined or averse to take such action. Simply explain the reasons for the step, point out the risks, and that the responsibility lies on them and not on the doctor. There is always a chance that certification may be the cause of legal action, and, in some rare cases, it may be necessary before certification to get a letter from some responsible person protecting you from such risk. As a rule, however, no action can stand if there is no reasonable ground for imputing to the doctor want of good faith or reasonable care. In the case of beggars and others sent up for examination by the police, etc., the chief responsibility undoubtedly lies on the medical man to whom the question of asylum treatment is referred, and on whose opinion the authorities are obliged to act.

In certification the first thing, of course, to decide is, "Is the patient insane?" Having decided this, endeavour to find what form of insanity the patient labours under, making use of any signs of mental disease observed by yourself, and also any facts proving it told to you by others who have seen the patient.

Next arises the question, "Is the patient a proper person to be detained under care and treatment?" The chief grounds for this are: (*a*) danger to himself or others; (*b*) disturbance of the public peace; (*c*) inability to care for or manage himself and his affairs; (*d*) acute mental symptoms of any kind; (*e*) amenability to curative treatment which cannot be applied without certification. Various questions—social, monetary, and domestic—have to be determined here. One has to decide the reasons for his removal from home; how he will regard it after his recovery; how it will affect his business; and, last and not least, what legal risk there is to oneself and his relations. If you cannot decide all these in one interview with the patient, see him, if necessary, several times, and make sure of your facts and reasons in every way. Having done so, then complete the first and legal part of the form with as much care as if you were answering an important question in an examination.

Then comes the "facts indicating insanity observed by myself." Think of what the patient says, and how he says it; of what he does, and how he does it; and of what he looks like. Put in first the most evident and indisputable insane delusions the patient labours under, as crisply and concisely as you can. Next note mutism, incoherence of speech, shouting, outrageous conduct, loss of memory, volition, or reasoning power. Where-ever possible quote verbatim from the patient some phrase or remark of convincing proof. In writing up delusions it is at times necessary to enter "Which is a delusion" after them; thus, "Says he owns 10 lakhs of rupees" might possibly be true, and would require explanation; but, "Says he is Allah," requires no remark. Note next the patient's appearance, expression, and manner, and, if you have known him before, note any changes from his normal condition. Avoid giving facts that do not indicate insanity; but in some cases, where such clear evidence as above is not available, lesser things put in a cumulative way might suffice us. Thus, "His manner is listless and his looks vacant. Speech incoherent and irrelevant. Takes no interest in anything. His whole appearance gives the impression of one unfit to manage his affairs," will quite suffice, even when unsupported by "Facts indicating insanity communicated to me by others," which are important as subsidiary but not essential points of the certificates. Here insert descriptions of aggravations of conduct and speech, of attempts at or threats of suicide or homicide, etc., and in every case note down the name of the informant. Having completed this, sign your name at the foot, and then go carefully over the whole document and ensure its accuracy.

In examining a patient previous to filling up and signing such a certificate a medical man is bound to exercise extreme care. The social stigma which attaches to any person who has been detained in an asylum is a terrible infliction to a sensitive mind, and makes it necessary that no case should ever be sent there without due cause, and that every safeguard should be taken to prevent the possibility of a sane person being incarcerated in an asylum. As remarked by Lord Coleridge (see Case II.), his examination should be a "real enquiry, a real weighing and sifting of evidence, a real serious and solemn exercise of judgment." Negligence or want of care on his part (not simply an error in judgment) renders him liable to be cast in damages, on an action being brought against him (see Hall *v.* Semple, Case I.). Obviously, a medical man, unless he has himself observed facts indicating insanity in the patient, is not justified in signing such a certificate; for to rely solely on the statements of others in such a case amounts to culpable negligence.

CASE I.

Negligence in Filling up a Certificate of Lunacy—Heavy Damages (Hall *v.* Semple, 3 F. and F., 337).—In this case the plaintiff had been discharged from an asylum on the ground of informality in the certificate. This certificate was dated July 29, but the visit and examination were made on June 13. The defendant was one of the medical men who had signed a certificate of the plaintiff's insanity. The evidence, however, went to show that Hall, although a very bad-tempered man, was not really insane, and that the defendant had relied too much on the statements of the wife and other interested persons.

Compton, J., in summing up the case to the jury, said: "The principal questions to which I desire to direct your attention are these: first, whether you think that he (the defendant) signed the certificate, untrue in fact, negligently and improperly, and without making proper and sufficient enquiries. It will be for your consideration what degree of care is necessary, so as to make out by the absence of it culpable negligence. It is not a mere mistake or error in judgment which would amount to such negligence, but you must be satisfied that there was culpable negligence. . . . And, again, you are not enquiring into an error in judgment, but whether the defendant has been guilty of that culpable negligence which I have explained and described to you—negligence in not making sufficient enquiries, the examination not having been sufficient in his own judgment." The jury found that there had been culpable negligence, and awarded the plaintiff £150 damages.

Further, the facts relied on and embodied in the certificate as facts indicating insanity must be facts which really do so. Numerous instances are quoted by Taylor,* on the authority of Dr. Millar, of certificates filled up with facts other than "good facts," or facts really indicating insanity. Some of these consist of mere statements of the existence of peculiarities of appearance or temper, not of themselves sufficient to show the existence of insanity—*e.g.*, Has an insane appearance; or, Is violent in temper, and very abusive; or, Refuses to take medicine. Others, again, are statements either to the effect that the individual labours under delusions, without specifying precisely what these delusions are; or statements to the effect that the individual labours under a particular belief, such as from its nature may possibly be true, unaccompanied by any definite statement to the effect that such belief has been enquired into and found to be untrue. A fact to be a good fact really indicating insanity must either clearly show the existence of a delusion, or the existence of such conduct as cannot be accounted for on the supposition of sanity.

Immense tact is often required to bring out the real condition of the patient's mind even when one knows on good evidence that he is insane, and still more so is this the case when he knows or thinks you are a doctor come to certi y him. In all cases find out all you can about a patient beforehand, and especially regarding hallucinations or delusions, if such exist; but even

* Taylor, "Medical Jurisprudence," ii., p. 512.

then in some cases you will find it hard—in fact, impossible—to get sufficient evidence for certification, even though you know the man to be a dangerous lunatic.

Degree of Mental Incapacity justifying sending to an Asylum.

By the law of both India and England, a medical man in relegating an insane person to an asylum must certify that the individual is insane, and that he is "a proper person to be taken charge of and detained under care and treatment."

Obviously a proper person to be detained under care in an asylum is one who, being insane,* is dangerous to himself or others; and medico-legal writers are agreed that this extends also to one who, by reason of insanity, is likely to injure his own property or the property of others. Taylor† infers that relegation to an asylum simply for the purpose of treatment is not justifiable; but from the remarks of Lord Coleridge, C.J., in the case of Neave *v.* Hatherley (see below), it would appear that relegation to an asylum simply for the purposes of treatment is justifiable in cases where the circumstances are such that efficient treatment cannot be employed unless the individual is so relegated.

CASE II.

Legal Justification of Restraint.—In this case Lord Coleridge, C.J., said that the examination of a person previous to placing him in an asylum ought to be "a real enquiry, a real weighing and sifting of evidence, a real examination, a real serious and solemn exercise of judgment," in order to ascertain whether an individual came within the definition of the statute of "a lunatic, idiot, or person of unsound mind, and a proper person to be taken charge of and detained under treatment. He emphatically dissented from the Attorney-General (for the plaintiff), that unless every other means had first been exhausted a person ought not to be placed in an asylum. The abuse of a thing was no proof that it had not a use, and early treatment in cases of unsoundness of mind was of the very greatest importance. People living in small houses had no power of making provision for such early treatment of relations who might be unsound in mind; while relegation, at an early stage, to a well-appointed asylum was calculated to have the best results" (Neave *v.* Hatherley, Q.B.D., *Times*, August 3, 1885).

* Not simply suffering from delirium of disease, which renders him a fit subject for a hospital, not for an asylum.

† Taylor, "Med. Jur.," ii., 709.

It may further be pointed out that when restraint by relegation to an asylum has been lawfully imposed, the responsibility for alleged unnecessary continuance of such restraint no longer rests with the medical practitioner under whose certificate the restraint was originally imposed.

Very rarely it happens that *certificates of sanity* are required from the medical man. These require the utmost care and circumspection, and very careful enquiry into the facts of the man's life and behaviour. I myself have known a patient leave an asylum and return some hours later with a certificate of sanity signed by some thoughtless doctor. The patient considered it a huge joke, but the doctor would have found himself in an awkward predicament if, after obtaining his certificate, the patient had killed himself or some other person. Such certificates are required to set aside an order for a committal of the person and estate (Chapters IV. and V., Act IV., 1912), and sometimes before a man can resume employment or public appointments. On discharge from an asylum in whatever condition, a discharge certificate should be always sent to the magistrate of the place to which the patient belongs, stating the fact of his discharge, whether on security or not, and his condition—*i.e.*, "cured," "improved," "unimproved."

Discharge of Lunatics.

(*a*) **Discharge of Boarders admitted on a Personal Application.**—A boarder received into an asylum on these terms cannot be detained for more than twenty-four hours after his having given notice in writing, to the person in charge of the asylum, of his desire to leave such asylum (Section 4, Act IV., 1912).

(*b*) **Discharge of Non-Criminal Lunatics.**—Three of the visitors of any asylum, one of whom must be a medical officer, may, by order in writing, direct the discharge of any person detained in such asylum. Notice of the discharge shall be immediately given to the authority under whose orders the lunatic was admitted (Section 31 (1), Act IV., 1912).

(*c*) **Lunatics detained under a Reception Order made on a Petition** shall be discharged on the application in writing, to the person in charge of the lunatic asylum, of the person who submitted the petition, provided the lunatic is certified in writing as not dangerous nor unfit to be at large (Section 32, Act IV., 1912).

(*d*) **A Person detained under the Orders of a Military Administrative Medical Officer** must be kept until his discharge under military regulations, or until the officer making the order applies for his transfer to the military authorities in view of his removal to England (Section 32 (2), Act IV., 1912).

Whenever such a patient appears fit for discharge on account of recovery, or his discharge becomes necessary for some other reason, such person must be brought before the visitors of the asylum. On the visitors confirming the recommendation for discharge, the G.O.C., or other officer authorised to order the admission of such persons into an asylum, shall forthwith direct him to be discharged in accordance with the military regulations in force (Section 32 (3), Act IV., 1912).

(*e*) **Discharge on Undertaking of a Relative.**—Any relative or friend of a lunatic may apply to the authority who signed the reception order for the release of the lunatic. A report is then called for from the superintendent of the asylum and the visitors, or one of them who must be a medical man. If this report be satisfactory the committing authority, after obtaining a sufficient undertaking (App. I., Forms VII. and VIII.) from the relative of the lunatic for his care and safe custody, may pass an order for him to be handed over to his relative (Section 33, Act IV., 1912).

(*f*) **Discharge of Persons admitted on a Magistrate's Order and subsequently found Sane on an Inquisition under Chapter IV. or V., Act IV. of 1912.**—When this occurs the alleged lunatic must be at once discharged from the asylum on the production of a certified copy of the finding (Section 34, Act IV., 1912).

Transfer of Lunatics in India.

A lunatic may be removed from one asylum to another in the same province at the orders of the Local Government, or to another asylum in any part of British India by order of the Governor-General in Council (Section 35, Act IV., 1912).

Transfer of Lunatics to England.

G.G.O. (H.D.), No. 598, dated September 17, 1875, No. 5-225 of March 29, 1877, and No. 1,289, dated August 5, 1899, lay down that **civil English lunatics** are despatched to England in June each year. The fullest and most accurate information regarding the medical history and relations of every insane patient sent to England should be transmitted with him.

Each case should be dealt with as it arises in direct communication with the G.O.C. the Division in which the asylum where the lunatic is detained is situated. Cases should be reported to the Government as they arise, care being taken to submit the medical history of the insane patient, and full particulars as to his relatives.

G.G.O. (H.D.) No. 413, dated May 4, 1905, lays down that the practice of sending a **European criminal lunatic** to the United Kingdom, under Section 1 of the Lunatics Removal (India) Act, 1854 (14 and 15 Vic., cap. 81), without previous reference to the Home Government should be avoided. Action for the removal of such a lunatic should hereafter be taken under the Colonial Prisoners' Removal Act, 1884 (47 and 48 Vic., cap. 31), under which a reference to His Majesty's Government is required before action is taken in India. When the transfer of such a lunatic to the United Kingdom is desired, a draft "order of removal" form, accompanied by a draft "warrant of removal" form, should be filled in and forwarded to the Government, with a request that the Secretary of State may be moved to make the necessary order (App. II., Forms I. and II.).

Escape and Recapture.

Any lunatic escaping from an asylum may be recaptured and brought back by any police officer, or by any officer or servant of the asylum. Except, however, in the case of criminal lunatics, or European lunatics subject to the provisions of the Army Act, this power does not extend beyond a month from the date of the escape (Section 36, Act IV., 1912).

Illegal Detention.

Act IV. of 1912, Section 93, further enacts that anyone who, otherwise than in accordance with this Act, receives or detains a lunatic, or alleged lunatic, in any asylum, or for gain detains two or more lunatics in any place not being an asylum, is liable to imprisonment for a term not exceeding two years, to a fine, or to both.

Management of Property.

Chapters IV. and V. of Act IV. of 1912 lay down the legal proceedings to be followed out in the disposal of a lunatic and his estate. Chapter IV. applies to those liable to the jurisdiction of the High Courts, and lays down that on the application of any person related, by blood or marriage, to the alleged lunatic, or on application by the Advocate-General, an enquiry may be ordered by the Court as to whether the alleged lunatic is of unsound mind and incapable of managing his affairs; also regarding his property, next-of-kin, and such other matters as may appear necessary to the Court. Such enquiry may be held by the Court itself, by any judge of the Court, or by any principal Court of original jurisdiction in civil cases within whose jurisdiction the alleged lunatic may be. The Court may require the alleged lunatic to attend at any place within twenty miles of his residence for the purposes of examination, or may authorise any person or persons to have access to the said lunatic for purposes of examination; except that where the person is a female such order will be regulated by the rules in force for the examination of such persons in other cases. The Court has power to amend the original report or to order a new enquiry if it appear necessary, and may also make orders respecting the costs of the enquiry. After the enquiry, if necessary, a committee of the person and estate of the lunatic is appointed by the Court, and the Court, by such order of appointment, or by subsequent order, grants such powers to the committee as shall be deemed necessary and proper, except that such powers shall not extend to the sale or mortgage of any part of the estate, or to the lease of any immovable property for terms exceeding three years.

The Court has power to make enquiries regarding the management of the estate, and can determine how many and which of the relatives of the lunatic shall attend such enquiry. The Court, on completing the enquiry, has power to pass such orders regarding the management, sale, or mortgage of the estate as may be deemed necessary, the committee having power to execute all such deeds and conveyances as may be necessary for the carrying out of such orders. If the lunatic be a partner of a firm the Court may order a dissolution of the partnership, and the committee carries this out in conjunction with the other members of the firm. Similarly, the Court may order the disposal of a business, of a lease or under-lease, or may assume charge of a lunatic's landed property with a view to the proper management of the same. The Court can also apply property for the maintenance of the lunatic and his family, without appointing a committee, if it be found necessary that this be done in an inexpensive manner, or in cases where the lunacy is reported as of a temporary character. The Court has also power to order a second enquiry if it be reported that the lunacy has ceased, and, if such be found to be the case, may then pass an order rescinding all past orders on such conditions as shall seem proper.

Chapter V. applies to persons not subject to the jurisdiction of the High Court, and delegates the powers of enquiry, etc., to the Civil Court within whose judicature the lunatic resides. The application in this case may be made by any relative of the alleged lunatic, or by any public curator appointed under Act XIX. of 1841, by the Government pleader, or by the Collector on behalf of the Court of Wards. Similar powers of enquiry are granted here as in Chapter IV. to the Supreme Court, and if the lunatic reside more than fifty miles from where the Court is held the enquiry may be delegated to any subordinate Court. The appointment of guardians of person and estate is practically the same as under Chapter IV., except that all proceedings in regard to the estate are subject to the control of the District Court or the Collector. The management of the estate also is to all intents and purposes similar to that laid down in Chapter IV., but, in addition, an inventory of the estate has to be submitted within six months, and an annual account of its management rendered within three months of the close of the year of the era current in the district. If the accuracy of such inventory or accounts be impugned, the Court may enquire summarily into the matter, or refer such petition to any subordinate Court or the Collector. Power is given to remove any manager, for sufficient cause, and order him to furnish accounts and hand over the estate to any other person appointed by the Court. In the event of the manager refusing to do this, or to furnish the inventory or the annual accounts mentioned above, the Court has power to impose a fine not exceeding Rs. 500. Power is given in certain cases for the Court to apply the estate for the maintenance of the lunatic and his family without the appointment of a manager, as under Chapter IV., and also to institute a second enquiry when the lunatic is alleged to have recovered.

CHAPTER III

MEDICO-LEGAL (*continued*)

Criminal Responsibility.

MEDICAL men are often called on to give evidence as to the presence or not of mental disease in persons accused of crime, to enable the law to fix or to absolve from responsibility. The forms of insanity mainly related to crime are: mania, epileptic insanity, delusional insanity, alcoholic insanity, sometimes puerperal insanity, acute melancholia, sometimes dementia and amentia, also the so-called "impulsive insanities"—*i.e.*, kleptomania, pyromania, etc.—which are very frequently seen in women during a menstrual period. Some of these cases, when complicated with the effects of drunkenness, are often most puzzling, both to medical men and lawyers, when crime has resulted. As a rule, however—and I think this is the experience of most alienists—crimes are usually committed in the incipient stages of insanity, the reason probably being that the more advanced cases have been placed under proper control and supervision, and it is those who have not yet given grounds for being restrained, and who are uncontrolled, who suddenly lose their senses or are seized by a sudden impulse and commit a crime, there being no restraining hand to withhold them. Drunkenness is not held to excuse but rather aggravate crime, though alcoholic insanity exempts from punishment.

The chief points usually stated to indicate homicide by an insane are:

(*a*) **The Absence of Motive.**—Case VII. is an example of this. Sometimes there is not only an entire absence of motive, but, as pointed out by Taylor, the act is done "in opposition to all human motives." A woman, for example, murders her children (see Case XXXVII.), or a man, known to be fondly attached to his wife, kills her. Caution, however, is necessary in judging from this character. In a murder by a sane person there may be an apparent absence of motive, simply because the motive has not been discovered. On the other hand, in cases of homicide by undoubtedly insane persons, a motive—often, it is true, incommensurate with the act—has existed, or has appeared to exist. Again, in cases of homicide by sane persons, especially in India, the motive leading to the crime is sometimes a very trivial one.

(*b*) **The Absence of Concealment of the Act.**—Cases III. and VI. afford examples of this. On the other hand, there may be considerable efforts at concealment of homicide by insanes.

CASE III.

Homicidal Mania in an Individual otherwise apparently Sane.—" William Brown strangled a child whom he met by accident, and then requested to be taken into custody. On the trial he said he had never seen the child before, and had no malice against it, and could assign no motive for the dreadful act. He bore an exemplary character, and had never been suspected of being insane " (Guy, " Factors of Unsound Mind," p. 181).

(*c*) **The Absence of Accomplices.**—This character is often present in homicide by sane persons. The existence, however, of accomplices strongly indicates sanity.

(*d*) **Numerous Murders committed at the Same Time.**—Little reliance can, however, be placed on this character. In homicide by insanes there is often only a single victim. On the other hand, in homicide by sane persons there are sometimes numerous victims, as in " running amok."

(*e*) **Absence of Elaborate Premeditation.**—To this, however, there may be exceptions.

CASE IV.

Homicidal Mania with Elaborate Premeditation under " Purity " Hallucination.—Bertha Peterson, aged 45, daughter of the Rector of Biddenden, was indicted for the murder of John Whibley. The deceased, a shoemaker, had been a teacher in the Sunday-school of Biddenden, and there had been rumours eighteen months before the murder of his having behaved indecently towards a little girl of eleven. The prisoner was much interested in the rumour, was a disciple of Mr. Stead, took a great interest in the Criminal Law Amendment Act, and appears to have allowed her attention to be absorbed by these subjects until she became even more crazy than the general run of the nasty-minded apostles of purity. She purchased a revolver and practised with it. She wrote to the deceased expressing her regret for the mistaken attitude she had adopted toward him, and asking him to meet her in the parish schoolroom in the presence of witnesses, and shake hands as a token of forgiveness. The meeting took place, and then, asking deceased to take a good look at a picture on the wall, she placed a revolver to the back of his head and shot him dead. Evidence was given of various eccentricities in the previous conduct of the prisoner, and Dr. Davies, Superintendent of the Kent County Asylum, and Dr. Hoare, surgeon to the Maidstone Gaol, in which the prisoner had been detained pending her trial, stated that in their opinion the prisoner was under the hallucination that she was ordered to shoot the man. At this point the Judge interposed and invited the jury to stop the case. The jury preferred to hear the commencement of the speech for the defence, but before its conclusion they returned a verdict of "Guilty, but insane."

This case shows the exaggerated effect that any emotional propaganda may have upon persons of unstable brain. The unfortunate woman's mind was obsessed by the pseudo-revelations of Mr. Stead's pornography, and her crime was the result of her obsession. The ease with which the plea of insanity was established is rather remarkable in consideration of the elaborate premeditation and contrivance exhibited. This case bears a striking relation to the Prendergast trial. The evidence of premeditation and adoption of means to ends shown by this unfortunate lunatic were of the same kind as those relied upon by the prosecution to prove the sanity and full responsibility of Richard Prendergast for the murder of Carter Harrison (*Journal of Mental Science*, October, 1899).

CASE V.

Murder of Lunatic for Insurance Policy (*Regina* v. *Ansell*).—Mary Ann Ansell, aged 18, domestic servant, was indicted for the murder of her sister, Caroline Ansell, a patient in Leavesdown Asylum. The prisoner insured the life of the deceased for £22 10s. Early in the present year prisoner purchased several bottles of rat poison, saying that her mistress had sent her for it. On February 22 deceased received by post a parcel containing tea and sugar; but when used they were found to have a bitter taste, and were thrown away. On February 24 deceased received a letter containing the false intelligence of the death of her father and mother, and purporting to be signed by a cousin, who, however, denied having sent it. On March 9 deceased received by post a jam sandwich, which she shared with two other inmates. All three were taken very ill, and

Caroline Ansell died. The prisoner advised her father not to allow a post-mortem examination to be made, and with his consent wrote a letter in his name forbidding the examination. The prisoner's mistress denied having sent her for rat poison or having used rat poison.

The plea of insanity was raised on the ground that, although the prisoner had never been insane, she had several relatives in asylums, and Dr. Forbes Winslow was the only medical man who could be found to say that the prisoner was irresponsible. The jury found the prisoner guilty After the trial considerable agitation was raised for the reprieve of the prisoner, and pressure was even brought to bear upon the Home Secretary by means of questions in Parliament with this object. The Home Secretary did not interfere, however, and the girl was hanged. We are clearly of the opinion that the verdict, sentence, and action of the Home Secretary were right. A more deliberate and cold-blooded murder has seldom been committed for a more sordid purpose. The deed was planned with cunning, and carried out with merciless cruelty. Of evidence of insanity on the part of the prisoner there was not a shred. It was said that she had several insane relatives, but this was denied by her father; and even if it were a fact, it is utterly out of the question that every person with an insane heredity should be held immune from punishment. Such a practice would be intolerable, as well as most unjust. That a medical man could be found to express an "emphatic" opinion of the prisoner's irresponsibility is much to be regretted, but it is satisfactory to find that no alienist could be found to endorse that opinion (*Journal of Mental Science*, October, 1899).

Case VI.

Homicidal Mania; previous Symptoms of Mental Disorder slight only.—"Prisoner, a quiet, inoffensive girl, a maidservant in a respectable family, was charged with the murder of an infant. She had laboured under disordered menstruation, and a short time before the occurrence had shown some violence of temper about trivial domestic matters." This was all the evidence of insanity exhibited previous to the act. "She procured a knife from the kitchen on some slight pretence, and, while the nurse was out of the room, cut the throat of her master's infant child. She then went downstairs and told her master what she had done. She was perfectly conscious of the act she had committed; she treated it as a crime, and showed much anxiety to know whether she should be hanged or transported. There was not the slightest evidence that at the time of the act, or at any time previously, she had laboured under any delusion or intellectual aberration. The prisoner was acquitted on the ground of insanity, probably arising from obstructed menstruation" (R. *v.* Brixey—Taylor, "Med. Jur.," ii. 564).

Case VII.

Homicidal Mania co-existing with a Quiet Exterior.—A Commissioner of Lunacy, deeply impressed with the conviction that a patient in the asylum which he was visiting was perfectly sane and fit to be discharged, in defiance of the physician's warning, trusted himself alone in the lunatic's company for the purpose, as he said, of a private conversation. In less than five minutes after they were alone, and, as the lunatic believed, unobserved, the Commissioner was throttled by his companion, and, but for the timely intervention of the physician, who had been a secret spectator of the scene, would have been strangled (Taylor. "Manual of Medical Jurisprudence," p. 743).

Examination of Alleged Insanes.

To ascertain existence or otherwise of insanity you examine:

1. **General Appearance of Patient.**—Especially (*a*) any cranial deformity (see "Amentia"); (*b*) the facial expression and gestures—these are often highly indicative of insanity, especially of its advanced or more fully developed forms; and (*c*) any peculiarities of dress, gait, or surroundings.

2. **Bodily Condition.**—Note specially (*a*) the condition of the digestive functions—these are often disordered in the early stages of insanity, the skin becoming harsh and dry; (*b*) the state of the pulse, and presence or absence of febrile symptoms—this is important in distinguishing between insanity and the delirium of disease; and (*c*) the presence or absence of insomnia, restlessness, excitement, depression, or defect of speech. Bucknill and Tuke observe that in a great many cases of chronic mania the hair becomes rough and bristling. A blood tumour of the ear (hæmatoma) ending in shrivelling, the so-called asylum, or "insane ear," is often noticed in advanced cases.

3. **History.**—(1) As indicative of the cause of the disease—the existence or absence of (*a*) congenital defect; (*b*) hereditary taint; (*c*) habitual indulgence in intoxicants; (*d*) disorders, especially in females, of the reproductive organs; (*e*) epilepsy, or other brain affection or injury; (*f*) excessive sexual indulgence; and (*g*) mental overwork, anxiety, or sudden shock. Enquiry should also be made as to whether anything has occurred likely to induce the individual to feign insanity. It must not be forgotten, however, that insanity may arise from the anxiety of mind resulting from a criminal charge. (2) As to existence of the disease, it should be noted whether or no (*a*) there has been any previous attack of insanity; (*b*) there has been any marked altera-

tion or change in the feelings, affections, and habits of the patient; and (*c*) enquiry should be made generally as to the symptoms observed at the commencement of the alleged outbreak of insanity.

CASE VIII.

Insanity due to Anxiety of Mind caused by a Criminal Charge.—A poor man, a shoemaker, was requested by two police-officers to assist them in conveying to prison two men committed on a charge of theft. The shoemaker took a gun with him, and on the order of the police-officers fired at one of the prisoners, who was attempting to escape, and wounded him severely. The shoemaker was committed to gaol as a criminal, and the event made "such an impression upon him that he became violently maniacal" (Taylor, "Medical Jurisprudence," ii., p. 496).

4. **Mental Condition and Capacity.**—Inferences may be drawn from patient's (1) answers to questions, (2) acts, and (3) writings.

As regards (1), the patient's memory may first be testeo. He may be asked, for example, his name; place of birth; as to the occupation of his parents; number of brothers and sisters or children; the date; the names of well-known persons; and may be asked to count in order from one upwards, etc. Next, his judgment may be tested; he may be asked to perform simple arithmetical operations; may be questioned as to his knowledge of the value of money, and generally as to the inferences he would draw from particular facts. While questioning him, his power of fixing his attention should be observed. Next, the existence of delusions should be searched for: if these are known, the conversation should be led to them; if not, the conversation should be led to various topics in succession. Lastly, the state of the moral feelings should be enquired into by directing the conversation to the subject of the patient's friends and relatives. This testing of the mental capacity by questions is of special importance in cases of supposed feigned insanity. Except in complete amentia, advanced dementia, or possibly also in an actual paroxysm of maniacal excitement, in true insanes, consciousness, memory, and reasoning power, especially as regards matters unconnected with their delusions, remain, at any rate to a certain extent, intact. Case XIII. is an example of feigned insanity, detected by persistently silly and erroneous answers to simple questions. Care should be taken that the questions asked are not too complex, but are such as the individual under examination might reasonably, from his education and position, be expected to be able to answer.

Case IX.

Ogston relates a case in which a medical witness put forward as evidence of mental incapacity the fact that an alleged imbecile could not tell how much per cent. £20 interest on £1,200 amounted to, though he himself (the witness), when asked to answer the same question, was unable to do so (case of David Yoolow, (Taylor, " Medical Jurisprudence, ii., p. 535).

A knowledge, too, of the person's religious beliefs and superstitions is important, as ignorance of these may often lead to grave injustice. This is particularly important in a country such as India, where so many castes and religions exist.

Case X.

An Anglo-Indian girl was certified as insane and sent to an asylum. The only evidence of insanity adduced by the doctor signing the certificate (a Protestant lady missionary) was that the patient had the delusion that some saint had given her her baby. On interrogation it was found that the girl was a Roman Catholic and, being unhappy with her husband, had prayed to her patron saint that a child might be borne, as she hoped this might bring happiness into the home. She had casually mentioned in conversation to the lady doctor that this saint had obtained the baby for her, quite a natural statement to anyone understanding the Catholic religion, but quite sufficient to be snatched at as a delusion by the narrow-minded missionary (A. W. Overbeck-Wright).

During the course of the examination it should be noted whether the individual, as is usually the case with impostors, appears to be trying to make himself out to be mad. True insanes will often argue with considerable ability that they are not mad. Others are conscious of their condition. A constant putting forward, however, of evidence of insanity should always be looked on with suspicion.

(2) As to the evidence of mental disorder afforded by the acts of the patient, it should be recollected that these in a true insane are the results of his disordered mental condition. Where delusions exist, his acts and antics are connected with them, even although the connection may be apparently inexplicable (see Case XI.). Sometimes, as Dr. Guy remarks, " the acts of the maniac evince the same forethought and preparation as those of the sane " (see Case XII.); and lastly, true insanes are generally easily imposed upon.

Case XI.

Acts apparently Inexplicable the Result of Delusion.—"I expected to be guided to prayer, but a spirit guided me and placed me in a chair in a constrained position, with my head turned to look at the clock, the hand of which I saw proceeding to the first quarter; I understood I was to leave the position when it came to the quarter. Another delusion I laboured under was that I should keep my head and heart together, and so serve the Lord by throwing myself with precision and decision head over heels over every stile or gate I came to" (Guy, "Forensic Med.," p. 186; quotation from "Autobiography of a Religious Maniac").

Case XII.

Homicide by an Insane; Forethought and Preparation shown.—"A patient confined in the Manchester Lunatic Asylum had been cruelly treated by a keeper, and in revenge killed him. He related particulars of the transaction to Dr. Haslam with great calmness and self-possession. He said, 'The man whom I stabbed richly deserved it. He behaved to me with great violence and cruelty.' After detailing the treatment, he went on: 'I gave him warning, for I told his wife I would have justice of him. On her communicating this to him he came to me in a furious passion, threw me down, dragged me through the court-yard, thumped me on my breast, and confined me in a dark and damp cell. Not liking this situation, I was induced to play the hypocrite. I pretended extreme sorrow for having threatened him, and by an affectation of repentance prevailed on him to release me. For several days I paid him great attention and lent him every assistance, and he became very friendly in his behaviour towards me. Going one day into the kitchen, where his wife was busied, I saw a knife; this was too great a temptation to be resisted. I concealed it about my person and carried it with me. For some time afterwards the friendly intercourse was maintained between us; but as he was one day unlocking his garden door I seized the opportunity, and plunged the knife up to the hilt in his back" (Guy, "Forensic Medicine," p. 187).

Case XIII.

Feigned Insanity; Silly Answers to Questions.—A widow who had bought a house, and, not liking it, wished to annul the contract, feigned insanity. When asked to count, she did so thus: 1, 2, 4, 6, 7, 8, 10, 11, 13, etc. Asked how many fingers she had on each hand, she said, "Four." Asked how many two and two made, she said "Six." To some simple questions, such as, How many children have you? How long has your husband been dead? What did he die of? What is your daughter's name? What have you had to eat to-day? What is your clergyman's name? she in each case gave an incorrect answer.

To other simple questions, such as, What year is this? How long is it since Christmas ? Where do you live ? etc., her answer was, " I don't know." Asked, What is the first Commandment ? she answered, "I am the Lord thy God." Asked, What is the second ? she gave the same answer. Said she did not know the third and fourth. Asked the fifth, she said, "Thou shalt not honour thy father and mother " (Woodman and Tidy, " Forensic Medicine," p. 900).

5. **Writings of the Patient frequently show Evidence of the Existence of Mental Disorder by the Patient.**—These may exhibit incoherence, or betray the existence of delusions; but except in cases of approaching general paralysis the legibility of the handwriting is not usually affected. Sometimes the approach of insanity is indicated by a person beginning to omit words from his writings, or spelling badly.

Feigned Insanity.

The chief points distinguishing feigned insanity are:

1. **Absence of Characteristic Facial Expression.**—In insanity, especially in the fully developed forms usually feigned by impostors, the facial expression is characteristic. In feigned insanity, this characteristic facial expression is usually absent, or if present is not persistent.

2. **Absence of Bodily Disorder.**—Bodily disorder is usually present in true, and absent in feigned, insanity. The presence or absence of insomnia should specially be noted. True insanes, except in a few types of insanity, sleep but little; impostors, exhausted by their exertions in feigning insanity, sleep soundly. Deafness and dumbness are sometimes feigned. These in true insanes are usually congenital; in feigned insanes they come on suddenly, and after the occurrence of an event likely to induce the individual to feign insanity.

3. **Sudden Attack without Sufficient Cause.**—In true insanity, if the attack is sudden, enquiry will, as a rule, show a sufficient cause for the attack. Feigned insanity usually appears suddenly, without sufficient cause, and is generally traceable to a desire to escape punishment, or to escape some undesired task or duty.

4. **Want of Uniformity in the Symptoms.**—In feigned insanity the symptoms are, as a rule, not uniform with any distinct type of the true disease. The impostor, for example, mixes acute mania with advanced dementia, etc. That variation from

distinct type is often present in a case of true insanity should, however, be borne in mind.

5. **Persistent Obtrusion of the Symptoms.**—Impostors nearly always try to convince you that they are mad, putting forward evidence of their insanity, especially when they think they are under observation. The fact of being under observation makes little difference in the behaviour of a true insane.

In many cases, a satisfactory diagnosis between feigned and true insanity can only be arrived at by subjecting the patient to prolonged observation. Suspected lunatics cannot be detained more than ten days under observation in the first instance, but the magistrate has power to prolong this period by subsequent orders for further ten days, up to a maximum of thirty days in all. It must not be forgotten that an expert witness, when called upon to give an opinion as to the mental capacity of an individual alleged to be insane, must be prepared, as in other cases, to state the grounds upon which his opinion is based.

Criminal Responsibility and the Plea of Insanity.

Every person is by law presumed to be of mental capacity sufficient to render him responsible for his acts. In criminal cases this presumption may be rebutted by proof that, at the time the act was done, the individual, by reason of unsoundness of mind, was mentally incapacitated to a certain defined extent or degree. The burden of proving this rests with those who assert it. The plea of insanity is often advanced dishonestly to escape from the legitimate punishment of crime, and this plea is sometimes too easily accepted for sentimental reasons.

The verdicts passed on such occasions are "Guilty," or "Not guilty because of insanity"; but a third verdict should be allowed—namely, "Guilty, but insane" (Sir W. T. Gairdner, Brit. Med. Assoc., 1898).

We have now to consider what is this degree of mental incapacity which must be proved before an individual will be held irresponsible, or entitled to an acquittal from the prescribed penalty of his crime on the ground of insanity.

These questions are embodied in Section 84 of the Indian Penal Code, which constitutes the law of India on the subject of the criminal responsibility of insanes. This section is as follows: "Nothing is an offence which is done by a person who, at the time of doing it, by reason of unsoundness of mind, is incapable of knowing the nature of the act, or that he is doing what is either wrong or contrary to law." The effect of this section may be stated to be as follows: Suppose it to be proved that an individual has done an act which, were he sane, would be an offence—say, for example, A. has killed B. Suppose, also, it to be proved that A. at the time of killing B. was insane. A. would be entitled to an acquittal if he, at the time of killing B., was by reason of insanity mentally incapacitated to one or other of the following degrees:

1. To such a degree as to render him "incapable of knowing the nature of the act"; as, for example, if A. in killing B. did so under the insane delusion that he was slaying a wild beast or breaking a jar; or,

2. To such a degree as to render him incapable of knowing that he was "doing what is either wrong or contrary to law"; as, for example, if A. at the time of killing B. was under the insane delusion that B. was attacking him (A.) for the purpose of killing him; for in that case A.'s insanity would render him incapable of knowing that he was acting contrary to law, seeing that A., were his delusion true, would be justified by law in killing B.

On the other hand, A. would not be entitled to an acquittal if all that was proved in regard to his insanity was that he killed B. under the insane delusion that B. had blasted his character; for in that case A., even were his delusion true, would not be justified by law in killing B.; and would be presumed, the contrary not being shown, to know the nature of his act, and also that he was acting contrary to law.

Another point requiring consideration is as follows: there is a general consensus of opinion among writers on insanity, first, that one effect of insanity may be a weakening of the affected individual's power of self-control; secondly, that in some cases the power of self-control is totally lost, the result being the production of an uncontrollable impulse—*i.e.*, an impulse, which nothing short of mechanical restraint will control, to do certain acts; and, thirdly, that such weakening or total loss of the power of self-control may occur, both in insanity accompanied by delusions and in insanity unaccompanied thereby. The question therefore arises: Suppose A. to have killed B., and the only thing proved about A.'s insanity is that, by reason of insanity, A.'s power of self-control was, at the time he killed B., weakened or entirely lost, what would be the legal effect?

To this question it may be answered:

1. That any weakening short of total loss of power of self-control would not entitle A. to an acquittal, either under Indian or English law.

2. That, according to Indian law, total loss of power of self-control would not entitle A. to an acquittal, except the court consider it proved that, by reason of such total loss, A. at the time of doing the act was, in the words of the section, " incapable of knowing the nature of the act, or that he was doing what is either wrong or contrary to law."

3. As regards the law of England on this last point, Sir J. F. Stephen* states that it is doubtful whether or no an act is a crime if done under the following circumstances: by a person suffering from mental disease, who at the time of doing the act was by such disease totally prevented from controlling his own conduct.

Hence, in a case where the question of criminal responsibility is concerned, a medical witness should not simply direct his examination towards ascertaining whether the accused is insane or not. He should, in addition, endeavour to form an opinion as to whether, by reason of insanity, the accused is mentally incapacitated to the degree specified in Section 84 of the Penal Code. He must, however, recollect that the real question at issue is the mental state of the individual at the time he committed the act. Hence he must be prepared if called upon to give his opinion as to this, and, as in other cases, must also be prepared to state the grounds on which his opinion is based. It may happen that, in order to arrive at a correct opinion, he has to take into consideration not only (1) facts which he has himself observed, but also (2) circumstances which he has heard deposed to in evidence, or of which he has been informed. It is obvious, however, that any opinion based upon circumstances not within the knowledge of the witness is worthless, unless such circumstances are admitted or proved to be true in fact; and such opinion, therefore, should be given on the hypothesis that these circumstances really exist, and should be stated to depend on such hypothesis.

Nevertheless, it should be remembered that few insane persons are wholly irresponsible. The insane in their routine treatment in asylums are punished for fits of temper or committing nuisances by withdrawal of privileges—such as stoppages of tobacco, for-

* " Digest of the Criminal Law," p. 21.

bidding them the weekly dance, or the infliction of pecuniary fines. The degrees and extent of immunity to be granted to an insane for his misdeeds have been thus formulated by Dr. Mercier:

(1) All lunatics should be partially immune for all their misdeeds; (2) every lunatic should be wholly immune for certain misdeeds; (3) very few lunatics should be wholly immune for all misdeeds (corollary, the plea of insanity, if established, does not necessarily involve the total immunity of the accused from punishment—it does necessarily involve his partial immunity); and (4) that in order to establish the plea of insanity it was necessary to prove the existence in the accused of one or more of the following mental conditions: (*a*) exonerating delusion; (*b*) such confusion of mind that the accused was incapable of appreciating, in their true relations, the circumstances under which the act was committed or the consequences of his act; (*c*) extreme inadequacy of motive; (*d*) extreme imprudence; and (*e*) the non-concurrence in the act of the volitional self (Brit. Med. Assoc., 1898).

Validity of Consent.

In certain cases the fact that an individual has given a valid consent to suffer what has been done to him affects the question of the criminality of the doer. But by Section 90 of the Indian Penal Code a consent is invalid if given by a person who "from unsoundness of mind or intoxication is unable to understand the nature and consequence of that to which he gives his consent." Hence, in certain cases, the question may arise whether a consent proved, or admitted to have been given, was or was not invalidated by the fact that at the time of giving it the giver was mentally incapacitated to the degree specified in this section.

This question may arise in rape cases, for the consent of a female to sexual intercourse may be invalid by reason of her insanity. By the law of India, proof of insanity to the degree above stated invalidates the consent. This is not so in England, where a female, even if she be insane to the degree specified in Section 90 of the Indian Penal Code, may yet be capable of giving a consent to sexual intercourse, sufficient to exculpate an accused from a charge of rape, and reduce the offence committed to a misdemeanour.

The same question may arise in cases where death or hurt has been caused. By the law of India, if a person over the age of eighteen suffers death or harm from an act done to him with his valid consent, the fact that he so consented may have the effect of reducing the offence committed from murder to culpable homicide not amounting to murder;* or may even, if the act be one coming under the description of Section 87 of the Code,† absolve the doer of the act from all criminality.

It should also be pointed out that, by Section 305 of the Indian Penal Code, abetment of suicide of "any person under eighteen years of age, any insane person, any delirious person, any idiot, or any person in a state of intoxication," is punishable with death or transportation for life, while the maximum punishment awardable for abetment of suicide of a person not coming under the above description is by Section 306 ten years' imprisonment. The degree to which a person must be mentally incapacitated to be an insane person within the meaning of Section 305 is not defined.

Capacity of an Accused to make his Defence.

In criminal cases the question may arise: Is, or is not, the accused "of unsound mind, and consequently incapable of making his defence"? (see Sections 464 and 465 Criminal Procedure Code). Obviously in such cases an expert called upon to examine the accused should direct his examination, not simply to the question whether the individual is or is not insane, but to the question whether or no the individual is mentally incapacitated to the extent indicated in these sections.

Somnambulism, or "Sleep Walking."

In this condition the higher or intellectual nerve-centres appear to be in a state of partial activity only, or, as in the higher form of somnambulism, in a state of full activity to one train of im-

* Section 300, Exception 5, of the Indian Penal Code is as follows: "Culpable homicide is not murder when the person whose death is caused, being above the age of eighteen years, suffers death or takes the risk of death with his own consent."

† Section 87: "Nothing which is not intended to cause death or grievous hurt, and which is not known by the doer to be likely to cause death or grievous hurt, is an offence by reason of any harm which it may cause, or be intended by the doer to cause, to any person above eighteen years of age, who has given consent, whether expressed or implied, to suffer that harm; or by reason of any harm which it may be known by the doer to be likely to cause to any such person who has consented to take the risk of that harm."

pressions, but inactive as regards others. In this condition, while bent on accomplishing one object, very elaborate acts may be performed, and dangerous ground traversed heedlessly, which would disconcert the mind when wide awake. Hence the mere fact of the performance of such an act does not of itself indicate that the higher or intellectual nerve-centres were in full activity at the time of its performance. This is obviously of much medico-legal importance, seeing that such acts, done during a condition of partial activity only of these higher centres, may result in the death or injury of others, and form the subject of a criminal enquiry.

If somnambulism be proved, the accused is exonerated from responsibility for any criminal act; and this is also the case if the person be suddenly roused from a deep sleep.

Case XIV.

Stabbing performed during Sleep.—"Two persons who had been hunting during the day slept together at night. One of them was renewing the chase in his dream, and imagining himself present at the death of the stag, cried out, 'I'll kill him! I'll kill him!' The other, awakened by the noise, got out of bed, and by the light of the moon beheld the sleeper give several deadly stabs with a knife on that part of the bed which he had just quitted" (Taylor, "Medical Jurisprudence," 2nd ed., ii., p. 600).

Case XV.

A Man stabbed by his Brother under Similar Circumstances.—"A Spaniard, aged 26, who had been a soldier, always of good conduct, and in tolerable health, was subject every spring to epistaxis, also to talking in his sleep. The spring of 1854 passed without epistaxis, and from this time, particularly during the night, he was subject to certain moral disturbance, for which purging was advised. Travelling with a brother, and sleeping in the same bed, he was attacked during the night by this excitement, fancied that his bedfellow was going to kill him, and, seizing a knife, he plunged it into his neck. He then went out and slept on the staircase two hours. When he awoke he had some obscure consciousness of what he had done, and on seeing his dead brother, he was in despair, and wounded himself severely. The flow of blood restored his reason, and he called for help, and after some time told all the circumstances. The man was tried for the murder, but was acquitted on the medical evidence" (Browne, "Medical Jurisprudence of Insanity," p. 241).

Hypnotism or Mesmerism.

Hypnotism or mesmerism is a condition in which hyperacuity of subjective ideation and of the power of receiving suggestions from other persons arises, owing to volition and objective restrictions having been thrown into abeyance through the influence of another individual. It is chiefly of medical interest in connection with cases of rape and testamentary capacity.

It is extremely doubtful if this state can ever be produced without the consent of the person affected, and all such claims should be investigated most closely and very strong corroborative testimony be required before they are accepted as fact. In addition, it must be remembered that, contrary to what is commonly believed by the general public, the hypnotised patient can always exercise volition to the extent of refusing to obey an injunction if he has sufficient cause to do so, or if he take exception to what is suggested. Hence the plea of hypnotism, even if proven, should have no weight in a question of responsibility.

Another form of increased suggestibility occurs fairly commonly among Malays, who know the condition by the name of "lātāh." I know of one case which occurred in Ceylon, and as possibly others exist in Southern India it is as well to mention it here. In these cases the symptoms apparently appear about the age of puberty, when, though perfectly normal in all other respects, an extremely hyperacute state of suggestibility manifests itself. With such persons it suffices but to attract their attention, and by word or sign suggest some action to them, and at once they act on the suggestion. Thus they will strike out blindly at anyone near them if suddenly told to " Strike ! "; they will fling themselves headlong into streams, and do all sorts of ridiculous deeds. From the tendency of their fellows to take advantage of them such cases are very commonly shy and retiring, but otherwise absolutely normal.

It is just possible some case of the sort might come up in connection with some crime. Ample evidence of the condition would, however, be forthcoming, and the guilt and punishment undoubtedly fall on the individual who made the suggestion.

Running Amok.

The work " amok " is a Malay word meaning, literally, " frenzied." But it is applied to the impulsive form of reckless multiple homicide, often without motive. In India it is usually associated with the delirious intoxication of Indian hemp, and is most prevalent amongst Muhammadans. In the Malay Archipelago it appears to occur independently of drug intoxication. Dr. Gimlette* considers the Malayan form to be pathological and allied to somnambulism, the individual being rendered "subconscious by the unrestrained action of his own automatic centres," and in some respects allied to the "procursive" form of epilepsy in which the patient starts to run. There is always, he says, (1) sudden paroxysmal homicide, generally in the male, with evident loss of self-control; (2) it is preceded by a period of mental depression; (3) there is a fixed idea to persist in reckless killing, due to an irresistible impulse of a purposive character; (4) there is a subsequent loss of memory. Another Malay observer† divided amok into two classes: (1) cases where the motive is revenge for a supposed or real wrong, where the assailant becomes perfectly reckless; and (2) what he describes as "orang beramok," which requires the intervention of the medical jurist to prevent irresponsible persons suffering from the penalty of the law. As the first persons injured are sometimes strangers with whom the accused is not at enmity, and whom he could have no motive in killing, the mental condition of the "amok" murderer should be subjected to prolonged medical observation with reference to the question of responsibility. In India, as in the Malay States, the law permits, or rather orders, that they be killed "at sight" owing to the extreme danger to the rest of the community.

CASE XVI.

In 1910, at Lansdowne, a dispute about gambling arose among the *kahars* attached to the hospital of the 2/39th Garhwal Rifles. One of them, becoming infuriated, seized his *kukri* and cut down his opponent in the argument. He then started on a mad run through the lines. A havildar and rifleman from the guard-room, hearing the noise, ran up to see what was wrong. They met the *kahar* careering down a steep hill path. The rifleman slipped down the *khud*, and escaped the blow aimed at him by the *kahar*, but the poor havildar was not so fortunate and was practically decapitated by the *kahar*, who continued his frenzied rush till, arriving at the guard-room, a timely bullet ended his murderous career (A. W. Overbeck-Wright).

* "Med. Archives," Federated Malay States, 1901.

† Dr. Oxley, in 1843, quoted by Chevers.

Criminal Lunatics.

In Indian asylums the so-called criminal lunatics are divided into three classes:

(A) Those unfit to stand their trial owing to their mental condition rendering them unfit to make their defence (Section 466, Criminal Procedure Code).

(B) Those who have stood their trial and been found to have committed the crime while labouring under mental disease (Section 471, C.P.C.).

(C) Those who have been tried and sentenced, and while undergoing their term of imprisonment have become mentally affected and had to be sent to the asylum (Section 30, Act III. of 1900).

Class A are detained, as a rule, until fit to make their defence, though the magistrate has it in his power to hand them over to relatives on their security if he deem it fit to do so. When fit to make their defence such cases are sent to stand their trial, and then either handed over to relatives or returned to the asylum as Class B patients according to the circumstances of the case (Sections 467, 468, and 473 C.P.C.). Under this class are included persons who, though not technically insane, are through the loss of some special sense, such as being deaf and dumb, deprived of the power to make their defence.

Class B have to spend a probationary period in the asylum without showing any signs of insanity, and then the cases are reported to the Local Government, which passes orders as to whether they may be released or not, and whether security must be taken from their relatives for their proper supervision and control (Sections 474 and 475 C.P.C.).

Act IV. of 1912 has repealed Sections 471 (2) and (3) and 472 C.P.C., and the period of probation in gaols prior to the release of Class B criminal lunatics is no longer necessary.

Class C, if they recover before the expiry of their sentence, are returned to gaol; if sane when the sentence expires, they are discharged as cured to their homes; otherwise they are transferred from the criminal to the non-criminal sections, and treated as ordinary lunatics admitted under Section 14, Act IV. of 1912.

Competency of Insanes to act as Witnesses.

In civil cases the law of India on this subject is embodied in Section 118 of the Indian Evidence Act. The "explanation" attached to this section is as follows:

"A lunatic is not incompetent to testify unless he is prevented by his lunacy from understanding the questions put to him and giving rational answers to them."

The "competency" of a witness to testify is a matter quite distinct from the "credibility" of his evidence. Hence, it may be that a lunatic who has been declared by the Court competent to testify, may give evidence which the other circumstances of the case may show ought not to be believed. As in the case of testamentary capacity, no amount of disease of the nervous system not affecting the mind renders an individual incompetent as a witness. Thus, by Section 119 of the same Act, "a witness who is unable to speak may give his evidence in any other manner in which he can make it intelligible, as by writing or by signs; but such writing must be written and the signs made in open court. Evidence so given shall be deemed to be oral evidence."

Testamentary Capacity.

Unfortunately, as a rule, we are not consulted at the time the will is made, when the real capacity of the testator could be examined into, but are placed in the witness-box after he is dead, with most imperfect and one-sided information to go on, and, probably more often than not, strong motives for those consulting us to prevent our getting at all the facts.

In regard to wills we have to take a larger and wider view of the disturbances of the mental functions of the brain than those comprised under technical insanity. The dotard, the man dazed and sodden with drink, the man racked with agonising pain, the man rendered mentally unresisting and facile from exhausting disease and the near approach of death, may all require to have their testamentary capacity tested. In such cases it is of the greatest necessity that an experienced medical man should examine impartially as to the testamentary capacity of the person before large sums of money are irrevocably dealt with in a document that above all things requires sound judgment for its validity. An important point to remember on this matter is that a lesser amount of mental capacity is needed for making a valid will than for managing property, or even for enjoying freedom from restraint. Patients in asylums during remissions of their disease, and with insane delusions that did not affect the provisions of the will, have been held to have made good wills by the highest tribunals.

When consulted in a matter of this kind one should insist on seeing the patient alone, or, at any rate, with no one but a nurse or the family solicitor present. The points then to be considered are:

1. *Is the patient free from the influence of drink or drugs, and in his usual state?*

2. *Does he know the nature of what he is about to do and realise the result of the document he is to sign?*

3. *Is he free of, and uninfluenced by, insane delusions in regard to any of its provisions, and also uninfluenced by a morbidly enfeebled mind?*

4. *Is there abnormal facility of mind from bodily disease, intemperate habits, weakness, or any other cause, or is there any undue influence exercised from without?*

5. *Make the testator then enumerate his possessions, and also all his relatives and any others he may wish to leave legacies to.*

6. *Then make him go over the particulars of the will he proposes to make, asking reasons for any disposition of property that seems unjust or out of the ordinary, or for any relatives being omitted.*

7. *Find for how long he has had these intentions, and if possible get independent testimony from others.*

8. *Ascertain, if possible, the nature of the mental disorder the patient is suffering from.*

Senile patients frequently are very emotional, and readily weep or become irritated, and this often indicates a lack of mental power and volitional resistance. Persons suffering from apoplexy or paralysis may have very varying degrees of mental power, from an almost normal mentalisation up to one of complete fatuity and want of memory.

In examining such a case one must be absolutely impartial, avoid any suggestions or expressions of opinion as to provisions to be made, and, above all, avoid influencing the testator in his views as to the disposition of his property. Also, the greatest care must be taken to avoid sanctioning a "bad will," no matter how good its provisions may be, and how much trouble and expense may be avoided by doing so, as such an act would be most improper and illegal.

Case XVII.

Validity of Will of an Insane.—Cockburn, C.J., in delivering judgment in this case, said: "It is essential to the exercise of such a power that a testator should understand the nature of the act and its effects; should understand the extent of the property of which he is disposing; should be able to comprehend and appreciate the claims to which he ought to give effect; and, with a view to the latter object, that no disorder of the mind should poison his affections, pervert his sense of right, or prevent the exercise of the natural faculties; that no insane delusion should influence his will in disposing of his property, and bring about a disposal of it which, if the mind had been sound, would not have been made. . . . But, when in the result the jury are satisfied that the delusion has not affected the general faculties of the mind, and can have had no effect upon the will, we see no sufficient reason why the testator should be held to have lost his right to make a will, or why a will made under such circumstances should not be upheld. . . . In the case before us two delusions disturbed the mind of the testator—the one, that he was pursued by spirits; the other, that a man long since dead came personally to molest him. Neither of these delusions—the dead man not having been in any way connected with him—had or could have had any influence upon him in disposing of his property. Under these circumstances, then, we see no ground for holding the will to be invalid" (Banks *v.* Goodfellow, L.R., 5 Q.B., 549; Browne, *op. cit.*, p. 191; and Maudsley, "Responsibility in Mental Disease," p. 117).

A person who is insane, therefore, may make a valid will provided at the time of making it he was not mentally incapacitated to the degree specified above. A valid will may, of course, be made by a lunatic in a lucid interval. Obviously, however, the shorter the alleged lucid interval the greater the caution which should be exercised in accepting evidence of its having occurred. Mere eccentricity will not invalidate a will, nor will any disease of the nervous system not affecting the mind. For example, a person speechless and paralysed from apoplexy may (his mind being unaffected) make a valid will. A medical man, in examining into the testamentary capacity of an individual, might ask him to repeat the principal provisions of his will, and explain their action. Ability to do so would show that the testator understood the nature, and was aware of the consequence, of the act he was performing. The existence of delusions, etc., likely to affect the provisions of the will should, of course, also be enquired into.

Undue Influence.

Undue influence exerted on a person of feeble intellect may be held to render a will invalid, although the feebleness of intellect, considered *per se*, be insufficient to invalidate it.

Aphasia in Relation to Testamentary Capacity.

The question whether a person suffering from aphasia is capable of making a will will depend upon the particular case. Each case must be judged on its own merits.

"It must be laid down as a general principle that no one could make a will who did not possess the power of understanding and producing language of some sort. In order to make a will it is necessary for an individual to be able to communicate to others by means of some form of language what he would like to be done after his death. It would not be held to be a will if a person simply indicated by signs before he died that he wanted such and such a thing to be done, nor would it be held to be a will if a person gave directions by word of mouth. A person must be capable of understanding language, so that he knew either what he said or what was read to him. That implied that he could hear and understand words if he could not read or understand pantomimic language; but if he could read and understand what he read, then it was not necessary for him to hear or understand pantomimic language. Given that a person understood what was in a document, it was not necessary that he should be able to speak in order that he might execute a testamentary deed. He might indicate what he wished by means of writing, or by pantomime, or in other ways. A complete case of auditory aphasia, which implied word-deafness and word-blindness, would be incapable of making a will, because, not being able to understand any form of language, he would, in all probability, not be able to communicate his wishes by producing any form of language. From a consideration of the whole subject he had come to the conclusion that organic disease of the brain might render a patient incapable of making a will, and that some forms of aphasia might be produced also as one of the symptoms of the organic disease; that some forms of aphasia might render a patient incapable of will-making; that auditory aphasia, if well marked, would incapacitate a patient from will-making; and that some other forms of aphasia, such as pictorial word-blindness, pictorial motor aphasia, and graphic aphasia, might render a patient incapable of making a will, although he was not necessarily mentally incapable" (Dr. W. Eider, Brit. Med. Assoc., 1898).

Validity of Contracts.

It may be sought to invalidate a contract on the ground of the insanity of one of the parties thereto. To succeed, two things must be proved—namely, (1) that the insanity existed at the time the contract was entered into; and (2) that by reason of insanity the contracting party was then mentally incapacitated to a certain extent or degree—namely, that he was incapable of "understanding it and of forming a rational judgment as to its effect upon his interests" (Indian Contracts Act [IX. of 1872], Section 12).

The law of England, however, makes certain exceptions to this general rule—namely, (1) an insane is "liable for the price of necessaries—*i.e.*, goods suited to his rank and position—actually ordered and enjoyed by, and *bona fide* supplied to him";* and (2) an executed contract will not be invalidated, especially if the parties cannot altogether be restored to their original position provided the contract is a fair and reasonable one, and the other party thereto had no reason to suppose the individual to be insane at the time of making it.†

According to the law of England, marriage is a contract. Hence, a marriage may be declared null and void on the ground of the insanity of one of the parties thereto at the time of entering into such contract. The degree of mental incapacity which must be proved in order to, *per se*, invalidate a marriage may be stated to be incapacity "to understand the nature of the contract and of the responsibilities and duties it creates" (see D. *v.* D., Case XVIII.). Weakness of intellect, coupled with undue influence, has been held to be good ground for invalidating a marriage (see Case XIX.); hence the suitability, or otherwise, of the marriage may be one of the points for the consideration of the Court.

CASE XVIII.

Question of Insanity in regard to Validity of Marriage.—In giving judgment in this case, Sir James Hannen said: "The question I have to determine is whether the respondent at the time of her marriage on the 28th October, 1882, was of sound mind, so as to be able to enter into the contract of matrimony. . . . I am of opinion that every case of this kind must be decided on its own facts. . . . I accept for the purposes of this case the

* Browne, "Medical Jurisprudence of Insanity," p. 7.

† *Ibid.;* Molton *v.* Zamroux, 4 Exch. 17.

definition [of soundness of mind] which has been substantially agreed upon by the counsel—namely, a capacity to understand the nature of the contract and the duties and responsibilities which it creates. It is to be observed, however, that this only conceals for a moment the difficulties of the enquiry, for we have still to determine the meaning to be attached to the word 'understand.' If I were to attempt to analyse this expression, I should encounter the same difficulties at some other stage of the investigation with reference to some other phrase, and I should still have to determine, on the review of the whole facts, whether the respondent came up to the standard of sanity which I must fix on in my own mind, though I may not be able to express it. I may say this much at the outset, that it appears to me that the contract of marriage is a very simple one, which does not require a high degree of intelligence to comprehend it. I agree with the Solicitor-General [for the plaintiff] that a mere comprehension of the meaning of the words of the promises exchanged is not sufficient. The mind of one of the parties may be capable of understanding the language used, but may yet be affected by such delusions, or other symptoms of insanity, as may satisfy the tribunal that there was not a real appreciation of the engagement entered into" (D. *v.* D., otherwise M., *The Times*, March 11, 1885).

Case XIX.

Undue Influence on Validity of Marriage of an Insane.—" In the suit for the dissolution of the marriage of the Earl of Portsmouth, on the ground that he was of weak, and afterwards of unsound, mind, it was proved that his servants were his playfellows, and that he was fond of driving carts loaded with dung or hay, that he was occasionally extremely cruel to his horses and domestics, etc. He was, although of age, in the hands of guardians. One of these, a solicitor, persuaded him to marry his daughter, without communicating with the relations or other guardians, and the marriage was afterwards declared void on account of the undue influence used" (Woodman and Tidy, "Forensic Medicine," p. 890).

CHAPTER IV

PSYCHOLOGICAL

To attempt anything like a full explanation of the mechanism of the mental processes in a work of this kind is, of course, out of the question. It is hoped, however, that the brief sketch attempted in this chapter may enable those who read it to form a framework sufficiently sound to act as a basis for further knowledge.

To gain an insight into the working of the "mind diseased" one must naturally have a prior knowledge of this mechanism in the healthy mind, and of this not only as it exists in its full development but from its earliest stages. Let us begin, therefore, by considering the mental mechanism of the infant, and thereafter trace out its further growth.

In the newborn infant we have but one factor, known to psychologists as **conation**—i.e., *the direction of the mental process towards the attainment of some aim*, though at first this aim is probably not recognised at all by the conscious subject. Thus, when the infant feels the pangs of hunger it probably has no idea of the special object it desires, certainly none as to its attainment. It therefore manifests its craving by purposeless movements and cries until the mother or the nurse comes to its aid and satisfies its desire. By degrees the infant, through experience, becomes more capable of supplying its own wants—from finding the nipple it advances to pointing to the bottle. As growth proceeds the mental powers increase, the use of knife and fork is attained, and, finally, the earning of money to buy sustenance.

This process is no mere raising of a structure of cognitive combinations on an unchangeable foundation—the "conatus." It is, on the contrary, the growth and development of the conatus itself: the vague craving for something (unknown), passing to a desire to suck, and thence through its various stages to the desire to earn a living.

Psychologists further demonstrate that as a conatus becomes progressively more complex each constituent part which emerges in the process itself becomes a conation—i.e., *to desire an end is also to desire the means of its attainment.* Again, it frequently happens that such partial constituents may assume an independent character, finding their satisfaction independently of the original conation, perhaps even becoming more imperative than the original conation from which they grew.

From the above it follows that *when the primary conation of a complex tendency becomes inoperative, the remainder is still capable of exhibiting a conative character.* Avarice, and various other undesirable qualities, are frequently examples of this, though this alone is not the full explanation of all cases of avarice.

A little consideration reveals in the above account two processes—an evolution of new desires *pari passu* with the decay of the original impulse, exemplifying the truth of the axiom that a *conatus in attaining its end ceases to exist.* In this way many such tendencies vanish completely; while others, falling outside the sphere of attentive consciousness, become wholly automatic.

The superposition of conation on conation described above explains the trait so manifest in human beings to " push on "— " having got so far why not go a little farther ?"

So far we have dealt solely with *practical conations*, with conations requiring for their satisfaction actual changes in the environment, or in the relations of the organism to the environment. *Theoretical needs*, on the other hand, only require an extension of knowledge and removal of doubt to satisfy them, and, for this purpose, observation and experiment, by removing conflicting alternatives, are the means of attaining the *unimpeded flow of ideas which is the object of the conation.* These gradually emerge from the practical conations as growing experience stores up " dispositions," the systematic co-ordination of which, as the child grows and develops greater complexity in the grouping of the cognitive elements, provides material for ideation.

As development continues conations arise which require prolonged trains of thought for their realisation, instead of merely bodily activity and its proximate consequences. For this it has to be foreseen when, where, and how action has to be taken to attain the desired end. In this way complex and sustained mental activity arises in the satisfaction of practical needs. Successful accomplishment of these conations brings pleasure; but difficulties which defy solution bring pain, as well because they impede the flow of ideation. as from the hindrance they present to the attainment of our desires.

The desire to assimilate himself with the society in which he lives, to talk about things which others talk of, to interest his fellows in him, leads man to try to acquire knowledge which may interest them and thus secure for him a place of honour in the social organisation. It is this motive, apart from that of practical utility, which forms the initial incentive to the pursuit of knowledge. This same motive also leads us to a sympathetic comprehension of the work of our ancestors, and incites us to endeavour to establish a similar claim on the gratitude of our descendants. In this way knowledge gradually accumulates and expands. What in one age has been attained with laborious toil and difficulty becomes in the next an accepted fact which serves as a starting-point for further investigation. Here, again, we are brought back to the fundamental position that *all mental process is conation*, and that the more complex and systematic it is the more it asserts itself as independent conation.

Cognitive synthesis is the term applied to the mode in which active tendencies define and differentiate themselves, as above described. Special emotions provide the best examples of this—the ideas or combinations of ideas arising in a mind under the influence of some strong emotion all tending to explain, justify, or gratify it. Such emotions may be stirred by some definite object; but not infrequently they are caused merely by some general organic condition, such as illness. Thus, when weak or in ill-health, a man is apt to misconstrue the behaviour of others, to resent incidents which, under other circumstances, would have been matters of indifference, perhaps even pleased him. In cases of "circular insanity" we have an admirable, though extreme, example of the influence of organic conditions in determining emotions, the alternating states of elation and depression with intervals of comparative quiet being most marked, and following closely on changes in the physical condition. Simple melancholia and simple mania also provide us with good examples of depression and elation respectively. In all these examples cognitive synthesis is impaired. In states of depression it is slow, laborious, and difficult, this very difficulty intensifying the mental pain.

In states of exaltation it is practically in abeyance—conations run riot, and disconnected impulse takes the place of the sustained pursuit of desire.

Cognitive synthesis may be said to consist of two main factors —" attention and apperception."

Attention is defined by Stout as " the direction of thought at any given moment to this or that special object in preference to others. This direction is a mode of being conscious, and, inasmuch as it is a direction of thought, it is a mode of being conscious with reference to an object." Attention is mental activity, and its work is commonly regarded as lying within the circle of consciousness. The results of its work are changes in the flow of ideas. Simple attention is best seen in the case of attention to an object, on account of the immediate pleasure it yields to the exclusion of ulterior aims. This simple attention, however, readily passes into conation by insensible gradations, and is indeed, never wholly separable from it, all ideas tending to fade, and become displaced by other ideas. In attending to anything we, as a rule, develop our ideas of it, so that the thought becomes more defined and expanded. It is clear that in this process the idea, as a content of consciousness, becomes altered. This tendency to expand the idea of an object is a conation, and is universally recognised as such, and by this means methodical trains of thought are originated.

Apperception has been defined by Steinthal as " the union of two mental groups in so far as it gives rise to a cognition." Its process closely coincides with attention, but attention is characterised by systematic unity, whereas apperception deals with the relation of the new to the old, in so far as it causes change in the old. In other words, the difference between attention and apperception is that attention is merely an attitude of consciousness towards a presented object, whereas apperception is a process of interaction between presentations and dispositions, whereby the apprehension of an object is arrived at.

Apperception involves the activity of an apperceptive system as a whole, tending thereby to produce changes in its constitution or some other appreciable alteration in it. For the due fulfilment of this some degree of attention is invariably requisite. *In the absence of attention, as in automatic action, there is assimilation but no apperception.* Stout lays down that, " Whenever, through habitual exercise, an organised group of psychical dispositions has become so preconformed to a special class of familiar experiences that it assimilates them with a certain degree of ease and celerity, apperception becomes needless." This power of assimilation and automatic action is a means of saving time as well as avoiding brain fatigue, as the exercise of the powers of attention and apperception would take a longer time than the processes of assimilation and association.

Under the term "apperception" are included all such processes as understanding, identifying, etc., and it may roughly be said to consist of the two factors, "noetic synthesis" and "retentiveness."

Noetic synthesis is defined by Stout as "that union of presentational elements which is involved in their reference to a single object, or, in other words, in their combination as specifying constituents of the same thought." According to the degree of organisation which presentational elements have already acquired, the terms *anoetic* and *noetic* are employed. For example, we must all have experienced the bewilderment of waking in a strange room, and our eyes, while we are yet only half awake, lighting on some object unknown to us. At first it is incomprehensible—a bewildering, confusing mass of formless details. This condition is an admirable example of *anoetic synthesis*. As our awakening becomes completed and we gather our wits together, we suddenly remember seeing perhaps a lady's hat, or a coat, hanging in that corner the previous night when we were retiring. So soon as we recollect what we recognised it for the previous night then all is clear, the details become defined, and our bewilderment vanishes. "*Anoetic" has merged into "noetic synthesis.*"

In other words, *anoetic synthesis* in its most characteristic form is to be found in the mind of an infant void of all experience by which those psychic dispositions, the calling up of which are essential for the process of noetic synthesis, are formed and stored away. *Noetic synthesis* is found, conversely, in its highest form in the well-read, travelled man of the world, who has lived under various conditions, in various climes, and not confined himself to one narrow groove. Between these extremes there are, of course, many grades, each gradually merging into another.

Dr. Bain ably defines **psychic dispositions** as follows: "All the permanent products stored up in the mental organisation have found their way there through a period of consciousness; they serve their function in the mental economy mainly during a return to full consciousness. Consciousness thus resembles the scenery of a theatre actually on the stage at any one moment, which scenery is a mere selection from the stores in reserve for the many pieces that have been or may be performed."

The "stores in reserve" here talked of by Dr. Bain may be regarded as *psychical dispositions* when they are considered from a purely mental aspect—*i.e.*, apart from any thought of a material nervous system, when the term *physiological disposition* becomes applicable, or if both aspects be taken into account the term *psycho-physical disposition* is made use of.

These dispositions are the results of **retentiveness.** The psychological law of retentiveness is stated by Stout as follows: "When and so far as mental development takes place through mental conditions, it does so because specific experiences leave behind them specific traces or dispositions which determine the nature and course of subsequent process, so that when they are modified it is modified."

Such dispositions tend to fade, and require to be renewed by the corresponding mental processes or by processes connected with them. Some people have greater power of retentiveness than others, the amount present in an individual being due very largely to original endowment.

Dispositions are stimulated into activity by present occurrences. At times distinct images are brought to our consciousness by such excitation, but these are by no means necessary for the continuance of our conscious life. Indeed, even when present, their influence, as a rule, is small compared to that exercised by their relations to other dispositions, near and remote, of which there is, at the most, only a vague sense experienced by the conscious mind. This is the *psychic fringe*, the halo or penumbra which surrounds the image, and on which Freud based his theory of the subconscious mind.

The excitation of dispositions is due to **association**, which may be roughly defined as the power a presentation has of arousing dispositions related to it by similarity or by contiguity. Association by contiguity is by far the commoner and most applicable for the wants of everyday life, association by similarity being only rarely met with, and then very frequently as an irrelevancy. The action of association is controlled by apperception, which confines consciousness to the centre of interest for the time being and prevents the intrusion of irrelevant ideas.

Memory is the term applied to this revival of dispositions which we have just discussed. The retentiveness of memory depends mainly on interest in the original idea or presentation concerned, frequency of repetition and congenital constitution having a determining influence in a very much lesser degree. *The serviceability of memory* depends largely on the formation of proper associations, thus enabling dispositions to be promptly aroused in their due relation to the presentation occupying consciousness for the time being.

Sensibility will be considered here under three heads: (*a*) *Psychical ; (b) Organic ; (c) Special Senses.*

(*a*) **Psychical Sensibility.**—In the earlier part of this chapter endeavour has been made to show that mental activity is the direction of mental process towards an end. In the attainment of this end the process exhausts itself, and when the end is attained the process *ipso facto* ceases to exist. The unimpeded progress of such processes causes feelings of mental pleasure, which are in proportion to the intensity and complexity of the mental excitement. Feelings of pain are felt when the process is in any way hindered or obstructed, the pain varying in intensity according to the degree of the mental excitement as well as to that of the obstruction. Thus smooth and uninterrupted progress towards an end gives pleasure, until, with the final attainment of the end, the conation ceases, and with it the pleasure terminates also. Psychic pain consists in the simultaneous stimulation and obstruction of a mental tendency.

In the waking state, therefore, it follows from the above that consciousness is never free from either feelings of pleasure or those of pain.

(*b*) **Organic Sensibility**—(i.) *Muscular.*—Muscular activity is most pleasant when the organism is fresh and in good health. The reason ascribed for this is that during rest nutriment is stored up; as this store increases there is *pari passu* an increase of excitability, so that a very feeble external stimulus may suffice to produce a large amount of muscular activity. This muscular activity tends to re-establish the neural equilibrium, which has been disturbed by the storage of nutriment, and hence the feeling of pleasure due to the satisfaction of the conatus thus originated. Where there is impediment to muscular action pain is felt. Both these feelings of pleasure and pain are not restricted to the muscles alone but diffused widely throughout the organism. This is well illustrated by the case of a schoolboy coming out of school full of life and its enjoyment, while an unfortunate classmate, "kept in" for some fault, furnishes an excellent example of the converse.

Muscular fatigue causes pain from the obstruction of conatus by tissue waste having outrun repair, as well as by the accumulation of waste products directly inimical to further action, in addition to being noxious to the body as a whole. Rest, therefore, gives pleasure in the first instance by withdrawing the attention from a conation whose satisfaction is impeded to another, which may ultimately prove a means of attaining the first, and in the second by giving the processes of elimination of waste products and repair and storage of nutriment an opportunity to re-establish neural equilibrium.

(ii.) *Sensibility of Special Organs* conforms to what has been said of muscular sensibility. Thus the feeling of hunger usually arises when, the usual hour for eating having arrived, food is not available. The stomach is stimulated to act in accordance with its special function, but its activity is obstructed, and hence hunger, or the relative form of pain, ensues upon obstructed conatus.

(*c*) **Special Senses.**—These are generally recognised as five in number—hearing, seeing, smelling, tasting, and bodily sensation. Under this last much subdivision can be done, the feeling of heat, cold, pain, pressure, etc., all of which are now known to be contained in separate minute areas of skin, and supplied each by its own individual type of nerve-fibril.

As a rule, stimulation of any of these organs becomes disagreeable when it is intensified beyond a certain point. The converse also has been maintained—*i.e.*, that all stimulations of these organs would be agreeable if not too intense; but this is not so easy of verification. According to Dr. Féré, pleasant sensations of this kind tend to increase the vigour of the nervous system generally, while disagreeable sensations have an opposite result. Pleasant sensations after lasting a certain time tend to become matters of indifference, and if prolonged still further may even become disagreeable.

When pleasing impressional experiences are revived ideally a demand for further stimulation ensues, and this explains the formation of *drug habits*, etc.

While discussing this part of our subject it will be convenient to define two derangements of sensation commonly met with in deranged mentality. The terms applied commonly to these are *illusion* and *hallucination.*

An **illusion** is a false sense perception in the presence of an external stimulus. For example, a patient in an asylum may mistake a visitor for the King or for Julius Cæsar. Another example of illusions is to be found in the diagrammatic advertisements often seen on the backs of magazines, which, on a circular movement being given to the magazine, seem to rotate.

An **hallucination** is a sense perception in the absence of any external stimulus. It is very common in asylums, where patients imagine they are visited by friends or relatives, either actually thinking they see them or that they can hear them talking to them. Delusions of poisoning and torture by unseen agency usually originate from hallucinations.

Emotion may be defined roughly as a state of mental feeling occasioned by occurrences which further or obstruct strong instinctive or acquired conative tendencies. It is generally accompanied by a nervous disturbance originating an organic reaction. It may arise from definite perceptions or may be originally caused by organic factors, such as ill-health or the consumption of drugs.

The range of emotion is enormous, the same emotional disturbances appearing in many and varied stages of mental development and for different kinds of stimuli. As a rule, emotion is agreeable or disagreeable according as the conative tendencies involved in it are gratified or thwarted.

Emotion is, as a rule, a secondary phenomenon, and presupposes the existence of some conception which causes it. The results of organic factors are, therefore, more correctly termed *emotional moods,* for in them there is but a certain general trend of mental activity which particularises itself according to circumstances.

An *emotional disposition* is the term applied to a persistent tendency to feel a certain kind of emotion in the presence of a certain object. These in the more highly developed intellects tend to become very complex, and are known as *sentiments* or *interests.*

In considering **impulse, desire,** and **will,** it is necessary to revert to the infant and the primary conatus. This conatus developing by cognitive synthesis, by degrees psychic dispositions become stored up and perception becomes possible. This may be called the *impulsive stage*, where perceptual and instinctive conations find immediate expression in bodily movement, guided by external impressions. In this stage of development there is no deliberation, no reasoning, conations are aroused by external stimuli, and action immediately ensues: the infant sees a match or candle burning, is pleased by the pretty flame and—burns his fingers. To such conations the term **impulse** is applicable, and such are generally termed **impulsive actions.**

As development continues and the store of dispositions increases in variety and amount, trains of thought, not wholly dominated by present external conditions, become possible. In this way some ideal conatus may originate an activity, itself either wholly or in part ideal, for its materialisation. To such ideal conations the term **desire** is most appropriately applied. Such desires develop in complexity *pari passu* with the general mental development. The fulfilment of rules of conduct, the attainment of ends realised previously only by ideal construction, and which can only be realised gradually and by repeated activities, ensue and reach their acme in desires which are recognised as unattainable in the present generation, perhaps never attainable in their entirety. Such conditions are very aptly known as **ideals.**

It has been shown above that impulsive action follows directly upon the conation. Under such circumstances, when two separate conations prompt to different courses of action at one and the same time, there is a trial of strength, as it were, and the stronger triumphs. With **voluntary action** such is not the case. There is deliberation. The conflicting tendencies are viewed in their relation to past, present, and future circumstances, choice is made of one or other tendency in view of these relations, and appropriate action ensues. It is really due to the development of the ego—the personality, the I—all such relations being regarded as related to self.

The term **deliberation** is applicable to this process of consideration, and when it ultimately ends in action the phrase *voluntary decision* is used. The antagonistic conation may, however, still persist and make the performance of the decision harder and more painful, giving opportunity to show the strength of the decision. To the power of thus adhering to a decision the term **will** or **will-power** is applied.

Self-control is a specialised form of will, and has been defined by Stout as "control proceeding from the self as a whole, and determining self as a whole. The degree in which it exists depends upon the degree in which this or that special tendency can be brought into relation with the concept of the self and the system of conative tendencies which it includes."

Failure of self-control may arise from three causes. The consciousness of self may not have attained a full degree of development. Organic causes may have disorganised a fully developed self conception and obstructed the full activity of its normal contents. The overpowering intensity of a relatively isolated impulse may hinder the evolution of the self concept, even though it be fully developed.

It will be as well to consider here a form of derangement of the will which is very commonly met with in asylums—constitutes, in fact, a separate type of insanity at times—and occasionally occurs to a certain extent in normal life. The derangement referred to is known scientifically as an **obsession.** It is a fixed or imperative idea which acquires and maintains such sway over consciousness that, contrary to all natural feeling and desire, perhaps even in spite of the strongest feelings of repugnance and aversion, it persists in consciousness and may even ultimately materialise its end.

In normal life this is best illustrated by the feelings of a man standing on the edge of a precipice and looking down into its depths. The idea of throwing himself down and the consequences of falling flash through his mind with intense vividness, and he feels impelled to carry out the idea, In normal life, as a rule, the will overcomes the fixed idea which has arisen independently of it, but it is always possible that the impulse to realise it may acquire sufficient strength to overcome volition and result in action.

Belief is a form of ideation involving objective control of subjective activity. **Imagination,** according to Stout, consists in a flow of suppositions connected in an ideally constructed whole, which, as a whole, is merely supposed and not asserted as actual fact.

In the pursuit of practical ends **objective restriction** is at its maximum, and in such cases we find full belief free from all play of imagination. In such cases only those ideal combinations that can be translated into corresponding perceptual experience are of use, and all others are excluded, therefore, as far as possible. The attitude of **disbelief** arises when ideal constructions break down on being translated into terms of perceptual activity.

It follows, therefore, that the lower the degree of psychical development, the less the objective control, the greater is the predominance of the subjective activity. Thus the primitive beliefs prevalent among savages are confined to the narrow circle of their practical interests, and often rest on what, to more highly developed minds, appear as very frail objective foundations. This predominance of the subjective factor in such cases is due to the mind ignoring objective data which do not obviously connect themselves with its aims and motives, and the primitive mind, with its infinitesimal store of dispositions and associations, fails to find relevancy, which becomes at once palpable with increasing knowledge, larger store of dispositions, and wider spread of associative ideas.

To the deliberation necessary for voluntary action, the weighing and summing up of objective perceptions which lead subjective activity to belief, the term **reason** is frequently applied, and the result of reason, or belief, is sometimes termed **judgment.**

Conation has a powerful influence on belief. Thus, if a negative decision were to obstruct activity, the whole force of conation is thrown on to the positive side of the scale, and *vice versa.* It is this factor which is apt to lead the strongminded to believe what they wish to believe, and is the basis of **stubbornness.** With the timid and those of a despondent nature the converse holds good, however. Such persons always look for trouble and prepare for the worst, believing that even if an alarm be false it is better to be on the safe side. This trait seems to give tone largely to the religious and superstitious beliefs of primitive races. In such cases subjective interests, combined with vivid and insistent associations of ideas, exercise unresisted control.

The **social factor** has a considerable influence in determining the beliefs of the individual common to the community in which he lives, the social acceptation of a belief serving to safeguard it against aspersions cast upon it by individual members.

The **associations of primitive races**, and their views regarding the constitution of personalities and things, differ from those prevalent in races with a greater psychological development. Whatever is habitually contiguous in consciousness with a person or thing is regarded by them as part of it and as having sympathetic communion with it. A knowledge of this belief in the personification of inanimate bodies, combined with the tinge of fear above mentioned and the influence of the social factor, helps tremendously when one comes to analyse the minds of such individuals.

It will be as well to mention here a derangement of belief which is commonly seen in many types of insanity, but found in its most characteristic type in one special clinical entity. This derangement is commonly known as a **delusion,** and may be defined as " a belief in anything which would appear impossible, incredible, foolish, absurd to people of the same race, caste, and class as the person expressing it, such belief persisting in spite of all remonstrance, argument, and proof to the contrary, influencing every action, affecting the whole thought and life of its exponent, and arising from derangement of the functions, or disease of the cerebral convolutions.

Instinct may be defined as a conate tendency of the nervous system whereby action is stimulated for the purpose of attaining definite aims. It fully occupies attentive consciousness, and from the outset brings into play whatever mental activity may have been developed.

From this it is apparent that instinctive conduct requires, as a matter of course, the exercise of attention, variation of behaviour to meet the effects of surrounding conditions on the various senses, and the power of learning by experience. **Reflex action** requires none of these; an external stimulus occurs—it is not, as a rule, even consciously noted—and the related action ensues automatically.

In accordance with the above, instinctive action becomes modified with mental development. It becomes discriminative, and, owing to its growing association with a larger number of dispositions, it becomes more generalised.

MacDougall gives the following list of instincts apparent in most adults: (1) *Instinctive fears.* (2) *Instinctive repulsions.* (3) *Instinctive pugnacity.* (4) *Instinctive self-assertion and self-abasement.* (5) *The parental instinct and the tender emotions.* (6) *The sexual instinct.* (7) *The gregarious instinct.* (8) *The acquisitive instinct.*

A more useful classification for those working among cases of mental disease is: (1) *The instinct of self-preservation.* (2) *The instinct to perpetuate the species.* (3) *The sexual instinct.* (4) *The parental instinct.* (5) *The religious instinct.* (6) *The gregarious instinct.* (7) *The instinct of self-assertion or self-abasement.* (8) *The ambitious instinct.* (9) *The acquisitive instinct.*

The *instinct of self-preservation* is far-reaching, including the obtaining of nourishment to supply the bodily wants as well as the fleeing from or warding off of threatened dangers. The first three entries on MacDougall's list are really traceable to and spring from this source.

The *sexual instinct* covers a very much larger field than that of the mere instinct to perpetuate the species. It covers all feminine and masculine traits—the gentle womanliness of the female and her desire for pretty and attractive objects around her to make home bright and cheerful; and the rougher methods of the male in his rôle as provider of sustenance and woman's natural protector.

The *parental instinct*, too, has a wider application than merely care of the family, and extends to the feelings experienced in the presence of the young, the sick, and the helpless.

The *religious instinct* is frequently wholly disregarded by many authorities. My wanderings, however, in several little-known parts of the world, and my experience in gaol and asylum work, have confirmed my belief that throughout mankind, no matter what he may profess, there is imbued a deep sense of one Supreme Being, One Who holds undisputed sway over the universe, One in Whose hands lie the powers of reward and punishment, Whose behests therefore it is incumbent upon man to obey, and Whom it is to his advantage to placate whenever possible. In those races commonly looked on as heathen and idolaters, this instinct, this belief, is still present. Such peoples, if their beliefs be carefully investigated, are found to have three clearly defined entities in the spirit world: (1) God, or Creator, Who is unique and unapproachable and on quite a higher plane than either of the two other sects. (2) Spirits, which are innumerable, are in communication with mankind, and can be controlled by mankind. These it is, or rather their representations, which form the idols of most heathen races. (3) Ghosts, or "shades," of deceased persons who are connected by origin with common humanity.

The *gregarious instinct* is manifest throughout mankind in the tendency to gather together into communities, to conform to the rules and regulations of the community, to work together for its common good, and to hold together to resist wrong and oppression.

The *instinct of self-assertion or self-abasement* is the one which shows most clearly the effect of early associations and experiences on the development of instinct. In all of us there is innate the tendency to suit our bearing or behaviour to surrounding circumstances, and as our experiences, our associations, are met with and formed in early life so do we develop into the "swanking braggart," the "knut," or the "cringing boot-licker." Not that I would by any means classify all mankind under these three types. Grade passes into grade by imperceptible degrees, but it is the experiences passed through in his childhood, the associations formed in his earliest years, that leave by this means an indelible imprint on man's character which persists throughout his life.

The *ambitious instinct* is present in everyone, no matter what his race, caste, or class, no matter what his occupation or position. King or beggar, petty pickpocket or man of science—each one cherishes the desire, has it born in him, to make his mark in his own special line whatever it may be, each one aches to do something to set himself above his associates, to make his name known among them, and have it acclaimed with honour.

The *acquisitive instinct* is present in a greater or less degree in all mankind. It is most clearly manifest in children, each one of whom has some collection—as a rule both useless and valueless—gathered together merely to satisfy the sense of possession, and with which nothing is, or can be, ever done.

CHAPTER V

PSYCHOLOGICAL DERANGEMENTS

HAVING touched briefly upon normal psychological processes in the preceding chapter, it is proposed to discuss now the results of disturbances of these processes which produce the mental conditions found among the aments and the alienated. Before entering upon this aspect of our subject, however, it must be noted that, though psychic causes undoubtedly have a large share in the production of certain cases of mental derangement, in by far the greater number of cases physical causes are the root of the trouble. The matter dealt with in this chapter, therefore, must not be looked on as an ætiological explanation of such cases so much as a description of the methods by which other causes, largely physical in character, derange the normal mentalisation and produce the pitiful wrecks which constitute the population of asylums.

In the preceding chapter we found the infant started life with a primary conatus and a certain innate capacity for the development of this by means of cognitive synthesis. Now, to develop anything the presence of a certain amount of material to work with is presupposed, and the development of the conatus is no exception to this rule. The material here is the **natural endowment** received from the parents, and varying greatly in degree from that bestowed upon the low-grade idiot, who never can advance beyond the stage of the first vague, unrealised conatus, to that conferred upon the man of genius whose name resounds in all the civilised parts of the globe, and whose work confers untold benefits upon posterity.

Failure, then, in cognitive synthesis may be taken as the explanation of the mental conditions found in idiots and imbeciles. This failure varies enormously in degree, and may be due to lack of innate endowment, to traumata incurred during or shortly after birth, or to intra-uterine toxæmias. Another class of such cases is found in those in whom the failure is due to the absence of some special sense, such as sight or hearing. In this class the failure is due to a want of sensory stimuli on which to form the dispositions so necessary for development. That normal mental power exists in a very large number of such cases is clearly proven by the knowledge they can acquire and apply to practical uses, when trained by some of the special methods now elaborated for the training of those so afflicted.

A type of insanity well known and recognised clinically is due to a failure of cognitive synthesis, more or less *in toto,* but at a very much later stage of life. Many of such cases seem to be absolutely normal when children, a few even brilliant and full of promise, but when late puberty or early adult life comes on there is a sudden failure. Like a lamp burning out its oil, the mental powers dwindle and fail, and, as a result, there is left much the same sort of spectacle as the idiot who has been afflicted from his birth. In such cases there is generally a strongly marked neurotic taint on one, perhaps both sides of the family.

A failure in cognitive synthesis occurs at a still more advanced age in cases of what is called senile dementia. In such cases the powers of attention and apperception fail, and the patient reverts to the condition of a little child. Many such cases, however, retain a wonderful memory for events of " the long ago," of the distant past. This is due to former dispositions persisting and, being unchanged by perception and the acquisition of more recent dispositions, they are naturally more clear if roused by association.

Derangements traceable to **disorders of the conation** itself mainly fall under the head involved in the axiom already touched upon in the preceding chapter—*i.e.*, to desire an end is also to desire the means of its attainment. Thus, if the original conatus cease from any cause the conatus for the means of its attainment may still persist and influence the whole life and conduct. Avariciousness, greed, and other undesirable qualities are often, though not always, traceable to this cause. For example, a man may have been toiling and scraping to provide a home for the girl of his heart. Before he has accumulated sufficient money for his purpose death robs him of his bride. Here the incentive to accumulate, to stint and deprive himself, is gone, but in spite of this the desire to accumulate money still remains, and he may still continue to pinch and scrape for the mere sake of accumulation. Other explanations of miserliness, however, are possible. The acquisitive instinct common to mankind, and specially noticeable in children, may become unduly prominent and give rise to avariciousness as well as other undesirable propensities. The innate love of power, too, furnishes another factor which has to be considered in such cases. Thus a child covets a penny for the sake of the sweets or other pleasures it can purchase. As soon, however, as the sweets have been devoured and the transient pleasures ended, he covets the penny again, but this time for its own sake and the feeling of power it gives him to purchase anew the pleasures which so soon have ended.

Attention may be: (1) *subjective* in so far as it is concerned with matters closely associated with and directly affecting the personality; (2) *objective* where it is directed towards an idea or perception having a direct interest of its own independently of any connection with the personality.

The main derangements of attention met with in mental disease consist in an intensification of one of these forms and a corresponding failing in the other.

In melancholia and similar conditions, subjective attention is predominant. All the patient's thoughts are wrapped in his own troubles, his ideas are fixed upon his own sorry fate, and he is indifferent to, regardless of all that passes around him. So marked is this that melancholic patients have been known to sit silent, brooding, inactive, while another patient has actually committed suicide before their very eyes, when a mere cry from the melancholic would have brought assistance and averted the calamity.

In cases of mania and mental exaltation, objective attention is intensified, and subjective at a minimum. As a result of this intensification of objective attention the slightest sound or movement acts as a stimulus for a fresh current of thought, the patient flies from one topic to another, and it is impossible for him to settle to any consecutive employment for more than a minute or so.

In normal conditions, when the consentience of mental and neural processes is undisturbed, the attention is directed chiefly to one subject alone at a time, and this direction is coincident with the main current of mental activity. This does not necessarily imply that two objects cannot occupy consciousness together, but merely that there must be some relation between them which can be thought of—*i.e.*, they must form a systematic combination. In normal persons it is possible for only one such systematic process to persist at any one time. In hypnosis, however, and certain functional derangements, such as hysteria, it seems possible for at least two such attention processes to coexist. Thus, an hysterical patient, while carrying on a conversation, at the same time may be writing replies to whispered questions regarding events of which she seemed unconscious at the time of their occurrence, owing to an hysterical seizure. It is this phenomenon that has given rise to what are called cases of "double personality"; but, as Stout remarks, such states seem to coincide with the existence of distinct individual minds of a very low order of individuality, and certainly not deserving to be termed personalities.

We have seen in the preceding chapter that **apperception** *consists in the blending of "dispositions" and "presentations,"* and results in the transmogrification of the disposition. Hence, for the adequate performance of apperception, dispositions are essential. Now *for the formation of dispositions the possession of the special senses is essential*, to originate the presentations from which our dispositions are evolved from our earliest hours. It therefore follows that *in the absence of these*, as sometimes occurs in those afflicted from birth with blindness or deafness, or in their derangement from pathological or functional causes, as frequently occurs in later life, the *development of the powers of apperception is either wholly prevented* or, in the latter case, apperception itself is liable to disturbance proportional to the affection of the special senses.

Alterations of acuteness of sensibility are common to both the sane and the insane. Thus, in convalescence after severe illness, patients are very liable to become hypersensitive as regards all the senses, and, as a result, are very commonly peevish and irritable.

In those afflicted with mental disorders alterations in sensibility are to be found in every degree, from complete absence to a high state of hyperacuity. Thus a complete absence of the sense of sight or hearing may render the person so afflicted little better than an idiot unless some of the special modern methods of educating such cases be available for his training. Again, quite apart from the shock experienced at its loss, deprivation of a special sense, especially of sight or hearing, is liable to upset the mental equilibrium of persons of normal psychic development, even when it occurs comparatively late in life. In such cases it is probable that the loss of the sensual stimuli affects apperception through a failure to arouse dispositions through association, and the mental tone is also upset and rendered irritable owing to lack of the stimuli which have become necessary to balance the stimuli received through the other organs of sense.

In states of mental depression psychic sensibility is intensified, though deranged; but, as a rule, physical sensibility, both organic and that of the special senses, is very much diminished. In states of mental exaltation, on the other hand, both psychic and physical sensibility seem to be hyperacute. These conditions are typically found in cases of circular insanity. I have seen persons suffering from this condition who, during the comparatively normal state occurring between the attacks of alternating exaltation and depression, required glasses of only one or two dioptres, and who could hear with but little difficulty. As the attacks of exaltation came on the glasses were discarded, the smallest print could be read with ease, and the hearing seemed to be, if anything, above the average. As attacks of mental depression supervened, perception seemed to fail, stronger and stronger glasses became necessary to enable the patient to read, and he heard with increasing difficulty. So marked is this diminution in physical sensibility among cases of mental depression that patients may burn and scorch themselves while sitting too near a hot fire and yet apparently feel no pain. In cases of stupor the powers of perception, during the attack, seem to be largely in abeyance; but, when recovery does occur, a little questioning often elicits the fact that, after all, the powers of perception were not so very much affected during the stuporose state. In cases of dementia sensibility is affected along with the general failing of the rest of the mental faculties, and in such cases external stimuli make but little impression. I have frequently seen one such case sitting in an asylum kitchen on a "hot plate" intended for keeping the meals of the inmates warm. The hot plate, as a rule, was so hot that it was impossible to place one's hand on it, and yet this old dame had to be regularly hounded away from it by the attendants. Instances, too, frequently occur of patients burning their fingers while using them as tobacco stoppers, and never noticing having done so, so far as can be gathered from their behaviour.

Two derangements of perception are met with, quite apart from any alteration in its acuteness. These are known respectively as (1) Illusion; (2) Hallucination.

1. An **Illusion** is a misinterpretation of a sensory stimulus which really exists. In the sane the reasoning powers, as a rule, rapidly correct the false perception. Thus, if seated in a train which is drawn up alongside another in a station, one of the trains begins to move, a normal person may be at first in doubt as to which train is moving but rapidly assures himself by looking out of the window away from the other train.

In the insane illusions are frequently not dispelled in this manner, and persist, giving rise, in many cases, to delusions. Thus the sound of the wind and rustling leaves may be thought to be enemies shouting out abuse and threats, or wireless messages, and in this way delusions of persecution may arise. Similarly, an attack of colic may give rise to the delusion that rats are gnawing at the vitals. In women, uterine or ovarian trouble is in this way a very frequent cause of delusions. I have had one such case in my charge—she suffered from leprosy too, poor soul —who had uterine fibroids and a chronic ovaritis. She suffered from delusions that the devil used to come and carry on obscene conversations with her at night, and frequently, as, " the black bugger, like a black snake, you know, doctor, " used to locate himself in her abdomen and amuse himself by gnawing at her entrails.

2. An **Hallucination** is a sense perception arising in the absence of any stimulus.

Hallucinations are important symptoms of insanity, for they greatly influence the conduct and behaviour of the patient. If any legal question be involved and it is necessary for the medical man to give evidence in court, one of the first questions to be asked regarding the patient is whether he has hallucinations. As a rule, patients suffering with hallucinations must be always classed as dangerous and carefully watched, for at any moment " voices " may incite them to serious acts of violence.

Hallucinations of hearing, besides being the type most likely to cause acts of violence, are the ones most commonly met with in asylum practice, and occur in infinite variety. From mere tickings and rustlings, they pass through whispered words of abuse to sustained conversations. Frequently the patient recognises the voices as belonging to people he knows, and he may accuse someone present of hurling abuse at him, or announce that he has just had a chat with some of his deceased relatives. Occasionally, as in the case already cited, the voices are loud and imperative, and urge the patient on to the commission of some act of violence or indecency.

Hallucinations of sight are also fairly common among the insane, and vary from mere flashes of light, through definite images of objects, such as rats, vermin, etc., to visions of departed relatives or the enactment of a whole series of incidents, generally terrifying and revolting in character.

Hallucinations of common sensation are occasionally met with among the insane, and give rise to delusions of persecution by "unseen agency," etc. In cases such as these, as well as in illusions of a similar type, it is always well to examine the patient thoroughly in order to ascertain whether some organic cause may not be present, the removal of which may at any rate alleviate, even if not cure, the mental condition.

Hallucinations of smell and taste generally occur together, and, in my experience, are fairly common in Indian asylums, where patients frequently complain of having seminal discharges mixed with their food. It has always been from male patients that I have had this complaint, and generally the complainant is a confirmed masturbator. Hallucinations of poison being mixed with the food are common to both sexes, and are liable to give trouble through the patient refusing food and requiring to be tube-fed.

Hallucinations most commonly occur at night, when all is quiet and the patient's attention is not distracted by genuine stimuli. In some cases, however, they occur at any time, no matter how the patient may be employed. I remember once sitting in my writing-room and hearing a lunatic, employed in my garden, apparently carrying on a loud conversation with some relative who had evidently just arrived to visit him. I listened; there was apparently no doubt about it. The lunatic's questions and comments were clearly audible and connected. I got up and went to the door to see this unknown relative and found my patient sitting down and emptying the earth out of some flower-pots whose contents were withered, and shouting out his questions and comments to the empty air. I asked him who his visitor was, and he informed me it was his father, who I knew must have died a good many years previously.

Hallucinations of several senses may occur at the same time, and are accepted implicitly as true by their victims. As a rule the patients are wholly unable to correct such false perceptions —in fact, they often resent vigorously all attempts to convince them of their inaccuracy, and in this way delusions originate.

It can generally be gathered, from the behaviour, statements, and complaints, when a patient is suffering from hallucinations. Occasionally, however, a patient may take great trouble to conceal them, either from a knowledge that they will be looked on as a symptom of insanity, or because they are in some way connected with some private or secret business. Such cases generally occur with auditory hallucinations, and careful watching soon reveals their presence; the patient sometimes stops short in conversation with a companion, and, turning his head sharply, he may smile or frown in a way inexplicable by ordinary circumstances. Sometimes, too, he may be heard talking to himself at night, not in the way many sane people do when they are thinking deeply, but as if he were carrying on a conversation over a telephone, of which the listener only hears one party's utterances.

Hallucinations persisting over a period of months are generally a very bad prognostic symptom, as are also hallucinations occurring in the very young. In epileptics, hallucinations of sight are fairly common, and at times constitute the so-called "aura," the same hallucination constantly appearing before a seizure, and so warning the patient of its approach.

Dreams partake largely of the characters of illusions and hallucinations: of hallucinations, in so far as the dreamer experiences what does not really exist—but, in general, dreams are without that dependence on motor activity which characterises percepts; of illusions, when they are the result of a certain state of the nervous system combined with the results of normal stimuli of the sense organs, as when a slight pain in some part of the body makes one dream of being wounded.

The best definition of dreams that I know of is that given by Sir George Savage, and quoted in the *Journal of Mental Science* (April, 1917)—viz., "mental action taking place during sleep, which is more or less recognised on waking." Hence, for a full apprehension of the nature of dreams it is necessary to have some knowledge of the nature and functions of sleep.

Sleep may be defined as a regularly recurring condition of unconsciousness designed by Nature for the rest and recuperation of the mind and body. The exact cause of sleep is not yet definitely known, though its concomitants are common knowledge. During sleep all the normal activities of the body are lowered, the blood-pressure falls, the pulse slows down, and respiration becomes more shallow and less frequent. Sir Robert Armstrong-Jones considers there is also probably a state of venous engorgement during sleep, allowing the products of fatigue to pass by osmosis into the bloodstream and lymph-channels. These, however, are all physical phenomena, and as yet little, if anything, is known regarding the condition of the brain during sleep, the condition of its blood-supply, changes in the cortical cells, and the relation of these changes to and their dependence on the ductless glands, such as has been found to exist with the pituitary gland during hibernation. Lépine, theorising, considers that the dendrites retract during sleep, leading to a separation of the contiguity of various neurons, cutting off nerve-currents, and thus inducing sleep. Lugaro, on the other hand, surmises a greater and more extensive outward prolongation of the dendrites, diffusing rather than concentrating nerve-energy, thereby lowering the nerve-potential, and producing a condition favourable to sleep. Whichever be correct, one thing is certain, and that is, that the whole of the nervous system presumably participates in this lowering of the activity of the circulatory and other systems during sleep, though whether this lowering is sufficient to interrupt the continuity of the unconscious as well as conscious life is not yet known.

The mental faculties are not lost simultaneously during the process of going to sleep, but are lost in a certain order. Judgment, attention, will, association, cognition, may be roughly said to be the order in which our chief mental faculties lapse. A little consideration, therefore, renders it clear that, if such be the case, in conditions of light, imperfect sleep, or dozing, where there is not a complete lapse of all the faculties, the remnants which remain lead to the weird, disordered, disconnected phantasies which we know as dreams.

Freud and his school promulgate the theory that dreams are "wish fulfilments," largely and grossly sexual in character, the resultants of a conflict between the "censor" and the "repressed idea"; that they are intended as a safeguard to unbroken sleep, and, being a compromise, can only be interpreted by an array of symbolism which practically attaches phallic import to every object in air, on land, or in water.

Such theorising seems to me utterly wrong, and to look on human nature as swayed by only one passion, possessed of but one instinct, and that the desire for acts of gross sexuality.

To my mind dreams seem to partake of the character of reaction to some sensory stimulus by the mental faculties in a condition of partial activity only, this partial activity being due to the soporific influence of sleep. There is much to support this view. Thus, the majority of dreams occur after 6 a.m., though an appreciable number, especially in children, occur in the early part of the night before sleep has gained complete sway over the mental faculties. Again, an analysis of dreams shows how closely they are related to what are commonly known as the five senses: thus, 60 per cent. of dreams relate to sight, 5 per cent. to hearing, 3 per cent. to taste, and 1·5 to smell—this difference in ratio being due probably to the much higher evolution of the senses of sight and hearing, which renders them more sensitive to stimuli. This high percentage of visual dreams is interesting when considered in the light of the results of Professor Ladd's researches, which have enabled him to trace the origin of even the most elaborate visual dreams to intra-organic retinal excitement. Thus, on several occasions when waking from a dream, wherein he had been reading consecutive words and sentences from a printed page, he has found that the minute light and dark spots, which the activity of the rods and cones occasions, had arranged themselves in parallel lines across the retina.

The contents of dreams, if closely examined into by the dreamers, will almost invariably be found to have relation to some incident of the previous three or four days—not an incident which has been of moment, requiring fixation of the attention and mental effort, but a happening of trivial import, which may even have passed without cognition at the time, or if it has entered on the field of consciousness has done so but to leave it again. This character of dream-contents is explicable by the law of association. Thus, those percepts which occupy the attention and have their place in trains of thought become exhausted and require much stronger stimuli to arouse them than those which have occupied the psychic fringe, which have been already rung up, as it were, and are standing by, tense and full of energy ready to respond to any call. This, and the lapse of volition and attention which occurs during sleep, are, I submit, the source of the phantasies which are initiated, if not in all, certainly in most cases by some intra- or extra-organic sensory stimulus.

Suggestibility is a condition which frequently accompanies mental weakness, whether this be due to congenital causes or to disorganisation arising from drugs or disease. It exists to a certain extent in the unformed minds of children where the mental systems are not yet fully enough developed to resist suggestion. In the drunkard restraining influences have been robbed of their power by alcohol, and in hypnotism the subject is placed in a similar condition by the operations of the hypnotist. It is frequently present in hysterical cases, and accounts for many of the manifestations met with in this disease, and is also fairly common among Malays, who speak of it as "lătāh."

It may be defined as a condition of the mind wherein apperceptive systems are excited almost wholly by the words, commands, gestures, etc., of another person, and not by their own mutual co-operation, competition, and conflict. In such states all kinds of strange hallucinations and delusions arise, as the patient is unable to find inconsistencies and fallacies in what, in a normal state of mind, would appear the wildest stretch of imagination.

In such cases external objects stimulate the senses, but unless the perceptions thus arising are congruous with the dominant system of ideas, with the group of ideas aroused by the suggestion, they are wholly suppressed and ignored. Sensory stimulation, nevertheless, far from hindering suggestibility, tends rather to aid it by giving sensuous vividness and definite localisation in space to suggested images.

In many neurotic and hysterical cases the suggestion seems to arise from previous thoughts, ideas, or day-dreams of the patient, and a little patience and tact in such cases of auto-suggestion may often elicit the whole cause of the trouble, and enable one to effect a rapid cure.

Suggestion, too, seems to be the cause of the cataleptic conditions so frequently met with in hysterical and katatonic patients, and accounts also for the allegorical modes of speech prevalent among the insane, as noted by Jung.

The ideal revival of dispositions constitutes **memory,** as noted previously. It has to be remembered, however, in this connection that this revival of a disposition need not necessarily be an exact reproduction of the original sensation or perception.

In some persons the visual sense seems to predominate in the formation of dispositions and their associations, whilst in others the auditory seems to hold greater sway, and so on. That this is so is well seen in ordinary life in the different accounts given by various observers of one and the same event.

The properties of a good memory are: (1) The rapidity with which the power of ideal revival is acquired. (2) The length of time during which a disposition persists without being renewed. (3) The rapidity and accuracy of the revival. (4) The compatibility, the relevancy, of the dispositions revived with the prevailing interest of the moment.

The rapidity of acquiring the power of ideal revival depends mainly upon two factors—interest, and innate endowment, though, literally speaking, innate endowment for remembering consists largely of an innate interest in what is to be remembered. This in a measure explains the power, sometimes seen in idiots, of remembering long lists of disconnected, wholly useless words and figures. They comprehend practically no relations except those of contiguity in time and space, and hence the power of recalling series of objects connected solely in this manner, a faculty still further accentuated by their excessively narrow range of interest.

The length of time during which a disposition persists without being renewed is determined also very largely by interest and innate endowment, but a further factor also influences this—*i.e.*, the frequency with which the presentation originating the disposition has been repeated.

The rapidity and accuracy of the revival are dependent on the formation of proper associations, the duration of the period of inactivity since the last revival of the disposition or its associations, and also on interest.

The utility of a memory is based largely upon the relevancy of the dispositions revived with the prevailing interest of the moment. Thus a man who is given to considering subjects from every point of view and in relation to all their surroundings acquires a wide field of associations, and, even though the general sum of his attainments be smaller, his memory may be infinitely more serviceable, both theoretically and practically, than that of a man crammed with cumbrous, disjointed erudition from textbooks.

From the above it necessarily follows that to improve a memory it is not the power to recall that requires education, but the strengthening of the power of attention, of interest. By increasing the attention given to any subject not only are clearer, more permanent dispositions formed, but their associations are increased, and the means necessary for their revival correspondingly multiplied.

For the purposes of the alienist *memory* is classed as (*a*) *recent*, (*b*) *remote*. *Recent memory* has to do with the formation of fresh dispositions and the power of their revival. *Remote memory* is applied to the power of recalling events of the dim, distant past.

Loss of memory is the most common derangement of memory found among mental cases. It is known as **amnesia,** and may be temporary or progressive.

Temporary loss of memory is of frequent occurrence after accidents, and I know of several cases where the victims of severe falls and other injuries have had no personal recollection of events which had happened some days, even weeks, prior to the accidents. Temporary loss of memory is also seen in epileptics. All such cases are always unconscious during the fit, and remember nothing of what has occurred, and in many cases this lapse is found to extend over some considerable time, both prior and subsequent to the seizure. In many acute forms of insanity, especially where confusion is present and the concentration of attention is at a minimum, there is an utter failure in the formation of dispositions, and days and weeks even may be blotted out of the patient's life.

Progressive failure in memory is found in many conditions, such as senile dementia, general paralysis, alcoholic and drug cases. In senile dementia it is chiefly the recent memory which is affected, memory for past events often remaining astoundingly clear and accurate—this, as already noted, being due to former dispositions persisting, and, being unchanged by apperception and the acquisition of more recent dispositions, they become intensified by repetition, and are naturally clearer when roused by association. In other types, however, it seems to be part of a general decay of the whole mental faculties, and both forms of memory seem equally affected.

A form of derangement of the memory which frequently arises, and is apt to give trouble to the medical adviser and nurses, is known as **paramnesia.** In such cases the patient, quite unknowingly, fills up the lacunæ in his true memory with entirely fictitious statements, in absolute good faith, as a rule, and without any intent to deceive. Incidents such as these have always to be looked for, as they may form the basis of a complaint against the attendant, and, though they are unlikely to lead to any serious consequences for the attendant, yet the latter is apt to feel dislike for a patient who has, apparently out of sheer malice, brought forward a most elaborate charge against him. In my experience cases of paramnesia, as a rule, occur in patients where temporary lapses of memory, or states of unconsciousness, are found to be present in combination with an increase of suggestibility. Under such circumstances any slight injury or bruise received during a fit or an automatic seizure is unnoticed at the time. On recovery of consciousness, however, the pain and inconvenience are realised, and some past experience of the patient's, or some incident read of in the papers or some novel is seized on, in absolutely good faith, as the cause of the injury.

Recognition is a form of memory which, in certain cases of mental disorder, is found to be deranged. It may be manifest as an inability to recognise faces, or the patient may be unable to localise his position, or fail to estimate correctly intervals of time. In extreme cases the patient may utterly fail to grasp his own identity. To such conditions the term **disorientation** is applied, and they are found in cases of delirium and confusion, and in those suffering from epilepsy, alcoholism, and drug habits.

Delusion has already been defined as "a belief in anything which would appear impossible, incredible, foolish, absurd to people of the same race, caste, and class as the person expressing it, such belief persisting in spite of all remonstrance, argument, and proof to the contrary, influencing every action, affecting the whole thought and life of its exponent, and arising from derangement of the functions or disease of the cerebral convolutions."

There are several ways in which such *derangements of belief* may arise.

We have already seen that belief involves the control of subjective activity by objective restrictions. This restriction of mental activity may take the form of actual obstruction, where, *nolens volens*, we are forced to think in a given direction, or there may be no attempt to think otherwise—no possibility of doing so. A man out at midday during the hot weather in the plains does not question whether the sun is blazing. The fact is only too perceptible to all his senses, and he yields unquestioned acquiescence to the objective coercion.

Objective restriction by actual obstruction may take the shape of a collision between a preformed anticipation, generally in the form of a conation, and actual facts. In a more advanced stage of development a further example of this is met with when an attempt is made to think of an opposing alternative to see how far it is tenable. In such a case, if the conditions of the belief are complete, it is possible for part of them to be outside the sphere of consciousness, and in consequence the negation may become thinkable. *It is, in fact, this dismissal from consciousness of apperceptive systems, which obstruct a desired belief, which accounts for the presence and persistence of many delusions.*

The effect of association upon belief is important when the subject is being considered from the present point of view. If objects have once been presented in a certain relation to each other, the thought of one tends to reinstate the thought of the other as in the original presentation, and a mental effort is needed to counteract this tendency. Under such conditions associations may offer objective restriction to subjective activity and, *ipso facto,* where the associations prove indissoluble they constitute beliefs. The persistence of such beliefs depends upon the presence and strength of counter-associations. Thus, a very feeble association, in the absence of any counter-associations, may suffice to constitute a belief. It is this class to which belong the primitive beliefs of children and aboriginals, as well as the suggested beliefs of hypnotised patients and the delusions of many cases of hysteria and of certain types of insanity.

The action of association being controlled by apperception, which confines consciousness to the centre of interest for the time being, and prevents the intrusion of irrelevant ideas, it follows naturally that, in cases of melancholia, of delusional insanity, and similar states, where the whole interest of the being is centred upon one topic, a powerful influence exists for the framing of delusions.

The *power of conatus upon belief* is considerable. If a certain objective combination seems the most favourable for obtaining a certain end, the active tendency towards this end is of itself a tendency to believe in the objective combinations. Hence the readiness with which man believes in what is pleasing to him and the difficulty of persuading him against his will. The effect of this often is to divert attention from counter-evidence, and the stronger the conation the more likely is this to happen. This is well seen in cases of delusional insanity or melancholia, where the mind is so occupied with one set of associations that whatever might conflict with them either never comes before consciousness, or, if it should succeed in gaining entry, it is but momentary, and only to be promptly ejected. Deducing from the above, it follows that the more vigorous and active the mind is the more ready it is to believe, and whatever heightens the flow of mental activity favours the believing attitude, as is well exemplified in cases of mental exaltation.

Beliefs thus formed under the influence of conatus are liable to be checked by counter-experiences, and where this check fails the belief not only persists but becomes the stronger for the momentary obstruction. The more frequently they are acted upon, too, the more they become an integral part of the conatus, and their power is proportionately increased. Associations also become strengthened and multiplied by frequent repetition, and so, in course of time, a whole system of beliefs grows and ramifies around the original one, strengthening and explaining away whatever tends to negative it. From this arises the wonderful array of arguments, etc., so characteristic of cases of paranoia (systematised delusional insanity).

Delusions at times seem traceable to general emotional states. Thus a patient may be feeling thoroughly depressed and wretched, and endeavours to find a cause for it, and probably fixes upon some past peccadillo for which his present misery is a judgment. Time passing with little or no relief to his misery, the delusion grows, and the patient becomes convinced he has committed the "unpardonable sin," and is lost for all eternity.

The possibility of delusions arising from sense perceptions has already been dealt with, and needs no further repetition.

Delusions frequently develop slowly and imperceptibly, and in many cases delusional insanity may be fully developed before relatives or friends suddenly realise the altered behaviour of the patient, and on consideration grasp the fact that the condition has been developing for some considerable period.

Delusions are said to be systematised when a whole system of secondary delusions has grown up and ramified around the original one, strengthening and extending it. When they are independent of each other they are known as non-systematised. A *fixed delusion* is one which remains permanent and unaltered from day to day, while fleeting delusions come and go and constantly change in character. Systematised and fixed delusions are those which cause most trouble in asylum practice, and they are generally of very grave prognostic significance.

Delusions may be classified either as regards their character —*i.e.*, delusions of suspicion, of persecution, of unseen agency, of thought transference, etc.; or as regards their objective relations—*i.e.*, delusions regarding the patient's personality, affecting himself in relation to his surroundings or his surroundings in relation to himself.

With delusions regarding the patient's own personality may be ranged delusions of identity, where the patient is convinced he is some other person; hypochondriacal delusions, where he falsely believes he is suffering from some serious ailment, in spite of repeated assurances to the contrary; or he may think some part of him has been changed for that of some other person, etc.

In cases where the delusions affect the relationship of the patient to his surroundings there is infinite variety. The patient may suffer from delusions of grandeur, when he fancies he is of high position or possessed of great wealth. A frequent form of delusions of grandeur is where the patient imagines he was formerly of exalted rank and possessed of countless wealth, but has lost it either through misfortune, his own fault, or the machinations of some imaginary enemy. Delusions of unworthiness, sinfulness, self-accusation and of impending calamity form the antithesis of delusions of grandeur. With such manifestations the patient thinks himself an outcast, unfit to speak to anyone, guilty of the " unpardonable sin," etc.

Delusions regarding the relationship of the surroundings to the patient may also be pleasurable or painful in character. Thus, a patient may believe all the surroundings belong to him and the asylum staff are his menials, his slaves, or, *au contraire*, he may believe he is in prison, and the attendants there for the express purpose of torturing and tormenting him. Delusions of suspicion or jealousy may rack his brain, as when he suspects his wife of deceiving him, or his friends of being his secret foes, or delusions of persecution may make his life a burden to him, with frantic unsuccessful attempts to escape from his imaginary tormentors. Along with delusions of persecution may be classed those of "unseen agency," where the patient believes he is acted upon by electricity, hypnotism, wireless telegraphy, or X rays, etc.

All delusions accompanied by mental depression are of grave import, and such cases require very careful watching, in order to prevent suicidal attempts. Suicide, too, frequently happens in endeavours to avoid impending calamities, or to escape from imaginary persecutors.

Delusions of suspicion render patients exceedingly difficult to manage. Everything done for them is misconstrued; every action is viewed with suspicion; everything that happens has a hidden meaning for them; and such cases are among the most trying one has to deal with, and strain one's patience and fortitude almost to breaking-point.

Those patients suffering from delusions of persecution have always to be carefully supervised, as suicide and homicidal assaults are very liable to occur in such cases.

Imagination is simply the retention of an ideal train in consciousness without questioning its accuracy or existence. It differs from dreams and the ideal representations of hypnotic trances in that the latter are absurd beliefs accepted, *pro tempore*, by the mental dispositions which would interfere with them being rendered inoperative for the time being by circumstances independent of the will. With imagination, however, these contrary dispositions are excluded by the direction of subjective interest. This holds also for the actions, etc., resulting from a fierce passion; but here the result is not imagination, but biased belief—the judgment, perverted by passion, is acted on and made the basis of reasonings leading to new beliefs. Imagination in the normal individual is never made the basis of an action with a view to an end, nor had recourse to in order to establish a fact. So soon as an attempt is made to utilise such floating ideas for the attainment of some ulterior end, mental combinations, which have previously lain dormant, spring into activity and nip the project in its bud. Thus imagination may be defined as "ideal combination, existing for its own sake, and not for the attainment of an ulterior practical end." Imagination, however, has an aim—an æsthetic end, tending to bring pleasing elements into relation so as to constitute a pleasing whole. In fact, imagination has been aptly described as "the mind at play"; it is essentially unpractical, and serves no purpose but the intrinsic pleasures which its exercise brings.

No human being is free from moments of reverie, of castle-building, or day-dreaming. The normal individual can indulge himself in such reveries without raising the question of their possibility, but with the neurotic, the hysterical individual, it is different. In such cases the tendency to castle-building, to fall into day-dreams, is markedly exaggerated, and generally the subject is one of absorbing interest to them. This constant dreaming tends to render the ideas more vivid and persistent, raises up in time even associations around them, so that, at length, what was primarily a mere floating idea may become looked on as having actually occurred. This process, too, is aided undoubtedly by the increased suggestibility found in such cases.

Even in normal individuals, however, day-dreaming may have a marked influence upon the conduct. Such day-dreams often partake of the character of a drama, in which the dreamer himself figures as the hero. To many it seems a harmless thing to let the mind dwell on the idea of an act which is recognised as wrong. By raising the idea into consciousness, however, we intensify it, and render it more persistent and more powerful to realise itself. By such methods many are led into temptation and fall an easy prey to it, even among normal individuals, and their effect upon neurotic and hysterical subjects is naturally much greater.

Professor Sidgwick has brought forward two other methods by which man may fall an easy prey to temptation, under circumstances where a seductive feeling leads him to act contrary to a general resolution. In one case he erroneously, but sincerely, persuades himself that the rule is inapplicable, whilst in the other he deceives himself, being all the time aware of the deception. As a rule, in these latter cases the validity or invalidity of the inhibiting perception is never considered. It is disregarded, treated merely as a floating idea, and the seductive feeling is given full sway to guard against interference in its determination of action.

Many cases of stupor, hebephrenia, and katatonia seem to me largely explicable by this last proposition. In such cases suggestibility is markedly in excess of the normal; they are given greatly to day-dreaming, and the stupor, the mental inertia, is in many cases apparently purely objective. This is due, I consider, to an extension of the disregard of inhibiting perceptions, noted above, to all objects irrelevant to the prevailing subject of interest—the subject of the day-dream, and a pathological intensification of this interest through the seductive feeling, to the exclusion of all extraneous perceptions.

A further disorder of imagination frequently seen in mental cases is the tendency of trains of imagination to assume practical form, for their topic to become an ulterior end, and its realisation the whole object of existence.

These last two factors, I believe, are largely responsible for habits of sexual malpractices, and the most common cause of masturbation, which prevails so commonly among the insane of both sexes.

In considering **will or volition** in the preceding chapter, it was noted that a condition of impulsiveness constituted an early stage of its development—*i.e.*, a state in which perceptual and instinctive conation find immediate expression in bodily movement, guided by external impression, and wholly uninfluenced by deliberation or reasoning, neither of which, indeed, ever forms an integral part of the process. In the insane such **impulsive actions** are often noticed, and are due generally to the higher apperceptive powers of reasoning and deliberation being in abeyance. Thus, these actions are commonly seen in cases of mental confusion or delirium, or in alcoholic or drug intoxication. They are frequently associated, too, with cases of epilepsy, where there often seems to be a mental seizure substituted for the ordinary physical fits, and in such cases appallingly brutal outrages may be committed without the patient having any subsequent knowledge of what has occurred. Sometimes such actions seem to arise as the result of aural hallucinations, the patient hearing some voice, generally described as that of God or the devil, commanding him to do something, and so authoritative is the command that without thought or question the deed is accomplished.

The extent of such actions is wide and varied, from trivial occurrences, like the breaking of flower-pots and windows, and trivial assaults, up to attempts at suicide or homicide. Sometimes the practically purely automatic character of such actions is very much more in evidence than at others, as in cases where patients may suddenly disappear and all trace of them be lost for days, and then news arrives of their discovery in some wholly unexpected place, the patient apparently having wandered away in a state of unconsciousness, and suddenly realised himself in an unknown part of the country.

A minor degree of loss of self-control or volition is found in the restlessness which forms so common a symptom in many forms of insanity. In some cases, such as the exhaustion psychoses, it is probably due to exhaustion of nervous energy and merely an exaggeration of the restlessness which accompanies over-fatigue even in healthy persons. In other cases, such as excited melancholia, it seems very often to be the manifestation of an unformed, unrealised conatus, impelling to action in any form in a vague, unseeing attempt to escape from the intolerable mental anguish. Restlessness may also be due to physical causes; thus it is a frequent accompaniment of cardiac disorders, and may be caused by toxæmias, both endogenous and exogenous, from the direct action of the toxines on the nerve cells.

A form of automatic action, mainly seen in adolescent cases, is manifested in *stereotyped movements*. A movement is said to be stereotyped when it is repeated over and over again in every detail and without variation. In most instances such movements are found in cases of stupor, hebephrenia, and katatonia, and they seem to constitute a part of, or a necessary accompaniment to, the reverie or day-dream already considered under Imagination. In many instances, especially where the movement takes the form of rubbing, with a circular movement, over the scalp, the patient is notoriously addicted to masturbation, and this movement seems in some way to replace the manipulation of the genital organs, and to arouse the seductive feeling necessary for the perfecting of his reverie. In other cases, as pointed out by Jung, the movement has some association with some past event, which forms the subject of the reverie, as in a case which he quotes where a young female, who had been disappointed in a love affair with a cobbler, fell into one of these stuporose states, and was continually carrying out the motions of a cobbler sitting sewing at his last. Peculiar noises are frequently repeated in this manner; thus, I have heard a young English lady who was afflicted in this way, and who spent her whole day and night screeching like a parrot; another patient, a Mussulman, who had been employed in railway workshops, used to dance up and down, roaring out to represent the throb of the engines; whilst a third, a Chamar, used to sit on the ground and imitate, and in a most realistic fashion too, the grunting of a herd of village pigs. Probably in all these cases careful enquiry would have elicited in time the subject of the reveries, and these noises would have been found to be associated with them.

Yet another form in which loss of volition or self-control may manifest itself is the lack of inhibition to be noted in so many of the insane, and frequently leading to gross immorality, intemperance, and vice. Such manifestations are especially common in cases of general paralysis of the insane, in the victims of drug habits, in maniacal states, and in many cases of dementia.

Other conditions are met with in asylums where the will, though not in abeyance, is deranged. These cases mainly come under two heads: (*a*) Lack of will-power, (*b*) resistiveness.

(*a*) Where patients are lacking in will-power they seem wholly unable to come to any decision about even the most trivial everyday matters. They cannot make up their minds, but hesitate and delay, and make endless false starts, until someone appears on the scene and makes up their minds for them. In other cases, the lack of volition shows itself in an inability to undertake ordinary work. Such conditions resemble greatly the effects of fatigue, but frequently are seen present even in the early morning. They may occur in otherwise healthy persons, and are a common symptom in neurasthenic cases. Such patients generally fully realise their condition; they are really anxious to work, and their inability to do so causes them poignant distress.

(*b*) In resistive conditions it is enough to suggest some action to the patient for him to refuse. He will refuse to get up, to go to bed, to take his meals, to take exercise. If left to himself, he will stand about aimlessly doing nothing, and in marked cases the calls of nature may be disregarded to such an extent as to necessitate recourse to enemata and catheterisation. Such manifestations are sometimes due to the lack of will-power already discussed, and the patient resenting his being made to do what he cannot do of his own accord. As a rule, however, some marked delusion is present, which occupies the whole consciousness of the patient, and resents greatly the intrusion of any other percept, and so leads to the state of "negativism," as it is termed; or it may be as a direct result of the delusion itself, which leads him to regard every attempt to lead and guide him as having some evil design upon his person or his liberty.

We have already defined an **obsession** or a **fixed and imperative idea** as " an idea which acquires and maintains such sway over consciousness that, contrary to all natural feeling or desire, perhaps even in spite of the strongest feelings of repugnance and aversion, it persists in consciousness, and may even ultimately materialise its end." In a minor degree we are all subject to such ideas, as when a fragment of some tune or some rubbishy jingle gets into our heads and annoys us because we cannot eject the intruder. In deranged conditions such distress may be caused by these ideas that the patient may be unable to perform his ordinary duties on this account. In such cases there need be no intellectual disturbance, merely this unwanted haunting idea which forces entrance into consciousness, and refuses ejection. The patient recognises the idea is morbid, and is in great distress on this account, and begs to be freed from it.

Many persons suffering from obsessions are quite sane and uncertifiable, being quite competent to carry on their ordinary duties and take their proper place in society. At times, however, the misery and depression arising from this cause are so great that the sufferer may be unable to carry on his ordinary business and social duties, and perhaps may even be impelled to seek freedom from his misery in suicide. In such cases the patient is undoubtedly certifiable, and requires to be put under proper restraint.

Among the insane obsessions are frequently met with, and patients thus afflicted get irritable, at times even violent, if they be thwarted.

Obsessions, as a rule, are classified under three heads: (1) Intellectual; (2) Impulsive; (3) Inhibitory.

1. *Intellectual obsessions* are characterised by the constant intrusion into consciousness of some idea, which frequently is foolish, quite irrelevant to any subject under consideration, and the patient is himself aware of its morbid nature.

2. A patient suffering from *impulsive obsessions* is constantly struggling against a conation to attain some end which he knows to be foolish or wrong. Such acts may be quite trivial, as in cases of impulsion to pick up scraps of paper from the road and read them. The results of the obsession may, however, lead to very serious endings at times if resistance to them breaks down.

I know of one case where the widow of a Hindu zemindar had an impulsive obsession to kill her baby daughter. She told the relatives with whom she was living, and begged to be kept away from her baby. It was of no avail, however, the relatives scoffed at her pleadings, and, misunderstanding the facts, and thinking the poor woman was shirking her duties as a mother, shut up the mother and the child alone in a room for the night. The result was the child was found dead in the morning, and the poor woman passed many weary years of her life as a criminal lunatic in an asylum.

Many of these impulsive obsessions have been given special names, such as "kleptomania," or the craving to steal; "pyromania," or the desire to commit incendiarism.

3. There are two recognised forms of *inhibitory obsessions:* (*a*) Morbid doubting; (*b*) morbid fears.

(*a*) A certain amount of doubting and hesitation is to be seen in everyone at times. In morbid cases, however, this may grow to such a degree, and the delay ensuing be so great, that practically every duty is neglected and nothing done. It is often some quite trivial matter that causes this, such as the question of a letter being put in the correct envelope, which entails opening and reopening letters countless times, or it may be a fear that bills have been paid with counterfeit coin, as in one case I know of. At other times it may be the correctness of a balance-sheet or the truth of religious convictions which is questioned. In all these cases no amount of investigation or explanation will set the mind at rest, but the same difficulty constantly recurs even though the patient recognises the absurdity, the morbidity of his condition.

(*b*) Morbid fears may arise which, although they be known to be groundless, may yet cause constant anxiety.

One very common form for such fears to take is the fear of contamination, which leads to the patient spending by far the greater part of the day washing himself, and renders him absolutely miserable if his ablutions be prevented. Other forms are the fear of open spaces, maidans, etc. (agorophobia); of rooms and buildings (claustrophobia); the fear of infection; the fear of travelling in a railway train or a motor-car, etc.

As already noted, the presence of an obsession does not by any means entail certifiable insanity. Those thus afflicted may still be perfectly competent to carry on their ordinary duties, even though their lives may be made a burden to them by the constantly intruding idea.

In considering the evolution of impulse, desire, and will, it was shown how, as development advanced, trains of thought, not wholly dominated by present external circumstances, become possible, and how from these ideal conations may originate. Many of these ideal conations are capable of materialisation, and are recognised as such by the apperception, and result in activity which leads to their realisation. Such ideal conations as we have already seen are most appropriately termed **desires.**

Others of these ideal conations are manifestly unattainable from their inception, as when on after consideration we wish that we had taken different action in some matter from that already carried out, or we wish our circumstances were different. Realising the unattainability of such conations, normally no more is thought of them beyond the expression of the wish and the thought of how pleasing it would be if only so-and-so could happen; certainly no action is ever contemplated or begun for their attainment under normal conditions. To these, recognised as unattainable conations, the term **wish** is fitly applied.

Such conations, though with but little influence in the ordinary normal individual, are potent factors in the production of mental symptoms among the neurotic and the insane. It is they that mainly constitute the subjects of the reveries and day-dreams which we have already seen are such a potent factor for evil in hysterical cases and certain types of insanity. It is the striving after their attainment, the translation of the conatus into activity which accounts for many of the symptoms found in such cases. This point will be considered later under "Psychic Causes of Insanity," but it was deemed expedient here to explain the term and its origin.

Emotions are a strong factor in the production of certain mental symptoms, as it is the mental craving connected with them, arousing and co-ordinating ideas which harmonise with the emotion, which gives rise to those reveries and day-dreams which we have seen are the basis of so many neuroses. It is noticeable, too, that neurotic and hysterical cases, in which the habit of day-dreaming is most marked, in which suggestibility is most apparent, are unduly emotional, "giving way to their feelings," as the saying goes, on the slightest pretext. It is important, therefore, for everyone to have full control of his emotions, as any disorder or loss of control may have serious results upon the mentality, quite apart from the reason just given.

In the preceding chapter it was shown that *emotional moods* arise from physical, from organic conditions, and how these are apt to tinge the whole view of life, as when one wakes irritable and peevish after a sleepless night in the hot weather, and can see no good in anything or anyone, anger and ill-temper being elicited by one object after another. This being so, it is no great step to say that, if some permanent lesion or derangement be present in the internal organs, emotional moods may originate which may markedly affect the patient's views of life in general, and notably alter his behaviour and reaction to his surroundings. This is especially so in subjects where the lesion affects the abdominal organs, and above all is this noticeable when the intestines are the seat of the lesion. We have all seen numerous cases of colitis and dysentery, and a little thought will prove how in practically every instance mental depression and groundless anxiety were present to a greater or less extent. The occurrence of such states in an ill-developed mind might well be the precursor to an attack of melancholia, or it is even possible to an outbreak of delusional insanity.

Emotions arising from psychic causes tend to enhance, to intensify, the conatus, the gratification or thwarting of which has originated the emotion. This being so, actions originated under the influence of strong emotions are less controlled by apperception, are lacking in judgment, reason and control, and frequently are the exact opposite of what would have been done if the person were not labouring under emotion. Thus, a man when in a fit of passion says and does things which in his cooler moments he would never dream of doing, and which may afterwards be a source of grief and distress to him. Hence, any increase in the intensity of the emotions may quite feasibly originate —at any rate, exaggerate—mental symptoms.

Emotion, however, is to a certain extent essential for the due performance of multitudinous social relations, and so any decrease in its intensity may also lead to the production of symptoms.

The chief mental disorders characterised by an increase of emotional intensity are: Depression; states of anxiety, exaltation, and excitement; and excessive affection.

A person is said to be *depressed* when he is sad or unhappy without sufficient reason. We all of us at times suffer from slight depression, are ill at ease or sad from no definite cause. Such attacks are the common lot of mankind, and in all probability the depression is due to biliousness, indigestion, a partial failure to excrete the waste products of metabolism, or some other physical derangement of too trivial a nature to attract attention. From such trivial everyday states, which are really no departure from good health either of body or mind, every stage of depression is to be found until that of the deepest melancholy is arrived at. In the deeper stages of depression the patient is in a condition of abject misery, and the mental pain and distress are persistent. In such cases the development of delusions is very common.

A condition of *anxiety and dread* of some unknown impending calamity is sometimes found associated with depression. I have frequently found this condition associated with various intestinal lesions, and observed that as the intestinal lesion disappeared under treatment, and the general health improved, there was a corresponding improvement in the emotional condition.

In *mental exaltation* the natural sense of well-being is increased. The patient is excessively happy and cheery, the slightest thing causes him untold pleasure, and he informs one and all of his extreme and wonderful happiness. In most of these cases there is an increase imagined both as regards physical and mental capacity, and a natural development of this is seen at times in the formation of delusions of grandeur.

Mental excitement is closely akin to mental exaltation, but in exaltation there is only the increased sense of well-being, and but for this and its results the mental faculties are clear. In excitement, in addition to this feeling of *bien être*, there is a clouding of apperception, a dulling of the higher faculties and instincts, a mental confusion which is never found in states of pure exaltation.

In cases of *mental enfeeblement* there is, as a rule, dulling of all the mental faculties, and with this there is a corresponding reduction in the capacity for experiencing the emotions. *Emotional indifference*, too, is an early symptom in many cases of adolescent insanity; such cases, though fully conscious of all that goes on, have no interest in anything, and pay no heed to the cares and anxieties of those near and dear to them.

Loss of natural affection is one of the commonest symptoms both in acute and in chronic forms of insanity, and one of the hardest for the family and relatives to bear. It is due to a decrease in the capacity for experiencing emotions,and is usually accompanied by a general lack of interest in the surroundings and daily occurrences.

Instinct has already been described as a conate tendency of the nervous system, whereby action is stimulated for the purpose of attaining definite aims, and it has been shown to fully occupy attentive consciousness and bring into play whatever mental activity may have been developed. For instinctive activity, therefore, the exercise of attention, variation of the behaviour to meet the effects of surrounding conditions on the various senses, and the power of learning by experience, are all essential.

From the above a little consideration suffices to show how any derangement of the psychic constituents, which we have already considered, how the formation of wrong or undesirable associations in childhood or youth, may have marked effect upon the actions originating from the various instincts, and lead to unthinkable, even to criminal, perversions of the same.

In the preceding chapter the following list of instincts has been given: (1) *The instinct of self-preservation.* (2) *The instinct to perpetuate the species.* (3) *The sexual instinct.* (4) *The parental instinct.* (5) *The religious instinct.* (6) *The gregarious instinct.* (7) *The instinct of self-assertion or self-abasement.* (8) *The ambitious instinct.* (9) *The acquisitive instinct.*

Very little thought enables us to deduce generally from the above list the large share that instinct has in determining our actions throughout our lives. How essential is its natural development in normal proper lines, free from unhappy, badly selected associations, follows as a matter of course, as well as the disastrous results liable to ensue upon its perversion, or the intensification or loss of power of any of its specialised forms. Speaking broadly, intensification of any of the instincts would originate a tendency to impulsive actions of the type associated with the instinct affected. Perversion of instincts is, as already stated, the result of wrong, of undesirable associations acquired in early youth. It, as a rule, is accompanied by an intensification of the special instinct affected, and frequently a loss of power is readily perceptible in some of the other special instincts, serving still further to accentuate the perversion. A diminution in the power of any instinct leads to careless indifference to and neglect of the subjects to which it is directed, and this it is which constitutes perhaps the saddest element in a case of insanity.

The derangement most commonly met with affecting the *instinct of self-preservation* is a deficiency which may manifest itself in a variety of ways and degrees. *Refusal of food* is an example of this in a small degree at times, but often in such cases this instinct is normal or even intensified. In many of such cases loss of appetite and deficiency of the gastric juices both in quantity and quality are quite sufficient to account for the refusal of nutriment, and, quite apart from this, there may be some organic disease of the intestinal tract to explain the attitude of the patient. The refusal in some cases may be due to a hypochondriacal delusion that the patient is unable to digest, and in such cases a little tactful but firm persuasion may suffice to remove the difficulty. Delusions of various sorts are to be seen accounting for this refusal of nutriment. Many patients refuse because they imagine they cannot pay for the food; others, because they think they are depriving fellow-patients by taking it, or that they are unworthy of such "luxurious repasts." In some cases the refusal arises from the delusion that the food is poisoned or contaminated; while the belief that the patient is God or is dead may be the reason given in other instances. This symptom at times is due to hallucinations of hearing "voices" ordering or warning the patient not to eat. In cases of dementia we see the extreme example of deficiency in this instinct, where patients have to be regularly fed by the attendants, owing to their total incapacity to realise their wants or the necessity of taking nourishment. Lastly, in some melancholic and delusional cases food is refused with a view to commit suicide, as an act of reparation for some imaginary sin, or with the idea of forcing the asylum authorities to send the patients back to their homes.

Self-mutilation is another way in which deficiency of the instinct of self-preservation manifests itself. The genital organs are very commonly the site chosen for such injuries, and generally with the idea of doing penance for some sin. All kinds and manner of injuries of this type are met with, and for various reasons, such as that of doing penance, or to rouse sympathy, or to support an imaginary accusation against the attendant or some fellow-patient. Dements frequently suffer injury from sheer carelessness, and this also occurs frequently in maniacal cases, while the habit many dements have of regarding their mouths as a rubbish pit, and promptly placing all they can lay their hands on, no matter what its nature, into these receptacles, often leads to serious but unavoidable injuries. Restlessness, as manifest in certain cases of dementia præcox and melancholia, by plucking at the hair, biting the nails, and picking at the skin, is often a cause of minor injuries of this type.

Suicide appears at first sight to be the manifestation of the highest degree of deficiency of this instinct—in fact, of its complete abeyance. It undoubtedly is in most cases; but in a few delusional and hallucinatory cases it is carried out in order to escape the machinations of imaginary persecutors, or in obedience to some "voice." Suicide may be purely an impulsive act, arising under the influence of alcohol or drugs, during an epileptic seizure, or in delirious or maniacal conditions. At times it may be the result of an obsession, and in this connection it is worth remembering that in many cases of depression the mere presence of an opportunity may originate a sudden suicidal impulse, even in cases where there has never been the slightest sign of such a tendency.

In cases of deliberate suicide the reasons vary tremendously. It may be planned to escape imaginary danger or persecution, or to relieve friends of the burden of the patient's maintenance, or save them from some imaginary disaster or disgrace. Very often in melancholic and delusional cases it arises from a desire to seek relief from the intolerable mental or physical suffering, the patient despairing of ever finding relief in this world. In some few cases there is no depression discernible, nor are any delusions ascertainable, the natural instinct of self-preservation being apparently replaced by a loathing of life.

In many cases, of course, patients may place themselves in dangerous positions, eat poisonous berries, drink lotions, etc., absolutely unthinkingly, and with no idea of committing suicide whatever—*e.g.*, as in the case of dements already noted under Self-mutilation.

Many cases, though deliberately bent on committing suicide, seem only to realise one way in which to accomplish their object; thus, with a case of this type bent on committing suicide by hanging, the patient might with perfect safety be left alone in a room with a case of razors or a loaded shotgun. Other cases, however, seize any opportunity that comes along, and their ingenuity in accomplishing their purpose is marvellous. I have known a patient hang himself with nine inches of cotton cloth from a bar so close to the ground that his knees had to be drawn almost up to his chin to let him get all his weight off the ground.

Besides the performance of directly suicidal acts, a deficiency in the instinct of self-preservation may lead persons to knowingly, willingly throw themselves into the way of danger in the hope that their desire for death may be gratified.

An *intensification of the instinct of self-preservation* may be the cause of gluttony, of cowardliness, miserliness, and many other undesirable qualities, which, though unpleasant for the persons who have to associate with such individuals, are certainly insufficient grounds for certification.

2. The *instinct to perpetuate the species* is the one which, when deranged, shows most clearly the effect of early associations in the development of the instincts, and provides some of the most disgusting, troublesome cases to be met with in asylums. I do not propose here to go into details concerning masochism, sadism, fetichism, and the like; enough, and more than enough, has already been written on such subjects. It is necessary, however, to deal broadly with this subject in order to emphasise the necessity of proper care and supervision over children, and their proper instruction regarding sexual matters when they arrive at an age when the first promptings of this instinct may be looked for—in both sexes at about the ages of ten to twelve years. For this to be effective, there must be frank, confidential relations between the parents, or teacher, and the offspring; and children from their earliest years should be encouraged to ask frankly and quietly questions concerning the necessities of nature. The instillation of false modesty and shame should be studiously avoided, and they should be brought to look on certain things as quite natural and ordinary occurrences, and recognised as such by everyone, though, at the same time, not made topics either of thought or conversation, any more than one would willingly think of or talk about any other unpleasant topic.

It must be realised that children are full of life and energy, and they should be encouraged to expend these in healthy recreation among suitable companions. The greatest mistake that can be made is to pen them up, to teach them that it is sinful to laugh and to be happy, to enjoy the sunshine and beauties of nature, and that all games are the work of the devil. This does, undoubtedly, occur in many families, and the children are robbed of their natural healthy pleasures, and given in their stead books to read dealing with a religion as cramped and distorted as the minds of the donors, depicting the Almighty as a God of wrath, only too anxious to consign us one and all to hell fire, and the most innocent games as snares and devices of the devil. Small wonder that such children either turn into utter blackguards, without a belief in anything except the wickedness of the world and their own determination to revel in it, or become lying, hypocritical mollycoddles, obtaining by reveries and day-dreams the happiness which is otherwise beyond their reach, full of distorted, erroneous views anent sexual relations, and addicted to masturbation and other disgusting acts of sexual perversion. Small wonder if such families provide frequent candidates for treatment by the mental expert. The dispositions, the associations they form from their earliest days, are cramped into one narrow, distorted groove; all their knowledge of natural processes has to be gathered from the promptings of their own instincts, probably intensified by the unnatural sedentary life they are forced to lead, and what they can gather by their own observation or snatch in surreptitious conversations with servants or equally undesirable associates.

The above is, I frankly admit, an extreme instance, and one meets with all grades of such errors in the upbringing of children. It is instanced here simply to emphasise the danger of such conditions, and to illustrate a frequent cause of masturbation, even in those who seemingly are healthy members of society, capable of carrying out their duties, and perhaps even looked on as highly religious people. When cases such as these become patients in asylums, can one wonder if masturbation is a prominent symptom in them?

It does not necessarily follow that all cases of masturbation are the sequence of such circumstances. Every perception forms a disposition, which persists with greater or less intensity throughout the life of the individual. This being so, we all of us must have a store of dispositions of unpleasant, offensive occurrences, which, so long as the powers of apperception are intact, remain buried in oblivion. In cases of mental derangement this restraining influence is removed; deranged instinct, stimulated perhaps by some irritation of the special senses or the genitals, has full sway, and the conversation, the whole behaviour, become shameless and indecent. This is one reason for the fact that, on the whole, the cases on the female side of an asylum are much more shameless and indecent than the male patients. The explanation is that man, being a coarser, rougher animal naturally, and seeing life from a much broader aspect than most women, looks upon occurrences of this nature as all in the day's work, and, in consequence, the dispositions arising from such perceptions are faint and more evanescent. In women, however, horror, disgust, and loathing intensify the perceptions of such occurrences, and in consequence render the ensuing dispositions stronger and more permanent. It is only to be expected, therefore, that, on apperception falling into abeyance, such dispositions would tend to have greater effect on the female mind and behaviour.

Lastly, masturbation may be purely a reflex act, due to some stimulation of the lower reflex centres of the spinal cord, such as would arise from irritation of the external genitals, or some similar condition. This, in cases where the restraint imposed by the higher centres in the brain has been removed, might well originate a purely reflex action without any participation by the higher qualities of the mind.

The *sexual instinct* is, I consider, quite apart from that of philoprogenitiveness, or that instinct which has just been considered. It is true there may be grounds for holding that the instinct of philoprogenitiveness is one of the attributes of what I look on as a separate entity, but, as my experience widens, I become more and more convinced of their existence as two distinct and separate instincts. Under the term *sexual instinct* I group the conate tendencies leading to the formation of all that common parlance indicates in the words "womanly" and "manly." The innate desire to please and attract, to soothe and comfort those around her are only some of the many results of this instinct in woman. These, and similar traits, I hold, are quite apart from any libidinous tendencies, and arise simply from woman's position, as man's helpmate and comrade, to cheer him when tired, soothe and comfort him when ill or worried, etc. Untold harm has been and is still being done by the teachings of Freud and others of his school, by instilling the doctrines that all these traits are due to one cause and one only—viz., that of desire for the sexual act. Such teaching seems to me to cast a slur on the purest, noblest traits of womanhood, to be a libel on the whole of humanity, and an insult to Him who made us.

In man the sexual instinct leads to the rougher characteristics necessary for one who has to compete in the struggle for existence, to provide a home and sustenance for wife and family, etc.

This instinct may be found intensified or diminished in cases of mental disorder. The results of such derangement can be easily followed, and are not likely to become a source of trouble nor to cause any serious manifestations. A knowledge of it, however, is essential, as it helps one to understand one's cases and to get in touch with them by realising more fully how surroundings, etc., will affect them.

The *parental instinct*, as already indicated, has a wider application than merely the care and protection of the offspring. To me it implies the relations existing between husband and wife, apart from the instinct to perpetuate the species, and extends to the feelings experienced in the presence of the young, the sick, and the helpless.

It is derangement of this instinct which is productive of some of the saddest manifestations of insanity. Diminution of its intensity, perhaps its actual abeyance, leads to coldness, complete indifference as to the condition of wife or husband and children. The wife, yearning for a word of love or a caress, is chilled by indifference, perhaps even cut to the heart by a brutal word of loathing or detestation, for in some cases of insanity this instinct seems to be completely reversed, and, instead of mere indifference, there is actual antipathy, hatred, and distrust for those who should be, and in his sane moments had been, all in all to the patient.

Such cases are naturally sad to see, and very trying for the friends and relatives of the patients. It is, however, soothing for such connections to learn that these symptoms are common in many forms of mental derangement, are simply due to the psychical disturbance, are by no means necessarily a bad prognostic sign, and are almost certain to vanish *pari passu* with the recovery of the patient.

The *religious instinct* is one of the utmost importance to the alienist in India, and a knowledge of the religious beliefs and customs of the various castes with whom he has to deal a matter of necessity. This question will be dealt with more fully under the section devoted to the "Psychic Causes of Insanity"; meantime, it will suffice to say that religious beliefs and customs are a very frequent cause of cases of hysteria and delusional insanity among Indians; and even among Europeans cases of delusional insanity and hysteria arising from such causes are frequently met with.

As a mere symptom in the course of some other form of insanity, this instinct may be intensified or reduced. The manifestations of such derangements can be readily imagined, and there is no need to unnecessarily lengthen this chapter by a discussion on such matters. Their chief import to the alienist is the influence they are likely to have on the behaviour of the patient, and patients showing any signs of intensification of religious feeling should always be carefully watched for the appearance of delusions or hallucinations which might lead to attempts at suicide or homicide.

Much stress has been laid on the *gregarious instinct* as a cause of insanity by writers of the Freudian school. A moment's consideration of the definition of insanity given in the beginning of Chapter II. also shows that, if this definition be accepted, it must follow as a matter of course that the gregarious instinct is deranged in every case of mental disorder or disease. In a very large majority of cases this derangement consists of a blunting of this instinct. This deficiency shows itself in various ways: carelessness of clothing and personal appearance, disregard of ordinary usages and customs, a preference for solitude and keeping aloof from others, delusions of persecution, are but a few of its numerous manifestations. As a cause of insanity I think its power has been tremendously overrated, both as regards cases in India and in Britain. As a symptom its deranged presence is met with in every case, and is, as a rule, of no prognostic value nor indication for special watchfulness. In recent cases of mental trouble, however, wetting the bed is often a sign of very grave prognostic import.

The *instinct of self-assertion or self-abasement* is, as noted in the previous chapter, present in us all from birth. It is largely through it that our reaction to our surroundings is affected, and from its development by the growth of experience and the formation of associations that our characters are formed. In some of us the tendency to self-assertion, in others to self-abasement, is more prominent *ab initio*, but growth and experience, education, and early surroundings have power to change any undesirable prominence of either.

Intensification of one or other is common in many forms of insanity, and may even prove a source of delusions. Thus, it is quite possible that delusions of unworthiness and of similar character may originate from an intensification of the instinct of self-abasement; while, on the other hand, intensification of the instinct of self-assertion would be liable to originate delusions of pride and grandeur. Delusions of persecution also might arise from this cause, for in practically all such cases the exalted ego is to be found, as, for such systematic persecution to be believed in, it is but a logical sequence to assume that the patient must presume himself of importance to have attracted such notice; and also in many cases there is to be found belief in former importance and opulence.

The *ambitious instinct*, when deranged, is only likely to attract notice when intensified. Sometimes its results would be really laughable were they not so pitiable. Patients from the lowest, poorest classes of society aping the airs and graces of the " upper ten " in order to impress their fellows and gain the position they imagine due to them; patients believing they are artists, successful inventors, great scientists, and that they daily turn out masterpieces for the gratification and benefit of applauding multitudes, constitute but a small selection of such cases. The cause of these manifestations lies in mental conflict, deranged imagination, and suggestibility in most cases, and their development will be gone into more fully later under the section " Psychic Causes of Insanity."

The *acquisitive instinct* is present in all men in a varying degree from our earliest days. Intensification of it is liable to produce avarice, miserliness, to lead to kleptomania and various forms of meanness, dishonesty, and other undesirable traits; while its abeyance is responsible for reckless extravagance, and those happy-go-lucky mortals who though drawing good salaries, never seem able to save, but spend every penny they earn, and probably even get into debt. Its intensification is well seen in cases of kleptomania, the early stages of general paralysis of the insane and in some cases of hebephrenia (one of the forms of dementia præcox). The derangement of this instinct, though apt to get the patient into trouble, as can asily be imagined, until the condition is recognised and proper steps taken for his care and control, is by no means likely to prove a source of danger, nor is it of any prognostic significance.

In the preceding chapter it was noted that **reason** determined voluntary action, and also constituted the process by which judgment or belief was arrived at. Reason consisting, as it does, in the weighing up of perceptions and their associations, and forming from this a conclusion, the judgment or belief, it follows of necessity that the mental faculties involved in the process—attention, association, the power of revival of psychic dispositions, etc.—must be present and unimpaired if we are to obtain good results. Hence, in cases of mental derangement, judgment and reasoning are practically always affected. The results of this are loss of business acumen, speech and action tend to become uncontrolled, and the patient is careless and irresponsible. In all forms of dementia reason is markedly in abeyance, while in delusional conditions there is marked perversion of this faculty.

The main processes affecting **apperception** having been considered singly, it is proposed now to devote a little space to the consideration of apperception as a whole. In the preceding chapter it was noted that apperception is the process by which a mental system appropriates a new element or otherwise receives a fresh determination. In most cases the appropriated element is only a part or aspect of the apperceived system; it is only in cases of subsumption of the particular under the general that the new element appropriated and the whole group apperceived correspond.

In practically every moment of our waking lives apperceptive processes are taking place. The presentation of any idea or object which attracts attention is at once apperceived, the aspects of the presentation which are congruent with the appercipient system acquiring special significance, while others remain outside the sphere of consciousness. Apperception throughout is conative process, and the mental groups or systems are grouped as systematised tendencies, the union of which is the confluence of different modes of mental activity. A system consists of partial apprehensions, of one and the same whole, in relation with one another, according as they are in relation with the central idea of the whole system.

The narrowness of consciousness and various other reasons preclude the full entry of a system into consciousness. Systems, therefore, even when they enter into conscious process, remain to a very large extent beyond the threshold of consciousness. These waiting dispositions are brought into consciousness as they are required by means of association controlled by noetic synthesis.

Mental elements sharing in the activity of one mental system are *ipso facto* for the time being unable to join in any other mental system or to act independently. From this arises the fact that our thoughts are, as a rule, in accordance with what we are saying or doing, and our adherence to one topic or subject until the attainment of its end.

On the dissolution of a mental system its elements have free scope to display the tendencies which had been suppressed by their combination—*i.e.*, by previous processes of apperception. This tendency is seen in certain stages of the hypnotic trance, in cases of hysteria, and in some cases of stupor, causing behaviour and delusions which would be impossible to the patient in his normal condition. The converse of this happens when a number of mental groups become combined into systematic unity. Here the action of each group is limited by its union, and one and all are regulated by the central idea of the system, as is seen in its extreme development in systematised delusional insanity.

An apperceptive process may be completed in a moment or be prolonged for years, and in practically every case a series of perceptions, a "mental train," is involved. This train may be wholly perceptual or wholly ideal, or it may partake of a combination of perception and ideation. As a general rule, two such mental trains take part in the process, the one, as a rule, ideal, the other perceptual. In positive apperception the process ends invariably in the confluence of these two trains into one. This blending is generally the result of relative suggestion, the evolution of one or both systems becoming gradually modified by their relation to each other until they become congruent and blend. Where the mental trains are purely ideal, this modification is wholly due to associative reproduction and relative suggestion; where one or other train is perceptual in any degree, then sense perception takes a share in the process.

Movements of fixation are important in producing and controlling the definite sequence of images which constitute these mental trains. They act by detaining the percept or image in consciousness so long as is required for the completion of that stage of the appercipient system which it subserves.

The class of images to which the signs of language belong make it possible to introduce into these mental trains, as separate and successive links, mental systems which otherwise would be merely apperceptive. This class of images excites the system as a whole.

while sense-perceptions, while exciting, also particularise it. Language gives birth to conceptual thinking, as a rule, only when words are combined in a context, only when words are so conjoined in successive order as to excite in combination distinct apperceptive systems, which apperceive each other and unite in a complex whole without losing their relative independence.

Stout applies the term *co-operation* to excitability roused in apperceptive systems by the activity of a related system. By this means these secondary systems are rendered alert and ready to act when called upon. At the same time as this occurs, it must be remembered that every mental system, in the exercise of its appercipient function, tends to prevent all other groups from becoming appercipient except such as are at the moment capable of combining with it in the same systematic activity. Another ground of competition between mental systems lies in the quantitative limitation of the total mental activity in each moment. This is the reason of the slow, difficult mentalisation found in cases of neurasthenia, melancholia, and the exhaustion psychoses. Mental activity in such cases is invariably greatly reduced; the little remaining to them is laboriously concentrated on the topic of the moment, and the effort to suddenly withdraw it to another subject is, in many cases, almost beyond their powers.

In so far as one appercipient system rouses others to excitability, it follows that by doing so it strengthens these other systems, even against itself; hence the power of an ideal group to compete with others varies inversely with the degree in which it co-operates with them. When co-operation affects a number of sub-groups in an equal degree, the one which has greatest affinity with the group to be apperceived is the one most likely to become appercipient. Again, when a number of objects, each having exclusive affinity with a different system of ideas, are simultaneously perceived, that group which is congruent with the most powerful system is alone apperceived, or if the same group is congruent with several systems the strongest of them apperceives it. These conditions have a strong bearing on the mental mechanism of melancholic and delusional cases, and go far to explain the formation of systematised delusions and the persistency of such states.

The strength of an apperceptive system is in direct proportion to the strength of the conation originating it. The stronger the conation the more likely is an interrupted process to recommence without external prompting, so soon as it ceases to be suppressed by other excitations.

Stout classifies the conditions favouring apperceptive activity as (1) Extrinsic; (2) intrinsic. Among *extrinsic conditions* he includes: (*a*) The co-operation of another system; (*b*) the recency of its own previous action; (*c*) the intensity of its previous action; (*d*) the influence of organic sensation; (*e*) its state of rest or fatigue. The *intrinsic conditions* he looks on as: (*a*) The comprehensiveness of the system; (*b*) its internal organisation; (*c*) the strength of the cohesion between its parts; (*d*) the nature of the sensory material which enters predominantly into its composition.

Some of these factors are of great importance in the ætiology of mental symptoms; thus the intensity of the excitement of a system may be intensely exaggerated, and even rendered permanent, as when a lady suffers a severe shock and continually thereafter harps upon it and believes she is continually suffering the same experience. The influence of organic sensation, too, is of importance to the alienist. Ideas connected with the satisfaction of an organic need assume predominance so soon as the corresponding organic sensation is felt with a certain degree of intensity. Every specific kind of emotion is accompanied by a characteristic organic reaction. These systemic sensations constitute an important part of the emotion, and also become associated with the apperceptive system, which is dominant when the emotion is felt. A recurrence, therefore, of a similar organic state, from whatever cause it may arise, will tend to revive the whole mental system with which it has thus become coherent.

Thus physical, organic conditions, by originating corresponding emotional states, revive past dispositions, and may reopen old sores, by brooding over which melancholic and delusional states may arise. On the other hand, however, a vigorous state of health favours hopefulness, and in its pathological expansion might lead to exaltation, etc.

The power of an apperceptive system depends on the organisation of its components, on the weight, the comprehensiveness of the system as a whole, and, lastly, on the comparative excitability of ideas derived from different senses. The more numerous, the closer the relations between the elements constituting the system, the more rapidly and completely will stimulation of a part spread and arouse the whole group. In some instances this close interrelation may be wanting, but a system may still gain strength and power from the sheer weight and mass of its components. This is exceedingly well seen in cases of systematised delusional insanity, where a mass of so-called facts are poured forth in support of the delusions, without any visible connection or relation whatsoever, either to each other or the central delusion. To the patient, however, the sheer weight and mass of these facts, which, for him, have direct connection with each other and his complaint, are irrefutable and the observer soon comes to the same conclusion, however much he may disagree with the statements in reality.

The *comparative excitability of ideas* derived from different senses is of importance even in normal life, serving to divide mankind into three main classes: (1) visuals, such as engineers, artists, etc.; (2) audiles, such as musicians; (3) motiles, as in athletes, soldiers, etc. In visuals, perceptions of sight are most vividly and readily produced; in audiles, auditory perceptions are more vivid and intense; while in motiles, the muscular sense predominates.

A fact of the utmost importance to the alienist is that apperceptive systems which are non-existent cannot be operative—i.e., *all new knowledge acquired must be a development of previous knowledge.* In many cases of insanity previous knowledge is conspicuous by its absence from congenital defect, want of early education, or as a result of derangements of the function, or disease, of the cerebral convolutions. In such cases knowledge has to be imparted from its earliest stages, and a full realisation of the position is essential for the exercise of the necessary patience, which such cases often strain to the utmost.

Destructive apperception occurs when one system, by appropriating a new element, wrests it from its former connection with another system. This may occur in two ways, according as it has its origin in a negative or in a positive apperception. Thus where a person has always been held in high esteem for his rectitude and honesty, and is suddenly discovered in some secret villainy, the new positive apperception introduces a negative one dissolving the old. Former associations, preformed connections, are thus disintegrated, and the nervous elements of the system are cast apart and, as already noted, given free scope to display such of their tendencies as had formerly been suppressed. In such cases, therefore, a double cause of derangement of psychic functions is present in the intense excitement caused by the discovery and the various mental elements liberated by the breaking up of the system.

In cases where the process of destruction has its origin in negative apperception the mechanism is somewhat more complicated, but terminates in much the same practical end from the alienist's point of view.

Mental conflict is defined by Stout as a state of more or less prolonged suspense between positive and negative apperception. It arises as a rule from the simultaneous activity of two or more systems, one and all striving to appropriate the same elements in such a way that the success of one means the defeat of the others. A frequent source of conflict arises from a plurality of systems all tending to enter into positive union with another system, though antagonistic to each other. This is the conflict of mere indeterminateness as opposed to the conflict arising from contradictions. Obstruction may arise from alternative modes of apperceiving being temporarily exhausted, or it may originate from the very multiplicity of alternatives without any indication to direct our choice. Lastly, and by no means least important, we have those cases of bewilderment springing from mere strangeness or unfamiliarity. This is akin to the old axiom that apperceptive systems which are non-existent cannot be operative; but in this instance it is the absence of an apperceptive subgroup, which is required to give a new mental combination its specific place in a wider system, which is the source of the trouble.

Conflict may work itself out to its natural termination, resulting in a new mental combination wherein the elements of conflict are eliminated, or it may be merely evaded or avoided. This forms a means of differentiating intellectual and moral character One type of individual meets doubts and difficulties bravely, and works energetically at their solution, while another type resents them and endeavours to avoid them whenever possible.

Conflict may be evaded either by a complete abandonment of the whole line of thought so soon as obstruction is met with, or by the suppression of its opponents by the system of greatest power. These two methods are again characteristic of two types of mind. The plodding, straightforward, practical mind shuns intellectual mazes and adheres to the paths of common-sense. The impetuous, excitable, unstable mind thrusts aside obstacles, overlooks difficulties, and rushes blindly towards its goal. Ideas and projects in such minds are rarely lasting: those domineering over it one moment are supplanted, forgotten the next, and so it proceeds through all grades till we come to the extreme of pathological exaltation.

As a stream when dammed seeks fresh channels for its currents, so our mental activity when obstructed seeks for fresh outlets. Thus the greater the difficulty, the more helpless the mind is in its presence, the greater will be the tendency to turn aside. Conflict at times may arouse a rapid and varied flow of ideas with a view to its own alleviation. Failing this, there is a deadlock, producing such a strain of mind as cannot be maintained for any length of time without very powerful motive. Under such conditions mental activity becomes diverted into other channels. In proportion to the power of the thwarted conation, in proportion to the intensity of the apperceptive activity obstructed, is the probability of the conflict being persistently maintained, or evaded by the repression of conflicting groups. This evasion is the more likely to occur if one of the conflicting groups be superior in extent, in the associative cohesion of its parts, and in its internal organisation to the others. Normally, one sees instances of this in the blinding influences of long-cherished convictions and hardened prejudices; in its pathological condition it is exemplified by cases of delusional insanity or paranoia. In many such cases conflict may even be conspicuous by its absence, for the power of the pre-formed system is so great that facts incongruent with it are either overlooked or transformed by coalescence from the outset. It has already been noted that an apperceptive system when active tends to eliminate from consciousness all that conflicts with it, and that the more intense it is the greater is this tendency. This is the cause of the hasty, ill-considered actions seen in fits of passion, etc., and is especially characteristic of the impetuous, unstable mind already referred to. Patients in the early stages of mania or the exaltation of folie circulaire are typical examples of this, ceaselessly promulgating all sorts of impossible schemes, resenting deeply any suggestion anent their impracticability, and yet incapable of persisting with any one scheme for any length of time, or working it out toi ts conclusion.

In fact, for healthy mentalisation is required a general excitability of all the mental systems composing the empirical ego, so that they can co-operate, compete, and conflict with comparative strength as determined by the factors already enumerated.

It is an inherent character of mental conflict to institute processes which ultimately lead to its termination. When the course of an apperceptive system is obstructed either a dead strain results, ultimately ending in stupefaction, or there is a regression of thought leading back to that point in the original train where the conflict emerged. In all these regressive processes the repetition differs from the original, being modified by the conflict, and seeking throughout to find some variation, some new channel in which the dammed-up stream of mental activity may flow. In conflict alone are these regressive trains of thought to be found, and in conflict therefore is to be found the source of all theoretical and practical knowledge. The importance of conflict as a factor in the psychic mechanism does not end here, however, for, as will be discussed in another chapter, conflict is one of the most common psychic causes of insanity.

CHAPTER VI

ÆTIOLOGICAL

THE idea most prevalent among the laity, among Europeans, as to the **cause of insanity,** is that it is due to an unstable brain readily thrown into disorder by physical causes, nervous shock, or mental strain, and that this instability is transmitted from one generation to another. Thus when a man who has suffered monetary losses, or a mother who has lost her child, becomes insane, the condition is at once believed to be directly due to the mental effect of such losses; and when a parturient woman becomes mentally deranged it is, to use Clouston's words, " due to the physical cataclysm, the pains of labour, the excitement, mental and bodily, the exhaustion, the loss of blood, septicæmia, the sudden diversion of the stream of vital energy from the uterus to the mammæ, the reflex disturbances on an unstable brain from the reproductive organs, these acting together or separately." To cases where no such causes are to be found the term *idiopathic* is applied, and supposed to be sufficient explanation; or, as in some cases occurring in adolescence, the cause is said to be cerebral involution.

Among Indians the causes most commonly—in fact, almost universally—given, are demoniac possession, a curse for slighting some faquir or sadhu, a visitation for the defiling of some grave, or a punishment for neglecting to sacrifice to some of their numerous deities, or desecrating some tree, tank, or shrine dedicated to them. Next in frequency, but a very poor second, indeed, comes disappointment in love, the patient in such cases generally having squandered, not only his own, but much of his employer's money on some well-known prostitute, who in the end has discarded him for some richer lover.

Other views, however, have been promulgated of late years and now the *toxic theory* of the causation of many forms of insanity is daily accumulating wider and stronger proof.

Twenty-two years ago Macpherson wrote: "The toxic basis of all forms of insanity is a presumption for which there is fairly good foundation but no proof." Since then Bruce has brought forward evidence which, to those who have studied bacteriology fairly deeply, must be at least most convincing presumptive evidence of the truth of this, though, as he himself says, "there is no direct proof, and never will be, because the only satisfactory and irrefutable proof would be the experimental production of morbid mental states by the use of toxines, and that is impossible."

Since this was written many eminent scientists—Mott, Orr, Rows, and others—have been working on this subject, and daily stronger and stronger evidence is accumulating to show that, though not all, at least the very large majority of mental and nervous cases arise from such causes.

Macpherson divides his causes of toxæmia into:

A. *Autointoxication*, as the result of (1) Physiological instability; (2) defective metabolism; (3) defective gland secretion; (4) autointoxication from the alimentary tract; (5) autointoxication from the liver and kidneys.

B. *Intoxication from micro-organisms* introduced into the system.

C. *Voluntary intoxication* by alcohol and drugs.

Though each of these causes is sufficient in itself to produce an attack of insanity, there is in most cases a combination of several of them. Thus with defective gland secretion or autointoxication from the alimentary canal, though primarily perhaps this may be the sole cause, yet soon the liver and kidneys become affected by the action of the toxines on them during the act of excretion, and in the end we have the double action. In the same way it can be seen that with the intoxications produced by micro-organisms, alcohol, or drugs, though the primary effects may be due to these alone, there is, sooner or later, superadded one of the subdivisions of Class A, owing to the action of these primary toxines on the rest of the organs of the body as well as on the central nervous system.

The term used to identify Class B—*i.e.*, "micro-organisms introduced into the system"—is in the majority of cases incorrect; for as a rule in most cases due to this cause the micro-organisms are found to infest some part of the alimentary canal, and it is their toxic products alone which are found to gain entrance into the general system and cause the nervous symptoms. Very often these organisms are normally present in the human alimentary system, and it is some impairment of the general vitality, some derangement of the glandular secretion or metabolism, which either may allow the micro-organisms to increase to a pathological extent, or may fail to destroy the toxines they produce, as is done in the healthy body. Very rarely indeed are micro-organisms to be found in the blood of insanes, and when found they are invariably of the streptococcic or staphylococcic group. That these invasions are not, as has been stated, terminal affections has been proved by Dr. Bruce, as the agglutinines produced by the action of the toxines of these organisms have been found in the blood of insanes who were not in the typhoid state.

Whatever the exciting cause of insanity may be, undoubtedly the **chief predisposing cause** is an unstable mental heredity. The sane are as liable as the insane to the exciting causes of insanity, but what in a man without hereditary predisposition will produce little or no effect, in one with hereditary predisposition will suffice to produce a severe attack of mental disease. Hereditary predisposition here has a wider application than to those born of insane parents only. It should be looked on as including such defects as extreme nervousness, eccentricity, alcoholism, hysteria, epilepsy, vagabondage, and any want of balance in the mental development—*e.g.*, extreme brilliancy in one direction combined with deficiency in others.

In addition to this, the truth of the old adage, *Mens sana in corpore sano*, is constantly brought home to us in asylum practice, where almost daily we see striking proofs of it. Thus the offspring of syphilitic, gouty, rheumatic, and phthisical parents are infinitely more liable to suffer from mental disorders than those sprung from healthy stock.

Probably the *working of heredity* is twofold, the patient starting life with an unstable nervous system which is readily influenced by toxines, which, in their turn, more readily gain access to the body owing to the inefficiency of its natural defences against them.

Hereditary predisposition manifests itself in various ways. The patient may be born an imbecile, or may retain his mental balance till old age sets in. In some cases two or three generations may escape, and one can in no way make sure of the manner in which the hereditary taint may manifest itself. Epileptics may beget imbeciles, alcoholics may beget maniacs, and maniacs may beget epileptics, and one and all of these may beget offspring who pass through life without showing any sign whatever of mental derangement. The maternal heredity is said to have the greatest effect on the disposition of the offspring, but the paternal heredity, too, is undoubtedly a strong factor in such cases. Asylum statistics in India on this point are most vague; owing to the meagre information as a rule received with each patient, fully 50 per cent. coming to the asylum without any family history whatever. Of the remaining 50 per cent. about 20 per cent. are noted as due to hereditary causes.

Child marriages, which are so common, especially among Hindu communities, are undoubtedly a factor to be reckoned with in the ætiology of mental diseases in India. In such cases the parties to the union are liable to suffer from the evil effects of premature sexual congress, the offspring suffer at first from the immaturity of the parents, and later from the vitality of the parents, lowered, as it must be, by such premature sexual indulgence. The lives of the widows of such marriages, often bereft of their husbands while yet even children, is wretched in the extreme, and well calculated to produce melancholic and delusional conditions as a result of the prolonged misery and mental strain.

Consanguineous marriages and the greater stress of modern civilised life are at times brought forward as predisposing factors in the production of mental disease. The former can only influence it as tending to intesify a bad heredity. The latter is a very questionable item, at least in countries where civilisation and learning have progressed slowly through the centuries and allowed of an equivalent development of the mental faculties. Where, however, the nation has vegetated for some centuries, and then, waking suddenly to its position, strives to attain at one bound the acme of civilisation and learning attained by other countries after years of laborious struggle, the result must be very different. In such cases there is no time for the necessary increase in mental development, early associations, customs, and beliefs are rudely torn away, and the minds are incapable of grasping adequately and complying with the new conditions. Such a country, therefore, must be prepared to pay a heavy bill in mental and nervous breakdowns in the course of the pursuit of its ambitions. The tendency, too, to quit the country and congregate in large centres, under unhealthy conditions, which is so prevalent nowadays, tends to lower vitality, weaken resistance to bacterial invasion, and render the outbreak of mental or nervous symptoms more probable.

In addition to the above, anything which **impairs the general vitality,** weakens resistance to bacterial invasion, may be called a predisposing cause of insanity—*e.g.*, worry, great mental strain, exhausting and debilitating illnesses, sexual and alcoholic excesses, the critical periods of life (*i.e.*, adolescence, the climacteric and puerperal states, and senility), faulty sanitation, abuse of drugs, such as opium and cocaine, etc. **Faulty upbringing and lack of moral training** are also two most common and potent factors in the production of mental disease, causing, as they do, a deficiency in the development of volition and self-control, as well as the formation of undesirable dispositions and associations, which exert an undesirable influence upon the whole of the after life.

Exciting Causes of Insanity—1. **Physical.**—Among male admissions into asylums in India undoubtedly the most common exciting cause of insanity is the abuse of Indian hemp (*Cannabis indica*) in some one or other form, some 9 per cent. of the total male admissions during 1913 being admitted for this cause alone. This, however, is a very much lower proportion than has been previously expounded, and the greater figures previously quoted were probably due to individual provinces being taken as the basis of calculations instead of all India. Practically no females are admitted owing to this cause, the most common causes among them being fever, lactation and childbirth, and mental stress.

As already stated, the most prevalent view held at present is that the disease originates *de novo* in the deranged cells and fibres of the cortex of the brain, and that the physical symptoms concurrent with such disease are directly the result of the pathological changes in the cerebral cortex. This on a little consideration will, I think, be admitted by all to be rather too sweeping a statement, as it palpably assumes that the brain is immune from the results of disease affecting the body as a whole, takes no note of the physical symptoms which in the majority of cases precede insanity, and ignores altogether the fact that, in practically all cases, physical improvement precedes any change for the better in the mental condition.

With the theory of the toxic origin of insanity no such fault can be found. Its very essence is that a physical cause in all cases must precede the mental symptoms, and, therefore, that a physical improvement must take place before any hope of improvement in the mental condition can be held. Bruce's work in this line also furnishes invaluable evidence in its favour, proving, as it does in certain cases, the presence of distinct hyperleucocytosis along with the presence of bacterial agglutinines in the blood. Still further we have in many cases changes in the integument and kidneys, which indicate that the excretory system is straining its utmost to remove some deleterious substances from the organism.

At times the mental condition seems more of a *functional nature*, depending possibly on the diurnal rise and fall of the *blood-pressure*, or even varying to a still greater extent and depending on the four-weekly curve hereafter noted as being present normally. In connection with this it is interesting to remember the derivation of the term "lunatic," which arose from an old-time belief that the phases of the moon were in some mysterious way connected with the course of insanity. This regular periodicity, however, is readily explained by the regular periodic rise and fall of the blood-pressure, the exacerbations of insanity, as a rule, occurring at its maxima or minima.

The exciting causes of insanity may be divided into two broad classes: (*a*) non-toxic; (*b*) toxic.

(*a*) *The chief non-toxic* cause is probably exhaustion, either as the result of severe physical or mental effort or severe illness, for when vitality is at a low ebb it is but natural that the brain should be affected, both structurally and functionally, as well as the other organs of the body, and the greater the hereditary predisposition of the patient the more readily will mental symptoms develop.

The other commoner non-toxic causes of mental symptoms are probably the results of hæmorrhage and traumatism. Other causes, as anæmia, cardiac disease, and narrowing of the lumen of the bloodvessels, are noted by some authors, but it seems to me incorrect to enter into these here, as in all of such cases there is not only a possibility but a very great probability of intoxication; in anæmia an autointoxication probably from the intestinal tract and defective metabolism, and in the others an intoxication due to the causes of the arterial and cardiac conditions. Sudden deprivation of the special senses of sight and hearing occasionally brings on attacks of insanity.

(*b*) *Toxic causes.*—These may be divided into three groups:

(1) *Toxines of Metabolic Origin.*—With these, as a rule there are symptoms of severe nutritional disorder, with diminished excretion from the skin, intestines, and kidneys.

(2) *Toxines of Bacterial Origin.*—In these cases there is hyperleucocytosis, and agglutinines and alexines are present in the serum. Besides these, there is a diminution in the amount of chlorides excreted in the urine, and at times boils, pustules, and irritative rashes are seen on the skin. The organisms producing these conditions are, more often than not, normal inhabitants of the body which become able to produce their effect through a weakening of the natural defences of the body against bacterial infection, and these, as already noted, are especially prone to break down in those of marked neurotic heredity.

It is supposed by many that the bacteria normally present in the intestinal tract are there for some purpose, and are essential for the due carrying on of certain physiological processes. Bruce, in his work, states that it is possible that their toxines act as a nervous stimulant, as he has noted in persons who, though not insane, are extremely nervous and irritable, that the blood-serum often contains agglutinines and alexines to such organisms as the staphylococci, etc., and cites cases of mental confusion and excitement, seen by him, indistinguishable from acute mania, arising as the result of acute poisoning by the *Staphylococcus pyogenes aureus* and the *Diplococcus pneumoniæ*.

(3) *Drug toxæmias* include poisoning by the various forms of *Cannabis indica*, opium and morphia, cocaine, chloral, and alcohol, etc.

More often than not the mental condition is due to a combination of these causes, an exhaustion condition combining later in the course of the disease with a toxæmic, or metabolic and bacterial toxæmias may be combined and produce mixed symptoms, and almost invariably alcoholic and similar drug toxæmias are combined both with metabolic and bacterial ones. It must also further be noted that the differences in working between two normal brains are still further exaggerated in disease, and that no two brains, therefore, can be expected to react in the same manner even to the same toxæmias. The effects of brain habits must be remembered also as affecting sleep and the general routine life of the patient, for bad brain habits are much more easily acquired than good ones.

2. **Psychic Causes of Insanity.**—In recent years much discussion has centred round the theories promulgated by the Austrian schools of Freud and Jung, but now psychologists are practically unanimous in affirming that their theories are unsound, and the probability is that in another twenty years their teaching will be forgotten or only stored as curiosities in scientific libraries. This being so, it is needless to cumber such a book as this aims to be with an exposition of their theories and doctrines. Many cases of insanity, however, are undoubtedly due to psychic causes alone, and it behoves the student to have a knowledge of these as well as of the physical conditions liable to cause mental derangements.

In Chapters IV. and V. we have considered briefly normal psychology, and the derangements of this which produce many of the symptoms found among the alienated and neurotic. It is proposed now to discuss the ways in which mental diseases may arise from such derangements alone.

It will simplify this question if we consider one typical and well-known class of such cases first, and then extend the knowledge thus acquired broadly to the rest of this division. Hysteria is naturally the type one would choose as coming most frequently into the sphere of the ordinary medical practitioner.

Reverting to Chapter IV., it will be found on consideration that every case of hysteria presents certain definite departures from the normal psychological standard. These are: (1) a hyperacute emotionalism; (2) an abnormally acute state of suggestibility; (3) an excessive tendency to indulge in reveries and day-dreams—*i.e.*, an abnormal imagination or an excess of subjective activity with a marked diminution of objective control; (4) hyperacuity of one or more instincts, and a deficiency of others.

With these facts to start with, the onset of hysteria can usually be traced as follows: Mental conflict arises from some cause, generally from the obstruction of some conation or desire. In the normal healthy mind, as shown in Chapter V., this condition may lead to abandonment of the whole line of thought, to a regression over the line of thought in endeavour to find a fresh solution of the difficulty, or to evasion of the conflict by suppression of one or more of the conflicting groups. This suppression of a conflicting group is more probable the more antagonistic conation is to it, and the greater the superiority of the opposing group in extent, in its associative cohesion, and in its internal organisation. In hysteria the state of hyperacute emotionalism tends to accentuate the conation, as has already been shown in Chapter IV. Hence the probability of such conflicts terminating in the suppression of the group antagonistic to the conation is greatly enhanced.

Again, in considering will, desire, etc., in Chapter V., it was shown that certain desires are recognised from the outset as unattainable, and receive no further thought from the normal person, and that to these desires the term *wish* is applied.

It is these wishes that in a very large majority of cases constitute the conatus originating the mental conflict in such patients. Realising the futility of the attainment of their wish, the victims of this condition, instead of abandoning it, as normal persons would do, resort to imagination as a means of satisfying their otherwise insatiable conation. In this way arise the reveries and day-dreams which form such constant symptoms in these cases. These reveries tend to increase the intensity of the conation, raise up associations around it, and, in time, owing to the increased state of suggestibility present in the patient, by a process of autosuggestion the contents of the reveries become looked on as actual facts, and to the patient constitute his real life, actual events, objective happenings, entering but little, if at all, into his consciousness. The derangement of the instincts serves to enhance the conation in much the same way as does the increased emotionalism, and thus introduces yet another factor, which leads to the evasion of the conflict by the suppression of opposing groups and objective activity.

The applicability of this theory is best demonstrated by a consideration of cases, and I will take the last three which have come under my notice. It will be noticed in them that, though in every case the above mechanism is present, in none of them is it absolutely as detailed, the conation and conflict assuming different form in every case.

Case XX.

A. B., aged 19, a Punjabi Mussulman sepoy in the ——th Punjabis, while on a night march across the desert in Seistan, fell out to micturate. Along the caravan routes in this region, if a death occurs in a *khafila* (caravan) the body is buried anywhere by the side of the track. As ill-luck would have it, this lad, in the darkness, chanced upon one of these graves, and unknowingly defiled it before its presence was discovered. His distress was great, naturally, as he feared the *bhut* (ghost) of the deceased would haunt or "possess" him for this desecration. His consternation was still further enhanced by his comrades, who sympathised with or flouted him constantly, some even going the length of writing to famous mullahs and peries at Lahore, Delhi, and other places for charms to be worn by the culprit as a safeguard against the *bhut*.

All this naturally increased his distress, and enhanced the conation to escape from this infliction at all costs. The emotion of fear caused organic reaction; he became dyspeptic and debilitated, brooded over his evil fate, and, finally, by auto-suggestion, became convinced he had been seized upon by some *bhut*, and an hysterical fit, pseudo-epileptic in character, occurred. He was thereupon brought to hospital, and I saw him then for the first time.

When I first saw him he was silent, morose, and depressed, and with the utmost difficulty could I get him even to tell me his name. The history I got with him was that he had had an epileptic fit the previous evening, and then gone mad (*pagal hua*).

I was by no means convinced of either of these statements, and with some difficulty got his story from him. Briefly, it was as already stated, the desecration unwittingly of the grave, and this "possession by the ghost" as a result. It was useless to try to persuade him there was no such thing as a *bhut*, as it would have been contrary to beliefs and superstitions imbued from his infancy. These had to be accepted as unquestionable. I spoke quietly but firmly to him, pointed out that the *bhut* would have a similar character to the man, and that no man would ever dream of inflicting such punishment for an unwitting act of the kind. He acquiesced in this after some little time, and then I explained to him carefully how his seizure had arisen, much as I have done in the preceding part of this chapter. He seemed much impressed by the explanation, and left me in a much cheerier, more hopeful mood. During the next few days he had one or two slight seizures, which were checked by strong smelling-salts. I saw him every day, and talked to him in the same strain, and in ten days he was back to duty, and has had no recurrence since, though this happened some eighteen months ago.

Case XXI.

C. D., a rifleman in the ——th Gurkha Rifles, was sent to hospital one morning. On asking about him I received the usual statement in such cases, "*pagal hua.*"

I found him in much the same general condition as Case XX. He was silent and depressed, but there was a distinct look of fear on his face, and his whole body shook with tremors, which he vainly tried to repress. At first I could not get even a word from him. At length, however, I gained his confidence, and he unfolded his tale of woe. Prior to leaving his village in Nepal, some two years ago, he had, in the foolishness of youth, omitted to sacrifice a fowl to the goddess of his village, and she had at last found him out, and was punishing him for his neglect. I noticed while he was speaking that he had a severe nasopharyngeal catarrh, and on examination found he had fever. Influenzal colds were rife in the station at the time.

A little consideration convinced me the case was as follows: He had felt the emotional depression due to the onset of influenza, and gone searching for a cause for it. With the restricted objective interests and associations of primitive races, he had struck upon this explanation for it, and the enhanced suggestibility and imagination found in such people had done the rest.

I treated him on the same lines as Case XX. No attempt was made to deny the village goddess and her power, but it was pointed out to him that she could be appeased if he would write to his father and get him to sacrifice two fowls instead of the original one. Meantime, until the letter could reach his home we would keep him in hospital, so that he would be safe from her revenge.

This acted like a charm. The letter was despatched, he was kept for a few days in hospital and treated for influenza, and ultimately discharged to duty bright and cheery, cured of his influenza, and free from any sign of his former trouble.

In this case I consider that influenza produced an emotional mood which became the origin of the mental symptoms in much the same way as Case XX. originated from the emotion of fear.

Case XXII.

E. F., a rifleman in the ——th Gurkha Rifles, is practically identical with Case XXI., but here the original emotional depression was due to pyorrhœa alveolaris and dyspepsia. He was treated on similar lines to Case XXI., and with equally good results, as he was discharged to duty within a week.

These three cases, unfortunately from my present point of view, implicate one instinct only—the religious instinct. This emphasises, however, the stress I have already laid upon the importance of this over other instincts, and illustrates well a type of case which figures very largely among the practice of alienists in India.

Case XX. shows the effect following immediately upon a conflict; Cases XXI. and XXII. illustrate how conflict may arise after long periods of apparent oblivion. In such cases some trivial incident, through association, or, as in these cases, ill-health through emotional depression, excites the dispositions which reawake the conflict, which, owing to altered circumstances, is not thrashed out as formerly, when bodily and mental health were normal, but continues unsolved in consciousness, making life a burden to the patient until aid is given to him and the difficulty solved.

Many, if not all, cases of paranoia, and a large proportion of cases of hebephrenia and katatonia (the three types of dementia præcox), are probably explicable on these lines, the apparent unconsciousness in the last two types seeming, in many cases at least, to be largely objective, and due to a wiping out of consciousness of everything irrelevant or antagonistic to the subject of the reverie, which has so absorbed the intellect as to give rise to symptoms necessitating the individual's incarceration.

Intense emotional shock, as already pointed out, may so intensify the activity of a presentation and the resulting disposition that its persistence in consciousness may be indefinitely prolonged, perhaps rendered even permanent. Such a case is seen when a mother sees her child snatched from the jaws of death from under a runaway horse, and insists continually thereafter that it has been killed, in spite of all proof to the contrary. Cases of rape frequently furnish examples of this ætiological factor.

The effects of derangements of cognitive synthesis have already been noted in the early part of Chapter V., and require no further notice here.

CHAPTER VII

THE PREVENTION OF MENTAL AND NERVOUS DISEASES

THE old saying, "Prevention is better than cure," is one the truth of which has long been recognised, and which has for long been applied to many branches of medicine. Till recent years, however, but little has been done towards the prevention of mental and nervous diseases.

Much undoubtedly can be done towards the prevention of such conditions, and it is the aim of this chapter to bring this briefly to the notice of the general practitioner and others in India, in the hope that through them much may be done to combat the ideas prevalent, though fast disappearing, regarding the causation of insanity, and the hopeless condition of those thus afflicted. In this and other ways, to be discussed later, a prophylactic campaign may originate against these conditions, which may prove of great value to posterity.

Owing to the atmosphere of conjecture and supposition which at present enwraps these conditions, the problems to be dealt with here are undoubtedly more complex than those which arise, let us say, in connection with the prevention of infectious diseases. Still, a certain number of mental diseases are known to be due to causes as definite as the bacterial invasions to which certain infectious diseases are known to be due. Thus in Korsakow's syndrome, or in G.P.I., we know that in the former case the condition is wholly due to alcohol, and would not have arisen had the patient refrained from alcoholic excess, while in the latter case the condition is due to syphilis, and its prevention consists solely in the prevention of syphilis.

In many, and, sad to say, the majority of types of mental disease, the ætiological factors are not so well understood. This is the main reason for the numerous classifications which exist at present, many of which are admittedly provisional, and promulgated with a view to the results of further research rescuing various entities from the provisional groups to which they are at present relegated.

In discussing this subject it is proposed to consider first some of the factors which are known to produce, directly or indirectly, mental disease, and at the same time to refer to possible means for their control. Thereafter other causes which it is believed have a considerable influence in the production of insanity, but whose action is not so clearly proven, will be considered. Finally, the means for a prophylactic campaign against such conditions in general will be discussed.

Infectious diseases are responsible for a certain percentage of cases, mainly of the types variously classified as confusional insanity, mania, exhaustion psychoses, or the infective exhaustion insanities. At various times I have had under my care cases due to malaria (which furnishes, in my opinion, a very much larger percentage of admissions to asylums in India than is generally believed, not alone as a result of the toxines formed by the parasite, but also, in many cases, from the quinine which people are in the habit of regarding as wholly innocuous and imbibing in enormous quantities), pneumonia, smallpox, typhoid fever, measles, influenza, and septicæmia, and there is no reason why any or all of the other infectious diseases should not have similar results. Influenza is known to be especially liable to produce mental derangements; sandfly fever, to my own knowledge, in many cases leaves a condition of extreme nervous exhaustion and irritability closely akin to neurasthenia, while dengue also has a marked effect upon the nervous system. The action of these conditions as secondary or contributory causes it is impossible to estimate; thus they may determine a recurrence of insanity in a patient subject, let us say, to "circular" or "manic-depressive" insanity, or, combined with other agents, may precipitate an attack, in which the infective disease plays only a minor part.

The preventive measures in such cases are already being undertaken in the general arrangements for the prevention of the infectious diseases themselves. Much, however, can still be done by improving our methods of treating *febrile conditions*. A knowledge of hydrotherapy, the pathology of delirium, and the evil results of continued high temperature on the nervous structures is essential to enable us to grasp the evil consequences which may ensue, and to lessen the number of cases of mental disease arising from this cause.

Dr. Mott, in his article in Allbutt's "System of Medicine," vol. vii., p. 213, writes: "When the temperature of the body rises above the normal there is, first, an excitation of the neuron, then exhaustion—the exhaustion is the result of the oxygen" (in the neuron) "being used up faster than it can be replaced and stored, and the neuron ceases its functional activity; it is not, however, destroyed unless the temperature rises to such a degree as to produce a heat coagulation of the neuroglobulin." Again, on p. 235, we find: "(1) That a temperature of 109·5° F. can produce this coagulation, and death of the protoplasm" (of the nerve-cell) "rapidly . . . . (2) that prolonged high temperature of 107–108° F. will produce the same coagulative process." Dr. Mott and Professor Halliburton, working together, found that a neuroglobulin in nerve-cells, which coagulates rapidly at 167° F. (75° C.), can be coagulated at a temperature between 107·2° F. and 109·4° F. if kept at this heat for about four hours. Goldschieder and Marineus have found experimentally that a certain amount of this coagulative change may take place without the death of the cells, and Dr. Mott considers this the explanation of the recovery which often takes place in some forms of hyperpyrexia when the cold bath is resorted to without delay.

Thus a high temperature affects the cells in two ways: (1) through their oxygen metabolism; (2) through the coagulation of the globulins and proteins of their cell-protoplasm. If in addition to these two factors we have a third, the presence of a toxine in the circulating fluids surrounding these cells, it does not require a very great effort to conceive why the mental faculties may be thrown out of gear in such conditions.

Syphilis is a much commoner cause of mental and nervous disease than is commonly supposed. In a most interesting and instructive article in the *Journal of Mental Science*, October, 1913, by Kate Fraser, M.B., and H. F. Watson, M.B., the results of their investigations into cases of mental deficiency and epilepsy by means of the Wassermann reaction are given. Their conclusions are as follows:

"1. Syphilis is the causative factor in a very considerable percentage of cases of mental deficiency of whatever degree of severity, as it is present in over 50 per cent.

"2. Syphilis is also the main causative factor in the production of that type of epilepsy which manifests itself at early ages. Syphilis is present in an equal degree in those cases in which epilepsy is associated with mental deficiency, and in cases where no apparent mental defect exists.

"3. The investigation by means of the Wassermann test into the families of defective children who have given a negative reaction has shown that syphilis is associated with a still higher percentage of cases than is ascertained by the examination of the patients alone. At the same time, an examination of ' the families of those children giving positive reactions affords further evidence of the presence of syphilitic infection.'

"4. A very small percentage of cases of mental deficiency and epilepsy giving a positive Wassermann reaction show external evidence of congenital syphilis, even where the family history and the examination of other members of the family afford practically conclusive evidence of the existence of syphilitic infection."

This alone would suffice, I think, to convince any reasonable being of the enormous scope there is here for prophylaxis; but when we consider its further effects on the central nervous system, the numbers who succumb yearly to G.P.I., locomotor ataxy, cerebro-spinal syphilis, acquired dementia, etc., we realise more fully the grim spectre which follows on youthful indiscretions, and haunts posterity even "unto the third and fourth generations." The only available statistics to show the incidence of G.P.I. among those who acquire syphilis are those of Mattauschek and Pilcz, published in the *Berliner klinische Wochenschrift*, February 19, 1912. As a result of their investigations into the histories of 4,134 officers of the Austrian army who had contracted syphilis during the period 1880-1890, they found that 4·67 per cent. of these officers developed G.P.I.

Tuberculosis is worthy of separate mention here, for, apart from the effects of exhaustion and debility, and the action of the tubercular toxine on the nervous system, one occasionally meets with a special type of mental derangement characteristic of disorder due to tuberculosis. The main symptoms of this type are those of slight melancholia, combined with ill-defined delusions of a hypochondriacal, persecutory type. No further action beyond that already begun for combating this disease is possible, but a knowledge that this is one of its possible effects might well be added to the information already disseminated about tuberculosis, for among the many benefits derivable from curing incipient cases and checking the spread of tuberculosis is undoubtedly to be entered the diminution, even to a small extent, of the prevalence of mental derangement.

Acute articular rheumatism and pneumonia at times give rise to mental disturbances. In the former case the mental symptoms appear commonly about the end of the second week, though occasionally they are postponed to the later stages of the disease. Associated with rheumatism and endocarditis, too, we have chorea and choreic insanity, which are points well worth keeping in view. Mental symptoms, arising from pneumonia, are generally antecedent to the outbreak of physical manifestations, and are usually of a delirious, maniacal order, and at times accompanied by deafness and severe supra-orbital pain; as a rule the mental disturbances disappear with the onset of the physical symptoms.

Having thus briefly touched upon the chief microbic diseases which may cause or give rise to mental disorder, let us consider for a little the **chief poisons from other sources** which may bring about mental or nervous symptoms.

In this connection arises one of the great stumbling-blocks in Indian statistical returns—viz., the distinguishing between habit disorders and ætiological factors. The majority of Indians, for instance, are in the habit of taking very small quantities of one or other form of *Cannabis indica*, especially in the hot weather, for the sake of its cooling properties. Such an individual is seized with symptoms of mental derangement, more likely than not due to some wholly different cause. A cursory enquiry is made into the individual's history, perhaps through a sub-assistant surgeon, more often than not through the police. "Bhang khata?" "Cheras pita?" are almost invariably the first questions asked. "Jee han!" comes the reply, and down goes *bhang* or *cheras* as the cause of insanity, and no further trouble is taken. In many cases one often has cause to wonder if even so much trouble has been taken. The result is that much of the information received with patients on their admission to asylums is meagre and unreliable in the extreme.

Cannabis indica has been said to be one of the greatest factors which swell the asylum population in India. Going by particulars received with patients it undoubtedly may be, and in some provinces it undoubtedly may play a much greater part as an ætiological factor than in others. In my experience, however, many cases are reported as due to abuse of *Cannabis indica* which, on close examination, show none of the typical symptoms, physical or mental, which one would expect in cases due to this drug, and further enquiry from the patient himself, if he recovers, or from his relatives, generally elicits some other cause as much more compatible with the symptoms exhibited, and in many cases a strenuous denial of ever having touched the drug in any form.

Opium is indulged in commonly by Indians, much in the same way as *Cannabis indica*, but in my experience cases due to this cause are few and far between. This, as already noted in Chapter I., I consider to be due to Indians taking the drug as pills, and very rarely, if ever, smoking it as is the custom in Persia and China. In this form the drug seems to have very much less noxious effects, and very rarely indeed do we find in India the physical, mental, and moral wrecks so vividly depicted by many writers as common to those who habitually indulge in this vice. *Morphia*, owing to its costliness, is rarely indulged in by Indians.

Cocaine is a drug which, before the war, was taking firm hold upon India. Much of the drug, however, was smuggled into India from Germany, and the war having dammed this source, the difficulty in obtaining it has increased tremendously. It is to be hoped that, now peace has been restored, steps may be taken to maintain this desirable state of affairs, and heavy fines and long terms of imprisonment render smuggling a much less profitable business. In India the drug is generally eaten mixed in *pan*, and hence the necrosis of the nasal septum so common among its Chinese, European, and Eurasian devotees, who commonly take this drug in the form of snuff, is rarely, if ever, met with.

Alcohol is not so frequent a cause of mental and nervous disorders in India as in countries where European races constitute the bulk of the population, mainly because of caste and religious customs, which prevent the Indian on the whole from indulging in it. The effects of alcohol vary greatly, not only between individuals, but between races. The form of liquor indulged in has been brought forward, and undoubtedly with some reason, as an explanation of this; others, however, support the view that a species of alcoholic immunity is produced in races who have drunk hard for centuries. The proof of this latter view is supported by the fact that most primitive races are intolerant of alcohol, and unless the supply be stopped it may threaten the very existence of such nations. Other points than these, however, have probably more to do with the matter. Thus the effects of alcohol are invariably greater upon those sprung from neurotic stock, and a very large number of habitual inebriates will be found, on enquiry, to have a tainted heredity. In fact, just as an alcoholic parent may beget an epileptic or an idiot, so a parent who is of weak nervous stability may beget offspring who readily fall into alcoholic habits. Besides its effects on the nervous system we must also remember its action on the body generally, and that by lowering the general resistance to infection by bacterial organisms it must of necessity be a strong predisposing factor to those insanities due to such causes. In fact, as Craig ably puts it, "alcoholism is so far-reaching in its results that in the individual we find a progressive tendency to mental and bodily deterioration and a lowered resistance to bodily disease—in the offspring a proneness to idiocy, epilepsy, and criminality, and in the race a higher disease rate, a higher mortality rate, and a lower birth rate."

Heredity, early associations, habit, and so on, may all account for alcoholism, and, whichever its cause may be, there is no doubt as to its unfavourable effects on each and all of the types of mental disease; and its influence cannot be too strongly insisted upon and borne in mind in any general scheme of prophylaxis undertaken against mental and nervous disorders.

The prophylactic measures indicated against these ætiological factors lie mainly in a strict enforcement of the terms of the Poisons Act, and registration and supervision of *pan* sellers in the case of cocaine. In this class of case, too, the punishment might well be enhanced, and made commensurate with the profits derived from such illegal traffic and the grave harm it causes to the race.

Cases of mental disease occasionally arise from **poisoning due to occupations.** These are cases mainly due to mercury, lead, carbon-monoxide and carbon-bisulphide. The means for their prevention naturally lies in the measures employed for safe-guarding workmen employed in dangerous trades.

Having thus briefly attempted to outline some of the main

extra-corporeal factors in the causation of insanity, let us consider for a little the **possible internal or endogenous factors.** Much work has of late years been done in this direction, but much still remains to be done, and while theories and suppositions are numerous, much proof still remains to be sought for here. Most of the factors are poisons, due for the most part to some *physical disease*—nephritis, gout, enteritis—which in many cases is beyond the scope of preventive medicine. In considering these points it is well to remember that *blood-pressure* often seems to influence mental symptoms, in many cases even as much as toxines. Thus in manic-depressive insanity attacks of depression are usually associated with a high blood-pressure, and those of exaltation most commonly appear when the pressure is relatively low; so also in women mentally affected, attacks of excitement generally accompany the menses, when the blood-pressure is at a low level. *Derangements of metabolism,* the influence of *internal secretions,* of toxines secreted in excess by *bacteria normally saprophytic* in the intestinal canal, are all being investigated as possible factors in the production of mental and nervous derangements, and our knowledge of the influence of these is increasing daily.

A history of **injuries to the head** is received with a certain small percentage of cases, and as proper regulation of traffic, especially in large cities, and proper measures for the protection of employees on railways and in large factories can minimise these to an appreciable extent, it is not out of place to bring this forward in an article on this subject.

Heredity is undoubtedly one of the most important factors in the production of mental disease. Statistics in India are of but little use in determining the percentage of admissions into asylums with a history of hereditary taint owing to the impossibility of obtaining any but the most meagre information in over 95 per cent. of cases. Indian statistics for 1913 show an insane heredity in some 18·71 per cent. of all admissions, while in England and America this rises to well over 50 per cent., probably owing to more reliable and fuller information being available. A brief summary of the results of recent theories and research on this subject is worthy of consideration.

The theory of the *continuity of the germ plasm* has caused much dissension. If it be true, then, as Weismann states, the inheritance of acquired characters is inconceivable. The occurrence of toxines, however, in the nutritional fluids surrounding the cell, as in syphilitics and alcoholics, may well affect the germ plasm. So soon, however, as the sperm cell produces fertilisation in the mother and is removed from such influences, there is the natural tendency for the cell to reassume its normal characters, and, even if the mother be similarly affected, so soon as birth takes place the child is removed from such influences, and the same tendency to return to the normal is apparent. The questions thus raised are at present still unanswered, mainly, as pointed out by Dr. White, "because up to the present time it has been impossible to define an acquired character." The most one can do therefore, in the meantime, is "to bear constantly in mind the fact that the individual is the result both of the tendencies which he acquired through the germ plasm of his ancestors plus the effects produced on him by his environment."

A study of the division of the chromosomes which occurs in the process of fertilisation led to the promulgation of *Galton's law of ancestral inheritance*, which is to the effect that each parent contributes one-fourth of the heritage, each grandparent one-eighth, each great-grandparent one-sixteenth, etc. This postulation, however, has been shown in recent years to be erroneous, a further study of the fission of the chromosomes and their determiners in the formation of new cells having largely contributed to discredit this theory.

The *Mendelian theory of inheritance* is, according to Dr. White, "based on the fundamental conception that there are certain characters of the individual, usually called unit characters, that are represented by the determiners of the germ plasm. These determiners are conceived of as being definite material entities, and, therefore, the inheritance of these special characters cannot be a blended inheritance in the true sense of that term, but must be an inheritance dependent upon the segregation and grouping of these determiners, and Mendel endeavoured to formulate with mathematical precision the ways in which inheritance would manifest itself by determining all the possible combinations in which these determiners could group themselves."

A further conception of Mendel's is that some of these determiners are dominant and others recessive; thus, if a flower contains a determiner for a red colour and a determiner for a white colour, if the red determiner be dominant the colour of the flower will be red, but its germ plasm would, nevertheless, contain a white determiner, which, even though recessive, might still enable the flower to reproduce a certain number of white progeny.

Mendel has worked out his theory exhaustively in the laboratory in connection with plants and lower animals which multiply rapidly and go through their cycle of existence in a comparatively short space of time. The situation as regards mankind is, however, different; small families, miscarriages, etc., are bound to throw out our calculations and make it impossible for us to foretell how any one child will develop. Its importance is considerable, however, and it is a point requiring much consideration when eugenics are being discussed. For example, let us take two cases of parents, in each case absolutely healthy themselves, but in one family both parents have a recessive determiner. By Mendel's law the results may be graphically shown as follows: If A represent the family with the recessive determiner in the parents, then the resulting offspring from Mendel's calculations will be one diseased, two with recessive determiner, and one healthy; whilst in B, the healthy parents free from tainted determiners, the family will all be healthy. If all the various combinations be thus worked out the influence of heredity on the human race and the impossibility of drawing eugenarian conclusions from a consideration of the individual alone are very apparent.

Galton's law of filial regression formulates the tendency of the offspring of a parent, abnormal in one way or another, to revert to the normal standard of their race in this respect.

Karl Pearson promulgated the *law of fertility:* "Fertility is not uniformly distributed among all individuals, but for stable races there is a strong tendency for the character of maximum fertility to become one with the character which is the type."

Lastly, and by no means least in this connection, we have the *law of anticipation*, on which so much work has been done by Mott. Briefly, it is that children of tainted nervous heredity become affected much earlier than their parents, according to Mott's results on the average at half the age of their parents. In this process Mott sees an effort on the part of Nature to eliminate bad stock, so that, if left untrammelled, in three generations there would be a regression to the normal, provided no further unsound elements were introduced by bad mating.

A consideration of the theories and laws briefly summarised above gives us some idea of the enormous influence heredity must have on the race, and how essential it is that some strong action should be taken on this point, to prevent the propagation of unsound stock. Not that I would recommend the lethal chamber or emasculation. Far from it! But I would advocate strongly the teaching of the elements of these laws in higher schools and colleges, and a gradual dispersion in this way throughout the country of this knowledge, whereby perhaps a certain number at least of unsuitable marriages may be prevented.

The **psychic causes of mental derangements** have already been dealt with in previous chapters, and there should be no need to recapitulate them here. Suffice it to say that they demonstrate clearly how necessary careful training and choice of environment is in children of neurotic types. The necessity of not instilling a false sense of shame and hypocrisy into such children is at once apparent. Their parents should endeavour to maintain the closest sympathy and understanding with them, which will allow of frank and sensible consultations on sexual questions when they arise, and prevent to a very large extent the serious consequences likely to ensue if such children be left to themselves. It is for such cases as these that psychiatric clinics would be of undoubted service; many of them in the early stages would, in all probability, be saved from further trouble, whilst in more advanced cases much relief could undoubtedly be obtained, and relatives and friends would be able to obtain timely advice on the upbringing of such children.

Other causes contributing to the ætiology of mental and nervous disorders are numerous, and in many instances their potency is most evident. *Child marriages* are undoubtedly to be reckoned with in the ætiology of mental disease in India. In such cases, where one or both parties to the union have not arrived at maturity, setting aside for the moment the disastrous effects to the offspring, the nervous and physical strain of such unions is bound to be enormous and tell heavily on the individual in later life. The offspring, too, in such cases are bound to be affected, at first by the immaturity of the parents, and later by the vitality of the parents, lowered, as it must be, by such premature sexual indulgence. *Unemployment*, *privation*, *over-*

work, child labour are but a few of the many causes under which weaknesses develop, which under happier circumstances might never have arisen.

Having thus briefly reviewed some of the main ætiological factors to be contended with, the next point which arises is the **views prevalent among the population in India** generally regarding insanity, its causation, its possible termination, and the character of an asylum, for, in my own experience, these are the earliest items to be dealt with in a prophylactic campaign of the type under consideration. Judging from the accounts given by the relatives and friends of patients admitted to the asylum, even by those of families of good position and standing, the persistence of the old views of "demoniacal possession," "a curse by a faquir for some slight," "a punishment by some deity for some neglect in religious observances, or for felling a tree or damaging some property dedicated to him," is practically universal. The effect of such beliefs on their views as to the course and progress of the disease and its proper treatment can be readily imagined, and requires no exposition here. As regards their views of asylums, two ideas seem to prevail, according to whether the person is a relative or merely a friend of some patient, or comes, perhaps out of curiosity, perhaps with a real wish to acquire knowledge, to "see an asylum." The former class appear to regard it with horror as a sort of place of perpetual confinement, where the inmates are either herded together in cages like wild animals, or shut up for ever in eternal solitude. The latter seem to look upon it as a sort of menagerie or circus, where they will see a lot of wild animals performing tricks, perhaps being fed for their amusement. To whichever class the visitor belongs, I think he leaves us with his views very considerably altered. In fact, one such visitor, well educated and intelligent, remarked, when taking his departure: "An asylum! This is not an asylum! It is a hospital where sick people are treated! Why is it not called a hospital, and its true nature spread among the community?"

And now let us consider on what lines **prophylaxis** should be begun. The first and most important step is undoubtedly to *uproot the old superstitions and prejudices regarding such cases and asylums.* To do this is not the work of months, but of years; but undoubtedly it can be done, not only by alienists, but by the general practitioner, through schools and in other similar ways. Let the title "asylum" be discarded. It will take longer to strip it of the old erroneous prejudices attached to it than to vest in a new title a proper belief in all the relief and benefits derivable from such an institution. "Mental Hospital" is not so much longer, nor so much more difficult to pronounce, and gives at once a true idea of the intention of such institutions, and one which can readily be grasped by the most ignorant ryot. Even though they dubbed it "paglai-ki-hospital," what matter? They know the benefits to be obtained at a hospital, and its purpose, and at once we attain two objects: we do away with the old ideas and prejudices attached to the term "asylum," and at the same time instil a dim perception of the fact that if it is a hospital then its inmates must be ill, and as all illness is not incurable why should not some of these invalids also recover? To still further carry out this view would be to start *out-patient departments* in connection with such institutions. Here incipient cases might be brought for advice and consultation—cases who have had previous attacks, relatives seeking advice, would all have the benefit of expert opinion. Such dispensaries would be found to afford many opportunities for the application of preventive measures and the dissemination of knowledge.

Theoretical and practical instruction could, and should, be given in such institutions whenever they are sufficiently near to a medical school to allow of this being done, and a course in mental disease should be as equally necessary in the curriculum of all such schools. In addition to this, *post-graduate clinics* could be held; and thereby the general practitioner would gain the latest views on the subject, and be better able to recognise the import of early symptoms and the necessity of expert opinion, as well as rendered more competent to help in inculcating a proper view of the subject among his clientèle, and to assist in this way in the general campaign.

All this would undoubtedly entail extra expenditure to the State, but in all probability the amount saved on account of the larger number of individuals thus rendered competent to earn a livelihood, and the lessened number of those rendered incapable by such conditions, and a helpless burden either on their relatives or the State, would fully equalise, if not exceed, the extra expenditure thus entailed.

In addition to the above, the medical staff of such institutions should avail themselves of every opportunity for spreading the true aspect of such cases when conversing with Indian gentlemen.

Lay societies also can do much in this connection. Europeans and Indians, Mussulmans and Hindus, all have societies and social bodies for promoting the welfare of the community. In many stations medical societies exist; clubs and various societies prevail in all stations, and many of them have periodical meetings where papers are read and discussed. Here, then, lies another fruitful source for disseminating information on this subject.

The introduction of little elementary articles on the subject into school primers—as has, I think, been done in connection with malaria and other similar subjects—would also be a useful means of disseminating such knowledge. An extension of this idea would be the preparation of leaflets and their distribution among those visiting asylums.

These are the main means at present possible in such a campaign as is the subject of this chapter. One other thing, however, is urgently called for in India, and that is the founding of *institutions for training mentally defective children.* Many such children, if taken in hand early, can be turned out useful members of society, capable of supporting themselves in some simple trade, instead of, as at present, swelling the ranks of the criminal, the loafer, the beggar, of those who not only prey upon the community, but, in addition, by the dirt and squalor of their persons and surroundings, prove a fertile source of danger in the dissemination of infectious diseases.

All this undoubtedly entails expenditure; but I venture to submit that the scope of such a preventive campaign is enormous, and the results to be expected are correspondingly large. The subject embraces a very much wider sphere than, let us say, a campaign against malaria, affects the community at least to an equal extent, and is capable, undoubtedly, of producing equally good results if taken up thoroughly and with patience.

CHAPTER VIII

ANATOMICAL AND PATHOLOGICAL

FOR correct appreciation of mental and nervous disorders an accurate knowledge of the anatomy and physiology of the central nervous system is of the utmost importance. It is proposed therefore to summarise here briefly some of the main points of these subjects.

The nervous system consists of two main divisions: (*a*) the *cerebro-spinal,* consisting of the brain and spinal cord along with the cranial and spinal nerves; (*b*) the *sympathetic,* formed by two chains of prevertebral ganglia, one on each side of the spine. The two systems intercommunicate, and react upon each other.

The nervous system consists of nerve cells surrounded and supported by connective tissue.

A **nerve cell** consists of the cell body and its *processes* or *nerve fibres.* These nerve fibres are divided into two categories: (*a*) *axons,* or fibres which conduct impulses away from the cell; (*b*) *dendrons,* or fibres transmitting impulses towards the cell body. The cell body, along with all its processes, constitutes the **neuron** of Waldeyer.

The cell body is composed of two substances, which are known as *chromatic* and *achromatic,* according to their reactions to staining reagents.

The *chromatic substance* is arranged in cube-shaped masses throughout the cell body, and constitutes the Nissl bodies, which form an important guide for comparative purposes in estimating the changes that have taken place in the cell bodies as the result of disease. The functions of this chromatophile substance are, as yet, uncertain, but it is generally assumed to be concerned with the nutrition and energy of the cell.

The *achromatic substance* forms a network of fibres apparently connecting the dendrons with the axons, and hence presumably has to do with the conduction of nervous impulses.

There is a *nucleus* generally situated near the centre of the cell body, and contained in this again is the *nucleolus*, which, as a rule, stains deeply with the ordinary dyes.

The *axon* is, as a rule, single, and larger in every way than the *dendrons*. As already indicated, it conveys impulses away from the cell body. Immediately after its inception the axon, unless it remains throughout its length in the grey matter, becomes encased successively in a sheath of myelin and the neurilemma, or sheath of Schwann; both of these evanesce shortly before the axon breaks up into its terminal branches.

The Neuron Theory.—According to this theory, every neuron is in itself a complete and separate anatomical unit, contiguous but not continuous with any other. These neurons are bound up by connective-tissue into various bundles and tracts, according to the different kinds of impulses they are to transmit These bundles and tracts have been differentiated and mapped out, partly from observation of the distribution of nerve degenerations, partly from the embryological development of the different units, which attain their full development at varying age periods according to the functions which they are to fulfil. The manner in which impulses are conveyed from one neuron to another is not as yet accurately determined. It is generally supposed, however, that the terminal arborescences of the dendrons and axons, upon many of which little excrescences can be seen, are capable of protrusion and retraction in an amœboid fashion, thus enabling contact to be made and broken as is necessary. The impulse transmitted is probably of an electric nature, and stimulates chemical changes in the cell bodies, such chemical changes largely assuming the character of oxidation processes.

To obtain a clear idea of the working of the central nervous system, neurons may be roughly divided into three groups: (*a*) *Association neurons* ; (*b*) *commissural neurons* ; (*c*) *projection neurons*.

(*a*) *Association Neurons*.—These neurons serve to connect the different portions of the cerebral cortex and various segments of the spinal cord with one another.

(*b*) *Commissural Neurons*.—These link together the two segments of the brain and the spinal cord.

(c) *Projection Neurons.*—These units join the brain with the spinal cord, and are divided into ascending and descending groups according as they conduct impulses upwards from the periphery to the brain, or *vice versa*.

The simplest manifestation of nervous energy is found in **reflex motor actions.** In these the impulse arises from the stimulation of some sensory end organ, travels up a sensory nerve fibre, through the corresponding posterior nerve root into the spinal cord. In the cord it passes from the cells of the posterior to those of the anterior cornu by way of an inter-communicating nerve fibre and cell in the grey matter of the cord. From the anterior cornual, or motor, cells an efferent impulse arises, travels outwards through the anterior nerve root and along a peripheral nerve to the end plates in the muscles of the part whence the original stimulus arose, and by this means appropriate action is brought about.

Many reflex acts occur unconsciously, but in other cases part of the afferent impulse passes upwards through the spinal cord, medulla, pons, etc., to the perceiving centre in the opposite cerebral cortex. By this means reflex acts can be voluntarily inhibited from above, and by further development of the same process the origination of voluntary movement from cells in the cerebral cortex becomes possible.

The Sympathetic System.—This division of the central nervous system is of importance in regard to its influence on and changes in derangements of mentalisation. Its effects on bloodvessels and viscera bring it into close relationship with the emotions, as it is largely through it that the physical symptoms and concomitants of the emotions arise, and it has already been explained in previous chapters how physical derangements may originate emotional moods which in time may even terminate in actual mental derangement. A knowledge of this system may be regarded therefore as essential for the alienist.

The sympathetic system consists of two divisions: (1) the *vertebral sympathetic*, comprising the chain of ganglia lying alongside of the vertebral column; (2) the *autonomic system* of Langley, which arises from three principal areas—viz., the mid-brain, the medulla, and the sacral region. The efferent fibres of these two systems are chiefly distributed to the unstriped muscle fibres of the heart and bloodvessels, to glands, and to the skin and viscera. Most of these structures receive a supply from both systems, and experiments tend to demonstrate that each system is antagonistic to the other.

The Vertebral Sympathetic System.—The efferent fibres of this system arise from groups of cells which constitute the *intermedio-lateral tract*, and are situated in the concavity of the ventral horns of the spinal cord. The fibres pass thence, as the *white rami communicantes*, into the ganglia at the side of the vertebræ. From the cells of these ganglia arise fibres, the *grey rami communicantes*, which join the fibres of the anterior roots,and thence pass down the mixed nerves to their various destinations.

The vertebral sympathetic system is constantly stimulated by adrenalin, a substance secreted by the medullary portion of the suprarenal body.

The Autonomic System of Langley.—The efferent fibres of this system are medullated, and those arising from the mid-brain and medulla reach their peripheral terminations by way of the cranial nerves.

As the vertebral sympathetic is stimulated by adrenalin, the probability is that the autonomic system is similarly regulated by some internal secretion; but further research is still required here. In this way a certain balance is maintained between the two systems, and if, from failure or change in either of the stimulating secretions, this balance be upset, symptoms of disease ensue. When the autonomic system is dominant the condition is known as *vagotonus*, while the similar condition of the vertebral system constitutes *sympatheticotonus*.

Many so-called functional symptoms are in many cases really due to disturbances of the sympathetic system—*e.g.*, flushing, formication, vertigo, syncopal attacks, etc.

The Cerebrum.

The principal functions of the cerebrum are to co-ordinate impulses from without, and to originate suitable action whereby the individual can adapt himself to varying conditions and surroundings.

Sensory impulses are conveyed to the cerebrum, and motor impulses away from it, by bundles of projection fibres. These projection systems are linked with one another and different parts of the brain by association fibres, and along these impulses pass to the higher centres, where they form the basis of psychic processes.

Bolton divides the cerebral mechanism roughly into three stages:

1. *Projection spheres,* which receive sensory impressions from the special sense organs.

2. *Centres of lower association,* which are situated in close proximity to the projection spheres, and convert the various sensory impressions into simple perceptions, and thence, by association, into higher complexes.

3. *The centre of higher association and co-ordination,* in the præfrontal region, where these higher complexes are grouped into harmonious series of concepts by means of voluntary attention and selection.

Cerebral Topography.—The localisation of specialised functions to certain special areas of the cerebral cortex has been studied by developmental, clinical, experimental, histological, and clinico-pathological methods.

By the *developmental method,* of which Flechsig was the chief exponent, the brain can be marked off into areas, corresponding to the different periods at which the fibres become myelinised. By this means motor and sensory projection tracts and association fibres can all be distinguished according to the period at which their myelinisation takes place.

The *clinical method* consists in correlating the symptoms noted during life with the lesion found post mortem. This method has been especially fruitful in mapping out the various motor areas of the cortex, and Hughlings Jackson has been particularly successful with it.

The *experimental method* consists in stimulating points in the cortex of an animal and observing the results. This, as with the clinical method, has borne most fruit in the localisation of the motor areas.

Histological examinations of the cortex show that the structure of different areas varies according to their functions. The names of Campbell, Brodman, and Bolton are specially connected with this method of research.

According to Bolton, the cortex may be divided into five primary layers:

1. Outer fibre lamina, or superficial layer.
2. Outer cell lamina, or pyramidal layer.
3. Middle cell lamina, or granular layer.
4. Inner fibre lamina, or inner line of Baillarger.
5. Inner cell lamina, or polymorphic layer.

These layers, Bolton states, can be identified in all layers of the neopallium, but they differ in their degrees of development in the various cortical areas, as instanced in the psycho-motor area, in which the third layer is of minimal depth.

The *præfrontal lobes* are especially associated with the performance of the higher mental functions, and, according to some observers, the left lobe is more important in this respect than the right. It is here the mental processes initiating or inhibiting movements seem to take their final form, and immediately posterior to it is the cortical area through which these mental processes appear to regulate the resulting movements. The mechanism through which the psychic processes appear to initiate the impulses for movement is apparently located in the posterior regions of the superior and middle frontal lobes of the left side, and these centres are joined to the corresponding ones in the right hemisphere by association fibres passing through the corpus callosum.

At the foot of the third frontal convolution on the left side is *Broca's centre*, which is closely connected with the motor mechanism for speech. In the frontal region, also, is situated an area regulating the movements of the eyes.

Immediately behind the frontal area lies the *præcentral* or *ascending frontal convolution*. This is commonly known as the motor area, and in it lie the large Betz cells which give origin to the fibres forming the pyramidal tracts, the main paths for the transmission of voluntary motor impulses.

Bounding the motor area posteriorly is the fissure of Rolando, which separates the præcentral convolution from the parietal lobe.

The *parietal lobe* seems to be wholly concerned with the reception of sensory impulses, though at one time the ascending parietal convolution, immediately posterior to the fissure of Rolando, was thought to be concerned in motor functions.

The *occipital lobe* is closely associated with vision, and two areas—the visuo-sensory, a lower projection area occupying the cortex of the cuneate lobe, and a higher centre, the visuo-psychic, occupying the angular gyrus—can be distinguished.

The *temporal cortex* has to do mainly with the auditory functions. In the posterior part of the first temporal convolution on the left side is situated the auditory mechanism of speech, and disturbance of this area gives rise to various degrees of auditory aphasia.

Sensations of taste and smell seem to be located in the *uncinate gyrus*.

The **optic thalamus** consists of an oval mass of grey matter situated at the base of each cerebral hemisphere, just above the crura cerebri. It serves as a station for the main sensory tracts passing up from the cord. From it fibres pass upwards to the cortex and downwards to the cord, in company with the rubro-spinal tract.

Head and Holmes consider that the thalamus is the centre of consciousness for certain elements of sensation, and that it responds to all stimuli capable of evoking pleasure, discomfort, or consciousness of a change in state.

The Cerebellum.—The cerebellum consists of the vermis, or central lobe, and two lateral lobes.

On inspection, each lobe is seen on section to consist of cortex, white matter, and central nuclei. The largest of these nuclei is the nucleus dentatus, others being the nuclei fastigii, nucleus globulosus, and nucleus emboliformis.

Afferent Fibres.—1. Fibres from the cells of Clarke's column on the inner side of the grey matter of the posterior horn pass up through the cord, and thence through the inferior cerebellar peduncles or restiform bodies to the vermis. Some fibres from the columns of Burdach and Gall also seem to follow this course, and among these a bundle passing to the nucleus of Monakow is of prime importance.

2. Fibres from the nuclei of the pons of the opposite side enter the cerebellum through the middle peduncles.

Efferent Fibres.—Fibres pass from the lateral lobes through the superior peduncles to the red nucleus and optic thalamus of the opposite side, and also to the nuclei of the pons. Communication with the fronto-parietal and temporal regions of the cerebral cortex is maintained through the nuclei of the pons.

Connections between the vestibular nucleus and the nucleus of Deiters in the cerebellum establish communication between the cerebellum and the vestibular nerve, and through this nucleus it is also closely associated with the ocular nuclei. Fibres also pass through the vestibular nucleus downwards to the cells of the anterior horns of the cord, and form a mechanism which assists in maintaining muscular tonus.

The *chief functions of the cerebellum* are the maintenance of equilibrium and muscular tone. Derangement of these causes vertigo, nystagmus, and hypotonus, and loss of synergia and eumetria are commonly seen in such circumstances. The most obvious symptom of cerebellar disease is ataxy of the coarser movements of the trunk and the limbs.

The **pituitary gland** lies transversely in the sella turcica of the sphenoid bone. It is enclosed in a pouch of dura mater, and is connected by the infundibulum to the floor of the third ventricle.

It consists of two lobes. The larger, *anterior lobe*, is purely epithelial and glandular in structure, and contains many chromophile cells of active, secreting nature. The smaller, *posterior lobe*, is subdivided into a pars intermedia, epithelial in structure, but without chromophile cells, and a pars nervosa, the continuation of the infundibulum.

The secretion of the anterior lobe, which is related to the general growth of the body, and especially of the skeleton, enters the blood-stream of the venous sinuses around the gland.

The secretion of the pars intermedia and pars nervosa is of a colloid character, and passes directly into the cerebro-spinal fluid of the third ventricle, and thence, through the dural sinuses, into the blood-stream. This secretion has a stimulant action on all varieties of non-striped muscle, and thereby raises the general vascular pressure; it is also a powerful diuretic and galactagogue. Experimental removal of a portion of the posterior part of the pituitary body increases the power of retaining sugar in the body. In a normal person, if more than 100 grammes of glucose be consumed at a time, temporary glycosuria ensues; but if the posterior lobe of the pituitary be destroyed, far larger doses of glucose can be taken without causing overflow glycosuria.

During pregnancy the pituitary gland undergoes temporary enlargement. As a result, hemianopia at times occurs in pregnant women; transient acromegaly has also been noted, whilst glycosuria frequently appears, probably owing to hyperactivity of the posterior lobe.

The **pineal gland** lies mesially in the depression on the dorsal aspect of the superior corpora quadrigemina. It contains a small cavity continuous anteriorly with the third ventricle. Involution of the gland ordinarily begins about the seventh year, and is complete at puberty. In the adult secondary calcareous degeneration progresses, and particles of "brain sand" are to be found scattered through its substance.

The pineal secretion has considerable influence upon growth and upon certain trophic functions. It inhibits development of the genital glands. Increased secretion, super-pinealism, retards the onset of puberty, and causes excessive adiposity, whereas diminished secretion causes sexual precocity and abnormal development of the male genital organs and of secondary sexual characteristics.

General Pathology.

The work of Dr. L. C. Bruce has largely revolutionised the views previously held in this branch of psychiatry, and has given an impetus to research in a new direction, which is steadily increasing our knowledge as to the causes of the majority of the forms of insanity. As a result, specific treatment on serum-therapeutical lines will probably arise for cases where at present the best that can be done is to treat them on sound hygienic principles, and endeavour to improve the condition by suitable feeding and employment as well for the body as the mind.

Up till late years alienists as a rule were content with finding gross lesions, such as thickening of the membranes, congestions of localised areas of brain tissue, atheromatous arteries, or various degenerations of cortical nerve cells, and bringing forth these as the causes of the various forms of insanity. It never seemed to strike them that such pathological changes could not originate *de novo*, that there must be some cause for such changes, and that any cause capable of producing such marked changes on comparatively gross tissues, would in all probability be capable of exerting a still greater effect on the highly specialised structures in the cortex, which, though not perhaps capable of demonstration microscopically, would still account largely for many of the conditions to be found in any of our asylums.

That these gross lesions exist and have an effect on the mental symptoms is undoubtedly true. To say that they have any effect in producing any one class of symptoms—*i.e.*, that any one, or indeed any group, of such pathological lesions is universally characteristic of any one type of insanity, is a fallacy which is daily becoming more apparent. Normal brains show such widely different reactions to exactly the same stimuli that it is only to be expected, and is indeed the case, that a still greater difference lies between the response of unstable brains to exactly similar conditions.

Gross Pathological Changes

The **cranial bones** may be uniformly increased in density, or this increase may occur in irregular patches or the converse conditions may be found, and they may be reduced to an extraordinary degree of tenuity.

At times, from degenerative causes, they may be unduly friable, and the cancellated tissue may vary in appearance according to whether anæmic or congestive conditions have been present. Increased density with adhesions of the dura mater is commonly seen in cases of chronic insanity and epilepsy.

The **dura mater** may be the seat of various lesions. Thickening, with adhesion to the skull-cap, is of common occurrence. Inflammations, with exudates and hæmorrhages, may occur and form cysts and discoloured patches, and at times adhesions between dura and pia mater denote inflammations of the serous surfaces of these membranes. Except as they affect the venous or lymphatic circulation through the pia, however, and thus react upon the nutrition of the brain substance, none of these lesions are of much significance.

Lesions of the pia mater are of very serious import, as into its meshes flows by far the larger portion of the blood and lymph of the brain. A certain amount of pial cloudiness is practically physiological in all persons over middle age, and must not be mistaken for a pathological condition. The most serious, and a fairly frequent, pathological condition is that known as *gelatinous thickening*, which is due to a congestion of the lymph flow, and causes atrophy of the cerebral tissue. In such cases the membrane is thickened and of a gelatinous consistence, the thickening being most marked over the vertex and in the neighbourhood of the Pacchionian bodies. On close examination, along the course of dilated arteries and veins the dilated lymph channels are to be seen as a fine bluish white line, which is absolutely characteristic of this condition, which it must be remembered is of a purely degenerative type. As the condition progresses, the lymph channels become more and more occluded, until finally the whole brain becomes bathed with the dammed-up waste products, many of which are undoubtedly toxic, and in this way atrophy and degeneration of neuroglia and nerve cells is produced as the final result.

Hæmorrhages into the pia are of fairly common occurrence

and may form hæmorrhagic cysts. They occur, as a rule, over the vertex, and are frequently associated with mental symptoms.

Inflammatory conditions are generally associated with dense adhesions between the brain substance and meninges, so that it is often impossible to separate them. This *meningo-cerebritis* resembles in appearance more an advanced degree of gelatinous thickening than an inflammatory process, and in many cases it is only by the presence of adhesions to the cerebrum that one can distinguish between them by the naked eye. Rupture of a pial artery, followed by extensive hæmorrhage, is of very rare occurrence, and when it does occur is as a rule rapidly fatal.

Gross lesions of the brain substance are common in many, but characteristic of no special form of mental disease. In chronic insanities, atrophy of the entire cortex, with serous exudation and gelatinous thickening of the pia mater, is very commonly present.

Thrombosis and embolism are common causes of localised atrophies, which may also result from arterio-sclerosis or the occlusion of arteries as a sequel of syphilitic disease.

Hyperæmic conditions are evidenced post mortem by vascular dilations, and varicose-like conditions of arteries and veins may be seen at times. Anæmic conditions, which are as a rule more commonly met with, may result from thickening of arterial sheaths.

Inflammation of the brain substance is very rare indeed as a local condition, and when present is generally due to thrombus or cancerous or tubercular growths. The site of the lesion is generally pinker than the surrounding healthy brain substance, though occasionally the converse is seen, and the affected area is much paler.

Atrophy of the hemispheres is found post mortem in all forms of chronic insanity, in the senile psychoses, and chronic alcoholism. It consists in atrophy affecting both the grey and the white matter, and, though as a rule diffuse, may at times be found localised in one or more lobes. It usually affects the cortex, medullary matter, and basal ganglia about equally, the result being that the grey matter is perceptibly reduced in thickness, and, the ventricles are more or less dilated, owing to shrinkage of the white medulla, without as a rule any compensatory granulation of the ependyma or dilation of the choroid plexuses. The convolutions are found to be thin and pointed as a rule in such cases, though at times, if there be much serous exudation, they may be found to be flattened. *Microscopically*, degeneration of the neuroglia is found to be present, the star-rayed elements being relatively increased owing to the disappearance of the other elements, and the nerve fibres present a varicose appearance. The nerve cells likewise show signs of degeneration, and are often pigmented.

Localised atrophy is seen in some cases of paretic dementia, or one hemisphere may be affected more than the other in such cases. When it occurs it is most frequent in the frontal lobes, the motor areas and occipital region coming next in frequency. At times patches of marked atrophy may be seen surrounded by apparently healthy gyri, and such cases are generally due to obstruction of an artery from some cause, or more rarely to a localised inflammation.

The **degenerations of the nerve cells** have been, and are even up to the present time, a fruitful source of discussion among pathologists and others, owing to the great difficulty there is in distinguishing lesions the result of disease from lesions occurring in the preparation of the specimen. This difficulty, however, is being gradually removed, and we are by degrees becoming more able to distinguish a true from an artificial lesion.

During recent years three methods have been mainly employed in this research: (1) *Nissl's alcohol-methylene-blue method;* (2) *the chrome-silver method and its modifications;* (3) *ordinary hardening with alcohol, etc., and staining by ordinary aniline dyes, hæmatoxylene, carmine, etc.* It is beyond the scope of this book to go into these processes minutely, and a mere summary of the degenerations most commonly met with will be given here. Those requiring further information on this subject will do well in consulting the books of either Bevan Lewis or Berkley.

Fatty degeneration is the most common pathological condition of the nerve cell found post mortem, and must be distinguished from the yellowish granules found normally in the large cells of the cortex after middle age, and whose true origin and nature are not as yet definitely known. In true fatty degeneration the pigment granules undergo an immense increase in numbers, and, pushing the nucleus before them, ultimately occupy by far the larger part of the cell. At this stage the outline of the cell is ill-defined, and the cell itself has enlarged and undergone alteration in its shape. Later, the nucleus, which remains practically unchanged in the first stage, rejects the basic stains, but takes up acid stains with avidity; later still its vesicular outline is lost, it becomes angular, stains deeply, and shows in its centre a bright refractile spot. Should degeneration advance still further, the nucleus shrinks, the pigment granules become a brownish colour, the protoplasm is absorbed, and, finally, the pigment granules are found lying loose in the intercellular space. This condition is common in congestive states, or where there is obstruction of the circulation in any way.

Simple atrophy of the cell is commonly seen in anæmic conditions, such as ensue after thrombus or embolism. The cell shrinks, its processes become angular, and the nucleus, gradually becoming roughened, eccentric, and indistinct, finally wholly disappears, and the cell undergoes absorption.

Coarsely granular degeneration is at times seen after inflammatory processes. The cell swells up and loses its definition, while coarse granular masses, staining readily with logwood or carmine, gather round the nucleus, which becomes eccentric, and at times even extruded from the body of the cell.

Vacuolation of the protoplasm may be due to either post-mortem changes or the result of disease, but is generally due to the former causes, and of very small import. It is sometimes, but not invariably, found in epilepsy, and usually also occurs after intense stimulation by an electric current.

Colloid degeneration is generally found in localised inflammations or in the neighbourhood of old-standing hæmorrhages. The cell is tumefied, and the colloid masses stain deeply with carmine or logwood.

Depigmentation and hyaline degeneration are closely allied to each other, and intimately associated with sclerotic changes in the cell substance. The angular appearance of the cell substance disappears, dyes are less and less readily taken up, the protoplasm becomes homogeneous, the cell barely distinguishable from the surrounding matrix, and finally complete atrophy ensues.

Finely granular degeneration of the cell is fairly common, and usually accompanies toxæmic conditions. The cells become tumefied, the protoplasm granular, and stains are but feebly taken up even by the nucleus, which itself becomes shrunken, distorted, and eccentric. The condition seems to be akin to a fatty degeneration, as in the perivascular spaces, in addition to broken-down leucocytes, there is a large amount of granular débris which blackens more or less readily with osmic acid.

Calcareous degenerations are at times seen as the result of irritations. Cells thus affected have a bright, almost iridescent appearance, owing to altered refraction, and their processes appear broken and irregular. If a drop of acid be added to the preparation bubbles of CO_2 are evolved, and characteristic crystals of the corresponding lime salts are deposited on the specimen.

Degeneration of the nerve fibres is mainly seen as the result of acute inflammations or irritative processes. It begins as a rule with swelling of the axis cylinder and a varicose condition of the medullary sheath; ill-defined retrograde conditions then ensue, ultimately resulting in the disappearance of the fibre.

Lesions of the neuroglia are frequently seen in all forms of mental disease. In irritative conditions an atrophy of the cellular elements is very commonly met with, the cell bodies and processes becoming granular and tumefied, and finally breaking down and filling the perivascular spaces with a finely granular débris. The cells of the neuroglia are more resistant to toxic processes than the nerve cells, except for the long-rayed spider cells, which seem possessed of wonderful vitality, and capable of existing under most adverse circumstances.

Lesions of the cerebral arteries and veins show no pathological differences from similar lesions found elsewhere in the body, and for descriptions of them the reader is referred to pathological textbooks, where the subject is more fully dealt with than can be done in a book of this type.

Clinical Pathology.

Some of the most common pathological conditions have been described above, and in recent years many more conditions of similar characters have been investigated, but, beyond showing that such conditions can be present, and apparently be connected with various types of insanity, we are no nearer ascertaining the causes of these pathological conditions, the true causes of the insanities, than when these histological conditions were unknown. The line of research which is being followed by Mott, Bruce, and others—a clinical study of mental diseases, supplemented by clinical pathology and laboratory observations—is undoubtedly one full of promise, and has already brought forth great results.

Temperature.—Various types of temperature are to be seen in the hospital wards of modern asylums, conforming to those of similar physical diseases among the sane. There are, however, two main features in the temperatures of insane patients which are worthy of note: firstly, that the febrile reaction is very rarely in proportion to the severity of the disease; and, secondly, that often with a high polymorphonuclear leucocytosis there may be no febrile temperature—*i.e.*, with every clinical evidence of a virulent toxæmia there is no corresponding febrile reaction.

Bacteria of the Mouth and Stomach.—Associated with all toxæmic insanities there is an accumulation on the lips, teeth, and tongue, of sordes, swarming with bacteria, mainly of the streptococcus group. These streptococci are found to be extremely virulent when injected intravenously into rabbits, doses of even 0·1 c.c. having proved fatal in three to four hours, though the streptococci grown from the saliva of a healthy man are not markedly virulent when injected into the lower animals.

Similar results have been obtained by Bruce in cases associated with excess of bacteria in the gastric contents. Here, too, streptococci are preponderant, and even more toxic apparently than those from the buccal sordes.

Coagulation of the Blood.—Many facts have been recently brought to light from systematic and long-continued examinations of this phenomenon. Thus in katatonia and acute mania the coagulation time is immensely delayed—in some cases of katatonic stupor twenty to thirty minutes being required to complete coagulation.

Hæmolysis has also yielded interesting results under Bruce's investigations; thus he cites a case where blood serum from a case of acute mania hæmolysed the washed red blood corpuscles of a case of general paralysis when mixed *in vitro* in the proportion of one part of red blood corpuscles to three parts serum. The same serum mixed in the same proportion with control red blood corpuscles did not alter them in the least in six hours, while control serum mixed in the same way with the red corpuscles of the general paralytic also had no action.

Leucocytosis.—With our modern advances in knowledge, observations on leucocytosis in mental diseases have a distinctly practical bearing, as it is now known that certain diseased conditions are almost invariably associated with alterations in the number of leucocytes per c.mm. of blood and in the percentages present of the various forms of these cells. Dr. Bruce, in his percentage counts, by Cole's method of counting by "fields," recognises the following forms of leucocytes:

1. *Polymorphonuclear leucocytes,* multinucleated cells with neutrophile granules (60 to 70 per cent. present in normal blood).

2. *Small lymphocytes,* averaging about the size of a red blood corpuscle, with a large, round, deeply stained nucleus, surrounded by an indistinct ring of more or less granular protoplasm (20 to 30 per cent. normally are present in the blood).

3. *Large lymphocytes* are larger than (2), and the protoplasmic ring is much more apparent (4·5 to 8 per cent.).

4. *Hyaline or mononuclear leucocytes,* large cells, with faintly staining protoplasm, no granules, and a round or lobed nucleus, which is frequently eccentric in position (3 to 13 per cent.).

5. *Eosinophile leucocytes,* multinucleated cells with large eosinophile granules (1 to 4 per cent.).

6. *Mast cells,* whose protoplasm contains large violet granules with a single lobed or double nucleus (0·5 to 1·5 per cent.).

Total number per c.mm. in healthy men, 5,000 to 9,000; in healthy women, 6,000 to 13,000.

Bruce also divides his counts into:

(*a*) *Leucocytic counts in non-toxic insanities.*

(*b*) *Leucocytic counts in insanities due to metabolic toxæmias.*

(*c*) *Leucocytic counts in insanities due to bacterial toxæmias.*

(*d*) *Leucocytic counts in epilepsy, general paralysis, and dipsomania.*

(*e*) *Leucocytic counts in insanities due to alcoholic or drug toxæmias.*

(*f*) *Leucocytic counts in states of mental enfeeblement.*

(*a*) *Leucocytic counts in non-toxic insanities* very rarely reveal a leucocytosis above 10,000 per c.mm. of blood; in men the polymorph percentage was generally well below 70, and in women below 60, while the large and small lymphocytes were proportionately increased. If in such cases hyperleucocytosis should occur, then the case is no longer of a pure non-toxic type, but some toxæmic condition has become superadded.

(*b*) *In uncomplicated cases of metabolic toxæmia* hyperleucocytosis is never present. The lymphocytes are always increased in number, the polymorph percentage as a rule is low, and eosinophilias are never to be seen. This leucocytosis seems to persist, and to be unaffected by recovery or relapse. At times, however, one does see cases with a transient hyperleucocytosis and a corresponding rise in the polymorph percentage, and also a high polymorph percentage may occur without any corresponding hyperleucocytosis. In these two last instances, it is probable some superadded transitory toxæmia is the cause of the high counts, though they differ from the counts in bacterial toxæmias, in that on recovery the hyperleucocytosis and high polymorph percentage disappear, and recovery is not marked by an eosinophilia, as is commonly seen in all bacterial conditions.

(*c*) Where insanity is due to *bacterial toxæmia* there is in all cases a marked hyperleucocytosis in some period of the disease. In *excited melancholia and acute mania* it is invariably present at the outset of the disease, and is accompanied by a high polymorph percentage, while eosinophiles are rarely seen. As the acute symptoms subside, there is a fall, more or less rapid, both in the leucocytosis and the percentage of the polymorphs. This fall in its turn is succeeded by a hyperleucocytosis, where, however, the polymorph percentage rarely rises above normal. Where recovery is rapid, this hyperleucocytosis is quick to appear, as a rule, and is accompanied by a rise in eosinophile leucocytes. In more chronic cases this hyperleucocytosis is less marked, and as a rule there is an eosinophilia, these corpuscles at times amounting to 20 per cent. of the whole. A bad prognosis is indicated by a fall instead of a rise of the leucocytosis after the acute stage is over, and if the polymorphs fall below 50 per cent. it is very bad indeed. In excited melancholia the leucocytosis is more irregular than in acute mania, and there is less tendency to a decrease in the polymorphs—*i.e.*, the toxæmia in excited melancholia has less tendency to produce secondary dementia than the toxæmia of acute mania. In recurrent attacks of either of these diseases the leucocytosis tends to fall just before the onset of acute symptoms, and the polymorph percentage falls with it, the reaction becoming less with each recurring attack. The polymorph percentage may fall far below the average, and coincidently the case may cease to be recurrent and pass into a continuous state of subacute excitement, with slight exacerbations corresponding to variations in the chronically persisting toxæmia.

In *folie circulaire* one sees quite a different leucocytosis. If the disease commences with a stage of elevation and is a first attack, the leucocytosis is irregular, not necessarily high, and the polymorph percentage is always well above the normal. As the elevation subsides the leucocytosis invariably falls with it. In the depression subsequent to this elevation there is recurrent hyperleucocytosis with a relatively low polymorph percentage, and frequently an eosinophilia, which may last for some weeks. There is, however, no persistent hyperleucocytosis when the patient recovers. If the attack commences with depression, the hyperleucocytosis is often well marked, but the polymorph percentage rarely rises above normal. When elevation supervenes on the depression, there is first a fall in the leucocytosis, and then a rise, culminating in the stage of elevation and then again falling to normal. From the above, therefore, it is evident that the toxæmia of folie circulaire is not persistent, but fluctuating in character.

The leucocytosis of *katatonia* is best dealt with in four stages:

(i) The leucocytosis occurring during the acute stage of onset.
(ii) The leucocytosis present during the stage of stupor.
(iii) The leucocytosis met with during the period of recovery.
(iv) The leucocytosis characteristic of katatonic mania.

(i) During the *acute stage of onset*, which rarely lasts more than three weeks, there is a marked hyperleucocytosis with, as a rule, an increase in the polymorph percentage, though this may at times be found unchanged. In typical cases this period terminates in a still more marked hyperleucocytosis, with a greatly increased polymorph percentage. Immediately after this, the patient passes into (ii), *the stage of stupor*, when the leucocytosis falls, and there is a corresponding fall in the polymorph percentage, though in cases which eventually recover this percentage remains well above 65 in both sexes. A low polymorph percentage at this stage indicates a bad prognosis. Later on in the stage of stupor there occurs in most cases a slight eosinophilia, up to about 15 per cent., and this is a hopeful sign of improvement. (iii) If recovery should take place the leucocytosis may rise, and the polymorph percentage always rises above the normal average. The eosinophilia always disappears on recovery, but a slight hyperleucocytosis without any increase in the polymorph percentage is often seen in patients discharged as cured. In cases which go on to dementia a low leucocytosis and a low polymorph percentage are always present. (iv) In cases where *the stage of stupor passes into one of mania*, or *maniacal symptoms* intervene after a lucid interval, the leucocytosis is irregular, and not marked by any increase of polymorphs or eosinophiles.

In *hebephrenia* there is generally a slight hyperleucocytosis, with every now and then a marked rise, reaching even as high as 30,000 per c.mm. The polymorph percentage is not necessarily high, an increase in the hyaline and large lymphocyte cells, up to 20 or 30 per cent. even, being more commonly seen. In the very rare event of a recovery taking place the leucocytosis always falls below 10,000 per c.mm.

(*d*) In cases of *general paralysis of the insane* the leucocytosis is of no fixed type, depending mainly on the type of mental symptoms complicating the nervous disorder. If the patient be maniacal, there is a corresponding leucocytosis, but if there be mental depression the leucocytosis conforms more to that of one becoming progressively weak-minded and paralysed.

If we generalise, the *first stage of G.P.I.* may be said to show an irregular hyperleucocytosis, with irregular increase in the polymorph percentage and transient eosinophilias. In the *second stage*, the leucocytosis may still be irregular; but where recurrent febrile attacks are present the leucocytosis tends to follow the temperature curve, and transient eosinophilias are to be seen about the time of defervescence. In the *third stage*, the leucocytosis is markedly irregular, the polymorph percentage is as a rule decreased, while the lymphocytes multiply and may even outnumber the polymorphs. If there be a *marked remission*, as occasionally occurs, then the leucocytosis invariably falls below 10,000 per c.mm. of blood, and the polymorph percentage is generally very low (40 to 50 per cent.).

In *epileptic insanes* there is invariably a hyperleucocytosis more marked in acute than in chronic cases.

In *dipsomania*, in one case examined, there was a hyperleucocytosis which disappeared on recovery. This case was also maniacal.

(*e*) In insanitus due to *alcoholic and drug toxæmias*, in Dr. Bruce's experience, there is never a hyperleucocytosis. My own observations on uncomplicated cases due to cannabis indica coincide with these results.

(*f*) In *idiots and imbeciles*, unless there be signs of toxic insanity superadded, there is as a rule no hyperleucocytosis.

In *secondary dementia* slight rises in the leucocytosis to 15,000 and 16,000 per c.mm. are frequently seen, but as a rule the polymorph percentage is low.

In all *insanities due to bacterial toxæmias* there are certain common features in the leucocytes, noted by Dr. Bruce as follows:

1. "During acute attacks, when the leucocyotsis is high and the polymorph percentage is above 70, the polymorphs are large, very granular, and deeply stained, and the nuclei subdivided into five or six lobes.

2. "As the acute stage passes off, the polymorphs become much less granular, and their nuclei show less subdivision. Frequently an eosinophilia occurs, and coincidently the granules of the polymorph cells appear to have a special affinity for the eosine dye.

3. "In patients who recover there is evidence that the leucocyte-producing cells are active, and especially those tissues which produce the polymorphonuclear cells. Such patients react vigorously to subcutaneous injections of irritants such as terebene.

4. "In patients who do not recover there is evidence that the power of polymorph production is impaired or exhausted. Such cases do not react to the subcutaneous injection of terebene or any other irritant. There is no exception to the rule that chronic cases of insanity of this class have a deficient polymorph percentage."

Agglutinines.—Agglutinines have been found, by Dr. Bruce, in cases of katatonia and mania, which appear to be specific for certain varieties of streptococci isolated respectively from the blood of a case of katatonia and of a case of acute mania. Adult rabbits injected with cultures of either variety of streptococcus showed more or less febrile reaction and hebetude, while rabbits of two or three days of age showed retarded development, and sooner or later developed paralysis of the hind legs, bladder, and rectum. Specific agglutinines were invariably present in the blood, but in no case has either variety of streptococcus been recovered from an infected animal. Dr. Bruce prepared a vaccine from these streptococci and injected it into certain cases with the result that in the majority of the cases specific agglutinines were found in the blood, but in no case was there any apparent benefit obtained, and the treatment was discontinued.

Paths of Infection.—Toxic material may infect the central nervous system by three paths: (1) by direct continuity of tissues; (2) through the blood; (3) through the lymph.

The two first channels of infection have been known for some considerable time, but only within recent years have the researches, more especially of Orr and Rows, revealed the possibility of lymphogenous infection. The results obtained by these observers show that infection may be conveyed to the central nervous system through the lymph channels of the peripheral nerves. Clinical observation has confirmed these results in cases where infection of the central nervous system has been traced to such local conditions as facial erysipelas, cancer of the tongue, tubercular abscesses, and even to inflammatory conditions of the urinary bladder.

Orr and Rows conclude from their clinical observations: (1) that the locality of the lesion in the central nervous system always corresponds to the nerve supply of the infective focus; (2) that the degeneration of the intramedullary portion of the spinal roots commences at the point where the neurilemma sheath is lost; (3) that the posterior root entry zone is always most affected; (4) that, as examination of the extramedullary portion of the nerves yielded a negative result, it seems correct to assume that toxines can, in certain cases, ascend along the perineural lymphatics without producing parenchymatous changes in the nerves.

When the changes found post mortem are considered along with the symptoms noted during life, it seems probable that absorption may proceed along the ascending lymph paths of the nerves for a considerable period before attaining sufficient potency to cause symptoms. This is probably due to the anatomical arrangement of the structures causing attenuation of the virus as it approaches the central nervous system, the highly vascular epidural tissue and the dura mater itself contributing largely to this result.

Orr and Rows lay down the following differences between hæmatogenous and lymphogenous infections:

In *hæmatogenous infections:* 1. The most highly developed structures—*i.e.*, the nerve cells—suffer least of all. 2. There is primary degeneration of the myelin sheath round the cord margin and on either side of the postero-median septum. 3. The myelin degeneration is greatest in the upper part of the cord. 4. There is œdema of the cord. 5. The vessel walls are hyaline, and thrombi of the same nature are present.

In *lymphogenous infections:* 1. Nerve-cell degeneration and neuronophage phenomena are present. 2. Scavenger cells are present where the myelin is disintegrated. 3. There is proliferation of the cells of the adventitial sheath of the veins and capillaries. 4. There is reaction of the cells of the connective tissues.

CHAPTER IX

DERANGEMENTS OF MENTALISATION

THE three most common conditions met with in asylums—in fact, one might almost say *the* three, for all cases can be roughly grouped under one or other head—are those of morbid depression, of excitement, and of elevation. These, though in all cases due primarily to some central disturbance, some disorder of the brain cortex, are frequently aggravated by derangements of the special sense centres, such as hallucinations, and most usually the senses of sight and hearing are those thus implicated.

Elevation and excitement are, as a rule, used as synonymous terms when maniacal conditions are being described, but this is incorrect, and should be avoided whenever possible. True *elevation* or *exaltation* of spirits is only seen in cases, such as the exalted stage of folie circulaire, where there is complete absence of confusion, and it is generally associated with a feeling of intense happiness and well-being. *Excitement*, on the other hand, is associated with more or less mental confusion, and is seen usually at the onset of an attack of any of the acute insanities, and most typically in acute mania.

Mental confusion is met with in varying degree in many types of insanity, from an inability to understand and answer simple questions to a state of absolute fatuity, where all power to grasp one's position and surroundings is lost. Some authors ascribe all conditions of mental confusion to toxæmias, but this is too sweeping a statement, for in mental exhaustion there is usually a condition of mild confusion in which no trace of toxæmia can be found. On the other hand, in the elevation of folie circulaire, where there is indubitable evidence of toxæmia, there is complete absence of confusion, so the two conditions are in no way necessarily connected. Mental confusion is best seen in acute melancholia, acute mania, katatonia, and toxæmias causing continued excitement.

Hallucinations, illusions, delusions, and obsessions have already been fully dealt with, and require no further notice here.

Stupor is defined by Clouston as "a morbid condition in which there is mental and nervous lethargy and torpor, in which impressions on the senses produce little or no outward effect, in which the faculty of attention is, or seems to be, paralysed, in which there is no sign of originating mental power, in which the higher reflex functions of the brain are paralysed, and in which the voluntary motions are almost suspended for want of convolutional stimulus, but where the patients usually retain the powers of standing, walking, masticating, and swallowing."

It must be distinctly understood that stupor is not in itself a disease, but only a symptom in the course of a disease, that it may complicate any mental disorder, and occurs as a definite stage in the course of all cases of katatonia. It may present varying characters during the course of a single case, and hence to treat it as a condition apart and subdivide it up, as many authors do, is most confusing, for, in by far the majority of cases, one condition merges into another: the non-resistive case to-day may be the resistive one to-morrow, etc.

Stupor is much more commonly seen in adolescence than during adult life, and varies greatly in severity and type. Thus there may be complete loss of consciousness and memory, or the patient may remain wholly conscious, and after his recovery be able to narrate in detail everything which occurred during his illness. In all cases of stupor there is impaired nutrition, alimentary disturbance, and defective circulation, with marked loss of muscular tone, leading to cyanosed and œdematous extremities. All cases of stupor must be carefully watched, as they are liable to sudden impulses which may be of a destructive, homicidal, or suicidal character.

Mental enfeeblement may be primary—*i.e.*, congenital—in origin (imbecility, idiocy, primary dementia or amentia), or secondary to acute mental disease, or be due to the natural failure of the mental powers in old age. It may be a transient condition resulting from ill-health or nervous exhaustion, from severe illness, shock, or physical or mental strain. It may be prominent as the result of cerebral lesions caused by accident, vascular changes, etc. It is met with in very varying degree, from a mere blunting of the intelligence up to complete fatuity, and may imply loss of judgment, of will-power and of self-control, blunting of the moral sense, impairment of the memory, loss of the powers of imagination and of attention and interest, all these being variously affected in every case, sometimes singly, sometimes in groups, and in all degrees.

Self-control is, perhaps, the one faculty which may be said to be essential for sanity, and loss of which characterises a man as insane. Even here one cannot dogmatise, however, for, as with every other mental process, so it is with this, and all shades of its enfeeblement are matters of everyday occurrence, from the merely passionate man up to the acutely excited maniac who tears up everything he can reach, shouts, laughs, grimaces and sings without any cause whatsoever. Each case must be judged on its own merits here. Thus it is absurd to expect the same self-control in a child as in an adult, from a person pulled down by illness and suffering as from a person in health. Still, it is a point invariably to be looked for and estimated in all cases, for, though of great diagnostic importance as an early symptom of mental breakdown, yet more often than not it is either overlooked or misinterpreted.

Impulsiveness, another common characteristic of the insane, may be defined as the committing of an act consciously but without motive or forethought.

Impulses may be of either reflex or central origin. Thus in the former case they may be stimulated by visual or auditory impressions; while in the latter case, the impulse is purely central or cortical in origin, and arises apparently without cause and quite unexpectedly.

The impulses may be of varied forms, those most commonly seen being to destroy anything and everything, to steal, to commit homicide or suicide. In some cases the patient feels the onset of the impulse, and calls out to those around to bind him or otherwise restrain him from committing the act he is feeling impelled to do, and if not at once restrained, it is a certainty that in a very short time, perhaps a few seconds, the action dreaded will have been performed.

The **faculty of attention** is variously affected in the insane. In some it is entirely *subjective*, every thought being occupied by the feelings of misery, depression, or sensory disturbances, while not a thought, not a glance, is given to what is passing around them. In other cases, as in the exalted stage of folie circulaire, the attention is wholly *objective*, being attracted by every movement or sound. Again, as in stupor and confused conditions, there is complete abolition of attention, the patient paying no heed to his own feelings and sensations, any more than he does to what is passing around him. In acute toxic conditions, both subjective and objective attention are impaired, and the capacity for work is in abeyance. This is also the chief mental symptom in hebephrenia, where there is complete loss of these, as well as incapacity to work or even to join in amusements. Similar conditions are noted in varying extent as a sequel to all the acute insanities, and are often the first indications of the onset of secondary dementia.

Derangements of instinct have already been fully dealt with in Chapter V., and I would refer my readers there for my views on this subject.

Volition is variously affected in mental disorders. It may be entirely lost, as in secondary dementia, where there is loss of power to originate action, or new ideas, in varying extent. In some cases of depression and confusion volition seems to be paralysed. Such patients can never decide on their course of action, everything becoming a source of doubt and indecision. In other cases, again, the derangement is seen as extreme obstinacy and resistiveness to every action suggested, though if the same action originate spontaneously it is readily and voluntarily performed.

Memory, both recent and remote, is more or less impaired in all states of confusion and loss of consciousness. In states of mental depression or exhaustion memory remains, but its use is a distinct effort to the patient, and it rapidly becomes exhausted, while in certain other states, as in the elevated stage of folie circulaire, the memory is abnormally active for both near and distant events. A failure of memory for recent events alone is characteristic of senile and alcoholic cases. *Amnesia* is the scientific phraseology for loss of memory, and it may be partial and complete, and affect either recent or remote memory. At times a condition of false memory, *paramnesia,* is met with, which is really more classifiable under the term Delusion. Its origin has already been discussed.

Speech, though it really originates, strictly speaking, in the motor centres, is so closely connected with all mental processes that it is usually implicated in the course of insanity. In states of excitement it is profuse, loud, and tumultuous, just as other motor centres through overaction cause restlessness and exaggerated muscular movements. From its mental aspect in these cases the speech is disconnected or incoherent, and the association of ideas accidental or fragmentary.

The mental condition, too, is often indicated by the character of the speech. Thus when delusions of grandeur and exaggerated self-importance are present the speech is pompous and boastful, as in general paralysis of the insane; and in depression, the speech is much diminished, and everything said is enunciated in scarcely audible whispers. In complete stupor speech is entirely in abeyance, while in less marked stupor, as is met with in katatonia, the implication of the speech centre is seen in *verbigeration*, or a repetition of numbers, words, or sentences in a rhythmical manner, and in *echolalia* or imitation of the words and tone of anyone speaking in the hearing of the patient.

Incoherence may be due to confusion, and result in a tumultuous rush of words without any marked cortical change being present, as in conditions of acute excitement; or it may be due directly to functional or structural changes in the grey matter. Impairment of speech, too, may be caused by muscular paresis, as in G.P.I.

A curious tendency existing among the insane has been drawn attention to by Jung. This is the habit prevalent among many of them of *talking in allegory*. This arises very largely from the habit of day-dreaming and auto-suggestion. Thus a patient with grandiose delusions regarding his own wealth and power, of which he has been bereft by his enemies, begins by comparing the similarity of his fate with that of Napoleon, and in a short time brings forth the apparently unfounded delusion that he is Napoleon. A little analysis, however, first as to the nature of the statements made, and, secondly, regarding the history of their elements, in very many cases brings forward the explanation of such announcements, and occasionally is of the utmost service in bringing to light symptoms which might otherwise have escaped observation, and puts the medical attendant on his guard against possible suicidal or homicidal attempts.

The *handwriting* often changes in character during attacks of insanity, being as a rule larger and bolder during excitement and elevation, with copious underlinings and numerous marks of exclamation. Indeed, at times the pen seems almost to "take charge," every available piece of paper being written on and sometimes crossed and recrossed two or three times. In states of depression it is as a rule thin, small, and straggling.

Disturbances of the emotions are very common in the insane, and indeed in certain types of insanity form the chief symptoms of the malady. Thus patients suffering from general paralysis of the insane and certain other forms of insanity are often unduly irritable, violent outbursts of passion occurring with little or even no provocation. In other cases the emotions seem to be in a condition of unstable equilibrium, the patients laughing one minute and perhaps crying the next without any apparent cause, as is frequently seen in cases of acute mania. As a general rule a tendency to hysterical weeping in men is of very grave prognostic import. In melancholia, on the other hand, the emotions seem to be dulled or even in complete abeyance, failing to respond to even the strongest stimuli—a mother perhaps hearing apparently unmoved of the death of her favourite child.

Fear and constant anxiety are symptoms often met with in many types of mental derangement.

With the onset of secondary dementia the emotions fail along with the other functions of the brain, and complete apathy is found as a rule in most dements, whether the condition be primary or secondary.

Jealousy is a common symptom of insanity, and most trying to those who have the misfortune to be its victims.

It is a frequent symptom of alcoholic insanities, and in these may at times lead to homicidal attacks on the wife or her supposed paramour.

It is seen at its most extravagant heights, however, in that form of delusional insanity commonly known as "ovarian or old maid's insanity." Widows and old maids as a rule are the sufferers here, fixing their affections on some man, generally a clergyman or famous musician or actor, and dogging his footsteps and pestering him with their attentions in a most shameless manner, and in spite of open rebuffs. Many a man has been seriously compromised by a woman of this type. I know of one unfortunate wight whose life for over two years was made a burden to him in this way, until finally he managed to get grounds for a criminal action, and when put on trial the woman was found to be insane and sent to an asylum, where she is still confined. The ordinary laity do not understand such cases, and as the women are often cunning enough to conceal their actions, and do not otherwise exhibit any marked eccentricity, the public always shows a disposition to champion the cause of the woman, pointing the finger of scorn at the unhappy object of her attentions, and hounding him out of society. To anyone having the misfortune to fall into such a predicament my advice is to acquaint the friends of the woman at once with the annoyance caused by her conduct, and to keep carefully all letters received and copies of all letters written.

Sleep is the function of the body most liable to disturbance in physical disorders, and, similarly, in mental disorders one may say no case occurs in which there is not some derangement of this function. This loss of the power to sleep is one of the most troublesome symptoms one has to deal with in asylums. In some cases of chronic excitement sleep is apparently absolutely abolished, and though they may be kept under observation for years, they will never be found asleep; in these cases, however, the probability is that sleep does occur, but is of so light a character that the slightest sound rouses the patient.

In other cases there is a regular periodicity to be noted; thus the patient may sleep one night and not the next, or sleep two nights and miss the third; and in some of these cases alterations of pulse and temperature may be noted on the day preceding or following the sleepless night.

Excessive sleep is seen at times, and is specially common in some stages of G.P.I., also during the stupor of katatonia and in some cases of epileptic insanity. Senile cases as a rule sleep heavily during the day and awake to abnormal activity at night.

The causes of *general sleeplessness* are innumerable. Very commonly it is due to a bad "brain habit," and nothing more, and in these cases a hot bath and a glass of hot milk taken just before going to bed work marvels. In acute insanities, however, it is generally due to a toxæmia, and as the case becomes more chronic there is superadded the acquisition of a bad "brain habit." In some cases the sleeplessness is due to the direct action of the toxine on the cortical grey matter, but in others, as shown by Dr. Bruce, the condition is due to the production of a high arterial tension and a rapid pulse rate, which of themselves alone are capable of producing sleeplessness.

Dr. Bruce states: "The normal arterial pressure, according to Hill, is about 110 mm. Hg with the patient in an horizontal position. In patients who have recovered from attacks of insanity I have found the pressure vary from 100 to 120 mm. Hg. Another characteristic of the arterial pressure in health is that it is always lower in the evening than in the morning. In natural sleep it was found that the arterial tension fell some 10 mm. Hg—*i.e.*, a patient who before sleep registered 110 mm. Hg during sleep registered 100 mm. Hg. The same patient, after a dose of one drachm of paraldehyde, fell asleep an hour later, and the arterial tension registered 80 mm. Hg. Two hours later the pressure had risen to 95 mm. Hg, and four hours later to 100 mm. Hg—that is to say, during the drug sleep the arterial pressure at first fell below that of normal sleep, but gradually rose again, the drug sleep apparently passing gradually into a condition of normal sleep."

In addition to this it should be remembered that there is a regularly recurring rise and fall in the blood-pressure, the whole period which this cycle takes lasting about four weeks, and occurring not only in women, in whom it seems in some way connected with the process of menstruation, but also in men. It is possible that this, too, may have some effect in producing attacks of recurrent insanity, and also in the production of the various stages of folie circulaire.

Dr. Bruce further states: "In all cases of metabolic poisoning and sleeplessness the arterial pressure in the evening was higher than that of the morning, and during the state of sleeplessness was as high as 140 to 150 mm. Hg; but if sleep occurred naturally the tension always fell below 110 mm. Hg. In a similar condition sleep induced by a drug, such as paraldehyde, was accompanied by a fall in pressure to at least 110 mm. Hg, but rarely lower. In patients suffering from excitement a high arterial tension was often associated with the state of sleeplessness, and in these cases also the arterial pressure always falls, whether sleep occurred naturally or from the exhibition of drugs. It was found, however, that some patients suffering from excitement with sleeplessness, and particularly cases of excited melancholia, had abnormally low arterial pressure, with a rapid pulse-rate. In such cases two drachms of paraldehyde raised the pressure and further excited the patient, while doses of 10 to 15 minims of paraldehyde, 30 grs. of sulphonal, or 20 grs. of trional lowered the pulse-rate and produced sleep without in any way altering the arterial pressure." This should be carefully noted, as the blood-pressure and pulse-rate are really most excellent indicators of what sedative to use, and in what dose, and my experience has led me to very much this line of action, though without having carried out the observations so carefully noted by Dr. Bruce.

CHAPTER X

PHYSICAL SYMPTOMS

If not in all, at least in by far the majority of cases of insanity there are well-marked physical symptoms in addition to those of mental derangement. These in most cases precede the onset of any mental disturbance, and, if rightly interpreted and treated by the medical attendant, an attack of insanity may in many cases be averted. This point has always seemed to me a most important one, and it has surprised me to find it slurred over, as it is, in so many standard books on insanity. I would therefore impress on my readers as far as possible the necessity of being able to read and interpret aright these symptoms.

Alimentary System.—As already stated, many cases of insanity due to bacillary toxæmia arise from bacilli normally habitant in the alimentary canal. Hence it is a natural sequence to say that in many forms of insanity the alimentary canal is found to be deranged in some way, and that, if this condition be treated, an improvement in the mental symptoms is noted.

Carious teeth are common adjuncts among the inmates of asylums even in England, and, judging by my own experience, much more prevalent among the inmates of Indian asylums than among the same classes in the general population. In such cases the removal of carious teeth and proper treatment of septic buccal conditions often causes marked improvement in the mental symptoms.

A furred or coated tongue, indicative of *dyspepsia*, is nearly always seen in the acute insanities; and a dry, brown, cracked tongue is an invariable concomitant of insanity, due to exhaustion or septicæmia, which has passed into the typhoid state.

The appetite for food and liquids is practically always lost in the acute insanities, and is a common call for artificial feeding. In most of such cases there is a *failure in the secretion of digestive juices*, and I have frequently seen such patients vomit a meal of eggs, milk, and meat-juice practically unchanged, even two hours after administration through the feeding-tube. In cases of acute melancholia or mania the gastric juice, when withdrawn, has practically no action on foodstuffs even when left in contact for two hours or more. Thus an important point to note is that dyspepsia, with all its symptoms, is a common concomitant of, and may often precede, any of the acute insanities.

Intestinal parasites at times play an important part as factors in cases of insanity. My experience in this respect has led me to make it a routine matter for every case admitted into my asylum to be treated at once with santonine and castor-oil. I have had some startling results in consequence. One case, I remember, admitted with acutely maniacal symptoms, after the above treatment passed over 130 round worms, and his mental condition was practically normal next day.

Hæmopoietic System.—The *thyroid gland* has been proved, through the experiments of Horsley and others, to have undoubted and important relations with nervous diseases. Thus its complete removal in such an animal as the monkey causes a condition practically indistinguishable from the disease in man known as myxœdema, and, conversely, if a case of myxœdema be treated with thyroid extract marked improvement invariably ensues.

The chief mental condition in myxœdema is one of hebetude, and many cases of insanity characterised by a listless inertia react most wonderfully to a course of thyroid extract. It is also at times of great use in cases of depression, excitement, or elevation, due probably to deficient or altered secretion of the thyroid. Such cases, however, are very hard to distinguish, and in the majority of them the treatment is begun tentatively at first, and only continued if good results follow its exhibition. At times, too, I have seen the depression much increased, and at others an almost maniacal condition produced by this course of treatment.

Leucocytes, as shown by recent research, are increased in number above those normally present in the blood in certain toxic conditions, and to this increase the term "hyperleucocytosis" is applied. This increase is not proportional in each and every type of leucocyte, but especially affects the polymorphonuclear elements, which in health normally amount to about 60 per cent. of the 7,000 or more leucocytes as a whole present per c.mm.

In toxic conditions the leucocytosis may rise as high as 30,000 per c.mm., or even higher, and the polymorphonuclears may increase to as much as 90 per cent. of the whole.

In addition to these leucocytic changes during toxæmias there is also the formation in the blood of *alexines*, or substances capable of neutralising the toxic bodies present, and when in addition to toxines we have to deal with the presence of bacteria in the blood-stream, there are certain other bodies present, of which the chief one for our purpose is known as an *agglutinine*. These substances, as most of my readers probably know, have the power of clumping the organism causing the infection, when mixed with it *in vitro*—*e.g.*, Widal's reaction for typhoid fever.

Dr. Bruce has examined the blood of many cases of acute insanity for bacteria, but in only one was he successful in obtaining an organism. One, a case of acute mania in a typhoid state, gave a pure growth of a small streptococcus, and the other, a case of katatonia, yielded a somewhat larger streptococcus. He tested the serum reaction of 23 cases of mania with both these organisms, in dilutions of 1 in 30, and in 19 cases obtained definite agglutination of the organism obtained from the case of acute mania. The serum of 6 cases of excited melancholia similarly tested gave agglutination of the same organism in 3 cases. Twelve cases of katatonia, when tested with the larger organism, gave a definite reaction in 6 cases.

Another point noted by Dr. Bruce, and one well worth remembering, is that for the production of agglutinines it is not essential that the organism should be present in the blood-stream, the mere digestion of the organisms in the stomach sufficing to produce this effect in a healthy animal. Hence it is probable that in many cases the source of trouble may be in the nasopharynx, or indeed any part of the alimentary canal, even the large intestine, for absorption takes place largely from it, and Ford Robertson has pointed out that atrophic changes in the mucous and submucous coats of the large intestine are common in all forms of acute insanity which present symptoms of toxæmia, and also in cases of general paralysis of the insane.

Red bone marrow has been examined by Dr. Bruce from cases which showed hyperleucocytosis in life, and in every case he found the marrow was leucoplastic and the cells undergoing active mytotic division.

Circulatory System.—The *heart* in the insane shows, on the whole, a larger percentage of valvular lesions than in the sane, and the onset of valvular incompetence, especially in old people, is frequently followed by mental symptoms.

The main circulatory disturbance accompanying insanity, however, is altered *arterial tension*, which may be increased or diminished, the former being more usually a concomitant of states of depression, and the latter of states of elevation and of excitement. In health the arterial tension is as a rule 115 to 120 mm. Hg, but in mental and nervous derangements it may rise as high as 160 to 170 mm. Hg, or fall well below 100 mm. Hg.

Pulse changes are best seen in acute melancholia, when a pulse-rate of 120 per minute may be associated with a temperature of 99° F., or even less. In cases of acute mania a fast weak pulse with subnormal temperature may be one of the earliest symptoms. In stuporose patients the tension and pulse-rate fall enormously, the latter falling as low as 50 beats per minute, or even less, and, with this, failure in peripheral circulation is shown by cold feet and œdematous extremities.

Respiratory System.—As phthisis has been noted as a predisposing cause of insanity, so conversely the diminished vitality so common among the insane renders them more than ordinarily liable to phthisis.

Integument.—Changes in the hair, the skin, and the nails are practically invariable concomitants of all types of insanity. Patients in the acute phases of the disease do not as a rule complain of subjective symptoms, but irritations of the skin and the scalp undoubtedly must be common, judging by the numbers who pull out their hair, scratch, and wash their heads on every available opportunity. The cause is difficult to explain; but, if we theorise, the only three tenable explanations seem to be, trophic changes due to implication of peripheral nerves or their centres, or a hyperexcitability of sensory nerves due to peripheral or central changes, or, lastly, the condition may be due to altered secretion causing irritation.

In support of the first of these theories we have the appearance of pigmentary deposits and the occurrence of phagedenic ulcers, both of which are common experiences in asylum practice. In support of the second it is not so easy to bring forward proof, but at times one meets with cases where, though the integument is absolutely normal in appearance, the patient constantly complains of insects running over or beneath the skin, or of having needles stuck into him, and there can be but little doubt, I think, that these delusions arise from disordered sensory nerves. The third of these theories is strongly supported by the hard dry skin seen in melancholics owing to deficient excretion of the waste products in the body, or the drenching perspirations seen at times in katatonia, or as a crisis in acute mania. A crop of boils sometimes occurs during the invasion period of an attack of acute mania, and as a rule such a condition can be looked on as indicative of a favourable prognosis.

In by far the greater number of cases of insanity, if not in all, the hair and nails become dry and brittle; and in some cases of mania the hair more or less stands on end, giving a finishing touch to the appearance characteristic of such conditions.

Urinary System.—The frequency of the act of micturition depends on two separate causes: firstly, on the amount of urine excreted; secondly, on the centres in the spinal cord and brain concerned in the reflex act of micturition being in a fit state to receive sensory impressions from the bladder and transpose them into the origination of the act. The first condition is exemplified well in cases of acute melancholia, where there is a suppression of urinary secretion and but little urine is voided in consequence, usually from 8 to 9 oz. in 24 hours, though at times less. In cases where consciousness is impaired the act of micturition may be delayed solely through the inability of the cortical centres to respond to the stimuli received from a full bladder, and in such cases a careful watch should be kept for the necessity of catheterisation, as the excretion of urine is in no way diminished.

Albuminuria is frequently met with, especially in cases of mania and melancholia, and as a rule is due to irritation as numerous leucocytes can be found microscopically in the urine. Very occasionally it is due to vasomotor disturbances.

Glycosuria, which is occasionally seen after epileptic fits and in delusional conditions, is invariably vasomotor in origin.

The *excretion of chlorides* is diminished in certain cases of toxæmic origin.

Reproductive System.—*Menstruation* among insane women, especially adolescents in Europe, is usually most irregular, by far the majority of them suffering from amenorrhœa. When menstruation, however, does occur it is as a rule accompanied by relapses and exacerbations in the mental symptoms, and no case can be said to have completely recovered till this function has become regular and normal in its occurrence. In India, however, as far as my experience goes, menstruation among the female inmates of asylums seems to correspond fairly closely with what one meets with in the same classes among the sane population, both as regards the number of the periods and the quantity of the flow at each period.

Masturbation is still regarded by many as one of the concomitant exciting causes of insanity. This view is now becoming a thing of the past, and rightly too, for, though it may tend to weaken the patient and exaggerate the mental symptoms, there can be but little doubt that in most cases masturbation is merely an early symptom, and due to impairment of the higher controlling centres of the brain allowing lower centres to come more into evidence.

The *testicles and ovaries* undoubtedly play an important part in the development and nutrition of the body and mind. Their removal in either sex before the completion of development causes complete arrest of the formation of both the bodily and mental sexual characteristics. It is probable, as suggested by Dr. Bruce, that deficient or altered secretory activity may coexist with an apparently, but not really, healthy state of these organs, and be the cause of the symptoms of arrested development seen so commonly in cases of insanity occurring during puberty and adolescence. Certain forms of insanity, such as "ovarian insanity" and "old maid's insanity," have been said to arise from derangement of the uterus and ovaries, but no proof has ever been deduced to show that there is even a connection between the conditions.

Vasomotor and nutritional disturbances are common in all forms of insanity. *Inequality of the axillary temperatures* occurs at times in cases of general paralysis, katatonia, and melancholia. In the first it generally occurs after congestive seizures more or less unilateral in character, but in the two last no such explanation is possible, and one has just to accept it as an undoubted fact.

Extremely low temperatures, seen in the course of mania, excited melancholia and katatonia, are probably due to vasomotor disturbances, while the flushing of the cheeks characteristic of the onset of mania, and pallor and lividity, seen in cases of stupor, acute melancholia, and at times dementia, are due to similar causes.

Excessive perspiration may be either reflex in character, as in the course of acute insanity, when it probably is due to fear caused by terrifying hallucinations or delusions, or a direct effort of nature to eliminate toxines from the system, as so often occurs in cases of katatonia or at the crisis of mania or melancholia. At times unilateral perspiration occurs in katatonia, especially after taking food, but the cause of this is unknown.

Lachrymal secretion is often suppressed, and one of the most extraordinary sights in an asylum is to see a patient wandering hither and thither, wringing his hands, sobbing and crying in an agony of grief, without there being even a trace of a tear visible. In such cases the first sign of improvement is often a flood of tears and the restoration of the lachrymal secretion.

Salivation may be modified, and as a rule when affected it is in excess, though how much is really in excess and how much only apparent and due to diminished reflexes causing its collection in and flow from the mouth is rather hard to decide.

The **Nervous System,** from which one would expect to obtain most information in this class of cases, is as a rule the most difficult to examine, owing to the patients being unable to afford us any assistance. In those forms of mental disease where consciousness is impaired it is impossible to test *sensation* owing to the inability of the patient to realise it—*i.e.*, the loss of subject-consciousness.

In certain forms of delusional insanity, especially those due to alcoholic excess, sensations of tingling and formication often give rise to delusions of a persecutory character, such as electrical agencies, hypnotism, or vermin in the bed or garments. In the few cases that can be tested, sensation is variously affected. It may be deficient or hyperacute, sense of heat may be lost, etc., and these symptoms are in no way connected with any type of the disease and are therefore no aid to diagnosis.

In folie circulaire the sense of sight at times varies enormously in the different stages, probably owing to variations in the power of concentrating the attention and in the excitability of the cortical centres. Similarly, the other special senses may be affected, giving rise to various delusions and hallucinations, such as unseen people abusing the patient, poisoning the food, etc.

The *pupils* are variously affected in insanity. Inequality of the pupils is common in various forms of insanity, especially in cases of long standing. In conditions of excitement, exhaustion, or fear, the pupils are widely dilated, and react sluggishly both to light and accommodation. In general paralysis, in senile cases where there are degenerative changes in the cortex, and in excited cases in a state of anger there are frequently pin-point pupils, though not invariably, as in G.P.I. no fixed condition of the pupil can be looked for.

Where consciousness is impaired control of the reflex acts of *defæcation and micturition* is lost, and uncleanliness results. This is not always the cause of uncleanliness, however, for often, as in cases of dementia, it is due to a blunting of the instincts and the patient can be re-educated to more cleanly habits.

Swallowing is at times impaired where there is loss of sensibility or advanced muscular paresis, as in general paralysis. Its impairment in katatonia, where the saliva often dribbles from the mouth, is due to an extension of the state of passive resistance to this function, as the reflex is not in any way abolished, and it is customary to feed such cases by hand and not by the tube.

The *superficial reflexes* are increased in all cases where there is a loss of consciousness, as in acute mania. They are decreased in cases where the reflex arc is severed, as in alcoholic patients, or in cases of stupor, where there is increased cerebral inhibition. *Deep reflexes* do not necessarily follow this rule, as there may be no increase in the knee-jerk in cases characterised by loss of consciousness. The tendon reflexes are increased as a rule in cases of general paralysis, in certain cases of stupor, especially katatonic stupor, and in old standing epileptics.

Paresis of the voluntary muscles is seldom met with except in advanced general paralysis, organic and secondary dementia, traumatic insanity, and certain variations of senile dementia. *Inco-ordination* is, however, present in all acute insanities, from mere failure of finely associated movements to the wild, purposeless movements of acute excitement. Mere sluggishness of movement, characteristic of hebephrenia and certain types of melancholia, is due to deficient volition, and no implication of the cortical motor areas can be demonstrated as a rule.

CHAPTER XI

COMPARISON OF EASTERN AND WESTERN PSYCHOSES

The Influence of a Tropical Climate upon Europeans.—It is, I think, an established fact that neuroses and psychoses are more common among Europeans and their descendants in hot climates, and, in a way, the climate may be said to be an essential factor in their development. The average European in the tropics does not alter his mode of living in any material way. He eats an abundant flesh diet, imbibes alcoholic beverages freely, and displays an energy in the pursuit both of business and pleasure which is in strong contrast to the calm placidity of the Indian. As a result of this he sooner or later falls a victim to dyspepsia, and when this condition becomes chronic the subject is naturally more liable to metabolic or bacterial toxæmias, and a train of nervous symptoms arise which may pursue him until death. If Europeans, however, were to conform more to the diet and customs of the Indians around them such bodily and mental disturbances would be much less frequent. The same applies to the rising generation of Indians, who, being more highly educated, and coming into closer contact with the social life of Europeans, have adopted to a greater or less extent many European habits and customs, and these, on constitutions unused to them, have much more marked results than on Europeans.

The regular recurrence, too, of a long-continued high temperature for practically half the year, accompanied as it is for the latter three months by excessive humidity, tells heavily on people accustomed to a more temperate, drier climate, for constant heat combined with constant humidity is extremely hard to bear, and lucky indeed is the man who emerges from the ordeal unscathed. The most common result of these is an intractable insomnia, to which in time is superadded physical and mental lethargy and an unconquerable disinclination for physical as well as for mental exertion. All energy is lost, the man's mental faculties become dulled, irritability and depression follow on, and finally there is an ever-increasing excitability, culminating at times in explosions of open violence. As a rule maniacal conditions are more common than states of depression in such conditions, and are probably largely due to the abuse of alcohol and quinine so commonly seen in the tropics.

Psychoses peculiar to India.—The large majority of mental diseases are common to both Eastern and Western races, and only a few—in fact, very few—forms of insanity exist which can be said to be peculiar to India.

The abuse of preparations of Indian hemp and opium is much more prevalent among Asiatics than Europeans, especially the abuse of Indian hemp, and mental symptoms due to this cause alone form an appreciable percentage of the admissions into Indian asylums. "Running amuck," as it is termed in Northern India, or "amok" as it is called in the southern part of the peninsula, is almost invariably due to an excessive indulgence in *Cannabis indica*. The patient as a rule broods over some fancied wrong or slight until life becomes unbearable, and he determines to end it. With this object in view he has recourse to drugs, with the object of inducing a state of frenzy, and in most cases *Cannabis indica* is the one chosen. When absolutely beside himself with the effect of the poison, he seizes his weapon and rushes blindly forth, cutting and hacking at everyone he sees, killing or maiming all he meets, until a timely bullet or sword-cut puts an end to the slaughter by causing his death. At times, however, in those chronically addicted to the abuse of the drug, a state of irritability and loss of self-control arises, and in such a condition any small reverse or argument may suffice to start the individual on his wild career to death.

As cretinism is endemic in some villages in Switzerland, so we have in the Punjab a comparatively large number of microcephalic imbeciles of comparatively uniform type, and commonly known as "Shah Daula's mice." The term "mice" is applied to them owing to the conformation of the cranium, which, with the flattened skulls and prominent ears, gives them a certain amount of resemblance to these animals, and the rest of the name is obtained from the tomb or shrine of a *peri* of that name in Gujrat, under whose protection they are supposed to be.

Until late years the priests in charge of this shrine used to hire out the "mice" to faquirs and jogis, who took them round the country begging. This has now practically been put a stop to owing to the brutal ill-treatment which they met with as a rule at the hands of their masters. The "mice" are all well under average stature, but, except for the microcephalic head and outstanding ears, show no marked deformity otherwise. A large percentage of them, however, appear to be deaf and dumb, and strabismus is common among them, indicating probably some error in refraction or other visual defect. They are capable of being taught simple employments, and are by no means immodest or indecent, and as a rule exhibit none of the revolting tendencies or depraved appetites so commonly seen among other types of *aments*. Nothing is known as to how they originate, in most cases no hereditary influence being traceable; and a *chuha* may often be found with absolutely normal parents and three or four healthy brothers and sisters. They apparently almost, if not quite, all are sprung from the lower classes. It is possible they are due to the custom, prevalent in those parts, of childless women going to the shrine to pray and vow a dedication to the shrine if their prayers are heard and they are blessed with a child. Not that I fancy mental influence has anything to do with it, but as the women stay there several days, it is quite possible that the guardians of the shrine every now and then have recourse to one of the male microcephalics to ensure that some of the childless women who spend the night at the shrine may produce a *chuha*, and so maintain the reputation of the tomb.

It is a common belief that this condition is due to pressure exerted in infancy by means of iron caps; but there is no confirmative evidence of this, so far as I know, any post-mortems which have been done showing apparently normal bones, except for the contractions in every diameter of the skull.

Lătáh is a condition of increased suggestibility fairly common among Malays, who know it by this name. I know of one typical case in Ceylon, and it is probable others may be seen in Southern India, though it is unknown in the Northern Provinces. The condition makes its first appearance about the age of puberty, when its victims, though absolutely normal otherwise both physically and mentally, begin to show extraordinary readiness to react to suggestion. If walking by a stream with a companion, it is sufficient for the friend to exclaim, "Let us jump in!" and in the man will jump promptly, clothes and all. When walking down a bazaar it merely suffices to catch their eye, and shout, "Strike! strike!" at times even the mere motion of hitting suffices, and the victim of this derangement will hit out promptly at anyone who happens to be next him. Naturally such sufferers are constantly having their affliction taken advantage of by those around them, and, being generally mild and good-natured, this constant ridicule and chaff tends to make them shy and reticent, and inclined to shun society. Except for this, however, they are normal in every respect, and many, I believe, have done good work in the police and other official capacities. Nothing is known as to its ætiology, and heredity seems to have no influence as a factor in its production.

Differences of Incidence and Manifestations in Psychoses common to both the East and the West.—Owing to differences in habits, customs, and temperament the evidences of insanity among Indians vary greatly from what one looks for among Europeans. Thus if an ordinary Indian female of Northern India voluntarily appeared in public with her head uncovered, one would consider it strong presumptive evidence of mental derangement, though one thinks nothing of European females doing so. In the same way, if a European behaved as so many faquirs do, he in all probability would be seized promptly and confined in an asylum, while an Indian can act in this way and nothing is thought of it. Innumerable other examples of this sort, arising from differences in habits, customs, environments, and temperaments, can be quoted.

The differences in the laws prevailing in Great Britain and in India, though largely diminished by Act IV. of 1912, still affect very greatly the types of insanity met with in asylums in these two countries. This result is further accentuated by the innate objection, prevalent among the Indian community, to sending their sick relatives away from home. The result of these two causes is that the numbers of insane under asylum treatment in India form an infinitesimal percentage of the whole population. Also, if we set aside those cases suffering from secondary dementia after acute insanity, the remainder may be compared as a whole to a collection of all the most violent and destructive patients from British asylums. The natural tendency of the insane to revert to their original type of mentalisation undoubtedly has some effect also in producing this result, and explains to a certain extent the relative excess in the incidence of mania over that of melancholia, and the comparative rarity of suicidal attempts, while homicidal outbursts are so frequently seen.

Custom is, I think, mainly responsible for the disgusting way so many insanes in asylums in India besmear themselves, and indeed anything else they can reach, with excrement, for the habit of "leeping" their houses and the primitive sanitary arrangements so common in villages is not conducive to any very high standard of cleanliness. Here, however, one must remember that sanitary arrangements in Indian asylums differ greatly from those prevailing in Great Britain, and as a result there is more opportunity for uncleanliness in the former case. The religious beliefs and caste prejudices, too, largely affect not only the symptoms but the whole course of treatment in India.

Judging by asylum admissions as a whole, one would therefore be inclined to say that insanity is much less frequent and as a rule of a more violent, more maniacal, more incurable type in India. When, however, we remember the points discussed above, and consider that melancholics are, on the whole, quite amenable to treatment at home, and if we also note the comparatively large percentage of katatonia, hebephrenia, and paranoia, cases universally admitted to be sprung from neurotic stock, then, I think, one can but come to one conclusion—viz., that insanity is at least as rife in India as in Britain, and that, probably, if every case of insanity cared for outside of asylums were noted, the relative percentages of melancholia and mania would be materially altered, and approximate much more closely to European figures than is the case with our present statistics. In other words, though the class of cases met with in asylums in India is, on the whole, more maniacal than those seen in English asylums, yet, taking into account the considerations noted above, the probability is that there is really much less difference in type than would at first appear to be the case; also, though from asylum statistics insanity seems much less rife in India than in England, it is probable in the light of what has already been discussed in Chapter I. that insanity is infinitely more rife in India than would appear to be the case if we judge by statistics alone.

CHAPTER XII

CLASSIFICATION OF INSANITY

CLASSIFICATIONS on varying foundations have been promulgated from time to time. Classifications based on similarity of symptoms (mania, melancholia, etc.); classifications by general causation (alcoholic, puerperal, senile); classifications on mixed principles, as in that of the Royal College of Physicians, where the symptomatic headings are again subdivided by the ascribed causes (mania: puerperal, alcoholic, etc.), have all been brought forward at different times.

Savage lays down that the basis of any scientific classification of mental disorder should be the pathological changes in the nervous system which give rise to insanity (Allbutt's "System of Medicine," p. 827); while Bruce bases his classification on a regrouping of the affections broadly into those of non-toxic and those of toxic origin ("Studies in Clinical Psychiatry").

It is, I think, on these last lines that one fixed and recognised classification will ultimately be based, as it strikes at the root of the subject, defines the causes of the pathological changes on which Savage would base his classification, helps us greatly in deciding what lines of treatment to adopt, and, for our present purpose, helps us also in providing, in many forms of insanity, some corroborative testimony to our opinions, based on the apparent mental symptoms, by means of leucocytic counts.

At present, however, no one universal classification prevails, so I propose detailing—

I. The classification proposed by Drs. Clouston and Mercier for the Educational Committee of the Medico-Psychological Association.

II. That of the Royal College of Physicians.

III. Bruce's classification, because I have worked on its lines since 1908, and find it the simplest and best for general work and comprehension of the subject.

I. Classification of Drs. Clouston and Mercier.*

1. States of mental weakness:
   (*a*) Primary, idiocy and imbecility;
   (*b*) Secondary, dementia.
2. Stupor.
3. Depression.
4. Exaltation and excitement.
5. Systematised delusions with hallucinations.
6. Impulsive and moral insanity.
7. General paralysis of the insane.

II. Classification of the Royal College of Physicians.†

1. Mania.
2. Melancholia.
3. Dementia, including acquired imbecility.
4. Idiocy, *syn.* congenital imbecility.
5. General paralysis of the insane.
6. Puerperal insanity.
7. Epileptic insanity.
8. Insanity of puberty.
9. Climacteric insanity.
10. Senile insanity.
11. Toxic insanity, from gout, alcohol, lead, etc.
12. Traumatic insanity.
13. Insanity associated with obvious morbid changes in the brain.
14. Consecutive insanity, from fevers, visceral inflammations, etc.

III. Bruce's Classification.‡

(A) Insanities of Non-toxic Origin.

1. Exhaustion insanity, occurring as a sequel to exhausting diseases and typically seen as the result of prolonged lactation.
2. Insanity the result of gross brain lesion or traumatism.
3. Insanity resulting from brain anæmia.
4. Insanity resulting from deprivation of the special senses, particularly of sight and hearing.
5. Insanity from mental or physical shock.

* Allbutt's "System of Medicine," p. 827. † *Ibid.*

‡ Bruce's "Studies in Clinical Psychiatry," p. 44 *et seq.*

(B) Insanities of Toxic Origin.

(α) Insanities due to Toxines of Metabolic Origin.

1. Acute melancholia.
2. Insanity associated with deficient, excessive, or altered secretion of the thyroid gland.
3. Delusional insanity.
4. Chronic metabolic toxæmia.

(β) Insanities due to Toxines of Bacterial Origin.

1. Excited melancholia.
2. Maniacal excitement with confusion (acute mania).
3. Folie circulaire.
4. Katatonia.
5. Hebephrenia.

(γ) Insanities due to Alcohol and Drugs.

(C) Nervous Diseases frequently complicated by Mental Disease.

1. Epilepsy.
2. General paralysis of the insane.
3. Dipsomania.

(D) States of Mental Enfeeblement.

1. Idiocy and imbecility.
2. Secondary dementia.
3. Organic dementia.

In describing the symptoms typically seen in these various types I propose adhering to Bruce's classification, but in each case will give the nomenclature also both of the classification of Drs. Clouston and Mercier and that of the Royal College of Physicians.

CHAPTER XIII

CLINICAL EXAMINATION OF PATIENT

THIS is a matter requiring infinite tact and care, as an unfortunate manner, want of tact, or lack of observation may stultify the results of an examination and render you unable to certify a case, when with a little care the reverse might have been the case, and endless trouble, perhaps even danger, avoided for others. It is in the endeavour to give my readers a clear course of action, and render this duty, difficult at all times, as easy for them as I can that I lay down the following rules for their guidance.

1. Make sure of your patient's *caste and station in life,* and learn all you can about his caste prejudices and customs, his religious beliefs, superstitions, etc.

This may seem unnecessary detail perhaps, but the following experience of mine gives point to it. A lady was certified and sent to an asylum as insane on the grounds of "facts narrated by her husband and his relatives," and this one fact noted by the certifying doctor, "Suffers from the delusion that some saint gave her her baby." Briefly, the facts of the case were family quarrels and a Protestant missionary lady doctor who knew nothing of the Catholic custom of praying to our Blessed Lady and the saints for their intercession. Needless to say the matter was speedily rectified, but it taught me a lesson I shall never forget.

2. Ascertain all you can about your patient as regards heredity, temperament, habits, and his behaviour generally. Go into his medical history carefully; find out how he has changed from formerly; what his delusions are, whether he is morbidly suspicious, or suicidal or homicidal. In fact, get a clear, concise history of the case, noting especially the manner of its onset and its general course.

3. In interviews with your patient be fearless, frank, honest, and a good sympathetic listener, behaving outwardly as if your patient were sane and you were treating him for some physical ailment. Do not be afraid to lead up to his weak points and delusions after you have gained his confidence. Unless you wish to test his self-control, never contradict or irritate him, and, if possible, avoid any sign of deceiving him. Having made sure he is ill, try and convince him of the fact too. Above all things take plenty of time, and never seem to be in a hurry; you will only frustrate your object by doing so, and far from doing yourself good may do yourself incalculable harm.

4. Note carefully his speech, manners, and behaviour, how he enters the room, his bearing, gestures, etc., as all these constantly give us indications of the mental condition we have to deal with, and what tone to adopt to derive most information.

5. Test his instincts carefully and *seriatim*.

6. Test his mental faculties, his memory, power of cognition, his reasoning power, judgment, self-control, volition, etc., and look out for hallucinations and delusions, depression, stupor, or excitement, and altered feelings towards his relatives.

7. Observe carefully his expression and articulation, the nutrition of the body, the conformation of the head, and presence of deformities in head or body. The writing often gives valuable indications, and whenever possible should be examined carefully both as to the character of the hand as well as the nature of its contents.

8. Take the pulse and temperature, and examine into the condition of all the bodily functions. This is an important point to note, for, in my own experience, I have known a patient certified by a medical practitioner and sent in the usual way for admission into my asylum when the poor fellow was really suffering from enteric fever. Find out how he sleeps, and if he dreams, and the character of the dreams. Examine into the motor and sensory functions of the brain and cord, asking about headaches and neuralgic pains.

9. Consider the case from three aspects: (*a*) The *medical*, which concerns you as a physician about to treat a patient; (*b*) the *medico-legal*, which concerns you and the patient as regards depriving him of his liberty and the control of his affairs; and

(c) the *medico-psychological*, which includes all the mental problems that arise from a study of the case.

10. Exclude the following conditions from the case: drunkenness, drugging, meningitis, cerebritis, syphilis, the specific fevers, sunstroke, gross brain disease, traumatic lesions, delirium tremens, the effects of moral shock, or the delirium that precedes death.

11. In studying a case of insanity remember that physical and mental symptoms are common to all insanities, and do not look on them as due to separate entities.

12. Remember that your patient's statements can in no way be relied on, and that by your own observation, reasoning, and medical examination you must distinguish between the true and the false, and find what the false is due to, whether it be with intent to deceive, or due to delusions or to deranged consciousness.

13. In some cases, owing to the patient's cunning, etc., it is necessary, for his own safety or that of his relatives, for the preservation of his property, etc., *to conceal your profession* and the object of your visit. One must remember, however, that relatives and others often desire that guile should be practised where there is absolutely no need for it, and that deceit must not be resorted to except when absolutely necessary.

14. Silence, obstinacy, stupidity, and other negative symptoms should be noted, and are valuable aids to diagnosis and treatment.

15. Compare the patient as seen by you with your mental picture of the person you have known, or had described to you, and note wherein the difference lies.

16. Make a blood examination where possible, estimating the number of leucocytes per c.mm. and the percentages of the various types.

17. The chief problems you have to solve are: (1) Is the patient mentally affected or not? (2) If so, is he sufficiently affected to be regarded as irresponsible and insane? (3) What type of insanity are you dealing with? (4) What treatment should you adopt, and what is your prognosis? (5) What risks are there in the case, (*a*) to the patient, (*b*) to others? (6) Can the case be safely treated at home or should it be moved to an asylum? (7) If treated at home, can reliable attendance be obtained?

18. Inform the patient's relatives or guardians of the risks attendant on the case, and impress on them the extreme necessity for care and watchfulness. If there be cause for hope let them know it, but be guarded, as our knowledge of mental diseases is far from perfect as yet, and even the most experienced alienists make errors at times. Make the patient's relatives take their proper responsibility in curtailing his liberty and sending him to an asylum. If you undertake to treat the case in a private house, do so only on condition that proper attendants are arranged for and placed under your exclusive orders.

CHAPTER XIV

PSYCHASTHENIA, NEURASTHENIA, AND HYSTERIA

STRICTLY speaking, these conditions do not fall under the head of insanity, but the border-line between such sufferers and the insane is so ill-defined, and these conditions often prove such a source of confusion to the ordinary practitioner, that I think it as well to discuss them briefly before entering upon a description of the various types of insanity.

PSYCHASTHENIA.

Definition.—Psychasthenia may be defined as a nervous condition affecting those of a well-marked neurotic heredity, who, though they escape insanity, still show a characteristic train of symptoms, both mental and physical, which generally affect the sufferers throughout their entire lives.

Ætiology.—A *tainted heredity* is undoubtedly the chief—in fact, the only—predisposing cause of this affection. *Exhausting processes*, such as overstudy, prolonged lactation, pregnancy, and sexual excesses; *the result of severe illness ; chronic intoxication from drugs*, as alcohol and carbon disulphide; *sudden shock* and *long-continued mental strain*, etc., are all possible exciting causes of psychasthenia.

The large variety of possible exciting causes of the malady shows one that each case should be carefully studied from an ætiological point of view, and its treatment carried out on this basis, for it is obvious that treatment producing good results in psychasthenia resulting, say, from a railway accident is by no means the treatment one would adopt for a case due to chronic alcoholism.

Symptomatology.—Numerous as are the causes of this condition, still more so are the symptoms to which it gives rise, and every new case furnishes to a careful observer yet another combination to add to the multitude already accumulated. There are, however, in nearly every case certain prominent and fairly constant physical symptoms which may be picked out as characteristic of the condition. Among such may be noted *neuro-muscular asthenia, insomnia, mental depression, headache, pains in the back, cardiac disturbances,* and *dyspeptic troubles.*

Neuro-muscular Asthenia.—This is universally admitted to be the most frequent objective sign of the disease. The patient is always tired, the slightest exertion, whether physical or mental, seeming to cause an overwhelming fatigue, and as a result practically the whole day is spent on a lounge or easy-chair. An examination of the muscles of such a patient shows that, though flaccid perhaps, they are still capable of considerable energy, and the dynamometer at first shows no great diminution of muscular power. After the tests have been repeated several times, however, the muscles are found to have lost part of their potency, so that apparently the condition is one more of nervous than physical impotency. True paralysis or contractures never coexist with psychasthenia, the patient being able to execute any ordinary co-ordinate movement, but there seems an incapacity to store up dynamic force enough for prolonged exertion, The tendon reflexes, if tested, are found absolutely normal in psychasthenia pure and simple, and if there be any increase or diminution in these then the presence of some organic disease complicating the psychasthenia must be looked for. All degrees and varieties of this neuro-muscular asthenia are met with, from a mere physical and mental lassitude in the morning, which passes off as the day advances, allowing the patient to take some pleasure and interest in his duties and surroundings, to actual confinement to bed. As a rule the diminution of the cardiac force and the rèlaxation of the arteries are at their acme in the early morning, and as the day proceeds and the vessels become filled by the products of digestion the vascular tone increases, and accounts for the accession of nervous energy as the day advances.

Insomnia.—This is the most troublesome symptom of psychasthenia with which we have to deal, also the most unyielding to treatment. It is largely due to the gastro-intestinal disturbances present, though undoubtedly lack of muscular exertion, cardiac irregularities, and diminished vascular tone also participate in its production. It occurs in a variety of forms; thus the patient may fall asleep soon after retiring to rest, only to wake after two or three hours and toss about till morning, when he rises tired and unrefreshed. In other cases sleep does not come readily; the patient lies awake listening to the irregular tumult of his heart; obsessions disturb his tranquillity; formication, twitchings, or cramps drive away the longed-for sleep just as it seems within his grasp, and only towards morning does sleep overtake him and give him two or three hours of the longed-for rest. It is remarkable how slight the evil effects of this insomnia seem to be, and one is often inclined to believe, on this account, that the patient's statement is either wilfully or unintentionally false; but in all such cases a little watching will prove the truth of the statement. Few psychasthenics show much inclination to sleep in the daytime, but occasionally a case may be met with where, with the nocturnal insomnia, there is irresistible drowsiness during the day. Even the little sleep which is obtained is by no means restful or refreshing. Terrible and appalling dreams disturb repose, and time and again the sufferer wakes, terrified, and soaked in perspiration, from some nerve-racking vision. These visions arise from the anxious mind with which such cases seek repose, the mental processes being carried on in imperfect form when consciousness is partly lost.

Mental Depression.—One of the earliest symptoms of psychasthenia, especially when the condition is due to prolonged mental strain, is loss of memory and inability to recall events. Names of people go beyond recall; writing and conversation are cut short for want of words; books and papers are read without any recollection of their contents remaining; and the details of business fall into entire abeyance. The power of looking after oneself and one's business vanishes, and the whole attention remaining is concentrated upon the unfortunate and helpless condition one has fallen into. Such conditions are more frequently seen in women than in men, and, as with all psychasthenic conditions, they are more marked in the morning, tending to pass off as the day advances.

Headache.—About the onset of puberty those with a tendency to psychasthenia begin to show the first signs of instability in paroxysmal attacks of "sick headache." Girls as a rule suffer about the time of the menstrual periods; and with males too the attacks seem to come on with similar regularity, probably owing to the regular monthly rise and fall in blood-pressure already remarked upon in previous chapters.

The headache of psychasthenia is characteristic and present in greater or less degree in practically every case. It may be continuous over months or even years, though at times it is intermittent. Physical and mental exertion invariably increase it, and, as with so many other psychasthenic symptoms, it is always worse in the morning, tending to pass off as the day advances.

Painful sensation is as a rule absent or only slight in amount, the patient complaining of a feeling of weight or constriction around the temples. Slight vertigo, roaring in the ear, retinal hyperæsthesias, muscæ volitantes, and other phenomena accompany it. The headache is not diffuse in all cases, but may be localised to certain areas, the most favourite site being the occipital and nuchal regions, and here actual pain is complained of much more frequently than in any other region.

Pains in the Back.—This symptom of psychasthenia is met with much more commonly in women than in men, and any attempt at motion suffices to bring it out. It is aggravated by the occurrence of the menstrual periods, the pains and aches being materially increased by the congestion of the organs of generation, and ovarian neuralgias are its common accompaniment. In men it is frequently confounded with rheumatoid or pre-ataxic pains, and often gives rise to mental depression or hypochondriasis.

Accompanying the pains various hyperæsthesias of the genital organs, formication, and other derangements of sensation are met with.

Cardiac Disturbances.—An irregular and tumultuous action is the most common of these, and is probably due to a transient inhibition of the vagus fibres, arising in all likelihood from the weakness of the reflex centres peculiar to psychasthenia. The immediate cause is in most cases fright or anxiety, though probably sexual excesses, alcoholism, and mental strain contribute in producing it. In one type of case the rhythm is regular and not perceptibly above the normal, but the arterial tension is increased, giving rise to the various other symptoms so commonly seen in psychasthenics. In such conditions slight emotion may bring on a high degree of irregularity, with anxiety and præcordial distress, such attacks lasting for a few minutes, and leaving the patient as a rule much exhausted. In other cases the cardiac rate is increased sometimes up to 130 per minute, and there is a diminution in arterial tension. When a nervous seizure occurs in such cases the pulse becomes small, the tension is markedly diminished, and the pulse-rate is increased by twenty-five to thirty beats. Accompanying this there is extreme reflex irritability and a feeling of great lassitude and fatigue; and at times vertigo, trembling, and even unconsciousness may accompany the attack, which may last from a few minutes up to five or six hours. Warm baths, with cold applications over the cardiac region, and the exhibition of alcohol and the bromides, combined with aconite, are indicated during the acute attack, and between attacks full nourishing diet, tonics, malt liquors, etc., should be made use of.

Digestive Troubles.—These are practically an invariable accompaniment of all psychasthenic conditions, but their character and degree vary greatly with individual cases. In by far the majority of cases they take the form of a gastro-intestinal disturbance, atonic in character. In mild cases there is not much reduction in weight, but in the more severe cases loss of weight is often very marked, and it is a common cause of the anæmia so prevalent among psychasthenics.

In such cases, after the ingestion of food there is an immediate sense of comfort and well-being, which, however, is soon replaced by vague feelings of weight and distension in the gastric region, and frequent eructations of gas. After the food has passed from the stomach to the intestine the gaseous fermentation is partially arrested, and some relief is experienced for a time; but the intestinal contents soon become fermented too, and borborygmi begin, which may be so severe as to cause a sensitive person to seek solitude and shun all company. Severe colic often accompanies this stage and may be a great trial, lasting for an hour or more, until expulsion of the gas *per rectum* brings gradual relief, and the patient returns to his usual condition. Such symptoms as a rule follow after every meal, and utterly prevent the patient having any pleasure in life, though they rarely produce any marked emaciation. The cause of this atonic dyspepsia is the subacidity of the gastric juices, as shown by the phloroglucinol phenylin and other tests, this subacidity allowing fermentation to proceed which the presence of 0·3 per cent. of acid is quite sufficient to check for a long time. The fermentation is probably started by micro-organisms, which, having collected between the teeth, get mixed with the food during the process of mastication, and thus get carried with it into the stomach, where the absence of hydrochloric acid allows fermentation to begin, and this is still further increased by the alkaline juices of the duodenum.

Constipation nearly always accompanies nervous dyspepsia in all its forms, and when the bowels are moved by purgatives or enemata the fæces are expelled as hard scybalous masses. When there is chronic catarrhal affection of the small intestine, as sometimes happens, diarrhœa may replace the constipation, and much emaciation occurs, though life is rarely endangered by it. In most psychasthenic cases the tone of the muscles of the alimentary canal is fairly well maintained, and in consequence dilatation of the stomach is but rarely seen, the ingesta passing through at a fairly normal rate.

The dyspepsia from subacidity is most unyielding to treatment, and may continue for years without amelioration, though as a rule the exhibition of acids lessens the fermentation, renders the patient more comfortable, and promotes nutrition.

It is often extremely difficult to differentiate more severe cases from some gastric tumour. In both instances the hydrochloric acid of the gastric juice is diminished or absent, and the emaciation, the yellow, dried-up skin, the markedly progressive deterioration of the blood, are also common to both types of disease. The absence of a tumour in the gastric region, and the history of suffering from various other cardinal symptoms of psychasthenia for some months, are the main points which help us in our differential diagnosis.

Nervous diarrhœas are often seen in neurotic people, and often the mere thought of a railway journey or some public ordeal is sufficient to start an attack, which ceases so soon as the cause is removed.

The **mental symptoms of psychasthenics** are much more difficult to comprehend and elicit than the physical ones, and are by no means invariably present, though in a large proportion of cases a careful and tactful enquiry may bring them to light. These mental phenomena are extremely varied in character, but as a rule arise from obsessions or imperative ideas, and from these are evolved states of mixed motor-emotional agitation.

From the imperfect adjustment of the brain equipoise certain dominant ideas obtrude themselves, and, owing to the imperfect volition of the patient, assert and reassert themselves at all times, gaining a morbid clearness which impresses them so on the mind of the patient that, unless some change of habits or surroundings intervenes, the patient's whole life is influenced by them. These imperative conceptions are recognised by the patient as absurd, but to resist them only produces mental distress, while yielding to them merely increases their power over the unhappy individual, and in either case his condition is almost unbearable. They are palpably in no way connected with hallucinations, and being recognised as false by the patient cannot be classified as delusions.

Motor-mental Agitation.—The obsession forcing a patient to some foolish or revolting act often brings on such a state of agitation that incessant motion can alone relieve it. In such circumstances the patient walks about his room, wringing his hands, and weeping and praying in an indescribable state of mental hyperæsthesia, until gradually a sense of relief is experienced and he becomes again calm and collected. These attacks resemble greatly the exacerbations seen so often in acute mania and excited melancholia, but are much more transient and less intense.

Psychasthenic Anxiety and Compulsory Ideas.—These, as with the majority of the mental symptoms of psychasthenia, are due to a loss or diminution of the power of volition. They arise usually either as a result of half-conscious dream states giving rise to a form of autosuggestion, or from long-continued habits, which gradually gain more and more dominance until finally they affect the whole life of the patient. As a rule the patients recognise their absurdity, and at times even make feeble attempts to overcome them; but their volition is too weak to sustain the struggle long, and they soon return to their former condition of terror and anxiety. These obsessions therefore are markedly different from those of the paranoiac, who is convinced of the truth of his delusions; but, at the same time, the constant presence of one train of thought has an undoubted influence upon unstable brain matter, and occasionally assumes pathological proportions.

The imperative ideas of the anxious psychasthenic may assume an infinite variety of form. Some may arise from perfectly natural aversions, such as the dread of filth, of poison, of infection, of solitude, etc. To many such forms distinctive names have been given—*e.g.*, *agorophobia*, the fear of open spaces;

claustrophobia, the fear of being in a closed room; *zoophobia*, the fear of animals, etc.

The *délire de toucher et de doute* of some authors is simply one form of this affection. In the first the sufferer has an irresistible desire to touch a certain type of article; thus, for example, he may have an intense desire to read every piece of writing he comes across, torn scraps picked up in the road or from a sweeper's basket, private documents on an official's desk—it is all the same to him; read them he must and does, and naturally he is constantly in hot water. The reverse of this is frequently seen; thus there is a marked antipathy to touch certain articles, and forced contact arouses a lively disquietude which can only be assuaged by repeated ablutions.

The *folie de doute* is a condition where every object and action is a cause of interminable arguing and reasoning, and often renders the sufferer unfit to continue his work owing to the apprehensions that some error may arise which might have a serious effect upon his career.

As a rule psychasthenic symptoms show a tendency to be intermittent in character, and the majority of cases show a tendency to temporarily improve in the hotter seasons and recrudesce during the colder months, owing to the effects of vasomotor paresis being less marked during the hotter seasons.

Diagnosis.—As can be readily understood, it is often a matter of great difficulty to distinguish psychasthenia from *incipient general paralysis of the insane, cerebral syphilis, tabes dorsalis*, and various other forms of organic cerebral and spinal disease, especially if a distinct history of venereal disease be obtained. One has also to distinguish it from various types of insanity; and lastly, and probably the most important of all, it has to be diagnosed from neurasthenia. In each case one must go most carefully into the history of the case from childhood upwards, asking especially about the symptoms, both physical and mental, detailed above. Next, a careful examination of superficial and deep reflexes must be made, and signs of paralysis or contractures looked for. Having ascertained all these fully and carefully one has then to go over the notes made during the examination and estimate to the best of one's power the condition present, and if the cardinal symptoms and conditions above mentioned be kept in mind, a fairly correct diagnosis will sooner or later be arrived at.

Treatment.—This is invariably a matter of much difficulty in psychasthenics. Every case must be carefully considered on its own merits and the treatment based on this, for what may prove beneficial in one case may prove useless or worse than useless in many others. Each case must therefore be studied carefully by itself, careful enquiry made as to the presence of any hereditary taint, and the incidence of acute diseases, and any of the cardinal symptoms of this condition during the earlier years of life, as to the possibility of the symptoms having been aggravated by excessive venery and indulgence in alcoholism and masturbation, and whether there be indications of secret indulgence in any drugs.

All these having been carefully enquired into, the treatment can be divided into four heads—*hygienic, dietetic, moral,* and *medicinal.* Weir Mitchell's treatment is based on the first three of these.

Hygienic.—The sanitation of the patient's surroundings should be carefully looked to as regards drainage, ventilation, and lighting. The water-supply should be seen to, and examined both chemically and bacteriologically; and proper bathing should be insisted on, careful instructions being given as to the time and temperature of the baths. Some psychasthenics improve wonderfully with cold baths and douches in the morning, while with others cold bathing does more harm than good, and lukewarm or even hot baths are required. In these last cases night-time as a rule is the best time for the bathing, as it calms obsessions, and has good results in promoting sleep.

Climate, too, has to be considered, and as a rule it will be found that excitable, emotional cases do best at fairly high altitudes (2,000 to 3,000 feet), while depressed cases, with slow, imperfect digestion, are better at lower levels. Removal from all business cares and change of scene to a free life in the country, from the hot, monotonous existence of a town or cantonment in the plains to the bracing air and lovely scenery of some quiet hill station, often works wonders in the restitution of a broken-down nervous system. Removal from his own family circle to the society of strangers in some bracing, quiet place, where there is, however, distraction sufficient to prevent brooding, is what we should aim at, as well as regulating the patient's life so that every hour of the day may have something to stimulate his flagging energies and give him an interest in life.

Dietetic.—By far the majority of psychasthenics are anæmic and run down, and really require what we may call a surplus of food, and it is a mistake to think that because dyspepsia is present food should be exhibited only at long intervals. It is true that in a certain number of cases with slow digestion three meals a day have excellent results, but as a rule in all psychasthenic cases it will be found better to remove them from ordinary diet and feed them on slops for a time, adding gradually one foodstuff after another until we find what is most suitable for our patient and gives the best results.

Milk, eggs, a moderate amount of meat, both red and white, fish, vegetables, especially cabbages, carrots, and those rich in chlorophyll, may all be added gradually to the diet, but potatoes it is better generally to eliminate. Fruit can be given fairly freely, and especially so if cooked. The imbibing of fluids should be carefully regulated, and only a limited amount allowed at meals, as otherwise indigestion is almost sure to result. A useful means of quieting the patient and inducing sleep will be found in the administration of some hot broth, milk, or cocoa just at bedtime, though it may not answer in all cases.

Moral.—The influence the physician, by unfailing tact, care, and sympathy, is able to obtain over the patient is of invaluable aid in his treatment of the case. Only too often is the condition of the patient made worse by his relations and friends misunderstanding the state of affairs and deriding his depression and feeble will-power. This as a rule, far from stimulating him to fresh efforts at self-control, only makes him still more miserable, and he sinks farther and farther into the depths of despair. A little sympathy and kindliness, combined with the firmness requisite for carrying out the treatment laid down, is what is required, and our efforts should be directed to attain this end, and, though exhibiting the necessary sympathy, yet avoid a leniency which by extending too far might equally militate against the results we aim at.

Hypnotic suggestion has been advised by many continental authorities, but experience has shown it to be more harmful than beneficial, as it tends to still further weaken the already deficient will-power. All that should be attempted in this line is to impress on the patient by well-considered words and actions that he is by no means incurable, and his malady is purely a functional one, the cure of which rests largely in his own hands.

The pathogenesis of the "phobias" and other imperative conceptions should always be carefully explained to intelligent patients, and their aid sought in overcoming them.

In many cases of the severer types it is absolutely necessary to take the patients away from their surroundings and place them under the care of a nurse who, under proper medical supervision, has complete control of the case. Complete isolation is only necessary in a few cases, and in the large majority rest, massage, and dieting make up the essentials of our treatment. The mental qualities of the nurse should always be carefully ascertained before any arrangements are made, for a firm but sympathetic nature is essential to the cure of such cases.

Therapeutic Measures.—The exhibition of medicines is not so much required in this condition as the prevention of the patient lavishing money on endless quack medicines and imbibing them, probably with disastrous results to himself. Any new advertisement seen or drug mentioned by friends sends the patient flying to the chemist to purchase it, and many thus become addicted to some drug habit or alcoholic indulgence which is often much more difficult to overcome than the primary trouble.

Psychasthenia being due to lack of a reserve of nervous energy, rest in bed is an absolute necessity in all cases for a few days at least. When by this means a certain modicum of energy has been stored up, carefully regulated walking or driving may be indulged in. With a certain number of chronic cases, however, too prolonged a rest is harmful, and they should be gently forced to take interest in what is going on around them and be roused from their self-absorption. Massage and electricity are often excellent adjuvants during the period of enforced rest, though at times, and in certain cases, they seem to have a debilitating effect, and are therefore contra-indicated.

Hydrotherapy.—As already noted, carefully regulated baths are often of the greatest service in treating such conditions. Extremes of temperature and too prolonged immersion are always to be avoided. Wrapping the body in a wet sheet for from fifteen to thirty minutes has often most beneficial results, especially if it be followed by a brisk rub down with a coarse towel. The temperature for this pack should be 85° to 90° F. as a start, the water being gradually cooled or heated as the patient's condition requires. Cold douches and very hot plunge baths are to be avoided, though a tepid plunge at bedtime is often most useful in inducing sleep.

Drugs.—All psychasthenic cases require some tissue-building tonic owing to their state of extreme physical weakness. In addition to this some harmless sedative, as tincture of valerian, paraldehyde, or trional may be given to soothe the patient and prevent his sending to the chemist for all sorts of quack medicines for one and all of his fancied ailments.

The most useful *forms of iron* are the peptonates of iron and manganese, or the subcarbonate of iron, especially in combination with other drugs, as is the case with several tabloids and capsules prepared by Messrs. Burroughs Wellcome and Co.

Preparations of phosphates are useful adjuvants. Glycero-phosphates in combination with cod-liver oil or somatose give good results, but for some years Huxley's compound syrup of the acid of glycero-phosphates in one or other of its combinations has been my mainstay in such cases, and I have had most excellent results from its exhibition.

Strychnine, from its general tonic effects, is good, especially so in cases of gastro-intestinal atony. It must, however, be used cautiously in the severer cases, or it may cause more harm than good by its action.

Hydrochloric acid, alone or combined with pepsin, is invaluable when fermentative dyspepsia is present.

Prognosis.—A permanent cure of psychasthenia is in all cases most problematical. A certain number improve sufficiently to enable them to take an active interest again in life, but relapses are frequent. The prognosis should, therefore, in all cases be a guarded one.

Neurasthenia.

Neurasthenia is a condition of nervous exhaustion resulting from sudden or prolonged mental or physical strain, or appearing as the sequel to shock or exhausting illnesses, in those with no marked hereditary taint. It is practically a similar condition to psychasthenia, but in it there is no hereditary taint; symptoms are absent until after the occurrence producing the derangement, and the prognosis is infinitely better. In practically all cases of neurasthenia a few months' rest, change of climate, and treatment, generally produce a perfect recovery, and the danger of subsequent relapses is infinitesimal.

The necessity, therefore, of diagnosing carefully between neurasthenic and psychasthenic cases must be palpable to everyone, and needs no further emphasis here.

Psychasthenic and Neurasthenic Psychoses.

Mental symptoms playing such a large part in all such cases, and the liability to toxic absorption during their course being so great, it is surprising how few, among the large numbers of such cases, overstep the boundary and become insane. When such cases do occur they are, as one would naturally expect, of the melancholic type, maniacal states very rarely being seen. The attacks generally occur at the climax of an exhaustion paroxysm, and quickly respond to rest, feeding, and sedatives, though a certain small number with markedly tainted heredity may run on to secondary dementia.

Masturbation is a frequent cause of a more protracted form of mental confusion, amounting at times to stupor, and in such cases the prognosis is by no means hopeful.

Some cases, generally those of marked neurotic family, pass into a condition of paranoia. For these sufferers recovery is practically hopeless, and the frequency of aural hallucinations, with the resulting danger to the public, renders it necessary to place such cases in asylums.

Hysteria.

Though hysteria and psychasthenia are, pathogenically, practically similar conditions, both being due to an incomplete development of the higher cortical centres concerned in mentalisation, yet, clinically, they differ widely in their manifestations, and when, as occasionally happens, the two conditions are found in one and the same individual, the diagnosis is often a matter of extreme difficulty.

The main points to look for are, in hysteria, the convulsive crises, the hemianæsthesias and segmentary anæsthesias, the contractures and paralyses, with narrowing of the field of vision and derangements of colour vision. In psychasthenia we have the constant dull headache, the motor asthenia, the rachialgia, the atonic dyspepsias, insomnia, and the other symptoms arising from defective vasomotor innervation. The mental conditions of the two diseases are also wholly different. In hysteria we see a marked reaction to emotion resulting in histrionic displays, or simulation, from autosuggestion or extrinsic suggestion, of paralyses and contractures. Defects of mental co-ordination and of the will-power render it almost impossible to catch the attention of the patient, and, owing to the defects of memory, as well as of the moral sense, it is impossible to rely on the statement of anyone suffering from hysteria. In psychasthenia, again, we meet with patients so self-centred that they are irritable and morbidly depressed, though not so much so as to constitute a true melancholia. They are the prey of innumerable impulses and obsessions, and suffer from transitory defects of memory, which, however, can be corrected if attention be drawn to them.

The **ætiology of hysteria** must undoubtedly be looked for in hereditary taint, aggravated by defective education, lack of proper control at home, and indulgence in either emotional or sexual passions in early life. The greater and less repressed emotional nature of women renders them the most frequent sufferers, and indeed certain characteristics of hysteria appear to be only exaggerations of well-known feminine traits.

The most common period of life for hysterical manifestations to appear is the post-pubescent age, teeming as it is with the natural longings that follow the change from incomplete to active development of the sexual functions. Especially great are its effects upon girls, who perhaps up to that time have lived the life of a tomboy, but are then bound down by the trammels of social life, and, meeting every hour with the repression of their natural emotions, are driven to concentrate their attention upon themselves, and in many cases upon those organs so lately sprung into functional being.

The **deviations from normal mentalisation proper to hysteria** are as a rule of a transitory character, and follow after the convulsive crises, with which they have a direct relation. They may be divided into two classes: (*a*) *those belonging to the inter-paroxysmal period ;* (*b*) *those immediately succeeding the attack.*

(*a*) *Interparoxysmal Period.*—The psychoses characteristic of this period are *amnesia, loss of will-power, aboulia, or loss of the power of attention, great emotional instability,* and *excessive reaction to suggestion.* The patients may be gay, active, and mischievous, or the reverse conditions may prevail, and they may be passive and apathetic.

Amnesia is generally present to a greater or less extent, and, as already noted, is one of the causes of mendacity so common in this condition. In severe cases, after frequent attacks, all remembrance of the past is lost and only recalled during the paroxysms.

The *loss of volition and faculty of attention* are found in other conditions, and by themselves are not pathognomonic of an hysterical state. It at times takes the form of a *folie de doute*, but as a rule simply incapacitates the patient from carrying on his ordinary daily duties, not from perversity or obstinacy, but simply from sheer lack of will-power. This, therefore, is in direct antithesis to the powerlessness arising from fixed ideas of repugnance so commonly seen in neurasthenia.

Mental hysteria, a condition where one sees all the mental but none of the physical stigmata of this condition, is common in India among Europeans, Indians, and especially among Anglo-Indians. It is characterised by an extremely emotional nature, which is always to be seen at work, as evidenced by capriciousness, sentimentality, irritability, and great changefulness of mood. Such persons have but little self-control, are morbidly nervous, quick at chaff and repartee, lack judgment, and are incapable of doing any work requiring great mental effort.

(*b*) *Post-paroxysmal Manifestations.*—These are numerous and varied, both in type and degree, stretching from various states of exaltation and depression, through delusional conditions to somnambulism and stupor. All of these are as a rule transitory, and but little or no remembrance of the seizure remains after recovery. Some, such as somnambulism and lethargy, are not necessarily preceded by a seizure, though a condition resembling *epilepsie larvée* is undoubtedly present in all such cases.

An almost constant symptom in such cases is the presence of hallucinations of sight and hearing.

In the delirium of *hystero-epilepsy* consciousness is lost, the patients at one moment shouting, singing, and dancing, being restrained only with the greatest difficulty; the next moment they are sunk in an almost stuporose condition. With this a maniacal condition at times is seen, with an inconceivable flow of language, in which, however, there is a tendency to the repetition of words and phrases which renders it unlike the logorrhœa of the true maniac.

Lethargy.—This may follow a severe seizure or come on without warning, and may last from a few minutes to a few weeks, in which latter case it is in all probability the equivalent of a seizure. Cataleptic conditions of the muscular system have been noted during such attacks, and if the condition lasts long, artificial feeding may be necessary, and emaciation becomes marked.

In some cases the excitement after an hysterical attack is prolonged over an indefinite period, assuming a chronic hallucinatory type very commonly seen in many of the " exhaustion psychoses "; but here the alternations of confusion and stupor with hallucinatory ecstasy, or even with hysterical convulsions, are extremely characteristic.

True mania and melancholia may complicate but never arise from a case of hysteria, and though a form of paranoia after hysteria has been described by Krafft-Ebing, I think most authorities at the present day are inclined to doubt its reality.

Suicide may occur in hysterical conditions, and undoubtedly many attempts are made, but most of these are simply to attract attention and sympathy.

Treatment.—The treatment is practically the same as for psychasthenia, and I would refer my readers to that section rather than cumber this book with a repetition of what I have already said there.

CHAPTER XV

GROUP A: INSANITIES OF NON-TOXIC ORIGIN

EXHAUSTION INSANITY.

(I. *Stupor.* II. *Consecutive Insanity.*)

Ætiology.—These as a rule are conditions of the late adult or senile periods of life, when the natural reparative powers of the body begin to fail, and with men these are practically the only periods of life in which it is seen. In women, however, the disease is often seen at much earlier age periods owing to prolonged lactation; and this is specially the case in India, where the habit prevails, certainly among the lower classes, of suckling the children for two or even three years.

Heredity, nervous diseases, and a neurotic temperament are all predisposing causes, while the exciting causes are innumerable, including all conditions which exhaust the physical powers.

Symptoms—*Prodomata.*—The attack begins insidiously, and often for some months before distinct mental symptoms manifest themselves a falling off in physical energy, dyspepsia, constipation, anæmia, atonic conditions of the circulatory system, irritability, nervousness, and insomnia have been noticed by the patient and his friends.

(*a*) *Physical.*—On seeing such a case one is at once struck by the appearance of malnutrition, the pallor and unhealthy condition of the skin, which has a cold, clammy feeling, and seems to have lost the elasticity normally appertaining to it. The eyes are dull, and the attitude and expression listless and apathetic and form a striking picture of the mental and bodily state of the sufferer. The temperature is generally subnormal. Dyspepsia and constipation are almost invariably present, and often much persuasion is required before the patient can be got to take nourishment. Anæmia is invariably present, there being as a rule a deficiency in the red blood corpuscles as well as in the hæmoglobin they contain. There is never any hyper-leucocytosis, and as a rule the polymorph percentage is lower than normal. The cardiac action is feeble, and functional murmurs are often present in the mitral and aortic areas. Œdema of the extremities is a common symptom. The skin has a dirty, sallow appearance, and any sudden noise may suffice to bring on profuse perspiration. The urine is practically normal in all cases, and there is no marked derangement of any of the sensory or motor functions beyond the results of the general atonic condition of the whole system.

(*b*) *Mental.*—The mental condition is invariably one of depression and confusion, varying from comparatively slight melancholic conditions to severer forms, combined with delusions of suspicion, or, in the more severe cases, to a semi-stuporose condition, where the patient sits listlessly all day long in one position, with a sad, vacant expression, and can barely be roused to answer questions. The slightest attempt at even the simplest mental effort causes intense exhaustion owing to the anergic condition of the cortical centres. Cognition of time and place is unaffected, but occasionally hallucinations of sight are met with. Delusions, though not an invariable concomitant, are often met with, and generally consist of suspicions of poisoning, or torturing by "electricity," "marconigrams," and "unseen agencies," or of other people talking about or laughing at the patient. The faculty of attention is deficient, as is also the power of volition. Self-control is lost, and the patient is obstinate and easily irritated, either getting angry or having fits of passionate weeping at the merest trifles. Memory is good both for recent and past events. The speech is lacking in life and character and seems to be a distinct effort to the patient, but it is never incoherent. The comprehension of questions and statements made by other people seems at times to be a matter of difficulty to the patient. Insomnia is present in every case, and is often a source of trouble in the treatment.

CASE XXIII.

Mt. Kallia, aged 35, Baniah caste. Admitted into Agra Asylum under Section 471, C.P.C.

This woman had been nursing her own child for some eighteen months when her sister-in-law died, and out of pity she began to suckle also her infant niece. Her circumstances were very poor, and the result of the poor diet and the heavy strain thus thrown upon her was that she became depressed, irritable, and run down. As her health deteriorated her mental condition became worse, and culminated one day in her suddenly dashing the head of her niece on the ground and killing it. She was arrested, her own child removed from her in case she might also do it harm, and she was put up for trial under 302 I.P.C. During the time she was under trial, being relieved of the heavy strain on her system, and getting good nourishing dietary, she began to improve rapidly, and by the time her trial was over, and she was acquitted, and sent to Agra Asylum under Section 471, C.P.C., she had practically recovered. She was in the asylum for some two years, during which she was always most kind, gentle, and sensible with the other patients, and a great help to the attendants (A. W. Overbeck-Wright).

Treatment.—Prolonged rest in bed is essential in all cases, and a cheerful, sympathetic, but strong-willed attendant is a most useful and necessary adjunct. The diet should be at first light, but ample and nourishing, milk, farinaceous foods, fish, chicken, soups, etc., being given in as large quantities as the patient can be persuaded to take. When recovery is well begun, ordinary full diet should be freely given, and if possible some of the malt beverages, such as beer and stout. As regards drugs, general tonics, such as iron, strychnine, and the phosphates are indicated for the general condition; and for insomnia, veronal, trional, sulphonal, or paraldehyde in small doses (10 to 15 minims) may be given, though in all cases before the exhibition of hypnotics the effects of a warm bath (95° F.) and a glass of hot milk at bedtime should be tried.

Prognosis.—This is influenced largely by the age of the patient and the cause of the exhaustion. As a rule the younger the patient is the better the prognosis which we can give. Cases due to prolonged lactation as a rule make a fairly rapid recovery, but cases arising from severe illness or physical or mental strain progress but slowly, and are apt to pass into a condition of mild secondary dementia.

Diagnosis.—This depends mainly on the history of the patient and of any previous physical or mental strain, such as prolonged lactation, over-study, prolonged nursing of some near relative, or some severe illness. The extreme physical exhaustion and the absence of any symptoms of toxæmia are the main symptoms we have to help us in this condition.

Insanity resulting from Gross Brain Lesion.

(I. ———. II. *Insanity associated with obvious Morbid Changes in the Brain.*)

The brain lesions most apt to be followed by mental symptoms are those affecting the motor areas of the cortex, especially those of the left frontal lobe which implicate Broca's convolution, and as a rule they are of vascular origin. The mental symptoms may follow immediately after the lesion, as is almost invariably the case when aphasia is present, or they may be delayed for some months. The early symptoms are invariably of a maniacal type, and may be very acute; they are due partly to cerebral irritation from extravasated blood, partly to derangements in the nutrition of the cortex, and partly perhaps to absorption of products produced by the breaking down of the effused blood corpuscles. The acute symptoms rarely last more than a few days, and are followed by a condition of irritable dementia. In some cases the first acute stage may be absent, and the childishness, emotionalism, extreme irritability, and causeless outbursts of rage characteristic of the second stage may come on gradually. Except for paralysis according to the areas affected there are no physical symptoms worthy of note in these conditions.

Lesions of the brain have been cited at one time or another as the cause of all sorts of brain disease, such as mania and melancholia, but in by far the greater number, if not all, of such cases the probability is that no attempt has been made to exclude the possibility of a toxæmic origin for these conditions.

Epilepsy undoubtedly does follow after brain injuries, and, as a result of the cortical irritation and epileptic discharges, one finds extreme irritability and impulsiveness in such cases, and on such brains alcohol has most deleterious results, producing attacks of wild mania which often end in brutal and revolting crimes. After repeated fits one at times sees a sort of stuporose condition with loss of memory and a blunting of all the mental faculties—a sort of secondary dementia, in fact.

Case XXIV.

G. W., male, aged 51, admitted into Murthly Asylum suffering from right-sided hemiplegia with aphasia and excitement.

History.—He had been a steady, industrious man, who rarely indulged in alcohol. Three nights prior to admission he went to bed complaining of headache and dizziness, and awoke in the morning paralysed in the right arm, and aphasic. In the evening his temperature was 100° F., and he appeared confused and talked incoherently. He was restless and delirious all night, and next morning his right leg was also paretic. During the next night he became maniacal and very noisy and difficult to manage.

On admission he was a big, well-made man, with tortuous atheromatous arteries. The right arm was completely paralysed, but the right leg was capable of some movement. He was quite aphasic. Mentally he was confused, restless, and, so far as he could be, violent, kicking and striking at those about him. He apparently did not understand what was said to him, and every now and then uttered inarticulate cries, apparently attempts at speech.

A week after admission he was no longer maniacal, but sullen, morose, and irritable. It was difficult to persuade him to take food. He seemed to live in a chronic state of irritability, and when spoken to would turn savagely upon his addresser and snarl, "You're a liar!" Any further overtures were invariably met by a volley of "You're a liar!" *crescendo*. These words and "damn" were the only four he was ever heard to utter. He used to try to read, but it could never be ascertained if he understood what he saw. He either did not recognise his relatives or did not care to see them when they came to see him. Sometimes he had causeless bursts of crying, howling and sobbing like a child. His general nutrition failed rapidly, in spite of his appetite remaining good. He died two years after admission (Bruce, "Studies in Clinical Psychiatry").

Traumatic Insanity.

(I. ———. II. *Traumatic Insanity.*)

The insanity following injuries to the head is a subject of moment from a medico-legal point of view, especially in so far as it concerns insurance companies, large employers of labour, railway companies, etc. Many of the traumatic neuroses are purely nervous, and many of them very obscure nervous complaints, and such cases are apt to be misinterpreted and looked on either as mere foolish fancies, or else construed as pure fiction and an attempt to obtain compensation by fraudulent means. The full comprehension of such cases is therefore a matter of importance to all medical men, as without it they may unwittingly do a man gross injustice, and, moreover, quite possibly place themselves in an exceedingly awkward predicament.

Ætiology.—The apparent injury to the head may be only slight, or, as occurs in many cases, not a trace of injury may be found, a severe fall on the feet or gluteal region having perhaps caused a concussion of the base of the brain quite sufficient to account for the mental symptoms, but leaving no subsequent trace; or even a severe fright may suffice in cases of hereditary taint. In many cases, indeed, absolutely no organic basis can be found to account for the condition, and most modern authorities are agreed as to the possibility of a psychical origin for such conditions. In such cases the mental condition may be apparent at once, or it may be delayed for some months, though even in these latter cases careful observation would probably reveal some slight change in character or mentalisation immediately after the incident. It is these cases, where the appearance of the symptoms is delayed, which form the great stumbling-block for the unwary, and against them I would earnestly warn my readers. In such cases, where there is an interval of apparent recovery between the results of the accident and the appearance of mental symptoms, the explanation is that the recovery is only from the urgent and acute symptoms, and that the later ones are of slow development. Moreover, the recovery is rarely complete, and careful observation usually reveals one or more signs of deranged mentalisation, chief among which insomnia may be noted. Alcoholics and syphilitics are especially liable to bad effects from head injuries caused by blows or falls, and in the latter type a cranial injury may very soon be followed by general paralysis, though the injury is only a determining and not a primary cause in such cases.

Sunstroke, too, must be included under this head, for the neuroses following on an attack of the sun are, to all intents and purposes, such as are met with as the result of blows and falls, as, for instance, cases where, after head injuries or sunstroke, the patient cannot take any alcoholic beverage without revealing marked temporary mental aberration, at times even approaching an attack of maniacal frenzy.

Physical Symptoms.—These naturally are mainly subjective. Headache is the most prominent, and may be almost continual, though in other cases it is confined mainly to times of work, or when any prolonged effort of attention is required. Defects of vision are frequently seen, the patient complaining of diplopia or of the letters all running together when he is reading. Noises in the ears are frequent, and may be a source of much annoyance to the patient. Derangements of sensation are often present, and the patient complains of pain in the back of the neck, or in the lumbar or dorsal region. Fine tremors may be present in the tongue, face, and fingers, and bladder troubles are frequently seen owing to some indefinite implication of the innervation of the involuntary muscle. Appetite is poor, and as a rule chronic dyspepsia is present in most cases, leading to general ill-health and emaciation.

Mental Symptoms.—These may either appear directly after the accident, or may develop slowly as the acute symptoms fade away, being delayed often for weeks or months. The patient becomes very irritable and querulous, and is always complaining and finding fault. He is readily fatigued by even the slightest physical or mental exertion. Memory is distinctly impaired, as is also his power of attention, and in some cases there is constant confusion and total inability to understand any communication, whether written or verbal. As a result of this depression is often seen, and even attempts at suicide may be made on account of this inability to work, and the feeling that he is a burden on all his relatives or friends. Insomnia is frequent in all such cases, and obsessions are often present. Many such cases, too, are hypochondriacal, and imagine they suffer from various forms of disease as a result of the accident.

The course of such cases is usually a long one, weeks and months often passing with little or no apparent improvement taking place. In favourable cases the powers of attention and thought gradually return and the bodily condition improves, while the continual sense of fatigue disappears, memory becomes more accurate, and by degrees the patient returns to his normal condition.

Diagnosis.—What is here mainly required of us is not so much to distinguish this condition from various others, such as neurasthenia or hysteria, as ability to detect the malingerer. Insurance companies and employers of labour often ask our advice regarding claims for compensation, and we must remember that though every care should be taken to frustrate the swindler, in doing so we must do all in our power to prevent injustice to honest men. It is the whole statement of the case on which we must rely for this and not on one or two details, for the malingerer as a rule overacts his part, and his statement of his symptoms teems with incongruities. See the patient and his friends separately, and note whether their statements agree, enquiring for the presence of unlikely symptoms, as by this means the malingerer is frequently induced to betray himself. Never show any surprise at any statement or answer received, but let the patient tell his own story first, avoiding leading questions, and remember that the patient may lay particular stress on certain points which seem to him of importance, and other mental and physical changes may be gathered from his friends.

Prognosis.—This disorder is invariably a severe test of the prognostic powers of the medical attendant. Not only the severity of the accident, but the past and present history of the patient also have to be taken into consideration, and every detail carefully weighed. Two judgments are invariably required of us: (*a*) What is the immediate prospect? (*b*) What is the ultimate prognosis?

In some cases complete recovery may take place after some months or even years, while in others, again, there may be complete incapacity for work and earning a livelihood, though the capability of enjoying life is recovered so long as they are free from work. These are the cases which are the cause of most litigation, because the lay mind wholly fails to understand the utter incapacity there is in such cases of fixing the attention for more than a moment at a time. Each case must therefore be carefully studied on its own merits, and it must be remembered that the power of concentrating the attention, the functions of memory, volition, and the like, may all suffer, and yet the grosser functions may remain undamaged.

Case XXV.

G. E., a Eurasian male, aged 27, was admitted into Agra Asylum in 1901. He had been an industrious, hard-working man, employed on the railway. A history was given of the beam of a crane having fallen on to his head some months prior to his attack. His attack began by his suddenly leaving his bungalow one morning and flinging himself into a well in the compound. His servants ran for assistance, and when it arrived he was found swimming about in the well. Ropes were flung to him, and he was told to come up, but his sole response was, "Go to hell!" At last preparations were made to send men down to bring him up, and when he saw these he grasped a rope, swarmed up it, and made a violent attack on those gathered round the well. He was captured and sent to the asylum.

For many months he remained in an acutely maniacal condition and subject to sudden seizures, when he would tear his clothes to ribbons, and march naked round and round his room, invariably from east to west, stamping his feet on the ground, and shouting at the top of his voice. During these seizures his head was always in a condition of left torticollis, and he used to slap violently with his open hand at the left side of his face and head—so violently, in fact, that it was quite a common thing to see subconjunctival hæmorrhages after such attacks. His maniacal condition has quieted down, and he is in a condition of quiet dementia now, but still liable to frequent seizures, which, however, are not so violent as formerly. He is now stone blind in his left eye, probably due to a slipped retina, for though he has a cataract there his blindness came too suddenly, and is too pronounced, to be due to it (A. W. Overbeck-Wright).

Treatment.—In all cases complete cessation of work and all business matters must be insisted on, and in many cases complete rest in bed will be found most beneficial. Baths, massage, and gentle exercise are often of the utmost benefit. Diet should be of a full and nourishing nature, meals being frequent (every two hours or so) and of small amount, and nourishment should be given through the night. Severer cases require treatment in some hospital, and complete removal from their friends is indicated. When convalescence is well advanced some light employment must be attempted, but fatigue must always be avoided, and it must be remembered that we should never attempt to hasten recovery, and that too early attempts to work only cause a relapse and are therefore worse than useless.

Insanity resulting from Brain Anæmia.

(I. ———. II. ———.)

Mental symptoms accompanying the constriction or occlusion of the cerebral arteries, arising from various diseases, may of course be due to the direct action on the cerebral tissue of the irritant or toxine which is the cause of the vascular lesion. It is, however, only reasonable to suppose that, apart from these conditions, which will be described later, the anæmia of the cerebral cortex resulting from such constriction or occlusion of the arterial supply is in itself sufficient to cause mental symptoms in many cases. In fact, such conditions are to be seen in every asylum, and there are certain characteristics, fairly common to the group, which enable us to distinguish them fairly readily.

Ætiology.—A neurotic heredity is traceable in the majority of such cases, and the exciting cause is naturally the blocking of the arteries causing the brain anæmia, this blocking being due to various causes, such as syphilis, gout, etc.

Symptoms.—The condition generally begins gradually, and partakes of the character of a gradually increasing failure of the mental powers, which imperceptibly proceeds to a complete dementia.

Physical Symptoms.—The heart's action is unaffected, the rhythm being normal both as regards rate and regularity. The arterial tension in such cases is, however, invariably increased. There is no hyperleucocytosis present, and the percentage of the various types of leucocytes remains about the normal. In fact, increased arterial tension is almost the only cardinal physical symptom in such cases, though at times various forms of paralysis are seen.

Mental Symptoms.—These consist of a gradually increasing dementia with progressive loss of intelligence and capacity for work. Combined with this, delusions of suspicion and unseen agency are often present, and disorders of common sensibility are frequent, and indeed are often the cause of many of the delusions, formication being interpreted as being due to electrical agencies employed by enemies to make life unendurable, and for this reason suicide and homicide have to be guarded against in such cases.

Treatment.—Treatment in such cases should aim at removing the cause of the anæmia as far as possible, and building up the general health by tonics and well-regulated exercises.

Insanity Resulting from Deprivation of the Special Senses.

(I. ———. II. ———.)

Of the five special senses sight and hearing are, by their deprivation, undoubtedly the most important in production of psychoses. By these two senses we adapt ourselves to our surroundings and the constantly changing conditions under which we live and work, and the loss of sight or hearing places us at once at a disadvantage with our fellows. Thus it is not surprising that, in persons of neurotic taint, the loss of either of these senses is followed very frequently by mental symptoms.

The man who has lost the sense of sight loses his sense of position and the true knowledge of what is happening around him, and experiences a sensation of absolute helplessness which he endeavours to remove by straining all his remaining faculties to the utmost. Similarly, the man who has lost his power of hearing is deprived of sensory stimuli necessary for healthy mentalisation, and is constantly endeavouring, by means of his remaining senses, to understand what is being said around him. Under these conditions the faculties which remain are excited to excessive activity and the brain receives an over-stimulation from these senses, and suffers a deprivation of stimuli from the sense which has been lost, and thus a condition of mental instability is set up. This instability, however, is probably not so often the cause of the mental symptoms as the sense of helplessness and loss of touch with the surroundings, which tends to make those who are blind or deaf at first suspicious and finally examples of delusional insanity. The delusions in all of such cases are those of suspicion, the blind man imagining his wife is flirting with a rival in his very presence, the deaf man that his neighbours are laughing and talking about him, and so on. Physical symptoms are rarely, if ever, associated with these cases, the condition being purely a psychical one.

Prognosis.—Rapid recovery is to be expected in most cases, but, as can be gathered from what has already been said, relapses are frequent in the majority of cases unless the utmost tact and care be exercised by the friends and relatives of the patient.

Treatment.—The treatment of such a case depends more on the tactful, sympathetic manner of the medical adviser than on diet or drugs. By gaining the confidence of your patient his suspicions become less and less acute and may in time wholly disappear. Want of tact, want of sympathy, and deceit on the part of those around him, however, will promptly cause the reappearance of all the old suspicions, so that in every such case we must explain things carefully to all those around our patient, and ask their co-operation in restoring him to his right mind.

CHAPTER XVI

GROUP B: INSANITIES OF TOXIC ORIGIN

I.—Insanities the Result of Metabolic Toxæmias.

THE term *metabolic toxæmia* is a vague and unscientific one, for the reason that not only the nature of the toxines, but the very toxines themselves are unknown. Probably the most important are the præurea bodies and perhaps the ethereal sulphates, as well as certain anæmic conditions where there is an accumulation of waste products in the body. The results of deficiency, excess, or alteration in the constituents of the internal secretions of the various viscera require investigation, as they undoubtedly exercise great influence upon mental conditions.

In all acute insanities there is distinct evidence of metabolic disorder, but in one type of disease—namely, acute melancholia—metabolic toxæmia is most markedly present, and to such an extent that there can be but little doubt that the mental derangement is mainly, if not wholly, due to this deranged metabolism.

ACUTE MELANCHOLIA.

(I. *Depression*. II. *Melancholia*.)

Definition.—Acute melancholia may be defined as a distinct physical disease, with definite physical symptoms, affecting mainly those in the decline of life, and only rarely seen in adolescence, when it is evidence of bad heredity. It is liable to recur and eventually end in a chronic delusional state.

Ætiology.—The chief predisposing cause is undoubtedly a bad heredity, but any weakening, fatiguing mental or physical conditions, such as overwork, anxiety, worry, and deprivation of sleep, may cause such a disorder. These latter conditions, leading, as they do, to derangements of metabolism, which directly cause the mental condition, may be also cited as exciting causes.

Symptoms—*Prodromata.*—The onset of the disease is slow and insidious, and indefinite symptoms of ill-health, gastric disturbances, loss of weight, and sleeplessness, are often present for months before any signs of mental symptoms are noticed. This prodromal period is one to which I would especially direct my readers' attention, for if it be recognised and the patient at once put under proper treatment, the chances are very great indeed that the attack may be stayed and the family perhaps saved from being tainted with the blight of insanity and all the horror and suffering which it entails.

Physical Symptoms.—By the time mental symptoms manifest themselves all such cases are thin and poorly nourished, owing to the lengthy prodromal period through which they have come. In the acute stage of onset the tongue is furred and foul, appetite is usually deficient or wanting altogether, owing to loss of the digestive power of the gastric juices, but excessive thirst is almost invariably present. The pulse-rate is rapid, irregular in force and rhythm, and the arterial tension as a rule is markedly increased. In pure uncomplicated cases there is no marked change in the leucocytes, both the total number per c.mm. and the percentages of the various types remaining about the normal; there is, however, always more or less anæmia present, due more to a deficiency in the amount of hæmoglobin than to a diminution in number of the red blood corpuscles.

The skin is hot and dry, and the temperature is often slightly raised in the evenings. The urine is scanty and passed at long intervals; the urea excreted is generally markedly deficient in quantity, and albumen is often present in small amounts. This falling off in the amount of urine excreted is remarkable when one considers the amount of fluids such persons drink in the course of a single day, and is probably due to the water being broken up in the system, as in the post-mortem on such cases the tissues are invariably abnormally dry. Restlessness and depression are marked at the onset of all such cases.

As the acute stage passes off the restlessness and depression gradually disappear, the tongue cleans from the tip and edges, appetite gradually returns, there is less tendency to constipation, and the gastric juice is more freely secreted and has greater digestive power. There are at no stage of the disease any signs of hyperleucocytosis, and nothing abnormal is to be found in the corpuscles in uncomplicated cases. The pulse gradually becomes slower and more regular, and the arterial tension falls, while the skin becomes moister and gradually regains its elasticity. Occasionally one meets with profuse perspirations in such cases, somewhat resembling the crises of acute specific diseases, but these are not very frequent, and are generally accompanied by excessive urinary secretion and marked increase in the excretion of urea, which, in some cases, may rise to even 800 grains in the twenty-four hours.

Nervous System.—Sensibility to heat, touch, and pain are very commonly diminished, more probably owing to the concentration of the whole faculty of attention on the feeling of extreme mental depression than to any failure in the peripheral innervation, and the special senses of taste and smell are frequently disordered. The organic reflexes remain as a rule under control, the diminution in micturition being directly due to diminished excretion; but the superficial and deep reflexes are frequently found to be increased. Voluntary muscular movements are sluggish, and the powers of fine co-ordination are impaired. As the acute stage passes off voluntary movement becomes easier and more natural, sensibility gradually reappears, and by degrees the patient returns to his normal condition.

Mental Symptoms.—The mental condition in cases of acute melancholia varies greatly in intensity. In an average case there is invariably well-marked depression, which the presence of marked hallucinations may increase greatly in amount. There is as a rule a varying degree of confusion, with a loss of the power of cognition, due probably, in great measure, to the deranged attention, which is wholly occupied in considering the wretched state in which the patient fancies he is situated. Vivid hallucinations of hearing are often present, and may give rise to delusions, but as a rule in the acute stage these are masked to a certain extent by the confusion, and only become pronounced at the later stages of the disease. In every case all sense of personal cleanliness and order is lost, there being apparently no thought or care for anything but the condition of mental depression which occupies the whole mind of the patient.

Loss of self-control is an invariable concomitant, and is evidenced by extreme restlessness and impulsive movements, which are commonly due to fright caused by terrifying hallucinations.

The attention, as already noted, is wholly subjective, and

self-control and memory on this account cannot be tested; and speech, when present, is jerky and spasmodic, though occasionally mutism is met with. Insomnia is invariably present in all cases.

The acute stage may last from two to three weeks to two to three months, and occasionally ends in a rapid recovery, with critical discharges as already noted, though as a rule it gradually merges into a subacute condition, the physical and mental symptoms gradually fading in intensity. This subacute stage may gradually improve and end in recovery; but relapses are frequent, all the symptoms of the acute stages then returning, and at times the condition passes into one of chronic depression with symptoms of nutritive failure.

When recovery occurs, memory of what has happened during the acute stage is as a rule but vague, and often absent altogether, though memory of the previous life is unimpaired. The physical condition invariably improves before the mental, the whole course of the disease and appearance of the patient reminding one of an exhausting physical disease.

When a state of chronic depression ensues the patient remains thin and unhealthy-looking. Digestion remains weak, and the patient suffers from dyspepsia, anorexia, and constipation. The pulse is weak and thready, and the extremities are cyanosed and cold. Trophic changes are evidenced by the dry pigmented skin, the brittle, lustreless hair and nails, and the great tendency there is for such patients to be carried off by pulmonary tuberculosis. The excretion of urine and urea is markedly irregular, and there is general impairment of sensibility and lack of normal tone throughout the body.

Death may occur in the acute stage, the patient passing into a typhoid state; or suicide may occur in any of the three stages, though most commonly during the acute stage of onset owing to the sudden impulses so frequently met with in that stage.

Diagnosis.—This depends largely upon the clinical symptoms; thus physically we have the disordered alimentary tract, the rapid irregular pulse, the high arterial tension, the deficient excretion of urea and urine, and the absence of hyperleucocytosis; while mentally we have the extreme mental depression with, as a rule, only a comparatively small amount of confusion.

Prognosis.—In adult life the prognosis is as a rule good, most cases recovering within six months; but in cases occurring in late adult life or in old age the prognosis is less favourable, the subacute stage being apt to be prolonged, and at times pass into a condition of chronic depression with delusions. In adolescence the immediate prognosis is good, but the condition is very liable to recur, and such recurrent attacks of melancholia are often the precursors of chronic delusional insanity.

Case XXVI.

C. A., female, aged 28, a domestic servant, admitted into Murthly Asylum suffering from depression. Illness had lasted only a few days. Her sister is insane; the patient had always been of correct and steady habits, but had already had two previous attacks of melancholia. Her illness commenced with sleeplessness, depression, and refusal of food.

On admission she was a well-nourished, well-developed girl, depressed in attitude and appearance, and with a muddy complexion. Temperature, 98·4° F. Her tongue was furred and her bowels constipated. She had no desire for food. Leucocytosis was 13,700, with a polymorphonuclear percentage of 69. Pulse was 90 per minute, and her arterial tension 130 mm. Hg. Her skin was greasy. During the first twenty-four hours after admission she excreted 12 ounces of urine, containing 190 grains of urea. During the same period she had ingested 60 ounces of fluid.

Sensibility to heat and cold, touch, and pain was present, but sensation was delayed. Pupils were medium, and reacted to light and accommodation. Muscles were well developed. Organic reflexes were normal; superficial reflexes slightly exaggerated; tendon reflexes were present.

Mentally she was depressed, with some slight amount of confusion, but free from hallucinations. Memory was dull. She did not speak, answered in monosyllables, and evidently disliked being talked to. There was marked insomnia. She was placed on fluid diet, and began to improve. On the tenth day after admission she was given a full ordinary diet, but immediately became worse, and in three days she was depressed and confused again. She was again placed on a fluid diet, and again improved. She made a good recovery, and was discharged within two months of admission (Bruce, "Studies in Clinical Psychiatry").

Case XXVII.

S., aged 18; caste, Lodha; admitted Agra Asylum, February 17, 1911. Class C., criminal lunatic; crime, murder.

He is stated to have killed his girl-wife with a chopper to prevent her relatives taking her away. On admission he is noted as being depressed but free from delusions. This depression lasted till December, 1911, when he brightened up considerably. In September, 1912, he again became deeply depressed, and is only now beginning to clear up. Subject-consciousness was greatly increased; he was wrapped up in his own misery, sleepless, listless, and refused food. Sensibility was delayed, and his skin was greasy and inelastic. He had no hallucinations (A. W. Overbeck-Wright).

Treatment.—In the stage of acute onset rest in bed and careful nursing by night and day are essential, while the condition of the digestive organs indicates an absolutely simple diet. Milk is the best food in all such conditions, and should be given in small quantities and at frequent intervals. Water should be given freely, and the patient allowed as much as he can drink, with a view to assist in the excretion of waste products from the system, as well as to meet the apparent destruction of water in the body. Constipation should be alleviated by large saline enemata.

As the condition improves, additions may be made to the dietary with caution, purin-free foods—such as bread, butter, sugar, eggs, rice, and potatoes—being added gradually at first, and later very weak tea, white meat, and fish.

Drugs.—For insomnia in this condition paraldehyde is undoubtedly the best drug we have. It should not be given every night, but ʒii. be given one night and then two nights allowed to elapse and the drug again given on the third night. In this way the risk of establishing a drug habit is avoided, and nature is given an opportunity to restore the natural powers of sleep. Sulphonal should never be given in acute melancholia, as it interferes with the elaboration of urea from the nitrogenous waste-products of the tissues. When the acute stage is over, tonics—such as quinine, strychnine, and dilute acids—should be exhibited, and the patient made to take exercise, which should, however, be begun by degrees and be carefully regulated so as to avoid fatiguing the patient.

Insanity of Myxœdema.

(I. ———. II. ———.)

In all persons suffering from myxœdema there is some mental change, in some perhaps so slight that it may be passed over unnoticed, while in others it may be so marked as to call for special treatment. One must, however, always remember there is a mental as well as a physical side to this condition, and not allow the prominence of the physical symptoms to make us forget the mental aspect of the case, as in this way some unforeseen accident may occur which a little care might otherwise have avoided.

Ætiology.—The condition is in all cases due to the failure of the performance of the normal functions of the thyroid gland. It usually appears about the age of thirty to thirty-five, and more commonly affects women.

Physical Symptoms.—Only a brief résumé of these will be given here, and for further details any medical textbook may be consulted. The hands become broad and spade-like, and the power of finely co-ordinated movement is lost. The hair and nails become brittle, the former often coming out in handfuls and leaving the patient bald, whilst the latter are always splitting and breaking. The teeth are very prone to decay, and trophic changes are common throughout the body. The fatty tissues under the skin are involved, the skin of the face becomes swollen and waxy, the swelling being elastic and unaffected by pressure or gravity. Irregular thickenings of the subdermal tissues occur in various regions, especially the axillary and the supraclavicular, while the abdomen becomes large and pendulous from the same cause. The mucous membranes become involved also, and the tongue is large and thickened. The pulse is as a rule very slow, and such cases are constantly complaining of chilliness, and are very susceptible to alterations of temperature. Anæmia is well marked in advanced cases, and women invariably suffer from amenorrhœa. Constipation is almost invariably present, and hæmorrhages from mucous membranes are by no means uncommon.

Mental Symptoms.—The early stages of myxœdema are invariably marked by a steadily progressive mental deterioration. Movement and thought become slower, and there is failure of general comprehension. Memory becomes defective for recent events, the power for work is diminished, mistakes are frequent, and outbursts of irritability are common. These patients as a rule are fully aware of this failure in their mental powers, and frequently complain about it, while with many it produces a condition of marked depression.

If left untreated the general lethargy increases, and the patient suffers from overwhelming drowsiness. He loses all interest in his personal appearance, and day by day he becomes more sluggish and clumsy in his movements and more and more easily fatigued. He loses all interest in his surroundings, and pays no heed to the wants of others. The greater majority of such cases suffer from a species of mild depression with vague, ill-defined fears for which they cannot account, though, in some cases, the early irritability develops into acute excitement. In advanced cases marked delusions and hallucinations are present, but such cases are rarely suicidal or homicidal.

Diagnosis.—The diagnosis is a matter of comparative ease, though, when acute mental symptoms have developed, the general condition may possibly be overlooked. Bright's disease is most apt to be confounded with it, but close examination reveals many points of distinction.

Prognosis.—If left untreated such cases go from bad to worse, death ultimately resulting from coma or some intercurrent disease. If treatment has been begun early in the course of the disease complete recovery may occur; but in the majority of these cases such is not the case, and there remains a certain amount of physical and mental enfeeblement, rendering them unfit to perform arduous duties.

Pathology.—In all cases the thyroid gland is either atrophied or diseased. In the earlier stages there is a small-celled infiltration into the walls of the vesicles, and the gland gradually passes into a condition of fibrous atrophy, small groups of cells and colloid masses being scattered throughout the fibrous tissue.

Treatment.—It is wise to begin with small doses of thyroid, and gradually increase the amount if necessary; firstly, because small doses may be sufficient for recovery; and, secondly, because with larger doses untoward results are likely to occur—3 to 5 minims of liquor thyroidei (B.P.), or 3 grains of thyroideum siccum, daily are quite sufficient for a commencement. During this treatment the patient should be kept in bed, and the temperature recorded daily in the morning and evening, the pulse-rate being also taken. If in a few days no improvement is seen, the dose must be gradually increased; but in no case should the drug be pressed with the idea of hastening recovery, as such a proceeding is most risky. Persistent frontal headache, dizziness, increased excitement, rapid heart's action, diarrhœa, fever, urticaria, etc., are indications for reducing the dose. If all goes well, the physical and mental symptoms improve rapidly, many undergoing complete recovery in about three months; but such patients must be made to understand that it will be necessary to continue taking thyroid throughout their lives, though usually comparatively small doses suffice; the amount necessary for each patient, however, is only ascertainable by careful observation.

Delusional Insanity.

(I. *Systematised Delusions with Hallucinations.* II. ————.)

Under this head I am grouping conditions variously described by other authors as progressive systematised insanity; mania of persecution; monomanias of pride and grandeur; megalomania and paranoia. This last condition is described by many as one of the forms of dementia præcox—katatonia and hebephrenia being the other two. A little consideration, however, convinces one of the error of this, for paranoia is of totally different origin from either katatonia or hebephrenia, which are both due to bacterial toxæmias; and, moreover, except that they all tend to affect largely young adults of marked neurotic heredity, they have not a single feature in common.

Dementia præcox, too, is a misleading term to apply to any of these conditions, for though most of the cases occur in early adult life, their incidence is not wholly confined to this period, cases by no means infrequently being postponed to much later age periods. For these reasons, therefore, and because the conditions mentioned above as described by various authors seem to me to belong to very much the same physical and mental states, I am ignoring the term *dementia præcox*, and grouping these various conditions under the one head of "Delusional Insanity."

Many forms of insanity tend to become complicated with delusions if the patient does not recover, but such delusions are mere indications of the chronicity of the disease and of the mental impairment, and their character is wholly different, as they are more changeable and fleeting, the patient has not arguments to bring forward in support of them, and they do not influence the whole habits and life of the patient, as is the case in the condition which I am now about to describe. In such cases, too, we have the history of the case, and in many instances physical symptoms also, which enable us to distinguish what condition we are dealing with.

Definition.—These conditions may be defined typically as mental states of marked delusions, generally of systematised persecution, at times combined with grandiose delusions, such delusions affecting the whole life of the patient, and being supported by fierce argument if their truth be in any way questioned.

Ætiology.—As already noted, hereditary taint is by far the most common predisposing cause, a history of this being obtainable in well over 50 per cent. of cases affected; a badly regulated education, unhygienic surroundings, want of proper care and supervision when children, sexual and alcoholic excesses, and venereal disease all tend to predispose towards an attack, though practically nothing is known as to the exciting causes.

The disease affects the sexes equally, and its incidence is most marked in adolescence.

Symptoms.—It is essentially a disease of failure of nutrition, with vague symptoms of malaise and sensory disturbances which gradually develop into hallucinations and delusions, which are invariably of a persecutory type.

In many instances the disease begins gradually, and passes unnoticed until attention is drawn to it by an assault, or some other crime, committed by the patient as the result of his delusions. In other cases, however, there may be an acute attack, with symptoms similar to those of acute metabolic poisoning, which may either pass into a chronic delusional condition, or from which there may be apparent recovery, the chronic delusional state coming on gradually, and months may pass before it is sufficiently developed to attract attention.

Physical Symptoms.—(*a*) The acute onset as a rule resembles an attack of acute melancholia, except for the presence of marked delusions. There is dyspepsia and anorexia. The pulse is fast and of high tension, and the temperature is frequently above normal. The urinary excretion is diminished, and frequently contains traces of albumin, while the excretion of chlorides and urea is markedly diminished. The leucocytosis is never raised, nor are there ever any changes in the percentages of the various leucocytic elements. (*b*) With the stage of chronic delusions there are well-marked physical symptoms. The patient is thin and sallow, and has a furtive, suspicious expression. There is invariably more or less dyspepsia, with furred tongue, foul breath, and discomfort after meals. The heart's action is slow and feeble, but readily accelerated, and there is a tendency to syncope, while the arterial tension is slightly increased. Leucocytosis is almost invariably below the average. The excretion of urine is increased, and with it there is an increase in the chlorides and urea excreted. The temperature is irregular, showing occasional unexplainable rises, which may be accompanied by indefinite complaints of malaise and discomfort. Sensory disturbances are frequent, and as a rule the patient looks on them as modes of persecution employed by his enemies to annoy or injure him. The pupils may be unequal, but react to light and accommodation.

Mental Symptoms.—(*a*) Acute onset. Depression with a certain amount of confusion is invariably present, and in nearly all cases there are marked hallucinations of hearing, and frequently delusions of persecution. Self-control is diminished, the patient as a rule being frightened and subject to sudden impulses. The memory, both for past and present events, is impaired, and attention to surroundings is in abeyance owing to its being bound up in the feelings and sufferings of the patient —*i.e.*, subject-consciousness is greatly increased at the expense of object-consciousness. Insomnia is invariably present.

Such cases may at times undergo apparent recovery, while in others there may be frequent attacks of this description before the onset of the delusional state, in which case there are marked hallucinations present, and persisting between the attacks. Other cases, again, seem to pass directly from the acute attack into the chronic delusional state, though as a rule some considerable time elapses before this condition becomes apparent.

(*b*) The condition of chronic delusions begins as a rule with hallucinations of hearing, which may at first be recognised as such by the patient, though in time they gain complete sway over him, and the other special senses become involved too. As judgment fails these hallucinations give rise to delusions, in support of which the patient has elaborate arguments always ready, and which govern his whole life and conduct. The patient's mood is very variable in this stage, being at various times depressed, irritable, sulky, or truculent in one and the same case. Cognition is never affected, nor is confusion ever noticed in such cases, but hallucinations are invariably present. These hallucinations at first are mainly those of hearing, the patient imagining people or voices are abusing him, or making accusations against him, or repeating his thoughts aloud, etc. Disorders of taste and smell give rise to delusions anent poison and foul gases being blown into the room, while derangements of sensation similarly cause delusions of hypnotism, electricity, etc. As a rule these imaginary persecutions are all ascribed to the machinations of some one person or sect, and in time everyone with whom the patient comes in contact is supposed to be influenced by his enemy. Along with these sensory hallucinations and delusions of persecution one sees in almost every case delusions of a grandiose type, due probably to failure of judgment and a deficient object-consciousness. As a result of these delusions all sorts of impracticable schemes are promulgated: one patient has discovered the elixir of life; another is going to convert all Brahmins to Mohammedanism; a third has found a means of converting stones and rubbish into gold, etc. In every case the patient is full of hope and convinced of the success of his plans, and when they miscarry cites it as but another example of the persecution he endures. In cases where there is much depression the delusions are at times of a melancholic type, and often religious in nature, and in such cases we must always be ready to prevent attempts at suicide. Self-control is never markedly impaired in these conditions, and patients generally can control their own actions. Assaults, however, are common, and are due to the delusions, the patient being cognisant of his actions and laying his plans carefully beforehand as a rule, though at times the action may have been unpremeditated, and then usually is due to an auditory hallucination, the reason being, in both cases, either a desire for revenge on his enemies or to rid himself from their constant persecution. The faculty of attention is good, and the patients converse sensibly on any subject apart from their delusions; memory also remains unimpaired. Insomnia is a common complaint in these cases, and is due as a rule to the sensory disturbances, which are more marked commonly at night.

Diagnosis.—In such cases the main points which help us in our diagnosis are the history of the case and the fixity and character of the delusions, as well as the comparatively normal mentalisation of the patient except on the subject of these delusions.

Prognosis.—Recovery from the mental condition is hopeless in such cases, and can never be looked for. There is, however, no risk to life, and as a rule but little mental deterioration, except in a certain number of adolescent cases of marked neurotic heredity, who rapidly become demented.

Case XXVIII.

Mrs. C. H., aged 30 on admission. This patient was married about the age of sixteen, according to her own statement, to a farrier-sergeant in a British cavalry regiment in India. Shortly after their marriage he got into trouble and was reduced to the ranks, whereupon he applied for his discharge, and they were sent to England, where he got a situation as commissionaire. On the outbreak of the South African War he joined the Imperial Yeomanry and went out to South Africa, took his discharge there, and she heard no more of him. From her own statements one can gather that her life in England was by no means what it might have been, and that prior to her husband's departure to South Africa their home life had not been a happy one. She was kept in a pauper asylum at home for some six weeks apparently, and on her recovery sent out with her three children to India (her domicile) by the War Office. Since her arrival in India her life has been a varied one—clerk in a railway office, barmaid and manageress at various hotels, a visitor of Zenana women, etc. In the railway office she met a poor unfortunate man on whom she seems to have set her affections, and from him now all her troubles arise. She states she was married to him secretly in England, under the influence of hypnotism; that he has collared all her papers, estates, maintenance, and accumulations (she never owned a penny according to her mother), "and has cruelly ill-used herself and her children." She wandered round for several years with this story, in which she firmly believes, making the poor man's life a burden to him, costing him endless money in lawsuits which were instituted against him by her, for in the beginning she was plausible, and the number of well-known lawyers and others who were taken in and believed her stories is incredible. After some years he managed to get her arrested and certified as insane, and she is now in the Agra Asylum. She now declares that the secret marriage in England was declared null and void in the Magistrate's Court the day she was committed to the asylum, and has transferred her affections to the Superintendent of the gaol where she was confined as an under-trial prisoner. She states he is the father of her three children, that they became "legally engaged" in the Magistrate's Court the same day "her secret marriage was cancelled," and that he was then appointed "legal guardian and protector" to her and her children, and received her "power of attorney to manage her estates and accumulations." These delusions have persisted now for over two years and are supported by vehement argument, and affect her whole life and conduct. She and her children are the victims of a conspiracy instigated by the person she first became enamoured with in India, and the Roman Catholics, and every day her persecutions and the number of her persecutors increase, everyone she comes in contact with being but a fresh conspirator come to increase the burden of her woes (A. W. Overbeck-Wright).

CASE XXIX.

Delusional Insanity; Persecution by Telephones.—M. L. G., Bengali Kayastha, aged 42 on admission in 1894, a resident of Calcutta, was formerly head clerk to the Inspector of Schools at the Presidency. Had a lawsuit with a distant cousin, P. N., which he lost, since which time (1890) he has been insane, exhibiting marked delusions that P. N. and his friends were constantly persecuting him with electric shocks, transmitted by telephones. In 1894 he attacked P. N. with an axe, and was consequently sent to the asylum, where he has spent nearly fourteen years without the slightest mental alteration. All his troubles are due to P. N. and his telephones. Quite recently he was unable to walk because of this persecution, and had to be moved about (C. J. R. Milne, 1908).

CASE XXX.

Monomania of Persecution detected with Difficulty.—" Dr. A. T. Thomson was requested to see a gentleman whose friends were desirous of placing him under restraint, being well assured of his insanity from the supervention of uncontrollable outbreaks of temper, to which he had never previously given way, though they could find no ostensible ground in his conversation or actions which would legally justify the use of coercive measures. Several medical men had been consulted, all of whom had failed to obtain any such justification. Dr. Thomson, struck with the evidence of violent passion afforded by the damage done to the furniture of this gentleman's apartments, 'felt convinced that there was some perversion of feelings or intellect which it was his business to discover.' For two hours he conversed with his patient on a variety of topics, and never enjoyed a more agreeable or instructive conversation, his patient being evidently a man of great attainments. Dr. Thomson was beginning to despair of finding out the mystery of his disorder, when it chanced that animal magnetism was adverted to, on which the patient began to speak of an influence which some of his relatives had acquired over him by this agency, described in the most vehement language the suffering he endured through these means, and vowed vengeance against his persecutors with such terrible excitement, that it was obviously necessary, alike for their security and his own welfare, that he should be placed under restraint" (Carpenter, "Mental Physiology," p. 669).

Chronic Metabolic Toxæmia.

(I. *Depression.* II. *Melancholia.*)

In the chapter dealing with the non-toxic insanities, I have considered the mental symptoms arising from conditions of brain anæmia due to occlusion of the cerebral arteries, and I there mentioned that the conditions causing this state of the arteries were quite capable of producing mental symptoms from their action on the cortical cells. It is this last condition with which I propose to deal now.

Ætiology.—This condition practically never occurs before middle life, as a rule commencing about the climacteric. In a large percentage of such patients a history of a previous mental attack is obtainable, and almost invariably this attack has been one of depression. A history of excessive alcoholism or drug-taking is obtainable in a large number of cases, and may be either a symptom, the drug having been taken to alleviate gastric discomfort, or a cause, the continued use of the drug producing metabolic disorder by deranging the functions of the intestines, liver, and kidneys.

Symptoms—*Physical Symptoms.*—The condition being wholly due to the accumulation of waste products in the system, it is but little to be wondered at that the symptoms, both physical and mental, approximate closely to those of chronic melancholia. The onset is gradual, and characterised by dyspepsia, anorexia, and constipation. The patient's appearance alters, the skin assuming a dull pallor owing to anæmia and œdema of the subcutaneous tissues. The pulse is thready, and of very high tension, and there is deficiency both in the number of the red blood corpuscles and in the percentage of hæmoglobin, though there is no alteration in the leucocytosis. Attacks of palpitation are frequently seen early in the disease, and as a rule are accompanied by vertigo and severe headaches. Sensory disturbances, too, are frequent, the patient complaining of formication, etc., which often give rise to delusions of persecution.

Mental Symptoms.—The mental state belonging to this condition is invariably one of depression combined with hallucinations and delusions. Confusion is a fairly prominent symptom in most cases, and judgment and memory are impaired. Attention, too, is deranged, and what little remains is so largely self-centred that it is impossible to attract the patient's attention for long, and conversation as a result is difficult. Attempts at suicide have to be guarded against in this condition.

Diagnosis.—The age and history of the patient and the physical and mental symptoms form an entity which in typical cases there is but little difficulty in diagnosing.

Prognosis.—In all such cases the prognosis is very bad. The patients are liable to be suddenly carried off by some intercurrent disease, and in those cases who do live some degree of mental deterioration invariably remains, and as a rule the last years of their life drag on in a state of more or less marked secondary dementia.

Case XXXI.

Chronic Melancholia.—B. A., Mussalman woman. At the age of thirty-two is said to have had five children at a birth, four of which were stillborn and one alive, which died shortly afterwards. During these births a urethral fistula was caused, and was left untreated. This caused her to be an object of disgust, and her mind gave way under the combined influences of bodily trouble and grief. In her insane state she set fire to a godown, and was sent to the asylum, where she has continued in a state of chronic mental depression. She is very irritable, and if thwarted may be aggressive. She is always in a state of abject misery, and no amount of kindness or comfort has any effect. Treatment of her urethral condition is negatived by her being in an advanced condition of pulmonary tuberculosis (C. J. R. Milne, 1908).

Treatment.—Rest; light, nourishing diet with plenty of fluid ingesta; and gentle regulated exercise are indicated in these conditions.

CHAPTER XVII

GROUP B: INSANITIES OF TOXIC ORIGIN—(*Continued*)

II.—Insanities in which there is Evidence of Bacterial Toxæmia.

INSANITIES due to bacterial toxæmias are much more serious conditions than those due to purely exhaustive or metabolic causes. An invariable concomitant of such conditions is a hyper-leucocytosis with a high polymorphonuclear percentage in the early stages, and whenever such a condition is found to prevail one can be sure one is dealing with a case of bacterial toxæmia. As a rule the most characteristic symptom of the group is excitement, associated with mental confusion, depression, or elevation, while relapses are frequently met with in these conditions. In practically all cases after an attack of this sort evidences of toxæmia persist in the blood for years, even after apparently complete recovery has taken place, and this, combined with the frequency with which relapses occur, can but lead one to the conclusion that perfect recovery from such conditions very rarely occurs.

EXCITED MELANCHOLIA.

(I. *Depression.* II. *Melancholia.*)

Until very recent years this condition always has been regarded as a type or variety of melancholia, and indeed this view is still held by many of the older members of the medical profession. There is undoubtedly a superficial resemblance between it and what I have described as acute melancholia, but a study of the physical symptoms, and an examination more especially of the blood, can lead to but one conclusion, and that is, that excited melancholia and acute melancholia are as separate and distinct diseases as are typhus and enteric fever, and that they should be similarly diagnosed and treated as two separate and distinct diseases.

Ætiology.—This condition is most liable to occur in late adult life, and occurs frequently during the climacteric period in women. As a rule heredity and alcoholic excesses have but little connection with this condition, long-continued worry, excessive mental strain, and the natural failure of the vital powers as life declines being the chief predisposing factors, while in all cases the exciting cause is a toxæmia of bacterial origin. How or whence the toxæmia arises is at present undetermined, but the probability is that the seat of infection is the intestine, and that the infection itself is caused by some of the saprophytic bacteria of the body becoming virulent and secreting toxines which act directly on the nervous tissues.

Symptoms—*Prodromata.*—In practically every case a history of great physical and mental strain is obtainable. As a result of this the patient becomes dyspeptic, sleepless, and anæmic, and complains of physical and mental lassitude, for which he frequently seeks medical aid. This condition gradually goes from bad to worse, the patient becomes unable to carry out his ordinary duties and unable to rest, and, if medical advice has not been previously sought, he is now driven to call for our aid.

Physical Symptoms.—The patient is always thin and badly nourished, and his expression is invariably one of misery or anxiety, and often of fear. Flatulent dyspepsia, with disinclination for food and drink, sometimes so marked as to necessitate artificial feeding, is very common, and constipation is invariably a marked feature of such cases. The temperature is as a rule irregularly febrile, the elevations usually occurring in the evening. The pulse is fast and weak, and the arterial tension is low. Anæmia is invariably present, and is accompanied by a hyperleucocytosis with a marked increase in the polymorphonuclear percentage. Trophic changes are evidenced by papular rashes, which the patient picks, causing unsightly sores, or by erysipelatous attacks, which at times seem to take the place of exacerbations of the mental symptoms. The urinary secretion remains fairly normal both in quality and quantity. Sensibility is frequently impaired, formications or flushings of heat and cold being often complained of, while sensibility, both to temperature and pain, seems diminished. The organic, superficial, and deep reflexes are as a rule all unaffected, though irritability of the motor area of the cortex is shown in restlessness, slight loss of co-ordination, and fine tremors in the muscles of the face and hands.

Mental Symptoms.—The main mental symptoms are acute

depression and anxiety, with practically no confusion or loss of consciousness; as a rule confusion is but rarely seen, and when present it is transient and coincident with the acme of the acute attack. Hallucinations and delusions are but seldom present, never in typical cases, and when they do occur are transitory and of little moment. Subject-consciousness is markedly increased, while object-consciousness is diminished, though not so markedly that attention cannot be obtained, but there is no capacity for occupation of any sort. Self-control is markedly diminished, as shown by the constant restlessness, noisy declamation, and attempts at suicide. The powers of speech and of comprehending written and spoken language remain as a rule unimpaired. Insomnia is invariably present during the attack, and often persists after apparent recovery.

Diagnosis.—Acute melancholia is the chief condition likely to trouble us here. Dr. Bruce has tabulated the distinctive features of these two conditions most clearly, and I quote his table here for the benefit of my readers:

	Acute Melancholia.	*Excited Melancholia*
Physical:		
(*a*) Alimentary	Marked disturbance	Less disturbance.
(*b*) Hæmopoietic	Moderate leucocytosis	Hyperleucocytosis.
(*c*) Urinary	Excretion of urine and urea deficient	No abnormality detected.
Mental:	Mental confusion with vivid hallucinations which affect the conduct	Little or no mental confusion. Hallucinations not necessarily present.

In acute melancholia, too, the patients as a rule are listless and quiet, whereas in excited melancholia the patient lives in a condition of constant restlessness, wandering aimlessly about, twisting or rubbing the hands, picking at the skin, hair, or clothes, and ejaculating or groaning in a rhythmical, somewhat staccato manner.

Prognosis.—The prognosis is in all cases a bad one, many cases continuing in a state of chronic depression for years. Recovery is seldom complete, but partial recoveries are not uncommon, though such cases are invariably subject to constant relapses.

Case XXXII.

A. H., aged 35, Mussulman; occupation, sub-assistant-surgeon. Has no ascertainable taint in his family history. Is said to have been always steady and industrious. For some months prior to the commencement of his present attack had, in addition to his ordinary routine hospital duties, been working very hard for his grade examination. Was admitted into Agra Asylum some three or four months after his attack began.

He was of average height and build, and somewhat anæmic and badly nourished on admission. His skin was dry and harsh, and his appearance and expression indicative of great mental anxiety and distress. He was dyspeptic and constipated, and required much coaxing before he would take any nourishment. Temperature on admission and some days after, 99° to 100° F. Sensation to touch, temperature, and pain were all diminished, but both superficial and deep reflexes were present and active. There was excessive muscular movement, the patient constantly walking about wringing his hands and clasping his head as if in extreme mental agony, and evidently in the deepest depths of despair. He absolutely refused to speak, and has never yet done so since admission (some three months). He is inclined to be impulsive, and on several occasions when being asked kindly about his condition has suddenly sprung up without any warning and attempted to run to the main gate. His attention is wholly subjective, and he takes absolutely no notice of anything going on around him. He suffers from marked insomnia (A. W. Overbeck-Wright).

Case XXXIII.

Melancholia of Recent Origin.—M. D., a young Hindu, aged 23, admitted from Midnapore on March 20, 1904. Except that his maternal uncle was an idiot, there is no other history of insanity in the family. In December, 1903, his house was burnt down, and at the same time his sister and other relatives died of smallpox, which was raging in the village. This caused him to become insane, and in January he attacked his mother and wife one day with a knife. He was then arrested, sent to gaol, and thence to the asylum, where he was admitted in a state of extreme mental depression, weeping constantly, declining to speak, and paying no attention to anything. He recovered gradually, and in November, 1904, was declared sane, and has continued in this condition (C. J. R. Milne, 1908).

Treatment.—In the acute stage complete rest in bed and a light diet are essential.

Calomel and a saline purge should be administered as soon

as possible in such cases, and, if necessary, repeated in three or four days' time. Hydrarg. subchlor., grs. iii., followed by mag. sulph. ʒiv., or a seidlitz powder after four hours, is what I usually order. On the subsidence of the acute symptoms general tonics with mild regulated exercise, and a full and plenteous dietary are indicated, and we should always endeavour to keep the patient's attention off himself by mild amusements or occupations, though avoiding anything likely to cause fatigue. In some cases small doses of nepenthe given three or four times daily give very beneficial results, but if improvement does not occur in a day or two it is wiser to stop the drug, as otherwise an opium habit may be started. In the more acute cases, sulphonal, grs. x., combined with potassium bromide, grs. xxx., and administered twice or thrice daily, has often most excellent sedative results, though both these drugs tend to increase gastric disorder and still further lower the nutrition.

ACUTE MANIA.

(I. *Excitement.* II. *Mania.*)

Mania, strictly speaking, is applicable to but one outstanding symptom, and that is excitement; but in practice it is also used to designate a distinct mental condition, which many authors subdivide into various forms. As pointed out by Dr. Bruce, however, a careful consideration of the physical symptoms present in this condition of acute toxæmia associated with maniacal excitement, can lead to but one conclusion—namely, that the disease is one and the same whether it lasts for a fortnight or a lifetime, whether it is recurrent or non-recurrent, and whether the symptoms are so severe as to deserve the term "delirious," or so mild as to be called "subacute."

As with all toxic conditions, so in this disease we have the symptoms modified by various factors, such as the individual power of resistance to the toxines, the virulence of the bacteria, and these factors themselves are affected by climatic and various other conditions. Thus the various conditions described by so many authors have arisen, owing partly to their classifying disease on a symptomatological instead of an ætiological basis, and partly to their having given undue prominence to mental at the expense of physical symptoms.

Dr. Bruce divides mania into two classes, viz.:

(*a*) " A condition of mental excitement, associated during its early stages with complete loss of consciousness (*i.e.*, confusion), with hallucinations and illusions, with complete loss of the powers of attention and memory, with incoherence of speech, and loss of comprehension of language spoken or written; while on the physical side there are evidences of very acute toxæmia." This condition he describes under the term " Acute Mania, or Excitement with Confusion.".

(*b*) " A condition of excitement without confusion, but rather associated with a hyperacute consciousness without hallucinations or delusions. The powers of attention are not lost, but wander loosely from subject to subject. The memory is often very acute. The speech, though rambling, disjointed, and inconsequent, is not, in itself, incoherent. The patient readily understands spoken or written language, and although the writing may be fantastic in style and in composition, the power of writing is not lost. Physically the symptoms of toxæmia are much less severe." This type is described by Dr. Bruce as " Folie Circulaire, or Excitement without Confusion."

In some cases of acute mania, when the condition has lasted for a considerable period, there is a return of consciousness with some capacity for attention and observation, and as a result the condition, viewed from the mental aspect, is not markedly dissimilar from folie circulaire, and mistakes in diagnosis are liable to occur. Notwithstanding this, the distinction between the two diseases seems to me so clearly established that I propose adhering to Dr. Bruce's classification and describing conditions of maniacal excitement under these two heads alone.

Typhoid or delirious mania is undoubtedly a misnomer, as any toxic insanity, whether metabolic or bacterial, may terminate in such a state, and as a rule there is a rapidly fatal termination to such cases. Simple mania, too, is a misleading term, being equally applicable to the early stages of acute mania or folie circulaire.

ACUTE MANIA.—Such conditions are most typical when affecting adults, and as a rule cases affecting adults are more continuous and less liable to remissions and exacerbations which are so common at other age periods.

Ætiology.—Hereditary predisposition is a well-marked factor in the production of this condition, British statistics showing a history of neurotic taint in at least 50 per cent. of the cases, and the presumption is that a similar condition prevails in India. The exciting cause in practically all cases is some condition which has lowered the natural resistive powers of the patient, such as mental worry or shock, bodily privation, unhealthy surroundings, alcoholic excesses, and, in women, childbirth.

Symptoms—*Prodromata*.—The onset usually is gradual, the patient complaining of malaise, insomnia, restlessness, and inability to concentrate his attention and thoughts for any length of time. Perversions of affection are common, patients taking unaccountable dislikes to relatives and friends. Headaches are constant in practically every case, and flatulent dyspepsia is a common cause of complaint.

In a few instances the acute attack is suppressed, the patient passing from the prodromal stage to an irritable moody condition, with a certain amount of confusion, and later on the development of delusions.

As a rule, however, an acute attack succeeds the above prodromal symptoms, and may be either acute in its onset or supervene gradually.

Physical Symptoms.—The patient's face is drawn and pale, the eyes are bright and staring, and the pupils dilated, but reacting to both light and accommodation. The temperature varies according to the stage of the disease; in the stage of acute onset and during exacerbations and recurrences the temperature is irregularly febrile, but after a week or so it becomes subnormal, and remains thus throughout the attack, and even after apparent recovery it may still be found about a degree below the normal. Paradoxical temperatures (*i.e.*, temperatures with their maxima occurring in the morning) are common in, but by no means characteristic of, this condition.

Gastric derangement is profound in the early stages of this condition, the teeth and lips are covered with sordes, the tongue is furred and foul, and for the first few weeks there is marked distaste for food, though as a rule excessive thirst is present. After this time, however, even though much of the excitement still remains, the appetite returns, and with it the digestive powers, the patient eating ravenously and digesting practically everything. These altered states of appetite are explained by Dr. Bruce, who has found that at the onset of the attack the secretion of the gastric juices is practically abolished, while at a later stage the gastric secretions are plentiful and very active.

The heart is as a rule normal; the pulse at the onset may be increased in rate and slightly irregular, but it is never so fast as in a case of excited melancholia, and rarely exceeds 100 beats per minute. If the attack is of long duration cardiac weakness may be seen and a tendency to syncope arise. The skin generally is dry, but excessive perspiration may affect the palms of the hands and the soles of the feet. Trophic changes are manifested by various rashes and pustular eruptions, while the hair and nails become dry and brittle, the hair at times standing on end and adding a finishing touch to the physical representation so typical of the mental condition.

Urinary excretion is scanty at the beginning of the attack, but the nitrogenous excretion is increased, probably owing to the incessant muscular movements; later in the disease, however, the urinary excretion is generally well above the normal. The excretion of the chlorides in the urine is diminished in the acute stage, but as improvement sets in there is as a rule a sudden rise in the amount excreted, the rise being in proportion to the amount of chlorides ingested during the acute stage of the disease.

Sensibility to heat and pain are diminished, but the sense of touch is as a rule hyperacute, as are also all the special senses except that of taste, which is often deficient. Superficial reflexes are generally slightly increased, but the tendon reflexes as a rule are unaffected, and the organic reflexes remain under control unless the attack be very severe. There is never paralysis or weakness of the voluntary muscles, and the inco-ordination, which is seen in all cases, and especially affects the facial muscles, is due to irritation of the cortical centres.

The blood presents characteristic features in this condition.

In the early part of the acute stages there is invariably a hyperleucocytosis, amounting to 18,000 or 20,000 per c.mm., and the polymorphonuclear percentage is never below 70 per cent. After a few days this hyperleucocytosis falls, occasionally to 10,000 per c.mm., but never lower, and as a rule to 14,000 or 15,000 per c.mm., and this fall is accompanied by a fall in the polymorphonuclears to 60 per cent., or even lower, whilst a corresponding rise occurs in the lymphocytes and a smaller rise in the percentage of the eosinophiles, though this last is not an invariable condition. Whenever distinct mental improvement sets in the leucocytosis again rises, and with it the polymorphonuclear percentage, which is practically always above 70 per cent. As recovery becomes complete the polymorphonuclear percentage again falls to between 60 and 70 per cent., but the hyperleucocytosis persists for long, probably indefinitely, and the presumption is that it is a protective leucocytosis necessary to maintain an efficient immunity against the source of the disease, which is still in the body of the patient.

When recovery does not occur the leucocytosis as a rule falls, and with it the polymorphonuclear percentage may fall to as low as even 30 or 40 per cent.

As a rule recovery occurs within six months of the onset of the symptoms, the severity of the attack gradually passing off, sleep returning, and the patient increasing in weight. Occasionally there is an unhealthy puffy appearance about the patient, somewhat similar to that seen in patients who have recovered from some septicæmia. At times, however, the patient passes into a condition of chronic excitement, with physical symptoms akin to that of the acute state, but less in severity. In a very small number of cases the acute condition passes into a state of delirious or typhoid mania, which is characterised by delirious excitement, followed by a stage of exhaustion, in which the patient lies helplessly picking the bedclothes, with dry, cracked lips and tongue, and sordes on the teeth. The patient wastes rapidly in this condition; the urine and fæces are passed unconsciously, and diarrhœa is a great source of trouble. Hypostatic congestion of the lungs occurs, and death is simply then a question of a few days.

Mental Symptoms.—Loss of self-control, mental excitement, and marked confusion are characteristic of this condition, and are as a rule associated with loss of the power of cognition both of place and person, loss of the faculty of attention, incoherent speech, insomnia, and extreme motor restlessness. Such patients too are, as a rule, very emotional, readily changing from laughter to tears or anger, but usually a condition of well-being and excitement prevails, tears being gusty and merely superficial, and not due to any lasting condition. Hallucinations both of sight and hearing occur in most cases, and may be associated with delusions.

In cases where gradual recovery occurs the symptoms lose their severity by degrees, and gradually short periods of comparative sanity occur, as a rule being seen in the morning after a good night's rest. These periods gradually become more and more prolonged until, with occasional moments of loss of self-control, the greater part of the day is passed in quiet and sanity.

Where the acute stage passes into a state of chronic restlessness, consciousness returns, and the patient is fully aware of all that passes; but there is no return of self-control or of ability for work of any sort, and in many such cases destructive tendencies are marked, clothes and furniture being destroyed, while the patients are readily pleased or irritated, and liable to impulses of an aggressive or erotic type. Such cases may drag on for years in this state until a mild dementia arrests the worst symptoms and renders the patients fit for ordinary unskilled labour under supervision.

In the comparatively rare state of "typhoid mania" delirious excitement is seen at the onset, but this gradually passes into a more or less comatose condition, which continues till death occurs.

Relapses and recurrences are frequently seen in this form of insanity, definite periods of sanity occurring in the latter cases between the attacks. In the continuous attacks immunity seems to be more slowly established, but, once it is established, the effects seem to be much more lasting than in the recurrent cases, where immunity is much more rapidly established but seems to be of only short duration. These differences in immunity periods are explained by Dr. Bruce as being due to variations in the resistive powers of the patients or to differences in the origin and virulence of the toxines causing the disease.

Diagnosis.—The only conditions likely to be mistaken for this are the elevated stage of folie circulaire and the excitement present in the onset of so many of the other insanities. In the former case the lack of confusion and the hyperacute state of the sensibilities serves to distinguish folie circulaire, but in the latter conditions it may be necessary to temporise for a time until the condition makes itself clear.

Prognosis.—As a rule, in most cases the immediate prognosis is fairly good, though the frequency with which relapses and recurrences are seen must render us guarded in our ultimate prognosis, which is, in truth, far from hopeful. Rapid emaciation, the presence of auditory hallucinations, and marked degeneracy, as evidenced by disregard of the calls of nature or the eating of filth, usually indicate an unfavourable prognosis.

If the attack occurs early in life subsequent attacks are to be expected as a rule, especially if there be a markedly neurotic history or some definite cause for the illness. In delirious or typhoid mania the prognosis is most unfavourable, death occurring in nearly every case.

The various types of mania described by the older writers on psychiatry are similar to the above description, but modified by variations in individual resistance or virulence in toxines as already mentioned.

The recurrent form is especially liable to occur in adolescents, and is characterised by its comparatively sudden onset, its short duration, and rapid convalescence, but it presents no other features beyond what are seen in the ordinary cases already described.

Treatment.—Rest in bed and careful nursing both by day and night are essential in the acute stages of the disease. Thorough evacuation of the bowels, preferably by calomel and a saline purge, should be obtained. The dietary should be light and as far as possible fluid, and, when necessary, artificially digested, and should be administered every two or three hours, with a liberal allowance of stimulants. Large saline enemata are often most beneficial in such cases, or, if these are not retained, subcutaneous injection of one to two pints produces equally good results. Insomnia is most troublesome in the acute stages, and the continuous hot bath at 100° F. is often marvellous in its effects. The benefits derivable from a hot bath are, however, evanescent, and every third or fourth night hypnotics may be required to produce a sound night's sleep, and I infinitely prefer paraldehyde in such cases, given in large doses, even up to ℥iv. if necessary. Hypnotics, however, should be used as little as possible, for they tend to augment the gastric derangements and still further diminish the self-control, and by stupefying the patient render him dirty in his habits.

In cases of mania following on the puerperium there are always very marked symptoms of toxæmia present. In some cases, where the uterus is tender or the lochia fœtid or suppressed, there can be no doubt that the uterine cavity is the source of this infection; but in others this is not the case, and in these latter relapses are more frequent, and there is the tendency to persistent hyperleucocytosis after recovery which is seen in other cases of acute mania. In mania following after the puerperal state both the physical and mental symptoms are very acute, and the patient is apt to be subject to impulses, and infanticide and suicide have both to be carefully guarded against.

The prognosis in cases due to a septic uterus is as a rule much more favourable, recovery occurring in about 70 per cent., while relapses are much less common; where, however, the toxæmia is not palpably due to an infected uterine cavity one should be guarded, as the prognosis in these cases is much the same as for ordinary cases of acute mania.

"Puerperal insanity" is a term better left unused. Any type of insanity may follow on the puerperal condition, and none are peculiar to it. It is but small wonder that cases do occur as its sequelæ, when one considers the exhaustion and pain of parturition, the loss of blood, and the liability to septic infection which occur in this condition. The last of these is, and can be, the only true exciting cause of the insanity, the others being more predisposing factors, owing to the exhaustion and diminution of the resistive powers caused by them.

Case XXXIV.

L. S., aged 25; caste, Chattri; admitted into Agra Asylum on April 6, 1913. Prior to admission he is reported to have "behaved in a very eccentric manner, waving his arms about, dancing and singing," and to be "always smiling and gesticulating." He was dirty in his habits, his powers of cognition were in abeyance, and there was marked mental confusion.

On admission he was in very poor bodily condition, thin and emaciated, with dry, inelastic skin. His evening temperature for the first few days after admission was between 99° and 100° F. There was marked dyspepsia present, and he ate but little food. His bowels were constipated. Mentally he was in a state of extreme excitement. It was impossible to fix his attention even for a moment; he kept up a constant stream of senseless chatter; any replies which could be elicited from him were absolutely irrelevant, and there was marked mental confusion present. He was extremely dirty in his habits and suffered from marked insomnia. He has improved greatly since admission, but is still confused and excited (A. W. Overbeck-Wright).

Case XXXV.

This case exemplifies a type of insanity which is not uncommonly met with in India, and which is perhaps the saddest of all the mental disorders to which human beings are liable. R. K. G., a high-caste Hindu of good family and superior education, formerly a schoolmaster, became insane at the age of twenty-nine through, it is stated, over-study. It is important to note that there was no hereditary tendency to mental disorder, and no marked previous alcoholic or other excess. Admitted in 1895, at the age of forty. Every three or four months he suffers from attacks of acute mania, whose duration varies from fourteen to twenty-eight days. During this period he remains naked, is extremely filthy, obscene, restless, excited, and is very noisy, shouting and singing constantly. His speech, a mixture of English and Bengali, is extremely foolish, sentences such as the following being uttered: "The pains of delivery are in my back!" He is very sleepless, and spends the night singing obscene songs. The attack begins suddenly, but for a day or two prior to it there is a curious alteration in expression which the attendants are well aware of as heralding an attack. He may be dangerously aggressive at the onset, and hence this alteration is carefully observed. Recovery is fairly rapid, and is complete. In the intervals the man is absolutely sane. His memory is good except for the attacks of insanity, of which he remains curiously oblivious (C. J. R. Milne, 1908).

In Case XXXVI. alcohol was a prominent factor as far as the first attack of mania was concerned. While suffering from this the patient was brought to the aslyum, and, beyond evidences of his recent alcoholic bout, there was nothing special about his attack. He then recovered almost completely; but on the fourteenth day after the cessation of the acute symptoms of the first attack he again developed acute mania, accompanied this time by fever and delirium. To this he succumbed. The following are the details of the case:

Case XXXVI.

A. P., Goanese, aged about 25, employed in a railway refreshment-room, was admitted into the asylum on April 3, 1905. His friends stated that he had always been considered a foolish person, talking nonsense on occasion, and having generally exalted ideas about himself. On the night of March 23, although a usually temperate man, he, assisted by a friend, drank about a bottle and a half of whisky, and after this he became acutely maniacal. He was very excited, abusive, and noisy. He broke a quantity of glass and plate. He became very filthy, and for three days he refused his food. He was brought to Lahore and admitted, as stated, on April 3. He was then in a state of exaltation, with delusions of being a great chief, of having served in great houses, of having visited the Pope at Rome. He said he had been sent to the asylum by Christ, etc. He had a vacant look, and was extremely restless and loquacious. He was very filthy with excreta, and tore his clothes and bedding into ribbons. He was noisy at night, and slept very little. Under treatment he daily improved, becoming cleanly in his habits, respectful in his attitude, and generally behaving quietly. He appeared to be reaching a normal state when, rather suddenly, on the night of the 21st, he became again acutely maniacal, destroying his clothes, etc., and incoherent, with temperature 101° F. On the 23rd still feverish (102° F.), and had become almost unconscious. On the 24th temperature rose to 104° F., when he was visibly delirious, and he died unconscious on the morning of the 25th. No post-mortem permitted (C. J. R. Milne, *Ind. Med. Gaz.*, 1906).

CHAPTER XVIII

GROUP B.: INSANITIES OF TOXIC ORIGIN (*continued*)

II.—Insanities in which there is evidence of Bacterial Toxæmia (*continued*)

FOLIE CIRCULAIRE.

(I. (*a*) *Excitement*; (*b*) *Depression*. II. (*a*) *Mania*; (*b*) *Melancholia*.)

Definition.—Folie circulaire may be defined as a mental condition characterised by alternating attacks of elevation and depression, though at times one or other stage of the disease may be suppressed or so transient as to escape notice. Confusion, hallucinations, and delusions are conspicuous by their absence in this disease. The condition as a rule commences in adolescence or early adult life, rarely originating at other age-periods.

Ætiology.—Heredity plays a marked part in the production of this condition, about 70 per cent. of such cases having a marked hereditary taint. There is, in most cases, no appearance of physical derangement to be made out, and as a rule neither moral nor physical causes seem to play an important part as ætiological factors.

For purposes of description this condition is best described in two stages: (*a*) the stage of elevation; (*b*) the stage of depression.

(a) The Stage of Elevation.

Symptoms—*Prodromata.*—As a rule in such cases we obtain a history of a gradual change in character and disposition, that the patient has become moody, and is sometimes elevated, at others depressed for short periods. Further, we are told that the periods of elevation have gradually become more frequent and pronounced until they have passed into the condition of continuous elevation in which we see the patient.

Physical Symptoms.—The majority of such patients appear healthy and by no means ill-nourished. The face is flushed, the eyes bright, and though unnaturally mobile, the expression is by no means unintelligent, and lacks the confused appearance so common in cases of acute mania. The skin is moist and greasy, and as a rule gives off a most offensive odour. The temperature is as a rule febrile, generally from 100° to 102° F., at the commencement of an attack. The condition of the alimentary tract varies; if the case be acute and be seen early there may be gastric derangement, anæmia, and complete distaste for both food and drink; but later on in the attack, especially if the patient has already suffered from this condition, the appetite becomes ravenous and the taste perverted, the patient craving for stimulants and condiments, and eating greedily things from which he would have turned with a shudder when in his proper mind. The pulse is of low tension and about normal in rate. The blood presents a hyperleucocytosis in the early stages, though not so marked an increase as in acute mania; the polymorphonuclear percentage, however, in a first attack may be well above 70. In recurrent attacks as a rule there is a fall both in the leucocytosis and in the polymorph percentage immediately before the onset of elevation. As the attack progresses the leucocytosis increases with the elevation, reaches a maximum at the height of the seizure, and then gradually falls to normal. The leucocytosis in such cases is, however, markedly irregular, and tends to fall as the attack passes off, and thus differs markedly from that of an attack of acute mania. The urine is diminished in amount, concentrated, highly coloured, deposits urates, and occasionally has traces of sugar and albumen.

Subject-consciousness is diminished, but sensibility to touch, heat, and pain is markedly increased, and the special senses are hyperacute. Superficial and deep reflexes are increased, as also the muscular tonus, while slight inco-ordination is present.

Mental Symptoms.—As already noted, the mental condition is one of pure elevation without confusion, and free from hallucinations or delusions. The hyperacute state of the special senses may, however, simulate hallucinations, and this must be carefully looked for to avoid error in diagnosis. Self-control is lost, but obsessions are rare in this condition, the diminished self-control being as a rule evidenced by extravagant but purposeful movement, noise, and mischievous teasing conduct, such patients as a rule taking great delight in baiting some poor unfortunate fellow-sufferer. Morality and decency are at a very low ebb in all these cases, and the conduct and speech are oppressively lewd and coarse. The memory in a first attack may be diminished both for recent and past events; but when the attacks are recurrent the memory in the stage of elevation is phenomenal, long articles being repeated from the newspaper, and every small word or action of some fellow-patient during a previous attack being brought up and used to tease and annoy him. Such cases are extremely divertible, and, though their attention can readily be caught, it is impossible to hold it for any length of time owing to their great divertibility and prompt reaction to each and every passing stimulus. The speech, though irrelevant, is by no means incoherent, and the power of reading and writing remains, though the latter is often fantastic in character and crossed and underlined in a way only an insane person would think of doing. Insomnia is marked throughout the attack.

The duration of the elevation is very variable, from a few days to months; but whether long or short the patient's condition during an attack is one of extreme restlessness, both physically and mentally; he is extremely capricious and flighty, irritable, and lacking in modesty, cleanliness, and honesty. The restlessness gradually diminishes, sleep returns, the physical condition, which is affected by the elevation, improves, and *pari passu* the patient returns by degrees to a condition of apparent sanity.

Diagnosis.—This stage of elevation has to be distinguished from acute mania and the acute stage of onset of many of the other acute insanities. The leucocytosis and the absence of confusion, hallucinations, and delusions are the main points which enable us to distinguish this condition.

Prognosis.—The immediate prognosis is good, recovery occurring in practically every case after a longer or shorter time. Recurrences, however, are inevitable, and with each attack the prognosis becomes more unfavourable, as the tendency to pass into a condition of more or less secondary dementia becomes greater with every attack.

Treatment.—Rest in bed is essential, tending, as it does, to lessen the acute symptoms. Free purgation should be resorted to at the commencement of the case, and where gastric derangement is present, light diet given in small quantities at frequent intervals is necessary; but where a good digestion is met with a full general dietary should be given to tide the patient over the acute symptoms with as little loss in physical condition as possible. In cases of extreme elevation and insomnia sedatives are indicated, and in my experience I have got best results from 10 m. of paraldehyde, or 10 to 15 grs. of sulphonal, given thrice daily. When the acute stage lessens, then exercise in the open air, tonics, and carefully regulated employment are necessary.

Thyroid extract has been used in the treatment of this condition, but its applicability is very circumscribed, as it is practically contra-indicated when elevation is present, and is only occasionally of use in cutting short or aborting the stage of elevation when it can be anticipated and the drug administered before its advent. Even then, however, it must be exhibited with caution, as its excessive or prolonged use tends to increase and prolong the elevation.

Subcutaneous injections of turpentine have been tried with the object of raising the leucocytosis and thus cutting short the attack, but the results have been disappointing, only a very small percentage showing any signs of improvement.

(b) *The Stage of Depression.*

Symptoms.—The stage of depression may either precede or follow the stage of elevation, and the physical state of the patient is markedly affected during this condition. There is marked gastric derangement, evidenced by anorexia, constipation, and a furred, flabby tongue. The heart is weak, and the pulse slow, irregular, and feeble, but the arterial tension as a rule is high. The skin is greasy and offensive, and the extremities cyanosed and cold, and at times even œdematous, in extreme cases tending to become stuporose. Hyperleucocytosis is nearly always present, but there is never any marked rise in the polymorphonuclear percentage. Sensibility to touch, heat, and pain is unaffected, but the special senses are less acute than is normally the case.

Mentally.—The condition is one of pure apathy and depression, without confusion or the presence of hallucinations and delusions. In some cases, where the depression follows after a stage of elevation, the apathy and depression are so marked after the restlessness and noise that one is almost led to think the condition one of secondary dementia.

As with the stage of elevation, so here the recovery is gradual and *pari passu* with the physical improvement.

Diagnosis.—The absence of confusion and of hallucinations and delusions enables us to distinguish this stage of folie circulaire from acute and excited melancholia.

Prognosis.—The prognosis here is the same as for the stage of elevation.

Treatment.—Rest in bed and a light nourishing diet are absolutely essential here. For constipation, large saline enemata are of great service, and should be given about twice a week. The enemata probably help in removing more toxic material from the bowel than would be done by ordinary purgatives, and, in addition, a certain amount must be absorbed, and thus the excretion of toxines by the skin and kidneys may be aided. For insomnia, paraldehyde, ʒii., is invaluable, if a glass of hot milk and a hot bath at bedtime prove useless, though they should undoubtedly be given a good trial before we resort to drugs.

Case XXXVII.

A. A., female, aged 47, admitted into Murthly Asylum suffering from excitement of some seven days' duration.

A brother and a sister had suffered from insanity. She herself was a woman of good habits, and had lived a healthy country life until a month prior to her attack, when she had contracted influenza. After this she became restless and sleepless, refused her food, and changed in appearance and manner. About seven days prior to admission she became excited and restless, and refused her food, which she said was poisoned. On admission she was a big, strong, well-nourished woman. Her face was flushed, her eyes widely open, and her expression unnatural. Temperature, 98·6° F. Her tongue was furred; she refused food, and the bowels were constipated. Leucocytosis was 16,000 per c.mm., and the polymorphonuclear percentage 84. Pulse-rate was 84, and the arterial tension 140 mm. Hg. The skin was moist and greasy, and the smell from the perspiration very offensive. Sensibility to temperature, touch, and pain was acute; the special senses could not be tested.

The organic reflexes, as well as the superficial and deep reflexes, were normal. Mentally the condition was one of pure excitement, without confusion or hallucinations. Her attention was attracted by any chance sound or movement, and she was noisy, erotic, and shameless in speech and conduct. After about two months she began to improve, but in a few weeks she relapsed for about a month, and then for two months was apparently sane though her expression was heavy and flat, and she often had a hyperleucocytosis. In October she began to complain of dyspeptic symptoms, and then passed into a condition of depression; her temperature fell; there was marked distaste for food, and she was much troubled with constipation. The leucocytosis was often as high as 20,000 to 30,000, but the polymorphonuclear percentage rarely exceeded 60. The heart's action was weak and slow, the hands and feet cyanosed and cold, and the body temperature subnormal. The skin was greasy and clammy. She complained of vague pains, yet was not sensitive to pain, though she felt draughts and cold acutely. The pupils were contracted but reacted sluggishly to light and accommodation, and there was some impairment of vision. Mentally the condition was one of pure depression without confusion, hallucination, or delusion, and it lasted for some five months. It was followed by a stage of subacute depression for some three months, after which she was discharged (Bruce, "Studies in Clinical Psychiatry").

Case XXXVIII.

S. D., aged 35; caste, Kayasth; occupation, clerk; admitted into Agra Asylum on February 6, 1913. Prior to admission he had been "talking nonsense and always smiling to himself; excited at times, and apt to wander if left alone; filthy in his habits, and abusive."

On admission he was a short, well-nourished man, with extravagant gestures and speech. His replies to questions, though relevant, were absurd and bombastic, and his ideas of his own importance were very great. His memory was good, and there was complete absence of mental confusion. He was very easily excited, however, and at such times became foul-mouthed and abusive. He made vague charges of persecution against his relatives, and was markedly erotic and shameless in his conduct. He remained in this condition, typical of the exalted stage of folie circulaire, for some three and a half months, when he began to show some mental improvement (A. W. Overbeck-Wright).

Katatonia.

(I. (*a*) *Excitement*; (*b*) *Stupor*; (*c*) *Excitement*.
II. (*a*) *Mania*; (*b*) *Dementia*; (*c*) *Mania*.)

This condition was first described by Kahlbaum in 1874, and derives its name from the muscular rigidity which is one of its characteristic symptoms. More recently Kraepelin has described it as one of the three varieties of what he terms "dementia præcox" (hebephrenia and paranoia being the two other varieties), and though I consider this classification unsound, grouping, as it does, three distinct and separate diseases under one head, as varieties of one condition, Kraepelin's description of this state is undoubtedly the more scientific of the two.

Definition.—Katatonia may be defined as an acute toxic disease, with a definite course and onset, characterised by a prodromal period leading gradually to an acute period of onset marked by mental confusion, aural hallucinations, paroxysms of fear and anger, obsessions, a katatonic spasm of the muscles, and a marked hyperleucocytosis, indicating an acute toxæmia. In the second stage a condition of stupor, without loss of consciousness, supervenes, which is characterised by marked resistiveness to passive movements, and is followed as a rule by the third stage of excitement.

Ætiology.—This condition is equally common among Europeans, Eurasians, and natives of India. As a rule it commences in adolescence, and so far as my experience in India goes seems more common among males; this, however, may be due to the habits of the Indian and the extreme reluctance with which he sends any of his women to an institution, for in Europe the incidence falls more heavily on females. Hereditary taint is present in the large majority of such cases; but any condition tending to lower the vitality and resistance to infective conditions renders the person liable to this disease.

Symptoms—(*a*) *Prodromata.*—In every case one elicits a history of insidious onset, with gradual loss of energy and failure of nutrition. Hallucinations of hearing are as a rule the first signs of mental aberration noted, and sooner or later give rise to delusions, obsessions, and complete loss of self-control. It is at this point the patients are usually sent to an asylum, and by far the majority are thin and badly nourished by the time we receive them.

(*b*) *Acute Stage of Onset—Physical Symptoms.*—Gastric derangement, evidenced by anorexia and occasional nausea and vomiting, is invariably present in such cases. The arterial tension rises as the symptoms become more acute, and the heart becomes irritable and its action rapid and irregular. The skin is moist and greasy, and drenching perspirations occur frequently, while blotchy pustular rashes are seen in many cases. There is a moderate hyperleucocytosis, and an increase in the polymorph and hyaline elements throughout this stage, and just prior to the onset of the stage of stupor there is a sudden rise in the leucocytosis, due mainly to an increase in the polymorphonuclear elements. Sensibility to touch, heat, and pain is diminished, and the senses of taste and smell are often completely perverted; but, so far as can be ascertained, the senses of sight and hearing react normally to outward impressions, though auditory, and occasionally visual, hallucinations are seen in this stage. The pupils are as a rule dilated, and react sluggishly to light, and the organic reflexes are deranged, such patients as a rule being wet and dirty, and requiring constant attention. The superficial and deep reflexes are invariably exaggerated, while the voluntary muscles are liable to pass into fits of rigidity or katatonic spasm, which may last from a few minutes to a few hours. Insomnia is invariably present to a varying extent. The temperature in these cases is irregular, at times paradoxical, but rarely markedly febrile during the acute stage of onset, though a distinct febrile attack invariably ushers in the stage of stupor.

Mental Symptoms.—In this stage of the disease the mental condition is essentially one of confusion, while vivid and terrifying auditory hallucinations affect the conduct and frequently lead to paroxysms of terror, during which the patient may make frantic attempts to hide from his imaginary enemies, or, finding attempts at concealment of no avail, may attempt to place himself beyond their power by committing suicide. In the intervals between paroxysms the patient may lie for hours with closed eyes, apparently oblivious to all that happens around him; or in other cases there may be brief periods of apparent sanity, in which, however, a certain amount of confusion still remains, and there is a lack of the faculty of attention and of memory for recent events.

Diagnosis. — The history of onset, the results of a blood examination, the temperature, and the marked state of mental confusion, with auditory hallucinations, are our main points in diagnosing this condition.

Prognosis.—The acute stage terminates as a rule, after four to six weeks, in a distinct febrile attack, which ushers in the stage of stupor. Death, however, may occur during this stage from exhaustion or from an exceptionally virulent toxæmia.

Treatment.—Rest in bed, with a light nourishing dietary, are essential in this stage. Nourishment should be given frequently and in small quantity at a time, and the patient should invariably have nourishment administered during the night. Normal saline solution, administered either subcutaneously or *per rectum*, seems in some cases to give a certain amount of relief, and even to induce sleep at times. If insomnia be trying, the effects of a hot bath and a hot glass of milk at bedtime should be tried, and if these fail then recourse must be had to drugs, and of these I prefer large doses of paraldehyde, ʒiii. to ʒiv., administered every third night, through I have at times had good results from sulphonal, grs. x., combined with potassium bromide, grs. xxx.

(c) *The Stage of Stupor.*

This stage of the disease occurs as a rule immediately after the febrile attack already noted as terminating the acute stage of the malady. In some cases, however, the febrile attack may be wanting, and the stage of stupor then occurs after the high leucocytosis which terminates the preceding stage.

Physical Symptoms.—Gastric derangement is still marked throughout this stage, and constipation is often most troublesome. The arterial tension falls below normal, and the cardiac action is weak and slow. Blood examination reveals a persistent hyperleucocytosis with a high lymphocyte percentage, and at times a transient eosinophilia. The extremities are cyanosed and cold, and the feet and hands are often œdematous. The skin is greasy, and gives off a close, offensive odour, and at times a fine branny desquamation occurs. The temperature as a rule is subnormal, with occasional sudden rises to 100° to 101° F. The organic reflexes are as a rule ignored, and retention of urine and fæces is therefore to be constantly looked for and treated. The superficial reflexes are active, but the deep reflexes cannot be elicited on account of the spasmodic muscular resistance caused by any attempt at passive movement. The sensibility and special senses, owing to the condition of the patient, cannot be satisfactorily tested during this stage; but, as the patient is fully aware of all that goes on around him, the probability is that the special senses at least are quite active. The power to sleep returns during this stage, and somnolence is often excessive, the patient being always drowsy and heavy.

Mental Symptoms.—The mental condition during this stage of the disease is one of semiconscious stupor. Hallucinations, both visual and auditory, complicate the condition, and give rise to various delusions. Obsessions, attitudinising, mutism, rhythmical movements and repetitions of words, letters, and numbers, sudden outbursts of excitement, and obstinate resistance to any attempts at movement or assistance in feeding and dressing, are invariably present in more or less marked degree in every case. Masturbation is very common in such conditions, but seems to partake more of the character of an automatic movement than of eroticism. Attempts at suicide or homicide occasionally occur, and must always be carefully guarded against; they are due as a rule to sudden impulses, and originate probably in some hallucination or delusion.

Diagnosis.—The condition of semiconscious stupor with fixed attitudes and an extreme state of negativism are characteristic of this stage, and when seen form an unmistakable picture.

Prognosis.—The stage of stupor is of uncertain duration, and may last from a few weeks to a few years. In favourable cases, which recover without passing into a stage of excitement, the leucocytosis remains high, and the polymorphonuclear percentage rarely falls much below 60 per cent.; and conversely, a leucocytosis much below 10,000 and a polymorphonuclear percentage of 50 or less occurring early in the stage ot stupor is a bad prognostic symptom. Where the stupor is of long duration the prognosis is always bad.

Treatment.—The stage of katatonic stupor is a most trying one for the alienist to treat. Fresh air, tonics, a full dietary, and patience are one and all essential for a successful issue. Beyond these and the observance of ordinary hygienic measures nothing can be done. Above all no attempt must be made to force the patient more than is absolutely necessary, for no good but only harm can accrue thereby: thus exercise must be purely voluntary on the patient's part and no attempt should be made to force him to it. When the patient shows signs of recovery hot baths with a little mustard in them may hasten the process, but caution must be exercised in their use, and a raised temperature or unduly increased rate or tension of pulse indicates their immediate suspension.

(d) *The Stage of Excitement.*

This as a rule occurs immediately after the stage of stupor, though occasionally there is an apparent recovery from the stuporose condition, and then the patients relapse after even two or three years. In some very exceptional cases, however, recovery seems to follow on after the stage of stupor, and no subsequent relapse occurs; but such an event is rare, and should never be spoken of too hopefully.

Physical Symptoms.—The excitement in this stage is by no means continuous but comes on in bursts, between which there are remissions to apparent sanity. Gastric derangement is much less marked, and the cardiac functions approximate more closely to the normal. There is still a tendency to fall into fixed attitudes or rhythmical movements, such as doing sentry-go, stereotyped movements of the hands, and irregular action of the facial muscles. Between the bursts of excitement, however, the patient is comparatively quiet, and shows no marked symptom of mental derangement.

Mental Symptoms.—Confusion is still present to a certain extent in this stage though much less marked than in the stage of stupor. Memory, both past and present, is impaired, and the power of attention diminished, the patient, in fact, showing all the signs of a more or less marked secondary dementia, which is only to be expected after the severe mental attacks he has already come through. Hallucinations and delusions are markedly pronounced in these cases, and are very liable to affect the conduct, so that patients in this stage of the disease require constant care and supervision.

Diagnosis.—Without a history of the previous stage of stupor such cases are practically impossible to diagnose with certainty, and hence arises one of our main difficulties in asylum diagnosis in India, for as a rule the information received with cases is most meagre.

Prognosis.—The older the patient the less tendency there is for the disease to terminate in marked dementia, but as a rule some mental enfeeblement invariably remains. In adolescent cases the outlook is very bad, and complete recovery rarely, if ever, occurs. (As a rule a little over 20 per cent. make complete recoveries, 20 per cent. partial recoveries with a certain amount of dementia, and the remaining 60 per cent. remain in a state of chronic irritable dementia till death occurs.)

Treatment.—A full nourishing diet with tonics, especially iron and quinine, is indicated during this stage. If the excitement be so intense and prolonged that the patient becomes exhausted, then rest in bed becomes necessary, and sedatives are essential.

In such cases sulphonal grs. x. thrice daily is useful, and I have also had good results from a combination of Tr. hyoscyami with Tr. cannabis indicæ.

Case XXXIX.

E. H. B. (European), an ex-soldier, admitted Benares Asylum April 16, 1901. On admission he was noted as being "peculiar in manner, sometimes refusing to talk, attitudinising, and making facial contortions, aggressive, and using filthy language. He is much excited." He remained in this condition until October 9, 1902, when he is noted as "dropping into the most extraordinary attitudes with almost cataleptic persistency, rarely speaks to anyone, and will not wear clothes." Since then he has continued in much the same condition, going about naked in his cell, apparently taking no notice of his surroundings, standing sometimes for hours on end in one position, and resisting passively all attempts to make him change it. He hardly ever speaks to anyone, and is filthy in his habits (A. W Overbeck-Wright).

Case XL.

Case of M. M. D. This boy, a Vaish by caste, aged about 22 years, was taken ill in the end of July, 1912. I was called to see him about a week after his illness was first noticed. The history I obtained was that about seven days previously he had returned from college in a peculiar condition, had been very irritable, and refused his food. This condition had continued; he had shown an access of religious fervour, and been noisy and troublesome for a day or two, and then the condition in which I found him had supervened. I found him sitting down, motionless and silent. When spoken to, one could almost feel the tremendous mental struggle to reply, but he remained silent. It was impossible to test his reflexes owing to the extreme state of muscular rigidity into which the slightest attempt at passive movement seemed to send the whole body. Pupils were medium and equal, and reacted to light. There was a marked tendency to catalepsy, and every attempt at voluntary movement was combated by intense muscular contraction. Reflex movements—*i.e.*, movements normally performed involuntarily and reflexly, such as swallowing, winking, etc.—were, however, much more readily performed, and seemed but little affected. The pulse was very slow, and the body and extremities cold. For a long time I tried to persuade his father to send him to the asylum, and at last he said if I could assert that I could cure him he would send him in. I explained what a very small recovery-rate there was in this type of insanity, and said it was impossible for me to say at such an early stage and from mental symptoms alone how the case would terminate, but if I might examine a drop of his blood I would give my prognosis in an hour's time.

A differential count showed: polymorphs, 82 per cent.; lymphocytes, 11·5 per cent.; hyaline, 3 per cent.; eosinophyl, 3·5 per cent.; mast cells, nil.

From this enormous increase in the polymorphonuclear percentage, as well as the extreme shortness of the first stage, I deduced that, though the toxæmia was probably a virulent one, the reaction was also very great, and that the attack would probably be short and sharp. I told the father this, and that I hoped for his son's recovery within a year, probably sooner.

The son was admitted into the asylum on August 6, 1912, still in the same markedly katatonic condition. His condition gradually improved until October, when he became excited and irritable for a few days. This, however, passed off, and in the beginning of November he seemed practically cured; but after a week or so he relapsed into a slight katatonic condition again. He remained thus for a week or so, and then had a slight attack of excitement, lasting for a few days, after which he again cleared up mentally. Two other similar but shorter and milder relapses occurred, one in December and one in January, and since then he has remained well. He was allowed to return home in the end of March, and we hear every now and then from either himself or his father, and his condition, both mentally and physically, seems perfect.

This case showed well the three typical stages both in the primary attack and the relapses, and is of importance also in view of the accuracy of the prognosis made on a leucocytic count, which is strong confirmatory proof of Bruce's theories regarding the toxæmic origin of certain types of insanity (A. W. Overbeck-Wright).

HEBEPHRENIA.

(I. *Dementia*. II. *Acquired Imbecility*.)

This term was first applied, by Kahlbaum or Hecker, to certain pathological mental disturbances which occur in puberty or early adult life. Kraepelin has included this condition, as already mentioned, in his description of dementia præcox, and the error thus entailed has been discussed already. It is only in recent years that this malady has been recognised in Great Britain as a separate clinical entity, Clouston grouping it among the insanities of adolescence, Macpherson wholly ignoring it, and many other authorities denying its existence. Gradually, however, it has forced itself upon the medical world, and now, instead of regarding the symptoms as due to premature brain involution leading ultimately to dementia, the majority of alienists recognise it as a distinct clinical entity.

Definition.—Briefly it may be defined as a disease of adolescence, in which the symptoms, both physical and mental, run a subacute but definite course, and in which the symptom of hyperleucocytosis is so frequently met with as to justify its inclusion among insanities due to bacterial toxæmias.

Ætiology.—This disease is essentially an affection of early adolescence, and I have never seen a case which began its course in adult life. It affects alike Europeans, Eurasians, and natives of India. In Europe females are more frequently affected than males, and, having regard to the customs and prejudices of the Indian and the possibility of treating such cases at home, I am convinced in my own mind that the same holds good out here, for though among Indians asylum statistics might lead us to think otherwise, yet among Europeans and Eurasians in asylums in India undoubtedly a larger percentage of females is affected by this condition than is the case with the males.

Hereditary predisposition is a marked ætiological factor in this disease, Kahlbaum's statistics showing it to be present in over 50 per cent. of cases.

The precise cause of this condition is as yet unknown. So far no evidences of metabolic toxæmia have been found, and the frequency with which hyperleucocytosis is seen in these cases leads Dr. Bruce to enter it among insanities due to bacterial toxæmias.

Symptoms—*Prodromata.*—The onset of this condition is invariably gradual and insidious, the patient, who as a child was probably intelligent and precocious, changing in character, losing the power of sustained attention and the capacity for work, and showing peculiarities in conduct varying from mere eccentricities up to undoubted mental derangement. As a rule such cases hate society and lead a friendless existence, wandering aimlessly about, unable to settle to any work or amusement, and more often than not becoming dissolute or mischievous. Such cases as a rule are given to masturbation, and may often be seen in a solitary corner, where they fancy they are unperceived, giggling and muttering to themselves, and indulging in this disgusting habit.

During this insidious onset the patient's friends and relatives are very apt to misunderstand matters, and resort either to spiritual exhortation or to physical repression for its cure, with the result that the condition becomes worse instead of better, as diminished self-control renders the patient liable to outbursts of irritability or violence with little or no provocation, and it is at this stage that the patients are usually placed under medical care.

Physical Symptoms.—Arrest of physical development is a striking feature in all cases, patients of twenty-five or twenty-six years of age looking immature and about fifteen or sixteen years old, or even less, and this abnormally youthful appearance lasts throughout life. The expression of the face is dull, heavy, and furtive. Movements are awkward, and there is marked disinclination for active exercise, such patients being as a rule lethargic, and preferring to sit idle all day long. Among Indians such cases are frequently enormously stout, and at times I have seen cases where there was no marked arrest of physical development. The temperature, on the whole, remains practically normal, though every now and then during an exacerbation, when the patient becomes restless and sleepless, the thermometer in the evening may, for a week or so, register about 100° F.

The pulse is normal in rate and tension as a rule, except during the exacerbations, when it tends to become faster and irregular. Dr. Bruce states that a small hyperleucocytosis of 12,000 to 14,000 per c.mm. is as a rule present; but in some cases this is greatly increased, the hyalines and large lymphocytes being apparently most implicated in the rise, the polymorphonuclear cells remaining about their normal percentage.

Amenorrhœa is constantly present among women, and both sexes are addicted to masturbation when suffering from this condition.

Sensibility to touch, heat, and pain is unaffected, and the special senses too seem normal.

The organic reflexes are under control, the superficial and deep reflexes are normal, and there is no paralysis or diminished co-ordination of the voluntary muscles.

Mental Symptoms.—The outstanding mental symptom in such cases is the gradually progressive dementia which overtakes the patient. Affection for relatives and friends is lost, the faculty of attention and *pari passu* the capability for work is diminished, the power of volition is gone, and such cases sit idly day after day contented with doing nothing, and, so far as one can see, not even troubling themselves to think. Memory, though fair for recent events during the earlier stages, becomes markedly impaired as the disease progresses. Speech is markedly affected; in the earlier stages it is hesitating and jerky, and as the disease advances this function becomes more and more impaired, till finally all power is practically gone, and the patient remains mute and silent, or, after much interrogation, simply jerks out, parrot-like, one or two phrases, no matter what question may have been put to him. Confusion is never markedly present in such cases, and the mood is variable, patients being perhaps one day dull and suspicious and next day irritable. Neither hallucinations nor delusions are common in this malady, and the former, when present, are usually hallucinations of hearing, and may lead to obsessions, impulsive acts, and general restlessness. Sleep is invariably abolished during the periods of exacerbation, and in some cases a curious condition may be noticed, the patient sleeping one night, being wakeful for the next one or two, and then sleeping again on the second or third night.

Diagnosis.—The previous history of the case, the hesitating, jerky speech, the gradual progressive dementia, and last, but not least, the retarded development of the patient, are what we must look for to help us in our diagnosis of such cases.

Prognosis.—This as a rule is indicated to a certain extent by the development of the patient, recovery being most likely to occur where development is fuller, and in those few cases which do recover there is invariably a marked improvement in development coincident with the abatement of the mental symptoms. In any case, however, the prognosis is by no means favourable. Kraepelin's statistics in Europe show a recovery-rate of about 5 per cent., and about 15 per cent. remain partially demented, though so far recovered as to be able to live at home; but the remainder pass into a condition of hopeless dementia. My little knowledge of such cases in India leads me to believe that the outlook here is much less hopeful even than the above; but statistics on this condition are hard to find, and, allowing for cases treated at home, possibly the prognosis may be much the same out here.

Treatment.—The treatment of such cases, until more is known as to its cause and origin, must be on merely general lines. During the acute exacerbations rest in bed may be necessary, but otherwise routine discipline, light regular work when possible and a non-stimulating, fattening diet produce the best results. In cases where sleep is deranged I have found sulphonal invaluable in breaking the periodicity and inducing a normal sleep habit.

Case XLI.

A. G. (Eurasian), aged 18 on admission. Admitted into Benares Asylum on March 10, 1900. History of two previous attacks. Noted on admission as "looking silly, and behaving in a foolish manner," and apparently had some transitory delusions of persecution. He had a history of previous masturbation, and has apparently continued this habit ever since. In 1909 his speech was jerky, and simply a repetition of the last few words of any sentence put to him. His condition of weak-mindedness has advanced steadily since admission, and he is now a mere log. Has no interest in anything, never speaks, never moves unless told to do so. His three aims in life are to eat, to sleep, and to masturbate (A. W. Overbeck-Wright).

CHAPTER XIX

GROUP B.: INSANITIES OF TOXIC ORIGIN (*continued*)

III. Insanities due to the Abuse of Drugs and Alcohol

INSANITY DUE TO ABUSE OF CANNABIS INDICA.

(I. *Mania*. II. *Toxic Insanities*.)

I HAVE given this drug first place in its class as it is the most common in use among the natives in India, in one or other of its forms, and is a frequent cause of the insanity in asylums.

"Indian hemp," as it is commonly called, is cultivated largely throughout India and Central Asia, and especially in the hilly country of Northern India. In fact, in these districts it may be found growing wild and apparently flourishing well at the commencement of the hot weather.

It is used in various forms, and many are the names applied to it in different districts. The four main preparations, however, are: (*a*) *Ganjah*, or *gangah* ; (*b*) *bhang* ; (*c*) *charas* ; (*d*) *hashish*.

(*a*) *Gangah* is the dried flowering tops, consisting of stem, leaves, and flowers, of the cultivated female plants, which, having been unable to set seeds freely, become coated with resin. It is the form most commonly used in Bengal for smoking, and is as a rule mixed with tobacco, its retail price being about Rs. 2 a seer (2 lb.).

(*b*) *Bhang* is a mixture of the dried leaves and capsule. It is the cheapest form of the drug, and is made into various decoctions. It is the form in which Sikhs commonly take the drug. It costs ordinarily about 8 annas a seer.

(*c*) *Charas* is the resinous exudate, obtained by rubbing the cut female heads, which have been previously dried for twenty-four hours, between the hands and then scraping off the resin which adheres to the hands. It is the most concentrated, and at the same time the most expensive, form of the drug, costing about Rs. 35 a seer. It is used either mixed with tobacco for smoking or is swallowed whole in pilular form.

(*d*) *Hashish* is a confection prepared from charas and more common in Arabia than in India, where it is practically unknown.

In addition to the above, many local beverages and decoctions exist, but the names of these are as legion as the preparations themselves, and it is useless to cumber the brain with them.

Ætiology.—It is quite a common habit among the general population to use a certain amount of bhang in the hot weather as a cooling drink, and taken thus in small quantity and in weak solution it is quite harmless. When, however, any form of the drug is taken in large quantity or for long-continued periods the results are disastrous, as is apparent in those who resort to it as a form of dissipation and indulge in it to a gradually increasing extent.

It is but seldom that any native, except perhaps a faquir, indulges in any form of the drug by himself. Thus it is a common custom among Sikhs to have one large vessel containing bhang in their temples or at their festivities, and from this all those present help themselves, and when among other castes the drug is smoked it is almost invariably enjoyed in company, one man pulling at the chillum till he becomes dazed, and then passing it on to his neighbour.

Many and various are the reasons I have heard given for the commencement of the habit; some say that it is to obtain a feeling of restfulness; others, that it aids digestion; while some affirm, after close questioning, that they use it on account of its powers as an aphrodisiac, or have acquired the habit from associating with faquirs. In this connection it is interesting to note that faquirs as a rule are addicted to the use, or shall we say abuse, of charas, and justify this by stating that while bhang and ganjah are undoubted aphrodisiacs, charas, on the contrary, is anaphrodisiac, and that it is for this reason they take it. Whether this be so or not, it is, however, an undoubted fact that the general population condones this indulgence of the faquir and his disciples, though they regard the other classes of its consumers, and rightly too, as dissipated loafers who have taken to the drug from idleness and viciousness.

Though so generally in use among Indians only a very small number are seriously addicted to the drug—about 0·5 per cent., according to the report of the Commission held on it in 1894. Its potency for evil, however, is great, though not so great as many would have it; for of all cases treated in asylums in India during 1913, 6·6 per cent. were of insanity due to Indian hemp.

Many Indians affirm that this habit has a great advantage over indulgence in opium, alcohol, or even tobacco, because it can be given up at any time without difficulty. To a certain extent this is correct, as I have noticed time and again that sudden stoppage of the drug, even against the will of the patient, is productive of none of the physical effects which occur after sudden stoppage of other drugs, such as opium, etc. It is, however, an undoubted fact that excessive indulgence in any form of the drug does produce a violent craving for it, and that the amount taken is gradually increased. Apart from the physical effects too, such as anorexia, debility, and muscular tremors, there is in those addicted to the abuse of the drug a general moral deterioration, very similar to that seen in those who indulge to excess in opium or alcohol, such people hesitating at nothing to obtain the drug, and spending their last pie on it rather than on food or clothing for their families.

Cases of insanity assigned to this cause show, both from the mental and physical aspect, a striking uniformity of symptoms, a uniformity indeed so striking that it at once precludes any possibility of error in the cause assigned.

Symptoms.—The description of the effects of over-indulgence in this drug is best divided into two groups:

(*a*) *Acute cases*, under which we may class the simple intoxication produced by a large dose of the drug in persons unused to it, and the transitory mania which often follows on after such intoxication.

(*b*) *Chronic cases*, under which head we may describe the effects of the drug on those who are well accustomed to it, and on whom the results are more marked and longer in duration.

(*a*) *Acute Cases.*

1. **Acute Intoxication**—*Physical Symptoms.*—In cases where a large dose has been taken by one unused to the drug a condition of intoxication is produced. The patient's eyes are bloodshot and the pupils dilated. General sensibility is markedly diminished, and there is a great inclination for muscular activity, and a marked tendency to perform acts of violence with a com-

plete disregard of the consequences, and cases of running amuck are frequently seen in this condition of intoxication.

Mental Symptoms.—The first effect of a large dose is a feeling of giddiness, which gradually wears off, and is replaced by a condition of ecstasy or excitement with which there is a marked degree of confusion. Delusions and hallucinations, both visual and auditory, flit through the patient's mind in rapid succession, keeping him entranced with delight, and by their rapid passage seeming to prolong time. This condition generally passes into a deep sleep, from which the patients awake to find that, but for the initial symptoms, they have no memory of anything that has occurred. This lapse of memory is very typical of intoxication from this drug, and occurs also after the transitory maniacal attacks which sometimes follow on the acute intoxication. The forgetfulness may last for some weeks after all other symptoms of intoxication have departed.

Treatment.—In a case of acute intoxication, when perhaps insensibility is setting in, the only remedy is prompt and complete evacuation of the stomach and bowels and the administration of stimulants. Vinegar, acetic, citric, and tartaric acids have been recommended as antidotes. The body should be kept warm by blankets and hot bottles.

A fact well worth remembering is that coffee, tea, and cocoa are said to increase the action of the drug, and should never be used in such cases.

2. **Transitory Condition of Excitement.**—This condition of acute maniacal symptoms as a rule follows after an acute intoxication in one addicted to the chronic abuse of the drug. It is an important one from a medico-legal point of view, for there is no condition in which acts of reckless violence and brutality are more liable to be committed, and it is apparently nothing but justice to hold such cases responsible for acts which were committed during a period of intoxication which they knowingly and willingly entered. It is the commonest asylum form of mental conditions due to *Cannabis indica*, and is generally of short duration, the symptoms ceasing so soon as the supply of the drug is stopped.

Physical Symptoms.—The temperature is as a rule slightly febrile, the eyes bloodshot, the horizontal ciliary branches being chiefly affected, the pupils dilated, and the face flushed, with an expression of demoniacal excitement.

Mental Symptoms.—The mental condition is one of intense excitement and confusion. The patients are intensely noisy and restless, and become irritated at the slightest attempt to control them. Hallucinations of sight and hearing are especially characteristic of this condition, and partake as a rule of a sensual character, lovely females being said to visit the patients at night and converse with them, etc. These symptoms as a rule subside quickly once the supply of the drug is stopped, and are followed by complete oblivion to all that happened during the period of excitement.

Diagnosis.—The history of the case, the marked confusion, and, above all, the recklessness and violence of the patient, are absolutely unmistakable, and form a picture which once seen can never be forgotten.

Prognosis.—The prognosis in this condition is invariably most hopeful, such cases recovering rapidly and perfectly once the drug is completely removed from them. It is as well, however, to keep them under treatment for as long as possible to make sure of their complete recovery from the habit, for if they again take to the drug when discharged relapses are sure to ensue.

Treatment.—Prompt and complete removal of the drug, with non-stimulating, nourishing diet, and careful supervision, to prevent acts of violence, as a rule suffice in such cases. At times sedatives may be necessary, and on such occasions I have got good results from paraldehyde, ʒiii. to ʒiv. every second day, or sulphonal, grs. x., morning and evening, but as a rule after a day or two of acute excitement the symptoms gradually subside, and no further trouble is experienced in treating the case.

CASE XLII.

N. G., a Hindu, aged 30, a criminal lunatic, was admitted into the asylum on November 26, 1900, being confined under Section 471 Criminal Procedure Code. On February 21, 1900, this man killed an old woman by beating her on the head with a stick, and remained sitting by the body after the deed. No apparent motive for the murder could be ascertained. Evidence was given to show that the patient's father had been insane, and the patient had on previous occasions exhibited signs of insanity. He was therefore acquitted on the ground of insanity, and confined in the asylum under the section quoted. No history of indulgence in drugs was forthcoming at the trial. When admitted he seemed dull and stupid, and his memory was apparently defective. Otherwise he appeared to be quite sane.

Eventually it is recorded in his case that the man is "an unprincipled, scheming liar." He was reckoned as sane until July, 1905. On the 14th of that month he was found in his cubicle smoking charas, being then in a dazed condition; a quantity of charas was also found in his room. He had, as was discovered, obtained this charas from the private servant of another patient, a sirdar of good family. Following this bout of charas-smoking he became acutely maniacal, being violent, noisy, and destructive. He remained thus for nearly three weeks, and then gradually recovered. He is quite sane at present, works well, but is an expert in the art of mendacity (C. J. R. Milne, 1906).

Case XLIII.

A Third Recurrence of the Drug Habit followed by Imperfect Recovery.—In Major Ewens' series this is No. 66, and the case is also noted in the text of his article. His two previous admissions are there recorded, and also his own concise history of his drug-taking habits. From April, 1903, until March, 1905, he was known to have not again resorted to bhang, and to have followed his trade in the city of Lahore. On April 21, 1905, he was admitted in a state of furious mania. He was extremely restless; very noisy, singing, and shouting constantly the choicest of abuse; he had destroyed all his clothes; he dug with his fingers huge holes in his cell into which he could disappear bodily, and he is not a small man; he attempted to extract the bricks from the partition walls of his cubicle, and this too with a horrible gangrenous finger, which eventually dropped off, and which could not be dressed, but was treated by the patient with smearings of filth. He was also extremely filthy with his excreta. With varying acuteness this state lasted for about four weeks, when he began to recover, allowing the stump of his finger to be dressed, and becoming generally cleaner in his habits. In June he had, without discoverable cause, another attack of acute mania, lasting about four days. Improvement followed this, but it has never been perfect, and his previous condition has not yet, ten months after his attack, been attained. Although he can talk sensibly to a certain degree, he is in a state of foolish exaltation, constantly making unreasonable requests, asking for bicycles, etc. His memory is very defective, and his speech childish. He has become very fond, when he gets the opportunity, of attiring himself in a fantastic manner, being particularly keen on pagris of grotesque design (C. J. R. Milne, 1906).

(*b*) *Chronic Cases.*

These occur in those much addicted to the drug, and generally as a result of a rapid increase in the amount of the drug consumed or of a too frequent indulgence in it.

Symptoms.—The symptoms are practically identical with the acute mania already described, but recovery is much slower as a rule.

Prognosis.—The majority of such cases recover after a time, but a certain number continue in a state of chronic excitement until death, while a still smaller number relapse into a condition of dementia, in which they ultimately die.

Case XLIV.

Chronic Mania following prolonged Indulgence in Bhang and Charas.—H. N. L., aged 30, a Brahmin employed in the Railway Mail Service, was admitted on April 11, 1905. He gave a history of having drunk a pice-worth of bhang daily for eight years along with others, and also of having smoked charas intermittently for two years. His motive was to make himself more fit for his work. His memory was, when he was admitted, less affected than these cases usually are, and by interrogation a coherent account of his past life was obtained from him, which was subsequently corroborated by his father and friends. His father stated that the son had become mentally altered four months prior to admission, and that, having threatened his wife and mother-in-law, they left him. He was also found at the Lahore station in a state of mania, and was brought to the asylum. On admission he was in a state of great exaltation and excitement, and was evidently well pleased with himself. He talked in a loud, sonorous voice, bursting out at the end of every sentence into a fit of exaggerated laughter, which lasted for a minute or more. He exhibited delusions of wealth and position. He has remained in this condition for about ten months, being at times more communicative than at others, but being easily aroused into a foolish declamation of his powers, interpolated with much amusing laughter. He is extremely proud, and is solitary in his habits. His physical health remains good, but he is mentally deteriorating (C. J. R. Milne, 1906).

Insanity due to the Abuse of Cocaine.

This was a matter of growing importance in India, as the cocaine habit was daily becoming more prevalent among a certain class of Indian. The war has greatly reduced this evil, but whether it will recur with the declaration of peace it is impossible to say.

The drug was generally brought in German ships to Bombay and Calcutta and smuggled thence to Delhi, where the headquarters of these illegal traders was situated. From Delhi it was distributed over the country and retailed in various ways, one of the most common methods being through sellers of *pan*.

Ætiology.—The habit is said to have originated in the *chawls* of Delhi, being used there first as an application to the glans penis to delay the orgasm and increase the pleasure of the habitués of these places. From this beginning its use has extended, till now it is extensively used by debauchees of the worst description, enfeebled by disease, vice, and debauchery. Its evil effects, when taken internally, on such constitutions can be well imagined; but how much of the mental symptoms is due to cocaine, and how much to the results on an already weakened constitution of the greater excesses it leads to, is an open question.

The amount of insanity directly produced by cocaine is, I think, greatly exaggerated, as in the last eighteen months, out of some 280 admissions into Agra Asylum, there were only two which could be definitely said to be due to this factor. Apart, however, from insanity, its evil effects on the nervous system are great, and it is hard to say what neurasthenic condition has not at some time been cited as its sequence.

Symptoms.—Like morphia, cocaine produces a loss of the moral sense in its slaves, who lie, cheat, steal, commit recklessly any crime to satisfy their craving, regardless of the punishment that may follow, and of the certain misery and suffering caused to those dependent on them. This is all that is seen in many of the cases, but occasionally, owing to a greatly increased indulgence in the drug, or large doses continued over a lengthy period, an attack of insanity ensues.

Physical Symptoms.—Such patients are in a very bad physical condition when admitted into the asylum. They are terribly emaciated, and the skin is cold, clammy, and inelastic. There is marked dyspepsia and gastric derangement. The eyes are bright, and the muscles of the face show fibrillary tremors and twitching. The muscles are tremulous and wasted, and occasionally convulsions occur. Cardiac action is feeble, and syncope may threaten to terminate the case. Marked insomnia is invariably present, and the patient has increasing desire for the drug to alleviate this. Sexual power is as a rule at a very low ebb in such cases, though occasional outbursts of eroticism and sexual excitement occur. In cases of chronic cocainism the patient often complains of a feeling as of "something creeping below the skin," which is especially referred to the fingers and palms of the hands.

Mental Symptoms.—In small doses the drug causes a condition of mild excitement with a sense of increased vigour; in large doses a condition of acute delirium occurs; and with prolonged abuse there is a general failing both of mental and physical power. The patient becomes talkative, suspicious, and irritable. His memory and power of attention fail, and vivid hallucinations may suddenly invade his existence without any warning of their approach, and are as a rule of a terrifying, awe-inspiring nature. As time goes on delusions of persecution may develop and the patient resort to carrying lethal weapons to protect himself from his imaginary foes, and homicidal and suicidal attempts have to be carefully guarded against.

Diagnosis.—The sensation of insects or sand under the skin is typical of cocainism.

Prognosis.—This is fairly good in early cases, but in cases of long standing recovery is by no means common.

Treatment.—This is practically confined to the withdrawal of the drug, which, in my experience, can be suspended at once and completely with but little danger of troublesome collapses, etc., as are sometimes met with in morphinism. Insomnia, restlessness, and excitement are best allayed by bromides in large doses. Constant and reliable supervision is necessary throughout the case, as well to avoid any risk of mishap in the acute stages of the condition as to prevent any chance of the patient obtaining the drug he craves for.

Case XLV.

C. P., aged 30; caste, Brahmin; occupation, patwari. Admitted into Agra Asylum January 19, 1912. No family history obtainable. Said to have been addicted to drugs (cocaine) and debauchery for some years. Had been "ill" for some time prior to his admission.

On admission was a poorly nourished man; wild and excited in appearance, and in a continuous state of restless activity. There was marked fibrillary twitching of his facial muscles, especially under the eyes, and marked intention tremors of the hands. Sensation to touch, heat, and pain were diminished as far as could be ascertained. Organic reflexes normal, superficial and deep reflexes somewhat increased. Questioning produced a vociferous torrent of complaint and abuse. His wife and neighbours were in league to poison and electrify him, they had done him out of his employment by "jadu." He was a most important man, and in high favour with Government; he must be released at once and appointed clerk in the asylum office. He had marked hallucinations of hearing, was morose and solitary, and could be seen at any time of the day walking in some remote corner of the asylum, gesticulating and vociferating loudly, while he carried on a conversation with some invisible companion. The acuteness of his symptoms have since subsided somewhat, but except for this his condition since admission remains practically unchanged (A. W. Overbeck-Wright).

Case XLVI.

K. K., aged 25; caste, Muslim; occupation, syce. Admitted into Agra Asylum. No family history obtainable. He himself had apparently been a vicious debauchee for years, addicted to cocaine, and the constant companion of prostitutes.

On admission he was in an extremely bad physical condition, nothing but skin and bones. His appearance and expression were wild and excited. His eyes were bright, and constantly on the move from one object to another, pupils contracted, and barely reacting to light or accommodation. His skin was greasy and clammy. Organic reflexes were disturbed, and he was dirty in his habits. Superficial reflexes were exaggerated, deep reflexes were decreased. Mentally he was in a condition of wild excitement with a certain amount of confusion. His recent memory was conspicuous by its absence, but remote memory was extremely good, and what he did not tell us about the cocaine trade was not worth hearing. For some time after admission he continued in this condition of acute excitement, accompanied by dyspepsia, constipation, and insomnia, and with marked hallucinations of hearing. During this period he was very emotional, crying one moment, laughing the next, and in the midst of his laughter suddenly turning round and pouring forth volleys of the vilest abuse upon any poor wretch who happened to be near him. He has improved greatly since admission, and there is some hope of his ultimate recovery from this attack; but a recurrence is certain, as on discharge he is sure to return to his former habits (A. W. Overbeck-Wright).

Insanity due to the Abuse of Alcohol.

There is no more common exciting cause of insanity among Europeans and Eurasians as a whole than alcohol, for though *Cannabis indica* stands prominent in India as an exciting cause among Indians, yet alcohol is freely used by Europeans and Eurasians, and besides its direct results on the individual leaves its taint upon the offspring, rendering them specially prone to intemperance, epilepsy, idiocy, and insanity. The crude liquor, too, so commonly seen in the bazaars, and in which certain classes of Indians and Eurasians indulge freely, is specially noxious, and produces much more disastrous results than the matured imported liquors.

The effects of alcohol vary greatly, not only between individuals but between races, and various explanations have been brought forward for this. The form of liquor indulged in has, and undoubtedly with some reason, been brought forward as an explanation by some, while others, again, say that a species of alcoholic immunity is produced in races who have drunk hard for centuries; and the proof of this is that most primitive races are extremely intolerant of liquor, and, unless the supply be stopped, it may even threaten the very existence of such races. Other points than these, however, have probably more to do with the matter. Thus the effects of alcohol are invariably greater upon those sprung from neurotic stock, and by far the majority of habitual inebriates will on enquiry be found to have a tainted heredity. In fact, just as an alcoholic parent may beget an epileptic or an idiot, so a parent who is of weak nervous stability, an epileptic, may beget offspring who readily fall into alcoholic habits, and the close connection between this habit and the neuroses cannot be too strongly brought forward.

A very small amount of alcohol, too, rapidly produces a most pernicious effect on persons who have previously suffered from head injuries or sunstroke, as well as on epileptics who have at any time suffered from insanity.

Besides its effects on the nervous system we must also remember its effects on the body generally, and that, by lowering the general resistance to infection by bacterial organisms, it must of necessity be a strong predisposing factor to most of the insanities due to bacterial toxæmias.

In fact, as Craig ably puts it, "alcoholism is so far-reaching in its results that in the individual we find a progressive tendency to mental and bodily deterioration and a lowered resistance to bodily disease; in the offspring, a proneness to idiocy, epilepsy, and criminality; and in the race, a higher disease-rate, a higher mortality-rate, and a lowered birth-rate."

Ætiology.—A neurotic inheritance is by far the most important factor. Some writers go so far as to state that an acquired taint is not transmitted to the offspring; but this certainly does not apply to alcoholism, and I know of several families where the tendency has been transmitted through three or four generations.

Habit is also an important factor in this condition, many persons first taking the drug from social or business reasons, and then gradually increasing the amount till they find themselves slaves to a habit from which they cannot free themselves.

Others, again, resort to alcohol to stimulate a worn-out brain and body to fresh exertion, instead of restoring them by the rest and nourishment they require, with the inevitable result that a mental breakdown sooner or later occurs, and is probably complicated by the alcohol taken to stave it off.

In this connection it must be remembered that alcoholism may be but one of the early symptoms of an attack of one of the acute insanities, or may be the sole remnant of a previous attack, and due to the diminished self-control resulting therefrom.

Varieties.—As with *Cannabis indica* so with alcohol, we meet with both acute and chronic intoxications. In the former conditions the symptoms are due wholly to the direct action of the poison on the nervous centres, but in the latter they are often due to structural alterations in the cerebral bloodvessels and nervous elements.

Roughly they may be classified into (*a*) *Acute intoxication ;* (*b*) *Delirium tremens ;* (*c*) *Mania a potu ;* (*d*) *Chronic alcoholic insanity ;* (*e*) *Dipsomania.*

(*a*) Acute Intoxication—*Physical Symptoms.*—These vary greatly with the individual, but, roughly, they may be classified into two groups. In the first of these sickness and subsequent gastritis are the main symptoms, while in the second motor inco-ordination and subsequent severe headache are most prominent.

Mental Symptoms.—Alcohol tends to exaggerate the normal temperament, the weakminded person becoming foolish, the morose man tending to weep or become sullen, and the excitable individual becoming merry and exalted under its influence. Many and varied, however, are the types of mental derangement associated with this condition, from stupor and extreme mental confusion to a state of wild excitement, and as the disturbance is as a rule over in a few hours there is but little need to cumber such a book as this with them. It is as well to note, however, that occasionally the mental disorder may last for days or even weeks, and in some cases epileptic convulsions may occur.

Treatment.—An emetic and forcible confinement to bed is all that is required in such cases.

(*b*) DELIRIUM TREMENS.—This condition may arise in several ways. It may be the result of an excessive amount of alcohol consumed in a comparatively short space of time; or, on the contrary, the sudden suspension of the drug may suffice to originate an attack; or it may occur after an injury or shock, or complicate an illness, such as typhoid or pneumonia.

Physical Symptoms.—Gastric derangement is the most marked physical symptom of this condition, and is evidenced by anorexia, a furred, tremulous tongue, constipation, and gastric pain and uneasiness, with occasional vomiting. The skin is as a rule moist, and drenching perspiration may occur at times, while the temperature rarely rises above 100° F. Muscular tremors are marked, and the speech is often affected thereby, while in a few cases epileptic convulsions may occur. Sleeplessness is invariably met with in such cases, and when marked is of great prognostic import. There is nearly always a moderate hyperleucocytosis in such cases.

Mental Symptoms.—The onset is not as a rule sudden, as is popularly supposed, but is preceded by a condition of neuro-muscular irritability. The patient is excited and impulsive, becomes timid, suspicious, and restless, and is generally very irritable. Night as a rule intensifies this condition, and the patient passes the hours of darkness in an agony of terror, misinterpreting every sound, and haunted by hallucinations both of sight and hearing. Animals and insects crawl around and on his bed, while devils torment and jeer at him, and it is characteristic of this condition that the hallucinations are invariably of a terrifying, awe-inspiring kind. As the case progresses these hallucinations appear by day as well as by night, and the patient spends the hours in one continuous agony of fear.

In very rare cases for a few brief hours these terrifying phantoms disappear, and the patient passes into a condition of exaltation with grandiose delusions as to his own position and importance; but soon this state vanishes, and the patient returns to his former attitude of terror. Where this condition is seen the case as a rule terminates in complete dementia. In such cases cognition is as a rule poor, and memory, though fair for remote events, fails altogether when recent events are brought forward for discussion. Attention is wholly self-centred and objective, and such patients spend the time wrapped up in themselves and their hallucinations and delusions. Suicide is often attempted in these cases, and one has to be constantly on one's guard against it.

Diagnosis.—Acute mania is the chief condition likely to be confused with this, and the history and the somatic symptoms, along with the character of the hallucinations, are our chief diagnostic aids.

Prognosis.—Recovery is in the majority of cases complete, and occurs in from six to ten days; but one attack renders the patient more liable to subsequent ones. Where the course of the disease is prolonged there are always certain dangers ahead; thus the patient may pass into a condition of stupor and coma and ultimately die (about 5 per cent.); the hallucinations and delusions may persist after the subsidence of the other symptoms; a certain degree of dementia may remain after the attack; or, lastly, the condition may pass into one of ordinary acute mania.

Treatment.—Rest in bed and frequent feeding with small quantities of fluid food, preferably milk and soda, are essential in all cases. In the very early stages a full dose of chloral and bromide may produce sleep and cut short the attack, but otherwise hypnotics must be used with the greatest caution, and paraldehyde is especially contra-indicated, as it seems to increase the excitement. Insomnia is best treated by hot draughts of milk and cold applications to the head. If there is a tendency to collapse, hypodermics of strychnine and warm saline enemata are invaluable. All such cases require careful supervision and control as there is constant danger of suicide and impulsive acts.

(*c*) Mania a Potu.—This is another but less common form of acute alcoholism, and a knowledge of it is important to the medical practitioner from a medico-legal point of view.

Ætiology.—There is usually in these cases a marked hereditary taint, and in many cases quite small doses of alcohol suffice to produce this condition.

Physical Symptoms.—The general health in such cases is as a rule good, and there is no appearance of illness, which is so markedly present in delirium tremens. Insomnia is practically the only physical derangement, and a very trying one it is, and sleep has constantly to be produced by artificial means. The leucocytosis is as a rule fairly normal.

Mental Symptoms.—The condition here is one of intense mental and motor excitement, sudden in onset and extreme in violence, homicidal attacks being by no means infrequent. Such cases are invariably exalted, boastful, and extravagant. Loss of self-control is evidenced by extreme irritability and sudden impulsive acts of violence. Hallucinations are by no means necessary concomitants of this condition, nor is confusion ever present to any marked extent.

Diagnosis.—This is as a rule easy when a clear history of the case is obtainable. The main conditions to be distinguished are other forms of excitement, epileptic furor, and the acute maniacal state which at times ushers in general paralysis of the insane.

Prognosis.—Rapid recovery is the rule in these cases, and once the patient is placed under proper care and treatment improvement progresses rapidly. Four to six weeks is the average duration of this condition, and I know of one or two cases where recovery occurred in a few days.

Treatment.—The question of certification and treatment in an asylum is always one of extreme difficulty in these cases. The extreme violence and excitement render them most difficult—in fact, dangerous—to treat at home; but, on the other hand, when placed on proper treatment recovery is rapid as a rule, and the patient and his relatives are apt to blame the medical man for having confined him unnecessarily in an asylum and brought the blight thereof on the family. In such cases therefore a family conclave to decide the treatment to be adopted is always advisable, and thereat the probable course and dangers of the illness should be fully explained to the relatives, and it should be left to them to decide, in consultation, what line of treatment is to be adopted.

Rest in bed is essential, as also a full, nourishing diet, and in these cases the alcohol may be withdrawn at once.

Restlessness, excitement, and insomnia call for the administration of hypnotics, but these must be given sparingly and with caution to avoid the commencement of a drug habit. The bowels require constant attention, as constipation is apt to be troublesome, and retention of urine has also at times to be guarded against.

(*d*) Chronic Alcoholic Insanity—**Ætiology.**—This form of intoxication arises as the result of steady drinking for months or even years. The symptoms vary with the individual; thus in one person the condition may be one of steadily progressive dementia; in others, a condition of stupor or confusion may be present; others, again, may reveal a condition resembling delusional insanity; while in some cases a condition closely akin to general paralysis of the insane may be present.

Physical Symptoms.—These vary greatly with the individual. As a rule the patient has a bloated, unhealthy appearance and a heavy, morose, and vacant expression. The eyes are bloodshot and may be slightly jaundiced, and the small subcutaneous veins of the face are congested.

Gastric derangements are invariable concomitants of this condition, and reveal themselves by anorexia, pain and discomfort after taking food, constipation or diarrhœa, and emesis, which is as a rule most frequent in the mornings.

The heart's action is irregular and weak, the arterial tension low, and valvular lesions are common in such cases. Blood examination never reveals a hyperleucocytosis in this condition.

Albumen and sugar are frequently present in the urine, and carbuncles and boils are often met with and cause trouble.

There is a general loss of muscular tonus, speech is blurred and defective, due to tremors of the lips and tongue, and tremors, twitchings, and cramps may affect any part of the muscular system, twitching of the supra-orbital muscles being especially characteristic of alcoholic intoxications.

The gait is uncertain and hesitating, and the knee-jerks are at times absent but may be exaggerated or unequal.

Peripheral neuritis may complicate this condition, in which case the patient may be unable to walk, and may lose all control of his sphincters.

The physical and mental failure follows the ordinary coûrse of events, the most recently acquired and most finely developed movements and faculties disappearing first.

The pupils are markedly unequal in many cases, and in a small number of patients the reaction to light may be markedly impaired, though some authorities deny this, and, if present, say it is due to some intercurrent disease.

Sensibility to touch, heat, and pain may be variously affected, but hypersensibility to pain is a very common symptom.

Perversions of the special senses are common, and frequently give rise to hallucinations and delusions.

Weight falls rapidly as a rule, and the various organs are all more or less impaired in their functions.

Mental Symptoms.—The delusional type is by far the most common form of this disease. The delusions arise in practically every case from hallucinations originating in the perverted sensibility, both general and special, which gives rise to suspicions of poisoning, mesmerism, electricity, etc., and soon the patient weaves out a wonderful romance as to who his persecutors are, their reasons for persecuting him, and the means they employ.

The emotional state varies in such patients. Usually a condition of depression prevails, but outbursts of excitement may occur, in which violent attacks may be made upon the supposed persecutors.

Memory is invariably affected in these cases, recent memory being most affected at first, the amnesia gradually extending to more remote events as the disease progresses, and, curiously enough, with this loss of memory there is in most cases a concomitant loss of the craving for drink.

Suspicion is a common factor in all cases of alcoholic toxæmia and gives rise to delusions of persecution, the patient believing his wife unfaithful to him, that he is being swindled in some outrageous manner, etc. It is characteristic of such delusions, however, that the patient's behaviour is wholly inconsistent with his loudly affirmed beliefs, for though firmly convinced of his wife's adultery, yet he will still continue to cohabit with her.

Irritability and violent outbursts of rage reveal a loss of self-control, and occur most frequently in the bosom of the family, being more or less suppressed before strangers.

In cases of the "progressive dementia" type, amnesia is marked from the beginning, the mental faculties fail, and the patient becomes dirty and immodest. Hallucinations, mainly aural and visual, are common in such cases, and occasionally delusions may be found, but these tend to disappear as dementia advances.

In the form resembling general paralysis of the insane the mental disorders vary greatly. One patient may be in a state of exaltation, with markedly grandiose delusions; another depressed, and haunted by delusions of persecution; while yet another type may pass into a condition of progressive dementia.

Diagnosis.—The diagnosis between this condition and G.P.I. is at times one of extreme difficulty. A reliable history of the case is of the greatest use to us in solving this problem, as is also the presence of rapidly developed hallucinations and the characteristic physical symptoms, though if physical signs of organic disease be present the question becomes at once a complicated one. A history of syphilis is, of course, an aid, though by no means conclusive, for alcoholics, owing to the effects of the drug on their powers of taking care of themselves, are very prone to venereal infection. A differential diagnosis by means of a careful examination of the physical symptoms is our best aid, and the main points to be considered are:

(*a*) *The Condition of the Pupils.*—Inequality and impaired reaction to light may be seen in both conditions, but the presence of the latter is in favour of G.P.I.

(*b*) *Examination of the Fundus.*—Primary optic atrophy favours G.P.I.

(*c*) *Tremors of the Tongue.*—Fine fibrillary tremors favour alcoholism; jerky ataxic movements G.P.I.

(*d*) *Loss of Expression.*—Favours G.P.I.

(*e*) *Speech.*—In G.P.I. is slurred, as if the mouth were full of marbles, and is more hesitating than in alcoholism, where the speech is thick and blurred.

(*f*) *Convulsive Seizures.*—More common in G.P.I.

(*g*) *Knee-jerks.*—Similarly affected in both.

(*h*) *Sensory Affections.*—Much more common in alcoholic conditions resembling G.P.I.

(*i*) *Hallucinations.*—Occur in both, but vivid visual hallucinations favour alcoholism.

(*j*) *Condition of Tremor.*—Indicative of alcoholism.

Prognosis.—Great care must always be taken in prognosticating in a case of this sort, for I have seen most wonderful recoveries when death or complete dementia seemed at one time the only possible termination of the case. Persistent hallucinations are always a bad sign, and in young people marked amnesia is as a rule an unfavourable symptom.

Treatment.—The patient must of necessity be deprived of his alcohol, and this is only possible in an asylum or a reliable nursing home, and all attendants on the case must be known to be thoroughly honest and trustworthy. Some recommend the gradual withdrawal of the alcohol, and others its immediate suspension. The latter is, I think, the sounder plan when, as in the majority of cases, the patient's condition permits of it, but where the patients are extremely weak and pulled down such a course is contra-indicated, and the alcohol must be withdrawn gradually. Various symptoms arise from the withdrawal which call for treatment. Collapse is by no means infrequent, but forced feeding and drugs, such as caffeine and strychnine, as a rule bring the patient round. Restlessness, nausea, and diarrhœa frequently give much trouble and call for the use of sedatives, while insomnia is an invariable and most trying symptom, and has to be combated by hypnotics.

All such drugs must, however, be given with the utmost caution, to avoid setting up a drug habit, and I always endeavour to vary the drug as much as possible, and avoid letting the patient know what he is getting.

The diet must be liberal, nourishing, and easily assimilated, and any tendency to refuse food must at once be met by forced feeding.

Case XLVII.

Alcoholic Insanity.—R. S., an aborigine from Midnapore, admitted in December, 1904, into Dullunda Asylum with the following history: For many years had indulged excessively in native liquor (*pachai*—a spirit distilled from rice). On two occasions he had had attacks of acute mania. During the second of these, which followed directly a bout of great intemperance, he came up one evening to another Santal, who was sitting in front of his house, and without saying a word killed him with an axe. He was then arrested and sent to gaol, where he was admitted in a state of wild excitement. He was then sent to the asylum. He was sane on admission, and continued to be sane until March, 1905, when he began suddenly to talk nonsense, and then fell into a state of stuporous depression. Some days later he was caught in the act of making preparations for committing suicide. This state of depression was followed by an attack of acute mania, which was characterised by noise, aggressiveness, and extremely filthy habits. This gradually subsided after a duration of nearly two months. He then recovered, and continued to be sane, and was sent for trial in September, 1905, and returned to the asylum in March, 1906. In May, 1906, another attack of depression, with another suicidal attempt, was again followed by a period of maniacal excitement, shorter in duration, however, than that of the previous year. He recovered completely, and continued sane for a year. In August, 1907, he had an attack of simple mania lasting for three weeks. In January and February of the present year he has had two successive short attacks, and his case is developing into one of recurrent mania (C. J. R. Milne, 1908).

(*e*) Dipsomania.—This, though usually classed among the alcoholic psychoses, is more properly one of the impulsive insanities, such as kleptomania, pyromania, etc. Roughly, it may be defined as an impulsive form of insanity, occurring periodically, and manifesting itself in an irresistible craving for alcohol.

In many such cases the patient, between the attacks, is a respectable, useful member of society, often a strict teetotaller, and thoroughly ashamed of his own weakness, against which he is constantly striving.

Gradually, however, the craving forces itself upon him, he becomes irritable and depressed, loses his desire for food, and a constant fear of impending trouble casts a shadow over his life. At this time the patient is frantically striving against the craving, and frequently implores his friends and relatives to assist him; but, unless such aid is promptly given, the desire proves too strong, and a bout of desperate drinking commences. This may continue until an attack of delirium tremens supervenes, though in some cases the drinking may last for a few days or weeks, and then terminate spontaneously for no apparent cause.

A condition of marked depression usually follows after such attacks, during which there is considerable risk of suicide, and this must always be carefully guarded against.

The intervals between attacks vary greatly, sometimes only three or four attacks occurring in a lifetime, but each attack renders a recurrence more probable.

Insanities due to the Abuse of Opium and Morphia.

The consumption of opium is a widespread habit among the inhabitants of India, and especially so among the people of Northern India; but practically no evil results ensue, and the number of cases of insanity directly due to its consumption are practically nil.

This state of affairs is due to the fact that the Indian invariably takes his opium by the mouth and in pilular form, and with this method of consumption the evil effects of the drug habit are practically eliminated. Thus there is no tendency to the constant increase of the dose, and the marked physical, mental, and moral decay so common among those who smoke it, as in Persia and China, or who take it by hypodermic injection in the form of morphia, as is common in Europe and America.

In small and limited doses, as is generally the custom among Indians, it is of great use as a restorative after fatigue, a stimulant, and a means of obtaining a general feeling of comfort and well-being. Large doses, however, derange digestion, diminish assimilation, and so lower the general health, and in this way may undoubtedly prove a secondary cause in the production of insanity. Apart from this physical result, a man addicted to the habit becomes selfish, neglects his duties, wastes his time in the dreamy state caused by the drug, which he squanders his substance to procure, and is forgetful of his family and the calls of duty.

Beyond this, however, and the intense hold the drug has over him, no other mental symptoms occur among Indians, and even these are by no means commonly seen, and though treatment in some home or institution is undoubtedly necessary to break such patients of the habit, their medical attendants would be foolish rather than brave men if they were to certify them insane merely for these symptoms. In fact, the influence of opium in causing insanity has, on the whole, been intensely exaggerated, as a glance at asylum statistics in India will convince anyone who is inclined to doubt this statement.

Indulgence in Morphia.

Owing to its costliness this is beyond the reach of the average Indian, but among well-to-do Europeans its abuse is fairly common, and undoubtedly produces a definite train of symptoms, both mental and physical, for which confinement in an asylum and removal of the drug is undoubtedly the only cure, though at the same time it is an open question whether such cases can be classed as insane or not.

As a rule the habit develops between twenty and thirty-five years of age, and both sexes seem equally prone to it. In most cases careful questioning will reveal the fact that the drug was first taken to relieve pain, and the result was found so successful that the operation was repeated on the slightest excuse, till the patient found it absolutely essential for his existence. A certain number, however, there are who have not even this feeble excuse, but take the drug first out of sheer idle curiosity, "just to feel what it is like," as they say, and, finding too late that their power of resistance is weaker than they thought, pay the penalty for their curiosity and become slaves to the drug.

Physical Symptoms.—Prolonged use of the drug produces general gastric derangement, with anorexia and constipation. The patient loses weight and becomes sallow and unhealthy in appearance. Salivary secretion is arrested, and the mouth becomes dry, creating a feeling of thirst, which explains why chronic alcoholism is so often associated with chronic morphinism. The pulse is slow and irregular, and there are frequent attacks of palpitation and threatenings of syncope. Secretions generally are arrested, and the skin is dry and loose; but from time to time sudden drenching perspirations seize the patient and render him liable to chills.

Loss of sexual appetite and impotence is present in both sexes when affected by this habit, and in the female amenorrhœa is an invariable concomitant.

Hyperæsthesia is invariably present over the whole body, and in severe cases is so marked that the lightest touch causes the patient to wince or even scream.

The pupils are contracted, their action both to light and accommodation is deficient, and defective vision is often present in such cases.

Superficial and deep reflexes are invariably exaggerated, and there is a general lowering of vitality and impairment of muscular power.

Mental Symptoms.—Except for a short interval immediately after the taking of a dose, the general mental condition in such cases is one of depression. Confusion, hallucinations, and delusions are by no means common in morphinism, where the condition approximates to one of slight dementia with impairment of volition and morality, amnesia, and carelessness of personal cleanliness and appearance. Sleep in such cases is most irregular, and frequently broken by dreams and visions. Occasionally such cases pass into a delusional condition, on which dementia as a rule rapidly supervenes.

If the patient suffers from acute intoxication hallucinations may be present; but these are not often seen unless the drug is combined with cocaine, as often happens.

When the drug is suddenly withdrawn a condition closely

resembling delirium tremens is caused, the patient becoming anxious and restless, suffering agonies of fear from terrifying hallucinations of sight and hearing, and often passing into a condition of coma and collapse. There is marked anorexia and emesis, with abdominal pain and diarrhœa, and often profuse perspiration and salivation. Death may occur in such cases from syncope or collapse.

The feelings of exhaustion and discomfort may persist for weeks after the disappearance of all mental symptoms.

Diagnosis.—This may be by no means easy, as morphinists are extremely cunning in concealing their vice. Scars resulting from careless septic injections should be looked for, but the only certain way is to confine the patient to bed in the care of a reliable nurse and wait for the development of deprivation symptoms.

Prognosis.—No patients are more troublesome to treat than alcoholics and morphomaniacs, and in no case can one be certain of no relapse occurring. If the patient be in good health and willing to be treated, we have a fair prospect of success; but I have known such cases relapse after months of abstinence, so the outlook is never very hopeful.

Treatment.—This is practically confined to the withdrawal of the drug, which may be done suddenly or by degrees. The sudden withdrawal is more likely to be followed by symptoms of syncope and collapse, but in either case the discomfort and misery are the same, only more prolonged by the gradual withdrawal, so one has to make a choice between two evils, and I certainly advocate the former method except when extreme weakness in the patient absolutely contra-indicates it. During the first few weeks of treatment the patient should be confined to bed and fed with milk, eggs, egg-flip, meat-juice, etc., and if collapse threatens, alcohol, sal volatile, or hypodermics of strychnine may be employed. Insomnia, restlessness, and discomfort are best allayed by bromides. After the disappearance of acute deprivation symptoms, tonics, cold baths, regular exercise, and constant supervision to avoid backsliding are required for some months.

Ether and Chloroform Abuse.

The symptoms arising from the abuse of either of these drugs are practically identical with those caused by abuse of alcohol. A single dose of chloroform may in neurotic subjects set up a condition of mild excitement with hallucinations, and at times delusions, under the influence of which charges of rape and assault have at times been brought against the anæsthetist.

Datura Stramonium.

I have seen two persons with mental symptoms as the result of an overdose of this drug. One case was a woman who had attempted suicide by eating the berries; the other case a man who had been heavily drugged with it by some thieves, who decamped with his property while he was unconscious.

Physical Symptoms.—In both the cases the patient was flushed and feverish. The pupils were widely dilated, and the eyes bright and shining. The tongue and skin were very dry. The pulse was rapid, and the heart's action tumultuous.

A marked symptom in each case was the derangement of vision, and it was curious to see them attempting to touch objects with their finger and missing them by inches.

Mental Symptoms.—Each of these patients was in a wildly maniacal state when first seen, and practically uncontrollable. In both cases emetics had already been given, and the condition gradually quieted down, and in two to three weeks the patients were convalescent.

Treatment.—Emetics and purgatives are called for to remove any of the drug lying unabsorbed in the alimentary canal. Thereafter confinement to bed with a plentiful liquid dietary is necessary until the acute symptoms have subsided. Potassium iodide and small doses of opium are the most useful drugs in such cases.

Prognosis.—Is good, in the cases of non-lethal doses, recovery generally occurring rapidly.

Paraldehyde Habit.

A knowledge of this is of importance to the alienist, as it is one of the most useful hypnotics at his disposal. Its prolonged use as a hypnotic produces a habit so that sleep cannot be obtained without recourse to the drug. It at times produces vivid auditory hallucinations, and invariably increases any tendency there may be to hallucinations, especially those of hearing.

Mercurial and Lead Poisoning.

Mental symptoms due to chronic poisoning by these metals are practically confined to those constantly working with them, and consist of intense mental depression with delusions. At times, however, such cases may be due to badly *kalaied* cooking-pots, the *kalai* being sometimes applied mixed with lead.

The classical physical symptoms of chronic poisoning, such as salivation, a blue line round the gums, peripheral neuritis, neuralgic pains, headache, etc., should be known to all medical men, and need not be detailed here. For the same reason it is unnecessary to discuss the treatment.

Iodoform Poisoning.

This is at times met with as the result of absorption from surgical dressings, etc. The condition is one of low muttering delirium, with tremors of the voluntary muscles, and lasts for about three weeks, recovery as a rule being perfect.

Carbon-bisulphide Poisoning.

Occurs chiefly among those working with rubber. The physical symptoms are those of marked malnutrition and anæmia, while mentally the condition is one of delusional insanity with, at times, vivid auditory hallucinations. The treatment is mainly tonic, iron and arsenic being especially serviceable in such conditions. Recovery generally ensues, but the condition tends to be chronic, and as a rule has a long course, lasting over a year. Relapses are sure to occur if such cases return to their former work after recovery.

Thyroid Poisoning.

This may result from the prolonged administration of thyroid in nervous cases. The condition is generally one of transient elevation, and soon passes off when the drug is discontinued.

CHAPTER XX

GROUP C: NERVOUS DISEASES FREQUENTLY COMPLICATED BY MENTAL DISORDER

Epileptic Insanity.

(I. ———. II. *Epileptic Insanity.*)

This is a condition of the utmost importance to a medical man, not only from a medical but also from a medico-legal point of view.

Epilepsy has been defined by Gowers as "a nervous disease characterised by a sudden discharge of nervous energy from the grey matter of the cerebral cortex, this discharge occurring without normal stimulus."

The latest theory on the subject, and one with a good deal to support it, is the theory of the toxic origin of epilepsy. The grounds in support of this are varied. Thus the temperature of epileptic patients is irregular and liable to become febrile at intervals, independently of any outward bodily or mental symptoms. The pulse is also liable to similar irregularities, affecting its rate, its rhythm, and its tension. The leucocytosis and results of blood examinations before, after, and during the fits also strongly favour this toxic theory of its origin; thus the polymorphonuclear percentage falls, and there is a corresponding eosinophilia immediately before the appearance of a fit, after which the polymorphonuclear percentage rises above normal, causing a temporary hyperleucocytosis. These changes in the blood point more to an autointoxication from deranged metabolism than to a bacterial toxæmia. Moreover, several European scientists have recorded that the urine drawn from epileptic patients during a fit produces convulsions when introduced into the venous circulation of animals.

As to the nature of the toxine, this is still a matter of conjecture. Haig regards it as due to uric acid poisoning, and it is an undoubted fact that the uric acid excretion falls before a fit, and that a corresponding rise occurs in the excretion after the fit is over. Krainsky, however, holds the view that the essential irritant is carbamate of ammonia, and brings forward strong evidence to support his theory.

Whatever may be the nature of the essential irritant, however, it is certain that in epileptics metabolism tends to be imperfect; the average excretion of azotised products, phosphoric acid, and chlorides is below normal in the interconvulsive periods, and is still further diminished in the prodromal periods.

After a fit the urine is more concentrated, contains a larger proportion of all the regressive products of metabolism, and is much more toxic than normal urine when injected into the lower animals. In the period immediately preceding a fit this toxicity of the urine increases greatly, and is proportionate to the amount of gastro-intestinal disturbance present, while after a fit the urine is hypertoxic. Gastro-intestinal disturbances seem to favour the formation of the toxine, and indeed seem able to determine the occurrence of a fit, as the use of gastric lavage, intestinal disinfectants, purgatives, etc., is a great aid in holding the fits in abeyance.

The gastro-intestinal changes consist chiefly in the occurrence of abnormal putrefaction among the contents of the alimentary tract, and the amount of this occurring can be roughly obtained by an estimation of the amount of ethereal sulphates excreted in the urine, which invariably increases prior to the occurrence of a fit.

Along with the accumulation of toxines in the blood there is in such cases a corresponding diminution in the alkalinity of the blood.

How these toxines act, whether directly on the nerve cells themselves, or indirectly by producing cerebral congestion or anæmia by vasomotor spasm, is still unknown, but it is, I think, universally admitted now that there are two undoubted factors in the production of epilepsy: (*a*) a special defect of cerebral organisation which predisposes to the epileptic discharge; (*b*) a toxic action which determines this discharge.

Ætiology.—Hereditary predisposition to nervous diseases is very marked in these cases, being present in well over 50 per cent. of patients. Age, too, has a considerable influence on the appearance of this disease, more than 75 per cent. of cases occurring in the first twenty years of life, of which about 35 to 40 per cent. occur in the first decennium. The sexes are affected practically in equal proportions.

The exciting causes are various. It may arise from a bad brain habit following the occurrence of infantile convulsions; cerebral injuries or sudden mental shocks may suffice to originate it, as also mental anxiety and strain, while at times it occurs as a sequel to such acute specific diseases as scarlet fever.

Symptoms—*Physical.*—The physical health always suffers much in cases of epilepsy. There is as a rule gastric derangement, evidenced by furred tongue and constipation; nutrition is impaired, and loss of weight ensues; while sleep is restless and broken. Automatism is a common condition in epileptics, especially in the petit mal, and as a rule follows the fit, the patient invariably going through the same movement or action immediately after the seizure while still in a condition of unconsciousness.

The fits are the most important physical symptoms, and may be described as of three types: (1) *Grand mal*, or major epilepsy, where the fit is of severe character; (2) *Petit mal*, where the fit is comparatively mild in character; (3) *Jacksonian epilepsy*, where the convulsions affect primarily one limb and spread from thence to the whole body.

1. *Grand Mal.*—Here occasionally there is an aura or warning, the patient having hemicrania, various neuralgic pains, gastric discomfort, localised analgesias, or some other sensory manifestation immediately prior to the fit. As a rule, however, the fit comes on suddenly; the patient, with a cry, due to the forcible expulsion of air through the glottis, falls helplessly to the ground in a state of tonic convulsions. The tonic convulsions, after twenty to thirty seconds, pass into the clonic convulsions, in which the muscles move in violent jerks, the tongue is apt to be extruded and bitten, and the patient foams or froths at the mouth. The condition of clonic convulsions passes into one of more or less marked stupor, with stertorous breathing, which passes into normal sleep, from which the patient awakes with no recollection of anything which occurred during the seizure. As a rule such patients on awakening are confused and dull and complain of muscular pain and stiffness.

2. *Petit Mal.*—In its typical form this consists of a temporary loss of consciousness, without visible convulsions or spasms, during which the patient may or may not fall to the ground.

On returning to consciousness the patient may at once continue his occupation as if nothing had happened, or may be confused and ask what has happened or what he was doing. These minor seizures are very apt to recur, and several may ensue in the course of a single day. The tendency here, too, is for the mental faculties to fail rapidly, and if definite mental disorder supervenes the physical health as a rule becomes speedily impaired.

3. *Jacksonian Epilepsy*.—This condition was first described by Hughlings Jackson, from whom its name was derived. In it the muscular spasm commences locally, in a hand, finger, or foot, and may be localised to this one region. As a rule, however, the spasm tends to spread until the whole body i, involved and insensibility supervenes, though at first when the spasm is localised there is no loss of consciousness.

Status epilepticus is a term applied to very severe forms of the grand mal, where the seizures occur in rapid sequence, consciousness does not return in the intervals between the fits, and a fatal termination is very frequent.

Mental Symptoms.—Many epileptics go through life without showing symptoms of mental derangement beyond being at times unduly irritable, impulsive, passionate, and emotional, especially on religious questions. When, however, mental disease does supervene it is practically always excitement with more or less marked confusion. The predisposing cause in such cases is undoubtedly the inherent or acquired mental deficiency, which allows the occurrence of the sudden discharges of nervous energy which constitute the epileptic spasms, while alcoholic excesses, mental shock, and strain figure as the chief exciting causes. Once an epileptic has suffered from even the most transitory mental derangement there is always a liability of its recurrence, and each attack increases this tendency and favours the occurrence of the same mental symptoms over and over again.

The earlier mental derangements are generally short bouts of acute excitement, from which the patient as a rule completely recovers, but gradually as the attacks continue the mental equilibrium becomes more and more impaired until a condition of chronic mental derangement is attained, characterised by hallucinations and delusions, wild excitement, loss of self-control, and obsessions and impulses, which are usually homicidal, though occasionally they may be suicidal, in character. Such cases are very liable to perverted religious emotionalism, and when in their religious moods are more liable to outbursts of frenzied rage and virulent abuse than at other times.

The moral sense is blunted in most epileptics, and such cases are invariably most untruthful and vindictive.

Sexual desire is commonly intense in such cases, and gives rise to masturbation and brutal assaults and outrages. Many of these patients are gluttonous, and given to overeating and alcoholic excesses.

In most cases of long standing there is more or less mental enfeeblement, which may pass into dementia of a most degraded type.

INSANITY ASSOCIATED WITH EPILEPSY.—Various types of insanity may be associated with epilepsy.

1. *Epileptic Idiocy and Imbecility.*—This may rise from arrested mental development caused by convulsions in early life.

2. *Pre-Epileptic Insanity.*—Occurs in certain cases where the mental symptoms precede the motor convulsions.

3. *Epilepsie Larvée (Masked Epilepsy).*—In this condition the motor convulsions are replaced by the mental disturbance, an attack of insanity taking the place of a fit, though some authorities state that a fit invariably occurs, but is so slight that it is overlooked in these cases.

4. *Post-Epileptic Insanity.*—This occurs as a sequel to the motor convulsions, and is generally of a very severe type.

5. *Chronic Epileptic Insanity.*—This is the most common form of insanity met with in epileptic patients.

In addition to the above mental conditions epileptics are liable to suffer from other acute insanities just as are other individuals. Indeed, with the epileptic the liability is rather greater on account of the marked hereditary taint present in so many persons thus affected, and also from the deranged metabolism weakening the natural resistance of the healthy body to bacterial invasion, and rendering the patient more liable to suffer from toxæmias.

1. **Epileptic Imbecility and Idiocy.**—These cases arise from the mental development having been retarded by the occurrence of epileptic fits in early childhood, and dentition is as a rule the exciting cause in such cases.

Such patients are usually very impulsive and irritable, and require careful supervision to prevent their injuring children with whom they may associate. If the fits continue long there is generally marked mental deterioration, but the fits may continue for some years without causing any marked intellectual degeneration, and if treatment be successful in arresting the fits there is in most cases marked improvement in the mental conditions.

2. **Pre-Epileptic Insanity.**—This is practically a mental aura replacing the sensory ones which have been mentioned in the description of the grand mal. Hallucinations of sight and hearing terrify the patient and give rise to delusions, under the influence of which assaults may be perpetrated and false charges formulated against entirely innocent persons. There is generally considerable excitement present in this condition, and refusal of food is frequently met with in such cases. The mental attack may precede a fit by a few hours or a few days.

3. **Masked Epilepsy.**—This is a term used to denote cases where there are no apparent convulsions, the fit apparently being replaced by mental symptoms. Cases of automatism have been classed by some under this head, but now it is generally admitted that the automatism is as a rule preceded by a slight fit.

4. **Post-Epileptic Psychoses.**—These are of various kinds, and are of the utmost importance to the medical jurist on account of the frequency with which acts of homicide have been committed by persons suffering from this condition. In such cases the stupor which usually follows after the fits may be replaced by a period of automatism. Such patients are as a rule confused, fail to recognise their nearest relatives, and wander aimlessly about, openly committing crimes of nearly every kind, and in such conditions brutal homicides and sexual assaults are very common, the patient on recovery rarely remembering anything he may have done.

In such cases of crime there is in most instances no traceable motive, and no attempt at concealment is made at the time of perpetration, though later, with returning consciousness, fear may give rise to efforts at concealment. There is, moreover, an unnecessary violence and brutality about such crimes, by which I mean a much greater amount of force and violence is shown than is necessary for their perpetration. This should at once give rise in a medical mind to a suspicion of the true state of affairs, and a careful enquiry into the antecedents of the culprit will generally bring forward ample corroborative evidence.

In some cases a violent attack of mania replaces the coma,

and while in this condition the patient is in a state of frenzy, shouting, kicking, biting, scratching, and committing even homicidal assaults on any and every one. As a rule this condition is quite transitory, lasting for a few hours only.

In a still smaller number of cases a period of mental depression follows after the fits. In such a condition delusions of persecution are common, and may lead to acts of homicide or suicide.

5. **Chronic Epileptic Insanity.**—The general tendency of epilepsy is towards a gradually progressive dementia. Memory fails, self-control is diminished, outbursts of passion and anger, exaltation and excitement, alternate with periods of misery and gloom. The patients become arrogant and boastful, and, though full of religious professions, and always forcing religion upon others, their whole character, their every action belie their sermons. Morals are conspicuous by their absence in such patients—liars, drunkards, and men given to the lowest forms of vice and sexual excesses, comprising the most degraded type of case to be seen in any asylum.

Diagnosis.—The diagnosis of epilepsy is by no means invariably an easy matter, especially when the fits are of the petit mal type. The seizures, too, often occur at night, and the history in such cases may be very obscure. Careful enquiry should be made for unconscious micturition or defæcation, and the tongue examined for scars and signs of injury in such patients. Sudden erratic conduct, incompatible with the former character of the patient, should always suggest epilepsy to the medical mind, and cause a closer supervision to be kept on the patient. Hysteria and epilepsy are at times difficult to distinguish in the earlier age periods, but the former almost invariably occurs when the patient is in company, and is commonly set up by some external influence, while the fall is not so helpless nor so liable to result in injury as is the case in epileptic fits. In place of the subsequent stuporose condition also, there is in hysteria a condition of extreme emotionalism and grotesque attitudinising which never occurs in epilepsy.

In later life a diagnosis has to be made between true epilepsy and the congestive seizures so common among general paralytics. In such a case the state of the pupils, the speech, the handwriting, reflexes, etc., must all be carefully gone into, and a careful enquiry made regarding the onset of the seizure, as in

G.P.I. the onset is as a rule more gradual, and the epileptic cry is wanting.

Prognosis.—Major epilepsy or grand mal is a much more curable disorder than the petit mal, and if it develops in childhood may often be successfully treated, though as the treatment is often a question of years it is difficult at times to get the patients to continue with it. Epilepsy resulting from gross brain lesions, and also petit mal, are practically incurable.

Case XLVIII.

R. R., an aborigine from Tributary Orissa, began to suffer from epilepsy at the age of twenty-five, in 1900. The first fit was a very severe one, and he fell into a fire, extensively scarring his left chest and arm. On August 7, 1905, he was sentenced to transportation for life for murdering his mother under the following circumstances: He was seen one day to drag his mother, who was bleeding from a wound of the head, from his house; in his other hand he had a bloody axe. Having deposited his mother's body, he sat down quietly by his door, and was arrested. It was then observed that he was in a dazed state. He admitted his crime, and said he had mistaken his mother for a tiger. He had dealt his mother four blows, any one of which might have caused death, and one over the right shoulder and neck had severed the spinal cord. It is not recorded, but it is possible that just prior to this murder the man had an epileptic seizure. It was observed in gaol that after his fits he became wildly excited and required restraint. He was then sent to the asylum. An irritable man who suffers from two or three major epileptic seizures monthly. Is dull and depressed before the fit, and is very excited immediately after for a couple of hours, and has then to be kept apart (C. J. R. Milne, 1908).

Case XLIX.

K., aged 32; caste, Mussulman; admitted Agra Asylum November 6, 1911, under Section 30, Act III. of 1900. Sentenced to penal servitude for life for the murder of his wife.

He had a history of epileptic fits for over ten years prior to the murder, the fits being both preceded and followed by attacks of maniacal excitement. About February, 1911, he had a quarrel with his wife over their daughter's marriage, and the same night he killed her with an axe. He was tried under Section 302, I.P.C., and sentenced to penal servitude for life, having apparently been considered not wholly responsible for his actions on account of epilepsy.

On admission into Agra Central Gaol, in April, 1911, he was a fine, well-built man, and showed nothing abnormal. Shortly after admission he became quarrelsome, and then excited, and then passed into one epileptic fit after another, all the fits being most severe in character, and consciousness never being regained between them (typical status epilepticus, in fact). He continued in this condition for several days, and then another attack of excitement supervened, during which he was most violent and aggressive. This was repeated every month or two, and finally, in November, he was removed to Agra Asylum. His condition has improved slightly as regards the frequency of the fits, but they still appear every six weeks or so, and are always accompanied by attacks of excitement. Mentally he is deteriorating and showing signs of slight dementia (A. W. Overbeck-Wright).

Treatment.—Much depends on the general hygiene of the patient's surroundings in cases of epilepsy. The diet should be simple, fattening, and non-stimulating, and overfeeding must be carefully avoided. Alcohol, flesh, tea, coffee, and tobacco should be given only sparingly, or, better still, withheld altogether. The bowels should be carefully regulated, and saline purges administered at intervals, while the patient should be encouraged to drink water freely so as to flush out noxious substances from the system. Regular open-air exercises should be insisted on whenever practicable, the patient's life should be kept as quiet and as routine as possible, and all undue excitement avoided.

Medicinally the only drugs of any service are the bromides, the bromide of potassium giving the best results. They are usually given in 30-grain doses thrice daily after food, and should be continued for long periods without a break.

Richet and Toulouse introduced, some years ago, an ingenious modification of the bromide treatment, based upon the theory that the privation of chlorides intensified the absorption power of the body cells for the two other halogens—*i.e.*, bromides and iodides. They therefore reduced the amount of chlorides in the diet as far as possible, placing their patients at the same time on about 50 grains of sodium bromide daily, with the result that the fits in these cases were largely reduced while under the treatment. I myself have tried withdrawing sodium chloride from the diet of such cases and replacing it with potassium bromide, and the result was most satisfactory. In these cases, moreover, except for the removal of the chloride, the diet was the same as that issued to the rest of the patients, and in itself must contain a fair amount of chlorides. Only 10 grains of potassium bromide was issued for each patient twice daily. This reduced the fits to a practically negligible number, the patients improved both physically and mentally, and bromism was unknown.

Bromism is apt to be troublesome after a lengthy course of the usual treatment, acute eruptions, gastric disturbances, and lethargy troubling the patient. In such cases purgatives and hot baths are indicated, while liquor arsenicalis, 2 to 5 minims, or salol, 2 to 5 grains, combined with the bromide, tends to avert the trouble. In severe cases soda biborate, 2 to 10 grains thrice daily, combined with liquor arsenicalis, 3 minims, is most effective.

Other sedatives, such as nepenthe, belladonna, Indian hemp, nitroglycerine, and erythrol tetranitrate, are all useful at times, especially in cases of *petit mal* in young persons.

When a sensory aura occurs in a limb, the subsequent fit often can be arrested wholly by tying a ligature tightly round the limb.

In cases of *status epilepticus*, chloroform inhalations are worth trying, also inhalations of nitroglycerine or erythrol tetranitrate, or hypodermic or rectal injections of chloral hydrate; but very rarely is any benefit obtained in this condition, which generally ends fatally from hypostatic congestion of the lungs.

Epileptic cases always require careful supervision, to prevent injuries occurring in the fits, to avert choking if the fit occurs during a meal, or to avoid suffocation arising from the patient, during a fit of stupor, turning over with his face on a pillow, etc.

Mental symptoms may at times be aborted by 5 grains of calomel followed by a saline purge, or 1 minim of croton oil, if the excitement be coming on gradually, or if the patient is given to overeating and only has occasional attacks. Where mental symptoms follow after a fit, 20 grains of chloral, combined with 30 grains of potassium bromide, may produce sleep and abort the mental attack.

CHAPTER XXI

GROUP C: NERVOUS DISEASES FREQUENTLY COMPLICATED BY MENTAL DERANGEMENTS (*continued*)

GENERAL PARALYSIS OF THE INSANE (*G.P.I.*).

THIS condition is found among Europeans, Eurasians, and Indians much more commonly than was formerly supposed. In the *Indian Medical Gazette* for January, 1912, this disease is said to be very rare among Indians. Yet at that moment in Agra Asylum there were twelve typical cases among Indians in the second and third stages of the disease, and several have been taken out on security by relatives, while one had died in the asylum since November, 1911.

So that I am of the opinion that if properly looked for and diagnosed it would be found to be much more prevalent among Indians than it is at present generally believed to be.

Definition.—The disease may be defined as a progressive degeneration of the central nervous system, but more particularly of the motor centres, in which remissions and arrest of progress of the symptoms are common, epileptiform or convulsive seizures often occur, and with which there is always associated a progressive mental enfeeblement.

G.P.I. is almost invariably fatal, the patient dying during a congestive seizure, from some intercurrent disease, such as phthisis or pneumonia, or as the result of exhaustion from advanced paralysis or bedsores.

Patients suffering from this disease are liable to attacks of any known form of insanity—indeed, according to Dr. Bruce, it is only very rarely that cases uncomplicated by mental disease are met with. This cannot be too strongly impressed upon the mind, for so frequently is it complicated by mental symptoms that many alienists have jumped at a wrong conclusion and described as one entity what is really two separate conditions, classing G.P.I. among mental diseases, when, from their description, they are really dealing with two diseases—a purely nervous one, G.P.I., complicated by an intercurrent attack of some form of insanity.

Ætiology.—General paralysis is seen much more frequently among urban than rural populations, and affects men more often than it does women. It may occur in childhood, adult life, or old age, but is most commonly and typically seen in men from thirty-five to forty-five years of age. Only a small number of cases (7 to 8 per cent.) have an hereditary nervous taint, but from 70 to 90 per cent. have a history of acquired syphilis, and all the cases I have seen which occurred in the age periods up to twenty have either had a history of congenital syphilis or, if this was denied, had all the physical stigmata of this condition.

The theory of an autointoxication of syphilitic or parasyphilitic origin was at one time strongly combated by Ford Robertson and others, who promulgated the theory that this disease and also locomotor ataxy were due to the toxines produced by a diphtheroid bacillus, which they described as of two types: (*a*) the *B. paralyticans longus*; and (*b*) the *B. paralyticans brevis.* This latter theory had at one time a fair number of adherents, and, if it be well founded, undoubtedly opens up a new field in the treatment of mental disease. The opinion at present generally held, however, is, I think, that the proof regarding *B. paralyticans* and its action is insufficient, and the tendency to regard G.P.I. and locomotor ataxy as terminal syphilitic manifestations is present in the majority of medical authorities.

Symptoms.—For purposes of description this disease is best divided into four stages: (*a*) *Prodromal*; (*b*) *First stage*; (*c*) *Second stage*; (*d*) *Third Stage.* It must be remembered, however, that there is no fixed line of demarcation, the disease being gradually progressive, and the one stage merging unnoticeably into the other.

(*a*) **Prodromal**—*Physical Symptoms.*—Before the definite onset of general paralysis there are as a rule certain more or less definite symptoms lasting for some months, or even years. The patient changes in habits and character, becomes either restless and unusually energetic, or torpid and sluggish. Alcoholic and sexual excesses are common at this stage, and are often wrongly interpreted as causal factors instead of symptoms. Definite complaints of gastric derangement, neuralgic pains, numbness and transient changes in hearing, vision, taste, and smell are often made, while passing attacks of aphasia, paresis affecting the muscles of the eyes, causing strabismus and diplopia, or of the extremities, are very suggestive of this condition. Attacks of syncope and congestive seizures, often mistaken for epilepsy, may occur early in this disease.

Mental Symptoms.—The mental symptoms at this stage are not marked, and might perhaps escape the notice of a total stranger. There is a general impairment of the more specialised powers of the brain, a loss of memory and of the power of attention, associated with a lack of judgment and a failure of volition which renders the patient liable to be led astray, to fall a prey to any swindler, and to plunge into absurd and foolish speculation. A loss of self-control leads to violent outbursts of rage and undue emotionalism, while honesty and morality are at a low ebb, and the patient is liable to commit thefts and other more criminal offences.

Occasionally G.P.I. may begin suddenly with marked mental or motor symptoms. The mental symptoms may be either of an excited or of a melancholic type, while the motor may present the form either of an epileptic seizure or of some form of paresis. In whatever way the condition first manifests itself, however, physical symptoms soon reveal themselves, and the diagnosis is apparent.

G.P.I. being, as already stated, more a nervous than a mental condition, it is proposed to discuss the physical symptoms of the three remaining stages first and consider the mental symptoms thereafter.

Physical Symptoms—(*b*) *First Stage.*—In this period of the disease the facial muscles are commonly affected, causing an alteration in expression, while the evening temperature runs from 99° to 101° F., falling to normal in the morning.

At times there are marked symptoms of gastric derangement, constipation being often a source of great trouble, but in other cases the patient enjoys comparative freedom from these and eats well. The pulse is rapid and irregular, the arterial tension high, while the leucocytosis, as already mentioned, is irregular with as a rule a high polymorphonuclear percentage. There is an exaltation of the sexual instincts in the earlier part of this stage, but later on these may be in abeyance. Sensibility to touch and temperature and also the special senses are rarely affected in this stage, but in about 50 per cent. of cases sensibility to pain is diminished. The condition of the pupils varies greatly. As a rule the pupils are unequal in size and irregular in outline, varying in size and shape from day to day. In some cases reaction both to light and accommodation is lost; in others, the Argyll Robertson pupil may be present. The pupils may be contracted to pin-points or widely dilated. One pupil only may show signs of being affected while the other may appear normal. In fact, no definite condition of the pupil can be laid down as characteristic of this condition, for any and every condition of pupil may occur. The superficial reflexes are exaggerated, as are also the tendon reflexes, except in cases with marked tabetic symptoms or those complicated by chronic alcoholism. There is general impairment of muscular movement throughout the whole body, causing marked inco-ordination, and affecting more especially the muscles of the face, tongue, hands, and lower limbs. The paresis of the facial and tongue muscles leads to loss of expression, and a typical slow, monotonous speech with slurring of the labials, or if the lingual muscles are more affected there is a blurred murmur as if the patient had his mouth full of marbles, such phrases as "Dusra lumba rissala," "Apke bap ka nam" being pronounced with difficulty. The muscular impairment of the hands and arms causes loss of co-ordination and of the finer movements, such as writing, etc. The gait is sometimes dragging, sometimes ataxic, but the patient always has difficulty in walking along a straight line, in placing one foot in front of the other, or in turning quickly—lurching or swaying occurring when any of these are attempted. Many patients, too, are unable to stand with their feet together and with closed eyes, and very few indeed can rise on tiptoe with their eyes shut.

According to the latest statistics available about 80 per cent. give a positive Wassermann's reaction with the blood, and practically all cases give a positive reaction with the cerebro-spinal fluid. In all cases there is an increase in the number of lymphocytes present in the cerebro-spinal fluid.

During this stage the patient loses weight, and insomnia is apt to be troublesome.

(c) *Second Stage.*—Here the involvement of the facial muscles is still more advanced, the face being absolutely expressionless no matter what the mood of the patient may be, and at times being pallid and puffy, as in cases of kidney disease.

The temperature chart in uncomplicated cases shows every second or third week recurrent attacks of slight fever, and gastric derangements are practically the rule. Appetite is often enormous, and at times perverted; the breath is exceedingly offensive, the tongue coated and furred, and alternating attacks of constipation and diarrhœa may prove an endless source of worry to the patient. The leucocytosis corresponds fairly well to the curve of the temperature chart; the polymorphonuclear percentage, however, as a rule remains about normal, the main increase, when the leucocytosis rises, being in the eosinophiles and the hyalines, so far as my experience goes.

The pulse is slow with a high arterial tension, and attacks of syncope are liable to occur, especially after a heavy meal or during exercise. The skin is unhealthy, greasy, and œdematous, and the hair and nails rough and brittle. Diminished sexual instinct and impotence are common in this stage, and form a marked contrast therefore to the first stage. Sensation, both general and special, is now much involved. The muscles are much more markedly affected and paretic, tremors are very apparent, and inco-ordination, etc., are well marked throughout the body. Congestive seizures are common throughout this stage, and are liable at times to be mistaken for epileptic seizures. Their incidence corresponds closely to the febrile attacks. During this stage the patient very commonly puts on weight, but the gain is not a healthy one, the tissues being loose and flabby. Primary optic atrophy is very common in such cases, and at times commencing symptoms may be found in the first stage even.

(*d*) *Third Stage.*—The claim of G.P.I. to be classed as a progressive nervous disease is undoubtedly most marked in this stage, emaciation and loss of power advancing with amazing rapidity. The face is thin, wasted, and expressionless; gastric derangements are practically the rule, diarrhœa and vomiting being constant and most troublesome factors to deal with. The temperature during this stage is most irregular, at times rising in the evening to 99° to 100° F., but as a rule being subnormal. The pulse is extremely feeble and irregular, arterial tension is low, and cyanosis and œdema of the extremities is common, and the lungs are apt to become tubercular. During this stage the leucocytosis is most irregular, and shows no association with the temperature; the polymorph percentage, however, is as a rule low, below 50 per cent., while the hyalines and eosinophiles always figure high in the count. The skin has the unhealthy look of old parchment, and trophic changes are manifest in the appearance of boils, carbuncles, and bed-sores. Common sensibility is practically lost, and the special senses are all more or less affected. Paralysis is now marked, and the patient is practically bedridden. Urine and fæces are voided unconsciously, and it is with the greatest difficulty the patient can be kept clean, while constant supervision may have to be exercised to prevent his choking over food, owing to impairment of the reflex act of swallowing. In the end of this stage the patient is a helpless, useless lump of what one can scarcely call humanity, and the disease soon terminates either from a congestive seizure, penumonia, accidents, or exhaustion.

Mental Symptoms.—In uncomplicated cases of G.P.I. the characteristic mental condition is one of gradually progressive enfeeblement, terminating sooner or later in dementia. As a rule, however, there is such marked derangement present that it is commonly believed that G.P.I. is invariably associated with insanity, or is in itself a type of insanity. Almost every type of insanity has at one time or another been described as associated with G.P.I., but in the majority of cases these mental symptoms have been intercurrent with and not symptomatic of the nervous condition.

The mental symptoms recognised as typical of the disease, however, are elevation, with grandiose delusions.

In the *first stage* the patient seems endowed with superabundant energy and an overpowering sense of well-being and self-satisfaction. There is slight mental confusion, and impairment of judgment leads to the wildest statements and delusions, and to the patient's launching out into the wildest projects and speculations; consciousness and the power of cognition remain, however, practically unimpaired. Loss of self-control leads to undue irritability and emotionalism, and when combined, as is generally the case, with an impairment of the moral sense, may be the cause of theft and other criminal offences. Memory is untrustworthy, and the power of attention is impaired, leading to incapacity for occupation. Such patients are as a rule garrulous but not incoherent, and the false sense of well-being leads to voluminous writing of poetry or imaginary business letters. Hallucinations are rarely, if ever, present in uncomplicated cases. Sleep occurs at times naturally, but in most cases this function is deranged, while nightmares are common in the earlier stages of this condition, which on the whole corresponds fairly well to the simple elevation of folie circulaire.

As the physical symptoms of the *second stage* become manifest the mental symptoms alter. *Pari passu* with the advancing paresis there is marked mental enfeeblement, the patient is less energetic and restless, and the general intelligence is markedly impaired. The special senses are less acute, and there is therefore less response to external stimuli; delusions, however, similar to those in the first stage, may persist, but they are as a rule less prominent and do not affect the conduct so markedly. The tendency to theft is increased, but the efforts of the patient are misdirected, and large piles of rubbish are accumulated which could be of no use to anybody. The patient becomes listless, careless of his appearance, and easily managed, while the advancing paresis and mental enfeeblement put an end to the volubility and the incessant writing of the first stage.

The mental symptoms of the second pass gradually into those of the *third stage*. The patient becomes more and more demented, gradually losing all human instincts and interests in life until he is practically a mass of flesh only kept alive by the constant care and attention of others. Congestive seizures are extremely common, and as a rule hasten the mental decay, though in one or two cases I have seen a distinct improvement in the mental condition occur after such an attack.

Diagnosis.—This is by no means always an easy question to decide. The conditions most likely to cause us trouble are: chronic alcoholism, cerebellar tumors, epilepsy, disseminated sclerosis, and poisoning by lead, chloral, or cocaine. In such questionable cases the only thing to do is to place the patient under careful observation, for some months perhaps if necessary, note carefully his behaviour and physical and mental condition from time to time, and also the results of treatment.

The results of recent research have placed valuable diagnostic aids at our disposal in this condition. The testing of the blood for Wassermann's reaction gives us valuable indications here, some 80 per cent. at least of cases giving a positive reaction. A spinal puncture and an examination of the resultant cerebro-spinal fluid gives valuable corroborative testimony when doubt arises and an accurate diagnosis is essential. Practically all cases of G.P.I. give a positive reaction with the cerebro-spinal fluid to Wassermann's test. Noguchi also has shown that globulin is markedly increased in the cerebro-spinal fluid of such cases, and half saturation with ammonium sulphate will practically solidify it while having little or no result on normal fluid. The lymphocytes, too, show a marked increase in the cerebro-spinal fluid from patients suffering from this disease, and an examination of it under the microscope thus serves to still further settle the question.

From a medico-legal point of view, too, it is important to remember that cases have occurred where atropine and cocaine have been given, in combination, to simulate general paralysis of the insane and conceal a murder. In the Agra murder case, where Lieutenant Clarke and Mrs. Fulham were tried for the murder of the latter's husband, the point was not definitely brought out owing to both of the accused confessing before the completion of their trial; but there can be little doubt from the reports of the case that it was on these lines the case for the prosecution was based.

Prognosis.—The duration of G.P.I. is extremely variable: one case may die within two months of the onset of the acute symptoms, while others may hang on for ten or even twenty years. As a rule, however, three to four years may be looked on as the average duration of a case. Much, however, depends on the character and cause of the remissions; thus, if a remission be due to an acute intercurrent disease, such as pneumonia or erysipelas, it may be of long duration and lengthen the course of the disease by months or even years. Recovery from this condition is at present unheard of.

Case L.

X. Y. Z., a native Christian, aged 33, was admitted on August 15, 1905. His father was a Hindu faquir who became a Christian convert, and who died many years ago. His mother is an apparently healthy woman, but is of a neurotic, excitable disposition. Has two brothers, who are said to be healthy. He was a very studious youth, of solitary habits, and was very much kept at home as a youth. He graduated as a B.A. of the University, and became a teacher. Shortly after this he married a young schoolgirl, by whom he had two children.

These are reported to be healthy. The couple after marriage lived a secluded life. Both complained of ill-health, and got into the habit of dosing themselves with quantities of patent medicines, and also indulging in port wine. He was twice inoculated for plague, and his friends say that a change was noted in him after this. Two years ago he was dismissed from his employment for falsifying registers, and he had difficulty in obtaining other work. This increased his morbidity, and mental and physical enfeeblement set in about a year prior to his admission. He became irritable and abusive towards his wife, and later careless and stupid. No history of syphilis elicited. On admission his condition was: A young man with a fatuous expression; eyes prominent and staring; smiles foolishly on being spoken to or being taken notice of; pupils pin-hole, apparently equal and irresponsive to either light or accommodation; tongue tremulous; speech thick, slurring, and slow; great difficulty experienced in pronouncing polysyllabic words. Recent memory for time and place very defective. Remote memory is not good, and he has forgotten a great deal of his previous knowledge. He has delusions of exaltation, saying that he is a very great man—he always was very proud of his attainments—and that he has great wealth. His gait is ataxic and his limbs tremulous. He became steadily worse. His habits were filthy, and he passed his excreta in his clothes or in bed. His speech became more blurred and thicker. Intelligence and memory at the end of three months had almost vanished. He could recognise his mother, and clung to her in a childish way. Hæmatomata of both ears developed ten days before he left the asylum, and I have learned he became progressively worse, and died at his home on February 25, nineteen months after the onset of his illness (C. J. R. Milne, *Ind. Med. Gaz.*, 1906).

Case LI.

S. T., aged 50; caste, Brahmin; occupation, pensioner of Military Police. Admitted Agra Asylum August 4, 1912. No family history obtainable. He himself had served his time as a sepoy in the Military Police in Burma. There, from his rambling statements, he had evidently spent all his available time and money with prostitutes, and had had at least one attack of venereal disease. Prior to admission he is reported to have been fighting and annoying people at the "kutcherry" in Fyzabad, and when placed under observation is said to have been "constantly muttering to himself something about Bhagta Bazar in Burma," "the British raj is no longer paramount in India," etc. He had some hesitation in speech at that time, but denied having had syphilis.

On admission, he was found a well-built man in apparently good bodily health, and well nourished. His face was expressionless usually, though at times he had a fatuous, self-satisfied leer. There were fibrillary twitchings of the facial muscles, and marked inco-ordination of the upper extremities, with intention tremors. Knee-jerks were practically normal. Speech was blurred, and the pupillary reflex to light was diminished. Mentally there was a marked degree of dementia with grandiose delusions regarding his wealth and physical powers.

Since admission he has deteriorated rapidly both physically and mentally. His knee-jerks are now markedly increased and his gait ataxic, his speech markedly blurred, and the upper extremities show a greater degree of inco-ordination. In spite of this, however, his former grandiose ideas still persist regarding both his wealth and his physical powers. He is occasionally subject to fits of excitement, and has had one slight congestive seizure since admission. He is now beginning to get puffy, and will probably soon come to an end of his troubles (A. W. Overbeck-Wright).

Treatment.—At present no specific treatment exists for such cases, which are simply treated on general hygienic principles, attention being mainly directed to combating the symptoms and alleviating pain and distress.

The effect of salvarsan on such patients has been, and is still, under investigation. So far as I know the only results yet attained show that salvarsan when injected in the ordinary manner has no effect on the disease—in fact, owing to the anatomical arrangement of the cerebro-spinal blood and lymph supplies it is extremely problematical if it ever reaches the site of the lesion. Research is now being directed to the results of injecting serum, from the patient, after his treatment by salvarsan in the ordinary way, into his own cerebro-spinal canal. So far the results of the few cases published are not very encouraging, but research continues, and it is to be hoped in time some panacea may be found for this evil. Good results have at times been obtained in the early stages of syphilitic nervous manifestations, but in more advanced cases, especially where there are signs of dementia, salvarsan seems to be worse than useless, merely tending to hasten the mental decay. Other antisyphilitic treatment seems similarly to be of but little use, but it should invariably be tried in all cases of this type. My favourite prescription for such patients is liq. hydrarg. perchlor., ♏ xl., and pot. iod., grs. v. to grs. x., thrice daily after meals, but I must confess I have never seen much benefit follow upon its administration.

The question of home treatment is often raised in connection with this disease, and, though possible in some cases, I cannot say I ever approve of it, especially in the early stages, for such patients are, at first at least, capable of begetting offspring, and it is most undesirable, both for the possible progeny and for the general public, that this should occur. I, therefore, strongly recommend asylum treatment for all cases in the early stages of the disease, or, when the patient can afford it, removal to some quiet place—in the hills, if possible—where he can have good attendants to care for him and will be away from his family as much as possible. In the later stages, quiet, demented cases can be quite suitably treated at home; but restless, excitable patients are much better in an asylum.

The diet should be stimulating and fattening, and alcohol should be entirely withdrawn. Tobacco may be allowed in the earlier stages, but should be withheld as the disease progresses, as it is then very liable to cause nausea and syncope. Constipation should be constantly looked for, and laxatives given when occasion arises. Restlessness and excitement, if acute, call for the use of sedatives, and sulphonal, grs. x., pot. brom., grs. xx., morning and evening will be found very serviceable in such cases. Sleeplessness should be treated with hot baths, hot draughts of milk at bedtime, hot bottles applied to the feet, etc., before hypnotics are resorted to, as these often suffice to give a quiet restful night, and by their means we can avoid having recourse to drugs.

CHAPTER XXII

GROUP D: STATES OF MENTAL ENFEEBLEMENT

Idiocy and Imbecility

(I. *Primary, Idiocy and Imbecility.* II. *Idiocy,* syn. *Congenital Imbecility.*)

SUCH cases comprise the "dementia naturalis" of lawyers, and are defined by Ireland as follows:

"Idiocy is a mental deficiency or extreme stupidity, depending upon malnutrition or disease of the nervous centres, occurring either before birth or before the evolution of the mental faculties in childhood. Imbecility is generally used to denote a less decided degree of mental incapacity."

Ætiology.—The ætiology of these two conditions can be treated of under two heads: (1) *Pre-natal*; (2) *Post-natal.*

1. *Pre-natal Causes.*—A neurotic inheritance exists in a very large percentage of such cases, insanity, epilepsy, alcoholism, and syphilis being commonly present in one or both parents.

Phthisis or other wasting diseases in the parents may be the determining factors of idiocy in the progeny. Syphilis, if contracted by the parents several years before the birth of the child, is not so liable to cause imbecility; but if the father be suffering from syphilis at the time of the conception, or the mother during her pregnancy, then the outlook is much more serious.

The influence of alcoholism as an ætiological factor here has given rise to much controversy, but, on considering the number of children who, though not actual imbeciles, still show more or less marked stigmata of degeneracy, one can but conclude that alcoholism is undoubtedly potential as a factor in the production of this disease, both directly as well as indirectly, by lowering the natural resistance of the organism and rendering it more liable to be affected by other causes.

Consanguinity has often been brought forward as a strong factor in the production of this condition, the laity especially being convinced of this. As a matter of fact, consanguinity only acts by emphasising and exaggerating weak points in the mental and physical characters of the parents, any failing common to both parents being more pronounced in the offspring, and more liable to be handed down through succeeding generations.

The age of the parents has an undoubted effect, however, for not only are the offspring of very youthful and very aged parents liable to show signs of physical and mental deterioration, but the offspring of parents of unsuitable ages, where a large series of years intervene between husband and wife, are also liable to be similarly affected.

During gestation any severe shock or accident, especially if the woman be of a neurotic type, may suffice to affect the fœtus *in utero* and produce an idiot; and a similar result may occur if the mother during pregnancy contract any acute specific disease.

Prolonged labour causing protracted pressure on the cranium is an undoubted cause of imbecility, especially among first-born children, and accounts in a measure for the predominance of male over female idiots, as male infants are commonly larger than female. Injuries by instruments during parturition are similarly responsible for a certain percentage of cases.

2. *Post-natal Causes.*—Infantile convulsions, no matter how they originate, are responsible for a very large number of cases of weakmindedness, not only from the damage and deterioration they produce in the nervous tissues, but also as they tend to arrest further development, and the child subsequently remains mentally enfeebled.

Gross diseases and traumata of the brain and meninges are responsible undoubtedly for a small number of such cases, while the influence of the acute specific fevers, as scarlet fever, whooping cough, diphtheria, etc., is still more marked and widespread.

Lastly, in some cases imbecility may be largely due to careless upbringing and bad home influences and education.

Thus the conditions likely to cause imbecility and idiocy are numerous and varied, and as a rule it is impossible to say that any one factor alone is responsible for this state, as two or three are generally acting in combination and forming, as it were, a vicious circle.

To sum up the matter, therefore, we may say, generally, that imbecility is due to anything which arrests cerebral development and the evolution of the complex nervous elements and the associated fibres which connect these centres with one another.

Cause and effect must be carefully distinguished when we consider such conditions; thus at one time in microcephalic idiots the cause was considered to be a premature ossification of the cranial sutures, whereas now observation has shown us that the primary condition is a failure in the cerebral development, which allows the premature ossification to occur.

Symptoms.—Various classifications of idiocy and imbecility have from time to time been promulgated; thus Ireland classifies the condition into various types according to the ætiological factors causing the arrest of development, whilst others classify them according to the severity of the symptoms and the extent to which mental development has proceeded. In the former the difference is mainly ætiological, and in the latter merely one of degree, and there is practically no difference between the symptoms of any two types, so that I propose, firstly, to consider the symptoms broadly and as one class. In doing so I would warn my readers that various grades of intensity in the symptoms are met with every day—from the idiot, whose mind is practically a blank, and who is incapable of learning, to the individual who, though simpleminded, has yet acquired some elements of education, and may even be an adept at carving or some other mechanical occupation. Having done this, then, a few lines will suffice to complete the various ætiological and other types.

Physical Symptoms.—The physical symptoms of idiocy and imbecility are mainly what are known as stigmata of degeneration, and include abnormalities and deformities in practically every region of the body. The stature is frequently below the average in size, and the long bones unduly curved. The skull may be unduly large, or abnormally small and misshapen, or asymmetrical. Thus the forehead may be receding, and give a pointed appearance to the head; or a non-development of the occipital region may cause the cranium to appear flattened. Premature ossification of the sutures may occur from arrested cerebral development, or the converse may occur, as in hydrocephalic cases.

The palate is as a rule high, narrow, and V-shaped; and a receding lower jaw is such a common concomitant that even the laity on seeing a man with such a feature are apt to exclaim: "What an idiot he looks!"

The teeth are generally badly formed, and readily decay, while they are frequently crowded together, and rarely show the complete complement.

The orbits may be either too close together or too widely apart, and at times approximate to the Mongolian type, while the pupils may be oval in shape. Strabismus and other visual defects are common.

The ears may be abnormally situated, or the pinna badly formed, or the rim, the helix, and other ridges and fossæ in the cartilage deformed or wanting altogether.

Congenital valvular deficiency is very common in the hearts of such cases, while as a rule the circulation is feeble and the fingers and toes cyanosed.

The tonsils are frequently hypertrophied in such cases, and adenoids are extremely common. Food is generally bolted without proper mastication, and causes dyspepsia. Constipation, due to altered or deficient intestinal secretion, is often seen; but at times obstinate diarrhœa may prove a source of endless worry. Hence nutrition in these cases is usually bad, and, in conjunction with the shallow respiration so common in the imbecile, renders them especially prone to phthisis and other pulmonary troubles.

The skin is often coarse, and the subcutaneous tissues thickened. The hair is thin and brittle, frequently absent from the faces of male idiots, but often present to an excessive extent on the faces of females. Pubic hair is commonly scanty or absent in both sexes. The nails are brittle and badly formed.

Various malformations of the genital organs are met with in such cases, and in females menstruation occurs very late or may be entirely absent. Sexual instinct is at times in abeyance, but more frequently it is abnormally strong, and leads to masturbation and other vicious practices.

Sensation is dulled, and from this and sluggish mentalisation the superficial and organic reflexes are affected, saliva dribbling from the mouth, owing to the impairment of the pharyngeal reflex, while the acts of micturition and defæcation are absolutely uncontrolled, and such patients are as a rule very dirty.

Motor phenomena are numerous and interesting. In infancy the microkinetic or spontaneous uncontrolled movements seen in healthy babes are absent, and the child is either abnormally quiet and motionless, or else goes through more automatic regular movements than the spontaneous ones performed in health. The voluntary movements are slow and badly performed, co-ordination is generally markedly deficient, and such children are very late in learning to walk, while more marked cases never learn to dress themselves. Muscular debility and paralysis of every kind is very common in these cases, and may render standing or walking impossible, while tremors may be present, either localised to one or other extremity or implicating the whole body.

Speech is markedly impaired in all cases of any intensity, and even in the milder forms is invariably very late in developing. This impairment is due in the vast majority of cases to defective cerebration, though in a certain number it is undoubtedly due to defects in the respiratory or laryngeal mechanism, and as a rule these latter cases are much more easily instructed and managed. Stammering is common among imbeciles; but deaf mutes are little, if any, more numerous than they are among the general population.

The features are as a rule coarse, out of proportion, and the head misshapen, while the expression in the majority is most degraded. Many are continually grimacing and laughing; others, again, look sullen and morose; while a vacant, senseless expression is found in some cases. Attitudes and postures are invariably awkward and clumsy, while the gait is waddling and the whole personality devoid of grace.

Many of such cases seem to be in a condition of continual torpor and drowsiness, spending practically the whole of their time in sleepy inactivity; in others, however, the converse is to be seen, a condition of restless activity prevailing, and the hours passed in sleep being few. Dreams and night terrors are very common among imbecile children.

Mental Symptoms.—The power of memory varies greatly in idiocy and imbecility, but even in the most intellectual of such cases there is invariably seen deficiency in this faculty. The causes of this are manifold; thus, as a rule such patients have a difficulty in associating ideas, and memory largely depends upon this. Lack of the power of concentrating the attention, too, is common among such cases, and has an undoubted effect on the memory; but probably the lack of language and "word ideas" is chiefly responsible for this condition in the majority of imbeciles. In some of the feebleminded, however, a highly specialised memory is present, which is, however, practically useless, as it seems to be developed at the expense of all other faculties.

Attention is one of the faculties of later development in the healthy child, and in the weakminded mental development is usually arrested before this faculty is fully acquired. Even passive or spontaneous attention, the first and most primeval form, on which we rely as a safeguard against sudden dangers, may be absent in some idiots, and as a result their powers of self-preservation are at a minimum. Inattention may be due either to defective cerebration, or to defective sense organs or their afferent fibres interfering with the strength of the stimuli which reach the brain. In some cases the stimulation of one sense organ may not suffice to attract the attention, but if the stimuli are such that they can act on two or more of the senses at once then attention is attracted, and this is specially the case when the visual sense is one of those acted upon.

Deficiency or perversion of one or all of the special senses is one of the common characteristics of idiots, and accounts not only for the difficulty experienced in training such individuals, but also is very largely responsible for the failure of mental development, as it is by sensation that knowledge is first acquired.

Idiots are as a class wholly devoid of emotion or sentiment, and it is only in the highest types of such cases that any great depth of feeling is developed. The idiot, in fact, responds merely to physical and not to moral pain, and as a rule is incapable of cherishing any feeling for a long time, the enemy of to-day being the friend of to-morrow, and *vice versa.* I know, however, of one or two cases where the reverse has been the case, and extraordinary love or hatred has been shown by the patient for some particular person, and with absolutely unselfish motives, too.

Religious feeling is absent in practically all idiots, whose thoughts are wrapped up in the present with no comprehension of a future. Morals, too, are markedly deficient in such persons; they lie and steal openly, and apparently without knowing they are doing wrong, and are as a rule most inquisitive, while many have an overweening idea of their importance which renders them easy dupes of unprincipled persons. A few of the higher imbeciles are extremely vain, and dress outrageously and extravagantly; but, as a class, the tendency is to marked carelessness of the personal appearance and clothing. The lower instincts, being free from central inhibitory control, run riot and lead to gross dissipations, and brutal cruelty at times to children and animals, and many idiots are extremely passionate and reckless, though others, again, are very docile, and, learning what pleases those in charge of them, always endeavour to please them.

The behaviour and conduct of the weakminded vary greatly. In the lowest types we meet with helpless individuals unable to feed or clothe themselves, who can take no interest in anything, can do nothing, and are dependent on those around them for their very existence. From this lowest level there are varying grades, shading impalpably into each other, from those unable to attend to the lowest functions of the body to those whose sole defect seems an inability to acquire knowledge of the social and moral laws of the community.

As regards the capacity for occupation and earning a livelihood, this, as can be readily imagined, is most variable. The lowest class of idiot is quite unteachable, and in fact seems at times to delight in destroying things, sometimes from sheer love of destruction, at other times aimlessly, and more for the sake of distraction and to pass the time. Next to these come those who are late in acquiring knowledge, and are incapable of any but the simplest occupation, but are yet able to maintain existence in their own particular line. In the higher types we meet with the "one-sided genius," the "wonderful infant musician," the "mathematical wonder," etc., which are all of this type—the one talent seeming to be developed at the expense of all other mental powers.

The great difficulty in teaching imbeciles is their inability to concentrate their attention, but once a trade or craft is learnt they generally prove excellent workmen, as they pursue their calling in an automatic sort of way, and are not easily led away from it.

The judgment, owing to lack of the power of observation, want of memory, deficient powers of attention, and absence of emotionalism, is deficient in all imbeciles to a greater or less extent.

Types of Idiocy.—The types of idiocy usually described are: (1) *Genetous*; (2) *Mongolian*; (3) *Microcephalic*; (4) *Hydrocephalic*; (5) *Hypertrophic*; (6) *Eclampsic*; (7) *Epileptic*;

(8) *Paralytic*; (9) *Traumatic*; (10) *Inflammatory, or post-febrile*; (11) *Syphilitic*; (12) *Cretinoid*; (13) *Idiocy from deprivation of the senses*. In India practically all these types are recognisable, and I have met with examples of them all except the cretinoid, but even it is seen at times, though apparently less commonly than in Europe, as Major Ewens, I.M.S., notes in his book on insanity that it occasionally is met with in India. Another class, however, requires mention in Indian psychiatry, and that is the individuals known as "Shah Daula's mice," for, though corresponding closely perhaps to the microcephalic type, yet there are certain differences which set them apart as a separate type and a distinct entity in themselves.

1. **Genetous Idiocy.**—This is the term applied by Ireland to congenital idiots, for whose mental deficiency no cause, beyond perhaps hereditary defect, can be assigned. Deformities of head and limbs are by no means common in this class, though many are stunted in growth. The child as a rule has a dull, degraded expression, the ears are large and defective, the palate is high and narrow, and the teeth bad; while the gait is clumsy and ungraceful. Rickets and scrofula are frequent concomitants of this condition. In many of these cases if the circulation and nourishment be good, sensibility not markedly impaired, and the power of attention present, there is a fair hope of educating the child to a certain extent and training him to some simple trade or occupation.

2. **Mongolian Idiocy.**—This is practically a subdivision of genetous idiocy, and draws its name from the physiognomy of such cases and the great resemblance they bear to the Chinese. The head is small and rounded, the features broad, and the eyes placed slantingly in the face. The figure is dwarfed and stunted, and the hands and feet broad and clumsy. Organic disease of the heart is very common among such cases, and the circulation in all is feeble. Such individuals are usually good-tempered and imitative, but have very little intellect, and there is practically no hope of training them to any trade or occupation however simple it may be.

3. **Microcephalic Idiocy.**—In these cases the head is always unduly small, and it may be taken as an axiom that where the cranial circumference is less than seventeen inches it is a sure indication of idiocy, though the condition is due more to arrested brain development than to cranial malformation. In this class

the head is narrow and oxycephalic in shape, and the subjects are usually unduly active and restless, though, strange to say, they are as a rule late in learning to walk. The large majority are very quarrelsome and aggressive, and are very deficient in mental capability and in the power of attention, so that it is practically impossible to educate them to even the simplest occupation. Morals and the sense of propriety are usually conspicuous by their absence in such cases.

CASE LII.

B., aged 17; caste, Hindu. Admitted into Lucknow Asylum in December, 1904; transferred to Agra Asylum in 1906.

No history obtainable.

A microcephalic imbecile, badly nourished, and of very poor physique. Circumference of head 17½ inches. Expression vacant and fatuous. Pulse slow, and blood-pressure low. Body and extremities cold and clammy. He can say a few words and understand a few simple sentences. Is quiet and good-tempered, and apparently quite happy and contented. When first admitted he was very dirty in his habits, defæcating and urinating in his clothes; but he has now been educated out of this, and taught to be of some use in carrying on the work of the section. He has epileptic fits every one and a half to two months, but not of a severe type (A. W. Overbeck-Wright).

4. **Hydrocephalic Idiocy.**—This must be distinguished carefully from the hypertrophic variety, with which it is very liable to be confused; but the shape of the head differs in certain particulars, and enables one to make certain of the diagnosis. It must be always remembered, however, that a large head does not always connote hydrocephalus, and that many normal children have abnormally large heads. I know, indeed, of a case where a father, who was himself a medical man, for some months underwent all the horror of believing his only child a hydrocephalic imbecile, and the grandfather too, also a medical man, when he saw the child on his arrival in England, experienced a similar shock. The condition was, fortunately, wholly different, and the child has developed into a bright, intelligent boy, without a single moral or intellectual taint.

As a rule the hydrocephalic head is rounded in shape, the widest diameter, if any, being situated about the temples, and the fontanelles are raised, whereas in rickets the antero-posterior diameter is the longest and the fontanelles are depressed. Hydrocephalus may cause death in early infancy, a few cases recover, but in the large majority the child hangs on a hopeless idiot, and usually blind or deaf, or both, from the intracranial pressure. Such cases are generally good-tempered and friendly, and a certain number may be educated to a slight extent, but the prognosis is practically hopeless as regards teaching the man occupation.

5. **Hypertrophic Idiocy.**—This is due to an abnormal development of the white matter of the cerebrum. The head is as a rule square, or elongated antero-posteriorly, the greatest width being above the superciliary ridges. The head never attains the size of a hydrocephalic head. The condition is very rare in India, and usually develops in early life. Individuals affected thus suffer from frequent headaches, are slow in their movements, and cannot learn readily. They can, however, be educated to a certain point, and many in time are capable of supporting themselves by some simple occupation.

6. **Eclampsic Idiocy.**—Here the condition is due to infantile convulsions, arising from teething or some other stress. Such cases are usually excitable and passionate, and, though they may seem bright and intelligent enough, owing to their abnormal restlessness and lack of power in concentrating the attention, it is practically impossible to educate them. The prognosis depends largely on the extent and severity of the convulsions, and where these have been fairly mild some small hope may be given to the parents. Such cases are as a rule devoid of morals, and their sense of propriety is at an extremely low ebb.

7. **Epileptic Idiocy.**—Epilepsy invariably tends to produce weakmindedness, either in early life by arresting evolution, or in later life by causing a process of dissolution. The fits may appear at any age, but in the majority of cases of epileptic idiocy they occur about the time of teething. Shuttleworth and Fletcher Beach divide such cases into three classes: (*a*) Bright, well-made children, who progress at school and take an interest in their work, whether educational or industrial. (*b*) Children who are also well-informed, but are listless, though they can talk and take an interest in what is going on around them. These cases as a rule progress well for a time, and then a succession of fits comes on and they become dazed and stupid, losing much of what they have already learnt. (*c*) Cases which on account of the frequency of fits make little or no progress with their education.

The faces of such children are commonly dull and more animal in type, and they approximate to the lower grades of idiocy. Such cases as a rule are passionate and violently impulsive, and require careful supervision to prevent their harming their playmates. They form by far the largest class of imbeciles in Indian asylums, and though the prognosis varies somewhat with the frequency and intensity of the seizures, it is never by any means hopeful.

Case LIII.

J., aged 9; caste, Rajput. Admitted into Agra Asylum on July 27, 1911.

All that could be learned about him was that he was an orphan, that the scars and injuries disfiguring him had been caused by falls during fits, and that he had attempted to throw himself down a well.

On admission he is noted as a "miserable-looking lad; many scars of falls on his face; external squint of right eye; necrosis of lower jaw; lame of left leg; can speak, but does not reply to questions. Fits daily."

In November, 1911, he was a wretched little mortal, having fits ten to fifteen times daily, and spending his time in between them crying his heart out. He never spoke, apparently understood nothing, and was filthy in his habits. Under a chloride-free diet and small doses of potassium bromide he improved rapidly, both physically and mentally. He has got right facial paralysis, and his right arm and left leg are paralysed, but he is a happy little fellow now in spite of this and his horrible scarring. He has quite fair powers of comprehension, cognition, and memory. His vocabulary is wonderful considering his state on admission, and he chatters away to everyone around him, and is a great pet with the rest of the patients (A. W. Overbeck-Wright).

8. **Paralytic Idiocy.**—In this type of case the damage to the brain may be either pre-natal or post-natal. The paralysis is as a rule one-sided, and the arms are generally more affected than the legs, the muscles being in a condition of spastic rigidity. I have, however, seen cases—indeed, one is at present under my care—where both arms and legs are affected and the patient is absolutely helpless. In the majority of such patients there is great impairment of the mental faculties, and education is impossible, but in a certain number of the milder cases a small amount of education may be possible.

9. **Traumatic Idiocy.**—This form may be due to protracted labour in a woman with an abnormally small pelvis, to injury caused by instruments during labour, or to a blow or fall on the

head after birth. The degree of mental incapacity is proportional as a rule to the amount of damage done to the brain, but at times an apparently slight injury may be followed by very severe symptoms. Cases where the injury occurs during birth are usually the most pronounced and incapable of being educated, while those in whom the injury occurs after birth may be physically strong, and even learn how to read and write, but retain the mind of a child throughout their whole life, and are only fit for the simplest occupations.

10. **Inflammatory Idiocy.**—This occurs as a sequel to the acute specific fevers, which are liable to set up inflammation of the brain and its membranes. The amount of mental deficiency is directly proportional to the amount of damage done to the cerebral tissues, and many cases improve greatly under careful training. Where, however, much damage has been done to the brain the child remains degraded, irritable, and uncontrollable, and cannot be taught.

11. **Syphilitic Idiocy.**—Hereditary syphilis is a very common cause of idiocy. As a rule the mental symptoms develop late, the child at first merely showing the physical symptoms common to such a condition and otherwise developing normally until about eight or ten years of age, when convulsive seizures supervene, mental development is arrested, and a definite deterioration ensues (*vide* Chapter VII.).

12. **Cretinoid Idiocy.**—This type of idiocy is occasionally met with in the hills and villages, where goitre and other affections of the thyroid gland are common. The infant appears at first normal, but as development proceeds physical abnormalities and mental deficiencies become apparent. Growth is retarded as a rule, and the figure becomes squat and dwarfish, with short thick limbs and slow clumsy movements. The skin is dry and harsh, the eyelids swollen, and the lips and tongue thickened. Dentition is delayed, and the teeth are badly placed and readily decay. The voice is harsh, and speech slow and limited as regards the vocabulary. The abdomen is flabby and protuberant from changes in the subcutaneous tissues, and the sexual organs as a rule are small and ill-developed. The circulation is feeble, and such cases constantly complain of being cold. These patients are usually good-tempered and affectionate, but their mental capacity is of the poorest, and they can be taught only by the exercise of much perseverance and patience.

Under thyroid preparations a marked improvement occurs in most cases, but the patient must continue the treatment throughout his life or he will relapse into his former condition. During the administration of the thyroid preparations careful supervision must be exercised, as in some cases rapid loss of weight ensues, while in others the temperature rises rapidly, there is great increase of the pulse-rate, and severe diarrhœa may terminate in a collapse.

13. **Idiocy from Deprivation of the Senses.**—To produce this condition an absence of two at least of the more important senses, such as sight and hearing, is essential. It is always possible to teach such children, and in Britain, where there are special institutions for such sufferers, remarkably good results are obtained. In India, however, without such institutions, and few, if any, people with the proper training and knowledge for educating such patients, the task is practically a hopeless one, and the prognosis in such cases is very far from hopeful.

14. **"Shah Daula's Mice."**—As cretinism is endemic in some villages in Switzerland, so we have in the Punjab a comparatively large number of microcephalic imbeciles of practically uniform type, and commonly known as "Shah Daula's mice." The term "mice" is applied to them owing to the conformation of the cranium, which, with the flattened skulls and prominent ears, gives them a certain amount of resemblance to these animals, and the rest of the name is obtained from the tomb or shrine of a saint of that name in Gujrat under whose protection they are supposed to be.

Until late years the priests in charge of this shrine used to hiré them out to faquirs and yogis, who took them round the country begging; but this has now practically been put a stop to owing to the brutal ill-treatment which they met with as a rule at the hands of their masters. They are all well under average stature, but except for the microcephalic head and outstanding ears show no marked deformity otherwise. A large percentage of them appear, however, to be deaf and dumb, and strabismus is common among them, indicating probably some error in refraction or other visual defect. They are capable of being taught simple employments, and are by no means immodest or indecent, and as a rule show none of the revolting tendencies or depraved appetities so commonly seen among other types of imbeciles. Nothing is known as to how they originate, in most cases no hereditary influence being traceable, and a *chuha* may often be found with absolutely normal parents and three or four healthy brothers and sisters. They apparently are almost, if not quite, all sprung from the lowest classes. It is possible they are due to the custom, prevalent in those parts, of childless women going to pray and vow a dedication to the shrine if their prayers are heard and they are blessed with a child. Not that I fancy mental influence has anything to do with it; but as the women stay there for several days, it is quite possible that the guardians of the shrine every now and then have recourse to one of the male microcephalics to ensure that some of the childless women who spend the night at the shrine may reproduce a *chuha*, and so maintain the reputation of the tomb.

It is a common belief that this condition is due to pressure exerted in infancy by means of iron caps, but there is no confirmative evidence of this so far as I know, any post-mortems which have been done showing apparently normal bones, except for the contractions in every diameter of the skull.

Treatment.—The treatment of idiocy covers a wide field, as it includes not only the treatment of the various factors which have caused the arrest of development, but also the physical, mental, and moral training of the child.

All possible causes of this condition must be carefully looked for and steps taken for their proper care and treatment. Nutrition is of the utmost importance in all such cases, and having arranged for the treatment of the cause our next care must be the diet. The food should be simple and largely farinaceous, meat being avoided as much as possible. Many idiots are given to over-eating and bolting their food in masses without properly masticating it, and such cases should have their meals supervised by a nurse, or some responsible person, to prevent choking or the gastric derangements which will otherwise inevitably occur. The clothing of such cases is also a matter requiring attention, for many are acutely sensitive to cold. It should be light but warm, and in cases given to masturbation or exposing their persons, garments like pyjamas, made without any opening in front, and of stout material, are often most useful.

In many cases the teaching of cleanliness is a most difficult matter, and it may be months before the child gives any sign when he wants to attend to the calls of nature. In older cases, bathing in cold water, or withdrawing some luxury whenever he offends thus, has often a wonderful effect in stimulating the memory. Personal ablutions and dressing are also matters requiring instruction. The former is best done by carrying out the ablutions at regular fixed times, someone being always at hand to see that the cleaning is properly performed; dressing, however, is a much more difficult performance, and quite beyond the powers of many idiots.

Swedish drill, etc., are of great use in developing the patient both physically and mentally, but such exercises should always be carefully regulated and supervised so as to avoid unduly fatiguing the patient.

Mental training must in these cases be begun gradually, and our first aim should be to develop the acuteness of the various senses as far as possible, and to strengthen the power of attention. Sight can be developed by using coloured balls and boxes, and making him put the balls into similarly coloured boxes, or matching coloured bricks or wools, etc. Hearing can be rendered more acute by means of musical notes, bells, etc. Touch is a sense requiring careful attention; it should be begun, in the first place, by coarse movements, such as putting balls or nine-pins into sockets; then smoothness and roughness can be explained by velvet and a file; and, similarly, sharp and blunt, hot and cold things can be explained to the patient. A most important lesson, and one that cannot be inculcated too early, is that fire burns, and proper care given to expounding this may avert serious accidents in later life. Finer movements may be taught as the child progresses by making him string small beads, or do a little simple, careful work. The senses of taste and smell are less important, but should be developed by means of various scents and solutions.

Attention is at times most difficult to attract, and much trouble is at times necessary before the child seems to gain the slightest control over it. Our efforts should invariably be directed to this object at first, for until some power is acquired in this direction practically nothing can be done. Brightly coloured or glistening articles, loud sounds, heat and cold, and, failing these, even mild electrical shocks, may all be resorted to that we may achieve this object.

Learning to walk is always a difficult task for the weak-minded, and the difficulty is due to various causes. In some the capacity to understand or to imitate may be wanting, while in others the incapacity may be due to some nervous or muscular defect. Thus, it is a matter of importance to ascertain in each case where the difficulty lies. Many and varied are the mechanisms evolved for the purpose of teaching such cases to walk, the most useful of which are specially constructed swings, or circular supports on wheels. Where muscular weakness is one of the obstacles to be overcome massage is a valuable aid in the treatment.

Learning to speak is a matter calling for great care and patience on the part of the teacher of such patients, and usually the children can understand what is said to them long before they seem to acquire the power of expressing themselves, probably because of a lack of ideas and thoughts to express. In all such cases the respiratory apparatus should be carefully tested, and all defects, such as adenoids and enlarged tonsils, rectified and removed as far as possible. Thereafter the child should be put through regular breathing exercises and carefully trained to distinguish sounds. The labial and lingual sounds and movements should next be demonstrated to the child, who should be made to imitate them from the teacher. In this way the child gradually extends his vocabulary, advancing by degrees from monosyllables to words of two or three syllables, until he can pronounce a complete sentence and express himself fairly clearly. The extent of the vocabulary that can be learnt varies greatly in the different types of idiocy, and as a rule it can be accepted as an axiom that if a child does not learn to speak before the age of six or seven his vocabulary will always be of the smallest.

Writing is a much more difficult accomplishment to acquire than speaking, on account of its greater complexity, and is far beyond the powers of the majority of idiots. Copying or even tracing of lines or figures is the best means available, but it must be remembered that an idiot may be able to write a word or even a series of words purely mechanically and without the slightest comprehension of the significance of his action.

Industrial education is a matter of great importance in the training of such individuals, and it is in this respect we are so lamentably handicapped in India by a complete absence of special asylums for the poorer patients of this class, and of kindergartens for those higher in the social scale and able to pay for their training. Many of these children have a wonderful aptitude for some special work, such as carving, and yet are wholly unfit for any other occupation, no matter how simple. As a rule, however, farming or agriculture is the work for which such persons are best suited, and with careful supervision most excellent results may be obtained in this line.

Moral training is perhaps the most difficult, though at the same time the most important, and no one who is not endowed with unlimited patience should attempt the post of teacher to an imbecile. Such children are abnormally apprehensive and timid, and one's sole hope of success is by gaining their affection, for by this alone have we any hold over them, corporal punishment being, in the majority of cases, not only useless but actually harmful. Good behaviour should be rewarded from time to time with little luxuries or rewards, and misconduct similarly punished by a withdrawal of these, but punishment should go no farther. A thing to be remembered too in such cases is the lack of the sense of morality which is practically invariably present, and careful supervision must always be exercised in order to avert some possibly serious catastrophe.

Many such cases are full of professions and promises, and mean them too at the time, but barely are the words uttered than they are forgotten, and the child is quite likely to transgress again, quite innocently, even in the presence of his teacher.

One can thus readily imagine what an uphill task the training of such a child is, and how much patience and perseverance is required to tackle it. Through it all, however, one has the knowledge that even the most hopeless cases may eventually learn something, and if this can be accomplished the greatest reward one can have is to hear the child talking, perhaps calling to one in terms of affection, and to realise that one has been instrumental in removing part at least of the dark shadow from the little sufferer.

Secondary Dementia.

(I. *Secondary Dementia*. II. *Dementia*.)

Dementia, or secondary dementia, is used, in contradistinction to primary dementia, amentia, or idiocy, to denote a condition of weakmindedness due, not to arrested development, but to progressive deterioration resulting either from gross brain disease or from degeneration of the nervous elements of the brain. A former state of higher intellectual power is therefore denoted by the term, and, provided life lasts long enough, it may be looked on as the final mental condition of us all.

The word "dementia" has been applied by various authors to many conditions, with a complete disregard of the possible duration of such conditions, and whether they were permanent or merely temporary in character. Such a use of the word is not only unscientific, but most confusing, and it is really more accurate and simpler in every way to look upon it as a distinct and separate entity, not as a disease in itself, but as merely the last and permanent mental state towards which so many of the acute insanities tend. Dementia is best classed under two heads: (1) *Secondary Dementia*; (2) *Organic Dementia*.

1. **Secondary Dementia** may be described as a state of mental enfeeblement, which may ensue after an attack of any of the acute insanities, and which has certain definite symptoms of its own, though these may be affected to a certain extent by the persistence of some of the characteristic features of the original mental disorder. The depth of mental enfeeblement may vary widely, from mere inattention and loss of the power of concentrated thought to a condition of profound degradation.

Ætiology.—A neurotic heredity is usually traceable in all such cases, and they are usually found most typically after those types of insanity which are most prone to occur in early adult life and in which a neurotic heredity is a common, if not a constant, factor. Alcoholism and epilepsy are especially liable to terminate thus.

Symptoms—*Physical.*—As a rule, when an acute attack of insanity is passing into dementia there is a marked improvement in the physical condition without any similar change in the mental symptoms, and when this condition occurs one should never be led astray and give rise to false hopes in the minds of the relatives, who are only too apt to be misled by it themselves. It should be explained to them carefully and tactfully that the mental prognosis is now even less hopeful than before the physical improvement, and they should gradually be brought to an understanding of the true state of affairs. As the condition advances appetite and sleep improve, and often the weight increases enormously, though if excitement and restlessness persist both the powers of nutrition and sleep remain deranged. Some dements, however, remain in a continual state of ill-health. Their circulation is feeble and their extremities cyanosed and cold. In some the appetite is voracious, but nutrition is deranged and weight is in consequence lost rather than gained, whilst in others a degraded appetite leads to the eating of mud, sticks, leaves, stones, and every kind of rubbish. The features of such cases are coarse and degraded, and the gait slow, clumsy, and shambling. All finer co-ordination is lost, and movements are in consequence slow and clumsy.

In short, the patient is mentally and physically degenerate, he looks degraded, his thoughts and actions are of a lower type than formerly, his appetites are perverted, his sensations dulled, and his lower instincts, being no longer under control, run riot, and what may have formerly been an intelligent, useful member of society becomes a moral and intellectual wreck and a heavy charge upon his relatives or the State.

Mental.—The mental symptoms of dementia vary greatly in intensity. In all such cases there is diminished self-control, and the patients are usually irritable and easily aroused; but a little tact quickly appeases their rage and restores them to good humour again. Such patients are very apt to lose their powers of cognition and of adapting themselves to circumstances, and thus are at a loss to support themselves in life, though in an institution such as an asylum, where life is regular and work properly supervised, such a man may prove most useful, working automatically almost day after day, apparently quite happy in his occupation, and never thinking of asking for a holiday. Advanced cases are, however, practically unfit for working, and if they do find anything to keep them busy, it is as a rule in the destructive rather than the constructive line.

The feelings and emotions are always affected in cases of dementia, subject-consciousness and object-consciousness both being diminished, and provided such cases are comfortable for the time being they have no thought of anything else; the deaths of friends and relatives bring forth not the slightest sign of grief; they may even be threatened with hanging next day and the only result is a grin or a demand for some little luxury. At times such cases may be most importunate in their demands to be sent home, but such a phase is but momentary, and a passing butterfly or the stub of a cigarette is quite sufficient to drive the idea out of their heads and for months one may never hear of it again. In cases the sequel to acute attacks of mania maniacal outbursts may occasionally occur; while others, again.

have an air of arrogance and decorate themselves most fantastically.

Homicidal and suicidal acts may occur from time to time in such cases, especially the former, and as a rule are due to sudden impulses, the patient being incapable of elaborating any definite plan of attack, or indeed of cherishing any ill-will for any length of time.

CASE LIV.

Bye, or Bhai, admitted on December 21, 1866, from Baellergurqe, E. Bengal. Neither his name nor his antecedents were known, and nothing has since been ascertained regarding him. Was then in a state of noisy aggressive mania, which became chronic, and which gradually led to his present state of dementia, in which he has remained for fifteen years. A childish vagabond with a very defective memory, and devoid of intelligence. At times irritable if interfered with. Has a voracious appetite, and is very indifferent to clothing (C. J. R. Milne, 1908).

Treatment.—With careful supervision and hygienic surroundings marked improvement may occur in many of these cases. It must be remembered that the minds of such persons approximate closely to that of a child, and much may be done to *educate* them, not only to cleanliness and a sense of morality and common decency, but even to some useful occupation. Thus at the present time most of the gardening, etc., of asylums is done by dements who are supervised by the warder staff.

2. **Organic Dementia.**—This is the term applied to mental enfeeblement arising from some gross lesion of the brain. The lesion may be diffuse or localised, and the intensity of the mental symptoms is due as much to the site of the lesion as to its extent. Mental symptoms are one of the many concomitants of such conditions, and are fairly late in developing, being as a rule preceded by various motor manifestations.

Where the lesions are diffuse, as in chronic meningo-encephalitis, a progressive mental deterioration is the rule, with marked loss of memory and derangements of speech. Such patients are generally irritable and liable to outbursts of violent maniacal excitement, while convulsive seizures may occur. The pulse in such cases is rapid and irregular, and arterial tension low, and many of these patients die from syncope or exhaustion.

Where the lesion is localised, as in cerebral tumours, hæmorrhages, embolisms, abscesses, etc., the later stages of the condition are always marked by more or less pronounced mental changes, and at times mental symptoms may be an early and important manifestation of the disease. In chronic cases, where the tumour growth is slow, the most common condition is one of gradually increasing lethargy and somnolence. Such cases think and speak slowly and with difficulty, their movements are slow and awkward, they take no interest in their surroundings, and have apparently no interest in life, and certainly seldom seem to have any wants or desires.

In cases of acute onset, as in hæmorrhage or embolism, where sudden alteration in the intracranial pressure occurs, the mental symptoms are much more acute. Restlessness and delirium are common in such conditions, and hallucinations of sight and hearing often terrify the patient. Lesions of the frontal lobes are more liable to be accompanied by early mental symptoms than are lesions in other parts of the brain, but it must be remembered that a growth may exist in the frontal lobes and yet give rise to no mental derangement whatsoever. Localisation, though at times possible from motor manifestations, is practically impossible from mental symptoms alone. The rate of growth of the lesion is of importance as regards the mental symptoms, a rapidly growing tumour giving rise to more numerous and more marked mental disturbances than one of slow growth.

In by far the majority of such cases a careful enquiry is sure to elicit a history of neurotic heredity.

Physical Symptoms.—The physical symptoms depend mainly on the character and site of the lesion, and will be found in any textbook on medicine, so need not be described here.

Mental Symptoms.—Progressive loss of memory and of the power of cognition are the most common mental concomitants of organic lesions of the brain, and may render the patient totally unable to look after himself, and apparently regardless of common decency. As the disease progresses the mental condition advances more and more, and the patient finally becomes bedridden and hopelessly demented. In cases of cerebral hæmorrhage I have at times seen severe emotional disturbances, both of excitement and depression, and in one case it seemed the starting-point of a series of maniacal attacks, and the patient is now in a state of comparative dementia with periodic exacerbations of excitement.

Diagnosis.—This can only be made from the physical symptoms, and is often a matter of difficulty. At times the mental disturbances are the first symptoms noticed, and may lead to the patients being sent to an asylum without the true condition having been diagnosed. Hysteria and G.P.I. may at times be confused with such states.

Prognosis.—Except in syphilitic cases or where operation is possible the prognosis is hopeless, and even in these cases the outlook is by no means favourable.

Treatment.—Syphilitic cases and those where operative interference is practicable are the only patients where treatment is possible; and for the rest, careful supervision and nursing, with general hygienic treatment, is all that can be done.

CHAPTER XXIII

1. MORAL INSANITY. 2. OBSESSIONAL INSANITY

1. Moral Insanity and Moral Imbecility

"MUCH has been written about instinctive criminals, and there is a school of writers by whom it is held that criminality is an innate quality, that it is recognisable by physical peculiarities, and that those who are thus distinguished are *ipso facto* irresponsible in the sense that they ought not to be punished. Of this doctrine it must be said that at present it is entirely wanting in proof, and is not likely to be generally accepted in Great Britain. Some even of its adherents have been repelled by the extravagances of its more enthusiastic advocates. Whilst, however, the doctrine is destitute of proof, or even of probability, so far as the vast majority of criminals are concerned, there is very plausible reason to believe that a few persons do now and then appear sporadically in whom the ordinary restraints of morality seem never to be developed. They are born with a congenital inability to become moral, and may be born of families every other member of which is normal. Such persons are liars, thieves, impostors, and frauds from the time they become able to talk and use their hands. Punishment, disgrace, affection have no influence on them—they are innately criminal" (Mercier). That such a condition does exist we have the authority above quoted to support, but that it exists without some other mental symptoms or changes seems hardly credible. I have certainly never seen such cases either during my service in the Gaol or the Asylum Department, and in all the cases I have seen recorded a clear history seems to be given of some definite type of insanity. Thus the case of W. R., cited in Browne's "Medical Jurisprudence of Insanity," p. 114, is on the face of it a case of epileptic imbecility; and that cited by Maudsley in his "Physiology and Pathology of Mind," p. 362, as well as that quoted by G. F. W. Ewens, *Indian Medical Gazette*, 1902, p. 230, both seem to me typical cases of Circular or Alternating Insanity.

Case LV.

"W. R., aged 27, had been eight times in the House of Correction. His father was an epileptic, and he himself had been subject to convulsions when teething, and at intervals during his after-life. He tortured animals, picked out the eyes of a kitten with a fork. He lied and stole. He was expelled from school as too bad to be kept. He afterwards consorted with the worst characters; was drunken, debauched, dishonest. He attempted, or pretended, to commit suicide. He was utterly false and untrustworthy. He delighted in torturing those patients who were, like himself, confined in the lunatic asylum, and who were too weak to resent injury with violence. He was indelicate in the presence of females, and attempted a rape on his mother and on his sister. Yet with all he was intelligent, exceedingly cunning, and, while actually the victim of epileptic seizures, he was prone to feign fits, and did it with considerable ability. In spite of careful watching, he repeatedly effected his escape; was exceedingly vain, and in the presence of some persons seemed to be exceedingly devout. He was ingenious in excusing his errors and, although exceedingly mischievous, was careful to avoid disagreeable consequences." This individual, Browne further remarks, was possessed of "an intelligence of such high order as to enable him thoroughly to understand the relation between a found-out crime and its punishment, for he invariably tried to conceal the commission of the criminal act by lies, hypocrisy, and various clever explanations" (Browne, "Med. Jur. of Insanity").

Case LVI.

"An old man, aged 69, who had been in one asylum or another for the last fifteen years of his life. He had great intellectual power, could compose well, write tolerable poetry with much fluency, and was an excellent keeper of accounts. There was no delusion of any kind, and yet he was the most hopeless and trying of mortals to deal with. Morally he was utterly depraved; he would steal and hide whatever he could, and several times made his escape from the asylum with marvellous ingenuity. He then pawned what he had stolen; begged, and lied with such plausibility that he deceived many people, until he finally got into the hands of the police, or was discovered in a most wretched state in the company of the lowest mortals in the lowest part of the town. In the earlier part of his insane career, which began when he was forty-eight years old, he was several times in prison for stealing. In the asylum he was a most troublesome patient; he could make excellent suggestions, and write out admirable rules for its management, and was very acute in detecting any negligence or abuse on the part of the attendants when they displeased him; but he was always on the watch to evade the regulations of the house, and when detected, he was most abusive, foul; and blasphemous in his language. He was something of an artist, and delighted to draw abominable pictures of naked men and women, and to exhibit them to those patients who were addicted to self-abuse. He could not be trusted with female patients, for he would attempt to take indecent liberties with the most demented creature. In short, he had no moral sense whatever; while all the fault that could be found with his very acute intellect was that it was entirely engaged in the service of his depravity. . . . At long intervals, sometimes of two years, this patient became profoundly melancholic for two or three months, refused to take food, and was as plainly insane as any patient in the asylum. It was in an attack of this sort also that his disease first commenced" (Maudsley, "Phys. and Path. of Mind").

CASE LVII.

V. B., aged about 22, admitted August 16, 1899, into Lahore Asylum, is an habitual criminal who has apparently never in his life maintained himself by honest labour. While in gaol for a term of imprisonment for receiving stolen property he was found so constantly troublesome, and given to making unprovoked assaults on the weaker prisoners, being filthy, and utterly unamenable to reason and punishment, that he was finally certified as a lunatic and sent here. Absolutely no previous or family history is obtainable of a reliable nature.

Beyond a certain amount of irritability he showed no sign of insanity, but he was soon found to be vicious, cruel, and animal, disobedient and revengeful, tearing up his bedding if checked, and destroying the materials of his work if spoken to. It was considered that his conduct denoted him at that time to be more of a criminal than a lunatic, and he was discharged at the expiration of his sentence, in December, 1900; but his conduct obliging the authorities to put him under security, he was sent back to gaol, and again, later on, was transferred here with the same history (early in 1901), and since then his conduct has never varied. He is a tall, well-built young man of most repellent aspect, being thick-lipped, with one ear cropped, and his face plentifully scarred as a result of old fights and injuries. He is clean, tidy, without any of the usual signs of insanity—that is to say, he speaks sensibly, intelligently, and coherently, is without delusion or hallucinations, and works well and skilfully with application when it so pleases him. He sleeps and eats well, is not an epileptic, and is in good physical health. But he is, on the other hand, most vicious, immoral, and unprincipled, a fluent liar, a thief, and though a coward, constantly found committing assaults on the weak and helpless lunatics; it is said that he assisted another patient to kick a man to death; he is perpetually endeavouring to commit sodomy, always ill-treating and bullying the weak dements and idiots, and daily concerned in some quarrel or grievance which the others come to complain about; mischievous, disobedient, absolutely unreliable and uncontrollable, the perfect pest of the whole asylum, on whom no training, no kindness, persuasion, or threats have the slightest permanent influence.

Now this man's actions have all the appearance of pure viciousness; he has perfect memory; he lies to excuse himself or for some other end; he does not steal from a magpie love of collection, but with a definite end and purpose; he is grossly immoral, and his acts of assault and cruelty are always on those weaker than himself, and not done out of pure insane impulse or in ungovernable passion. It is doubtful how much they are due to the failure of volition, for when caught and threatened with the deprivation of some privilege or the imposition of a punishment he will remain for some days quietly and orderly, but the effect gradually wears off, and he again follows his old evil courses. In his case his general intelligence is of such a high order as to preclude the possibility of suggesting his act as due to imbecility or weakmindedness. It may be also pointed out that, being so intelligent, it is reasonable to suppose that he would exercise more self-control to escape from his present uncomfortable position, and his failure to do so is a very strong evidence of his insanity. He is certainly irresponsible and incapable of seeing things as others do, and his general conduct for ordinary public security and comfort renders it imperative that he should remain secluded either in gaol or a lunatic asylum, even though his history may always give different observers opportunities for debating as to which particular institution he more properly belongs (G. F. W. Ewens, *Indian Medical Gazette*, 1902).

2. Impulsive and Obsessional Insanity.

It is often pleaded in defence of a person charged with crime that the offence was committed through a sudden ungovernable impulse. Such cases of necessity require most careful investigation. Sudden and ungovernable impulses cannot arise *de novo*; in every case where such a plea is warranted there must be some history of previous mental change, of which the impulse and resulting crime are only a part, and which a careful enquiry among friends and relatives is almost certain to reveal.

In many cases the mental condition alone, apart from the impulse and its results, would not suffice to warrant restraint. Thus psychasthenics, neurasthenics, and hysterical cases are at times apt to be seized with sudden impulses, which may or may not result in crime, and, as so many types of insanity are liable to be complicated by impulses, to lay down a hard-and-fast type of "impulsive insanity" seems rather like splitting straws.

Crimes due to such a condition are specially liable to be committed by women, especially about the time of their menstruation, and in women with this tendency the menopause is always a dangerous period of their lives.

Intoxication by alcohol, too, is especially productive of excessive impulsions, owing to the powers of inhibition being removed and the reflex centres in consequence running riot.

Clinically the following types of morbid impulse may be noted: 1. *General impulsiveness,* or the tendency to react immediately to all sorts of external or internal impulses. 2. *Epileptiform impulses,* where the patient is unconscious of, or, at any rate, cannot remember, his action or its cause. 3. *Sexual impulses,* which include tendencies towards excessive sexual intercourse, onanism, bestiality, etc. 4. *Morbid appetites,* where the patients are unable to resist eating and drinking all sorts of filth. 5. *Homicidal impulses.* 6. *Suicidal impulses.* 7. *Dipsomania, kleptomania,* etc. 8. *Impulsive conditions which alternate with forms of intellectual or moral insanity* (Hyslop).

In many such cases between the attacks the patients are respectable, useful members of society, and thoroughly ashamed of these recurring attacks, which they are constantly striving against. Gradually, however, the conatus forces itself upon them, they become irritable and depressed, lose their desire for food, and a constant fear of impending trouble casts a shadow over their lives. At such a period the patient may be frantically striving against the ungovernable desire, and frequently implores friends and relatives to assist him. Unless, however, the assistance be prompt the conatus is victorious, and some act is committed which may perhaps land its performer in the dock. Such cases are of the obsessional type of insanity.

A condition of marked depression usually follows after such attacks, during which there is considerable risk of suicide, and this must always be carefully guarded against.

CASE LVIII.

"A young man, aged 25, and of gentlemanly appearance, after giving his address, and declaring himself to be a schoolmaster in a certain well-known college (in Paris), begged that the Commissary of Police would take him in charge with a view to his confinement in the Asylum of St. Ann. He then explained that he was not mad in every respect; on the contrary, he possessed the full use of his mind, only while sleeping among the pupils confided to his charge he was seized with the most destructive inclinations. Night after night in an agony of fear he had struggled with himself, and it was with the greatest difficulty that so far he had succeeded in restraining his intense desire to strangle one or two of the little boys. Now all his energies were exhausted, he felt that this unknown power would ultimately triumph over him, and rather than commit the crime he placed himself in the hands of the police. At this moment a boy accused of theft was brought into the room. The eyes of the schoolmaster were immediately lit with a strange light; and had it not been for the timely assistance of a brawny policeman the boy would have been throttled before the eyes of justice" (Bucknill and Tuke).

CASE LIX.

Mt. J., a woman of the Baniah caste, and about 30 years of age. She had been the wife of a zemindar, but adversity came her way. Her husband died, and his property was taken by his relatives, with whom she continued to live. She had one child, a daughter, about whose future she was much concerned, as she could obtain no money to arrange for her marriage. Gradually she felt the desire to kill her child force itself upon her. In vain she fought against it, in vain she told her relatives and implored them to keep them apart. They only scoffed, and to emphasise their incredulity took to locking them up together at night. The result was that one night she killed her child, and was found in the morning in a state of deep melancholy by the body. She was tried under Section 302, I.P.C., certified as suffering from melancholia at the time of the occurrence, and sent to the asylum under Section 471, C.P.C. The melancholic stage wore off gradually, and she is now a quiet, gentle, industrious little woman, of great assistance in helping in the duties of the Indian Female Section (A. W. Overbeck-Wright).

The intervals between attacks vary greatly, sometimes only three or four occurring in a lifetime, but each attack renders a recurrence more probable. In other cases, the true Impulsive Insanity, the person affected is markedly neurotic, has previously shown signs of nervous weakness, such as psychasthenic, neurasthenic, or hysterical symptoms, and opportunity suddenly gives form to this irresistible desire for the performance of some act, which is committed at once, on the spur of the moment, without a moment's consideration of the nature of the act or its consequences. Such cases are extremely common in weakly or neurotic women about the menstrual periods or the menopause, and most cases of kleptomania and pyromania are of this type. *Kleptomania* is often brought forward as a defence to save persons of good standing from the disgrace which would otherwise come upon them. A true kleptomaniac as a rule confines the pilfering to some one article, or type of article, without any regard to its use or value, and, having gained possession of them, simply accumulates them, and as a rule makes no attempt to use or dispose of them.

CHAPTER XXIV

PSYCHOSES ASSOCIATED WITH PHYSICAL DISEASES

PSYCHOSES associated with physical diseases are as a rule classified under the heads of Exhaustion Insanity, Insanity due to Metabolic Toxæmia, Insanity due to Bacterial Toxæmia, or a combination of these, and, strictly speaking, such a chapter as I now propose to deal with is scientifically inaccurate. It is an undoubted fact, however, that many physical diseases have certain mental characteristics or concomitants, a knowledge of which is most useful to the physician, not only from a psychiatrical point of view, but also as it affects his treatment of and bearing towards the patient, quite apart from any question of sanity or insanity. For this reason, therefore, I propose to discuss in this chapter the mental conditions prevalent in some of the common physical diseases.

1. Phthisis and Insanity.

Apart altogether from insanity there is a peculiar attitude associated with cases of phthisis; no matter how ill the patient may be he is always full of hope as to his ultimate recovery, and this hope I have known to persist in cases practically until death. This being such a prominent feature in patients who are mentally sound, it might be supposed that in cases where insanity was a sequel to the physical condition the mental state would be one of excitement or exaltation. Such, however, is not the case, for as a rule such patients suffer from a mild depression, with delusions of persecution and suspicion.

In considering such cases it must always be kept in mind that though phthisis is such a common cause of death in asylums, in by far the majority of such cases the physical disease is secondary to the mental one, and may even have been contracted after the patient's admission, and has nothing whatever to do with the mental condition. It is only when insanity is consecutive to the lung disease that this state of delusional depression is seen, which is, however, by no means pathognomonic of phthisis.

The relationship between phthisis and insanity is a close one, a tubercular parent begetting children, some of whom are tubercular and others may be insane, while tuberculosis finds a much larger percentage of victims in asylums than in the general population.

Mental Symptoms.—Where the insanity is consecutive to the physical disease, the patients as a rule are peevish and irritable, and many are depressed and unable to settle to any occupation. Delusions are common, and may lead to refusal of food, so that tube-feeding becomes necessary. The faculty of self-control is diminished, and the power of attention and concentrated thought is lost, though memory is little if at all impaired, and if so, mainly for current events.

Attempts at suicide are common in such cases and have to be guarded against.

As the case progresses a condition of partial dementia ensues, but often, when the pulmonary trouble is far advanced and life is nearly at an end, there is a sudden and marked improvement in the mental condition which may continue until the moment of death.

Diagnosis.—The diagnosis of phthisis in an insane person is a matter of no little trouble as a rule owing to the difficulties experienced in auscultation. Generally, rapid loss of weight, especially if accompanied by an irregular febrile chart, should make us suspect this condition. Where the mental symptoms supervene in a case already diagnosed physically little if any trouble in diagnosis exists.

Treatment.—Beyond careful supervision and artificial feeding, if necessary, nothing beyond the ordinary treatment for phthisical patients is called for. I always endeavour to keep such patients away from non-tubercular cases, and, so far as possible, have the expectoration collected and destroyed. Such cases should be kept as much as possible in the open air, under a shelter, and a plentiful supply of good nourishing food allowed to them.

Prognosis.—This depends largely on the extent of the lung trouble, but is generally by no means hopeful.

2. Pneumonia and Insanity.

The pneumococcus at times produces a general toxæmic condition quite apart from the usual pulmonary affection. In these cases mental symptoms are very likely to occur, and I have seen two or three patients where undoubtedly the mental symptoms were due to pneumococcic invasion.

In my experience the mental symptoms in such cases either precede the pulmonary manifestations or supervene in the course of the disease, when as a rule they are accompanied by an apparent amelioration of the pulmonary symptoms, which usually occurs suddenly, and is unaccompanied by the usual critical discharges, etc., while the other physical symptoms, high temperature, etc., remain unaffected.

In such patients the mental state is one of restless mania. Insomnia is marked, the patient wanders restlessly about the room, or lies tossing and turning in bed, constantly chattering to himself a stream of disconnected rubbish. In this stage of the disease impulsive acts have to be guarded against and homicidal or suicidal attempts carefully watched for.

This condition may terminate fatally from cardiac failure, or, as is more usual, a sudden improvement in the mental state occurs, ushered in by the appearance or recrudescence of the pulmonary symptoms.

Diagnosis.—This is practically impossible where the mental symptoms precede the pulmonary affection, but where the pulmonary lesions already exist, or there is a previous history of pneumonia, the question is fairly easy to decide.

Prognosis.—As a rule the prognosis is by no means good, such cases usually ending fatally from syncope, either in the stage of mental derangement or in the later stage of pulmonary affection. I know of one case only that recovered from such an attack, and this one had a second attack some two years later which terminated fatally.

Treatment.—As for acute mania, where, however, the pneumococcic origin of the condition is apparent, subcutaneous injections of anti-pneumococcic sera should invariably be tried.

Case LX.

L. M., a Hindu from Muttra, aged about 29, agriculturist. Admitted into Agra Asylum in a state of acute mania; noisy, restless, destructive, and dirty in his habits. He continued thus for about ten days without any change, and no signs whatever of any pulmonary lesion. Suddenly one morning he was found lying quietly on his bed in a practically sane condition and complaining of intense pain on the right side of his chest. Examination revealed consolidation of the lung, with rusty sputum containing numerous pneumococci. His father came to see him a day or so later, and on interrogation gave a history of an almost exactly similar seizure, commencing with mental symptoms which ended suddenly in an attack of pneumonia, some two years previously.

The patient was treated for pneumonia, but in spite of all that could be done for him he died some eight days after the implication of the lungs.

3. Malaria and Insanity.

As with other acute specific disorders, so malaria, by the action of its toxines, as well as by the debility it produces, may be responsible for an attack of insanity. In the febrile stage I have seen patients who were at first in a condition of delirium gradually pass into a condition of maniacal excitement, with hallucinations which lasted from a few days to a week or more after all fever had passed off. The maniacal condition is certainly the most common, but I know of one or two cases where, after a chronic course of fever lasting off and on for some months, the patient quite suddenly has passed into a semi-stuporose condition, and wandered away from home, and, when found about a month later, hundreds of miles perhaps away from his own village, has been in a state of bewilderment as regards his surroundings, and his mind a complete blank as to his past.

The maniacal condition is probably directly due to the action of malarial toxines, and improves rapidly upon treatment with quinine, while the stuporose condition approximates more closely to the exhaustion psychoses, and calls for rest, tonics, and a full, nourishing dietary. Saline purges are useful in either type of case, aiding the elimination of the toxines from the blood.

A form of "exhaustion insanity" also occurs at times after malarial attacks, and, owing to the delay in bringing such cases for treatment, the majority are received into the asylum in a practically demented condition.

As a rule the prognosis is good in the maniacal and stuporose cases, recovery occurring in the course of a few months, but in the cases approximating to an exhaustion psychosis it is by no means favourable as regards recovery of mentalisation.

4. Sunstroke and Insanity.

Among Anglo-Indians sunstroke is one of the reasons most frequently given for an attack of insanity, but in the vast majority of cases such a statement needs qualification. Sunstroke alone would hardly suffice to cause insanity, and in the greater number of such cases careful enquiry elicits a history of alcoholic abuse, which is undoubtedly a potent factor in the production of insanity. Moreover, it is people of these habits who are most liable to be exposed to heat as well as to suffer from its results.

The cases of insanity from sunstroke alone are practically confined to that type of insolation described by Sir Patrick Manson, in his work on Tropical Diseases, under the term of "sun traumatism."

In such a condition the patient becomes ill while actually exposed to the sun's rays. A certain number of such cases may even die suddenly from cardiac syncope, but others are seized with high fever, vomiting, headache, and delirium, with a full, quick pulse, and intolerance of light, sound, and movement. A lengthy period of debility and ill-health may occur after such a seizure, and such cases are extremely liable to be affected with amnesia, tremor, deafness, amblyopia, constant headaches, and occasionally epilepsy and insanity are said to occur.

In practically all such cases after recovery the least exposure to heat and sun is liable to bring on a recurrence, while if the smallest quantity of alcohol be imbibed a condition of acute drunkenness is aroused.

Three types of this mental affection can be distinguished:

1. A form approximating closely to organic dementia, where after recovery the patient is left foolish, timid, and depressed, incapable of doing his former work, irritable and passionate, and peculiarly susceptible to the action of alcohol or to exposure to the sun. The symptoms vary from practically complete dementia up to little more than a change of temperament and a liability to intense fits of passion.

2. A form characterised by changes limited to practically only one of the mental functions, such as pronounced amnesia, or a social or moral change. In all such cases sudden exacerbations of the mental symptoms are likely to occur, and to be associated with loss of sight or hearing, severe headaches and paræsthesia

along the distribution of nerves arising from certain parts of the spinal cord. This latter symptom is especially prominent when the back has been exposed to the sun, as occurs at times when, during a day's shooting, the man is crawling along stalking his game.

3. A post-febrile psychosis occurring after the acute symptoms of sun traumatism have subsided. Such patients are as a rule excited and restless, and are troubled with hallucinations and delusions of persecution. As a result of the delusions they are irritable and passionate, unruly, and at times even homicidal. Such cases usually recover after some months, but never seem quite to regain their former mental equilibrium, being constantly moody and irritable.

5. Influenza and Insanity.

With this disease one may safely group the mental conditions which frequently are met with after dengue and sandfly fever. The toxines resulting from these three conditions seem especially prone to affect the nervous elements of the body, and very few people pass through an attack from any of them without revealing some more or less marked mental or nervous symptoms. As a rule the condition is one of mild depression with irritability and loss of capacity for work. Headaches and neuralgias may be a constant source of worry to the patient, while insomnia may call for immediate treatment to avert a mental breakdown, or neurasthenia may occur as a sequela.

The severity of the mental symptoms is by no means in proportion to the severity of the attack of the original malady, an apparently very mild attack frequently producing profound mental derangement, especially in persons with a tainted heredity.

Where the mental symptoms arise during the febrile stage of the disease the condition generally is one of acute excitement and of a maniacal type. The most common form, however, is where convalescence apparently is established, and after some weeks have elapsed from the abatement of the fever melancholic symptoms supervene.

Symptoms.—In the maniacal type the patient becomes noisy and restless, and troubled by hallucinations both of sight and hearing. Occasionally the excitement may become so intense as to necessitate removal to an asylum. As a rule such cases pass after a time into a depressed condition, during which refusal of food may call for tube-feeding, and from this depressed condition the patient gradually returns to his normal mentalisation.

In the post-febrile type the onset is often most insidious, and insanity may have been developing for some time before the relatives begin to suspect the true state of affairs. A history of insomnia is very common in such cases, and, combined with anorexia, this undermines both the mental and physical health. Work becomes a labour, and indolence and lethargy become marked characteristics of the patient. At this stage the patient is constantly depressed in the morning, and suicidal feelings gradually force themselves upon him. If the condition progresses still farther the patient passes into a condition of marked melancholia, with pronounced hallucinations and delusions, in some cases of a hypochondriacal type, in others those of suspicion and persecution.

Treatment.—This resolves itself into the treatment of the physical diseases which can be found detailed in any textbook on medicine, and the treatment of the mental symptoms which have already been described under melancholia and mania.

Prognosis.—Such cases usually recover quickly if treatment is begun early in the course of the insanity; persistent auditory hallucinations, however, are a bad prognostic sign, and should make us invariably guarded in our prognosis.

6. Rheumatic Fever and Insanity.

Rheumatic fever, like many other acute diseases, is capable of causing mental symptoms and affecting the nervous tissues in a similar way to that in which it affects the other tissues of the body. That this is so is not a matter of surprise when we consider the results of recent investigations into rheumatic fever, as well as into the causation of insanity. The probability is that the streptococcus described by Triboukt, Westphal, Wassermann, Poynton, Paine, and others, and known as the *Micrococcus rheumaticus*, is capable of forming toxines, which act on the nervous tissues, causing varied manifestations of insanity. Hence, here again we are probably dealing with a bacterial toxæmia, and have yet another reminder of the importance of closely investigating the origin of our cases so that we may be enabled to treat them more successfully. Moreover, apart from actual insanity, after an attack of rheumatic fever the patient may occasionally be found completely altered either mentally or morally. Savage, in writing on this very subject, states: "We have met with several patients, mostly women, who have ceased to perform their domestic duties, and have caused family discord in consequence of their changed habits, the industrious mother becoming indolent and negligent of her duties. It is certain, too, that some persons, who before rheumatic fever were sober and truthful, after it became intemperate and untruthful."

The mental disorder varies both as to the time of its appearance and its manifestations. The fever may pass on to acute mania, or mental symptoms develop at a later stage of the disease. In these latter forms either melancholia or mania may be present, but mania is the more common. Where cardiac complications are present, however, the type of insanity is largely affected by them, mania being more common with aortic and melancholia with mitral disease.

Treatment.—This turns on general lines, both as regards the physical and mental conditions; but the probability of cardiac disease should never be forgotten in these cases, and a careful search should always be made for valvular lesions.

Prognosis.—The immediate prognosis, as regards the mental symptoms, is always hopeful in these cases, as most cases make a good recovery. A recurrence, however, is always to be feared when any subsequent attack of rheumatic fever occurs.

7. Heart Disease and Insanity.

Except for the changes caused in the blood-supply to the brain little or no effect is produced by valvular lesions. Anxiety and restlessness are common concomitants of aortic insufficiency, and insomnia may lead to an attack of acute insanity in a person suffering from any form of valvular disease. As a rule cases of aortic insufficiency, with a low blood-pressure, usually suffer from symptoms of mania or excited melancholia; while in cases of early mitral disease, where the blood-pressure is high, the symptoms approximate more closely to those of acute melancholia. This is what one would expect from the state of blood-pressure, which is really the cause of the condition.

Prognosis.—The prognosis in such cases is far from hopeful.

8. Syphilis and Insanity.

The potency of the *Spirochæta pallida* as a factor in the ætiology of mental and nervous diseases has formed the subject of much research in recent years. In 1913 Drs. Fraser and Watson conclusively proved its close connection with cases of mental deficiency and its manifestations in other ways, and the danger it constitutes to the public health and welfare are now fully recognised and steps are being taken to combat it.

The modes in which it may give rise to mental symptoms are numerous. Thus a cachectic condition may be produced by the action of the poison on the blood-forming tissues; arterio-sclerotic conditions may arise from its action on the bloodvessels, or local or diffuse lesions of the brain and its membranes, such as gummata or sclerotic changes, may ensue; and, lastly, the possibility of its forming the subject of a mental conflict and causing mental derangement through a purely psychic channel must be kept in mind.

Like many other diseases, syphilis does not affect all its victims in a similar manner; thus, in one case the viscera may be attacked, while in another the vascular or nervous elements may be affected. Strangely enough, too, persons with a neurotic heredity seem by no means prone to be affected mentally by the syphilitic poison—in fact, the experience of well-known authorities seems to point in the opposite direction.

Savage has drawn up the following scheme of the relationship between syphilis and insanity:

1. Insane dread of syphilis.
2. Insane dread of results of syphilis.
3. Syphilitic fever, delirium, and mania.
4. Acute syphilis, leading to mental decay.
5. Syphilitic cachexia, dyscrasia, and mental disorder.
6. Syphilitic neuritis (optic), suspicion, and mania.
7. Syphilitic ulceration, disfigurement, and morbid self-consciousness.
8. Congenital syphilis, cranial, sensory, and nerve-tissue defects.
9. Congenital syphilis, epilepsy, and idiocy.
10. Infantile syphilis acquired.
11. Constitutional syphilis: (1) vascular or fibrous; (2) epilepsy;

(3) hemiplegia; (4) local palsies; (5) general paralysis, spinal (spastic and tabetic), peripheral.

12. Locomotor ataxy: (1) with insane crises; (2) with insane interpretation of ordinary symptoms.

The first class comprises those who have an insane dread of syphilis, and who may, in fact, never have had the disease in any form. It is, in fact, an obsessional insanity, and has been termed *syphilophobia*. The patient spends his days washing and scrubbing himself and his belongings, searching his body for symptoms of syphilis, and worrying himself into a depressed and delusional state, in which suicide is common.

In most of such cases enquiry elicits the fact that they have undoubtedly run the risk of contagion through promiscuous sexual intercourse, and it is the psychic conflict thus originated, the dread of being discovered, and the fear of anything which may lead to discovery, which in the majority of cases accounts for the mental symptoms. This type is fairly common among Europeans and Eurasians, but I have never heard of a case in an Indian.

The second class of this affection is also to be seen in Europeans and Eurasians, and leads to very much the same sort of symptoms. Besides being suicidal, however, such cases are liable to commit homicide, a husband perhaps killing his wife and child in the belief that he has given them the disease also, and being unable to contemplate the suffering and misery which he has thus brought upon them.

The third type is generally of short duration, lasting two to three months, and is practically an attack of acute mania. The action of the syphilitic toxines, combined perhaps with a careless administration of mercury, as is the common practice of so many hakims, leads in many cases to a cachectic condition with trophic changes in the brain and subsequent insanity. This may be either melancholia or mania at its onset, but as a rule such cases tend to rapid dementia.

In other cases, where the syphilitic lesions infest the face, the patient may become hypersensitive, imagine people abuse and avoid him, and finally pass into a typical state of delusional insanity.

Congenital syphilis may lead to any of the conditions treated of under idiocy and imbecility, and to these (Chapter XXII.) I would refer my readers.

True cerebral syphilis as a rule develops within ten years of the primary infection, and the greatest danger of its developing lies in the first three or four years after infection, the risk decreasing with each additional year. The patient may at times simply show a gradual and progressive mental decay, passing finally into a condition of profound dementia; but as a rule maniacal symptoms are manifest, at first probably interspersed with delusions of grandeur or at times of persecution. Such patients are as a rule very irritable and liable to sudden and violent outbursts of passion. The majority of such cases sooner or later join the class of those suffering from organic dementia.

Treatment.—This should invariably be begun early. Injections of salvarsan should be tried in all cases where no sign of dementia has yet appeared; but the appearance of dementia contra-indicates the use of this preparation. Where dementia is present, and indeed in all cases, potassium iodide, combined with mercury, is the most practical method of treatment, and large doses should be given—20 to 40 grains or more thrice daily if the patient can stand it. In some cases, where the vascular system is specially affected, iodide of sodium is a better preparation to exhibit, as the potassium salt tends to increase arterial tension.

Mercury may be prescribed as the liq. hydrarg. perchlor., or in the form of an inunction, and where headache is troublesome shaving the scalp and then rubbing in mercurial ointment often produces wonderful results.

During treatment the general health and diet should be carefully supervised, and special care must be taken of the patient's mouth, which should be cleansed after each meal and a gargle of chlorate of potash used at the same time.

The treatment should be continued for at least a year after the cessation of all symptoms, and the patient should be carefully informed as to the extreme necessity of his leading a regular, temperate life in the future, and going through a three months' course of treatment yearly for at least three years.

Prognosis.—In cases due to gummata, and where treatment has been begun early, the prognosis is decidedly hopeful, but in other cases, especially where there are marked depression and delusions, the prognosis is by no means good, only about 25 per cent. making any sort of recovery, and most of those relapsing sooner or later.

9. Chorea and Insanity.

There is no special type of insanity peculiarly characteristic of chorea or which properly can be called "choreic insanity"; but in reality chorea and insanity are very closely allied. In nearly every case of chorea there are some symptoms of mental disturbance, in some cases mere apathy and listlessness, with slight loss of memory—symptoms so mild, indeed, that they often escape unnoticed, all attention being directed to the severer physical manifestations. Sir William Gowers, too, has shown that chorea is much more prevalent among those with a neurotic heredity, and that insanity may either precede or follow after the physical symptoms.

Ætiology.—Mental symptoms are much more common in adults suffering from chorea than in children afflicted with the same complaint, and usually occur in persons with a tainted heredity. Women who develop chorea during pregnancy are especially liable to suffer from mental disorders. Chorea, however, rarely occurs primarily in an adult, most of such cases having already suffered from the disease in childhood, except in that type of the malady known as "Huntington's chorea."

Symptoms.—Various types of insanity may be associated with chorea.

1. *Choreic Mania.*—This as a rule occurs in the early stages of the physical disease, generally in the second or third week. The restless agitation of the chorea passes gradually into a condition of excitement, accompanied by loss of self-control and impulsiveness. Sleep is invariably markedly disturbed in such cases, and a condition of great confusion is present, while both auditory and visual hallucinations are common. At times such cases may be extremely affected mentally, with raised temperature, restless excitement, absolute insomnia, and refusal of food, and such patients are very liable to die from exhaustion and syncope.

2. *Choreic Stupor.*—This commonly occurs later in the course of the physical disease, the general lassitude and confusion common in choreic cases becoming gradually more profound until it merges into a condition of stupor.

3. *Choreic Delusional Insanity.*—In chronic cases of chorea a state of mental derangement with delusions of suspicion and persecution at times arises.

4. *Huntington's chorea* (hereditary progressive chorea) was noted first by Huntington in 1872.

It is an hereditary condition tending to be transmitted through several generations, and usually affects people between the ages of thirty and forty-five—*i.e.*, it is a disease of middle life. It affects the sexes equally, and may be transmitted either by father or mother. It is a progressive and incurable condition, accompanied by increasing mental deterioration, which finally ends in dementia. The muscles of the head and upper limbs are first affected, but gradually the whole of the voluntary muscles become implicated by the movements, which, though at first fairly well under control, gradually become more extensive and less controllable. The early mental symptoms of general apathy and listlessness soon pass into a condition of profound depression, marked by occasional outbursts of irritability and anger, which sooner or later merge into a state of complete dementia. Life is not shortened by this condition.

Treatment.—The treatment here should be on general principles. The diet should be liberal and nourishing, and meat should be avoided as much as possible. If food is refused forced feeding should be resorted to at once, and in severe cases stimulants should be given whenever the physical symptoms call for them. The action of the bowels should be carefully looked to, and kept rather on the loose side by means of salines or cascara. Sedatives are required for the insomnia, and chloral hydrate is the most useful in such cases where it can be safely used; failing chloral hydrate, paraldehyde or veronal is of great service.

Where the movements are violent and the patient restless or excited, care should be taken to prevent his being injured, and it is better to keep him on a mattress on the floor surrounded by other mattresses.

Prognosis.—Except for the acutely maniacal cases, which often have a rapidly fatal termination, the prognosis is as a rule good in the maniacal and melancholic forms of mental disorder, such cases usually recovering in a few weeks. In the stuporose form the prognosis should be more guarded, as the duration is longer, and such cases at times pass into a state of dementia.

Huntington's chorea is progressive and incurable.

In cases where chorea supervenes on an attack of insanity,

so far as I have seen the mental condition seems but little affected by the presence of the physical symptoms, but the choreic symptoms are as a rule chronic and incurable.

10. Pregnancy and Insanity.

Insanity frequently occurs during the course of pregnancy, and generally partakes of a depressed, delusional condition, though at times maniacal symptoms are met with.

The cases are divisible into two groups: (*a*) Those occurring during the first four months of pregnancy; (*b*) those occurring during the later months.

In the former type of case recovery generally takes place before the time of delivery, and in the latter the condition clears up several months after parturition. In neither case is recovery accelerated by inducing premature labour, and therefore this should never be attempted for mental symptoms alone.

11. Menstruation and Insanity.

During menstruation women are much more liable to suffer from insanity and various neuroses. An enquiry among female criminals in Europe elicited the fact that in a very large percentage indeed the crime was perpetrated during a menstrual period. Most cases, too, of kleptomania and other impulsive insanities among women occur during the process of menstruation. In asylums, in the female sections, maniacs are always more maniacal, melancholics more depressed during a menstrual period.

This point is well worth remembering, as it has important medico-legal bearings.

12. Intestinal Parasites and Insanity.

Experience has convinced me that besides being capable of causing fever and other physical symptoms, frequently closely resembling enteric fever, intestinal parasites at times are undoubtedly the sole cause of mental symptoms. The most potent in this direction are the common round worms. In fact, so strong is my belief in their power for evil in this direction that, knowing their prevalence among Indians, I have made it a rule that every case admitted into my asylum is at once put through a course of anthelmintics.

The most common form of mental symptoms arising from this cause is the acutely maniacal type, though I have at times seen cases in a depressed, stuporose condition.

Such cases clear up rapidly so soon as the cause is removed, and the prognosis is invariably good.

One case in particular impressed me early in my career. A patient was admitted into Agra Asylum in an acutely maniacal condition. One or two lumbricoides being observed in his motions, anthelmintics were exhibited. The results were startling, as next morning he was found to have passed some 180 round worms, and the mental symptoms were to all practical purposes cured.

CHAPTER XXV

PHYSICAL CONDITIONS COMPLICATING INSANITY

THE insane are as liable to physical disease as the sane—in fact, owing to the weakened resistance to infection so common among them, even more so; but it is not proposed here to go into a general disquisition on medicine and surgery, though, as from 15 to 20 per cent. of an asylum population are constantly in hospital, ample scope might perhaps be found for it, but merely to bring to notice certain conditions which seem especially liable to affect the inhabitants of asylums and others who suffer from mental derangements.

1. Hæmatoma Auris.

This condition, which is also known as Othæmatoma, or the Insane Ear, has given rise to much discussion concerning its cause, and three distinct opinions are mooted as to its origin. Some say it is due simply to an effusion of blood between the cartilage of the ear and its perichondrium, such as at times occurs in those who play Rugby football; others affirm that it is primarily due to trophic changes in the cartilage, which render hæmorrhage more likely on account of the weakening of the arterial and venous walls; while others say it is due to changes in the blood. Personally, I strongly favour the second view in most cases, for I have seen this condition in patients where little or no injury could have been sustained, and its prevalence among the chronic insane and general paralytics, where trophic changes are so common, and forced feeding seldom if ever required, strongly supports this theory. I undoubtedly have met with a few cases where the first theory is tenable, but as a rule the injury received is so slight that no result would have ensued had the ear been in a healthy condition, the injury perhaps consisting in the patient rubbing the ear with his hands, or even against the pillow. The third theory is ruled out of court by the fact that the condition is more commonly unilateral, whereas if due to blood changes the opposite would be the case.

Symptoms.—When first seen it appears as a smooth, tense swelling limited to the cartilaginous parts of the ear, and occupying the anterior or outer part of the auricle. It is acutely tender to the touch, and causes much discomfort to the patient. If left untreated the hæmatoma may rupture or become slowly organised, but in either case much wrinkling and deformity of the ear ensues.

Treatment.—I have heard some teachers recommend cutting down and evacuating the contents of the cyst; but by far the greater number of authorities advocate the use of a blistering fluid, and strongly deprecate the use of a knife. Certainly what I have seen of such cases has made me a strong adherent of the latter method, for I have never seen a case where the knife has been used recover without marked deformity of the ear remaining, whereas if strong counter-irritation be applied early the swelling subsides, and in the large majority of cases very little puckering ensues.

2. Lesions of the Osseous System.

Fractures are extremely liable to occur among the insane, not only from their being more liable to receive injuries, but also from injuries often producing fractures in the insane which in the sane would cause merely a contusion or sprain.

Extreme excitement, restlessness, irritability, and lack of cognition of place are the main reasons rendering the insane more liable to receive injuries, while a deficiency of reflex action—"delayed reaction" as it is often termed—as well as nervous lesions and changes in the osseous system, render a slight injury much more likely to cause a fracture in an insane than a sane person. Insane patients show a much larger percentage of cases of syphilis than does the normal population, and the presence of gummata in many of such cases has a distinct effect in rendering fractures more probable, especially when combined with the mental and nervous conditions already enumerated.

In cases of chronic insanity there is a tendency to absorption of the internal parts of the bones, especially of the ribs, and in time not only may the inner parts be absorbed, but even the inner surface of the external parts of the bones may become affected and riddled with cavities, the bone absorbed being replaced with a fatty material. As can readily be imagined, bones thus affected are brittle and easily fractured, and even attempts at artificial respiration may produce serious injury in such cases, no matter how carefully the manipulations are carried out. Chemical examination of such bones has shown a relative increase of organic matter to earthy constituents, and a decrease in the proportion of lime to phosphoric acid.

As a general rule, in spite of incessant restlessness and movement in many of the cases, fractures among the insane show just as good results as among the ordinary population, and there is no very marked increase in the number of ununited fractures in an asylum when the figures are compared with the statistics of other hospitals.

3. Wounds, Ulcers, etc.

Owing to trophic changes, the habit so common among many of the insane of constantly picking at the skin or hair, and the disregard of cleanliness displayed by so many asylum patients, ulcers are common among them, and any small wound or scratch is very liable to suppurate. It is impossible also in many cases to keep a surgical dressing applied for any length of time, for the patients tear them off on the first opportunity, and, scratching the wound, not only aggravate the condition, but carry the sepsis to other parts of the body, and in this way extensive glandular suppurations may result.

Cases of stupor or dementia require constant attention on this account, for such cases as a rule are indifferent to what settles on them, and any slight wound or abrasion is liable to become not only septic, but swarming with maggots for this reason.

Curiously enough, severe surgical cases among the insane generally run a more favourable course than minor ailments, probably owing to the greater pain and inconvenience compelling rest and attention, where a lesser hurt would be forgotten by the patient, or remembered only to be scratched.

My experience of minor surgery among the insane has given me a strong belief in the efficacy of iodine as a disinfectant. My habit is to use the linimentum iodi on the unbroken skin around the wounds, while the wounds themselves are washed either with boiled water or a weak boric lotion, and then swabbed thoroughly with tinctura iodi, a simple aseptic gauze dressing being then applied. The dressing is performed twice daily until convalescence is established, when once a day suffices. In very severe cases the dressing may have to be done thrice daily. I have never seen any bad effects arise from this method of treatment, and in all the results have been most satisfactory, and to my mind better than would have been the case from ordinary dressings, especially in one or two cases of chronic tuberculosis.

A fact to be remembered is that an acute abscess or carbuncle, or some similar condition, may often seem the starting-point of recovery in some of the acute insanities, probably owing to the effects on the leucocytic elements of the blood, and for this reason the subcutaneous injection of terebene is advocated by some authorities as a method of treatment in such cases.

4. Micro-organismal Diseases.

Though much more immune to the results of changes of temperature than the sane community, the insane are, owing to weakened resistive powers, much more liable to suffer from micro-organismal diseases, and to these by far the larger number of deaths occurring annually in asylums are due.

Phthisis.—This disease seems to be becoming gradually less common in asylums, owing to improved hygiene, etc. It is still, however, a source of much trouble at times, and its diagnosis in an insane patient, with little or no history, in the midst of the continual noise and clatter as a rule present in most of the sections of an asylum, and perhaps with the patient himself constantly moving and chattering, is, as can be imagined, by no means an easy task.

"Why not examine his sputum?" I expect some of my readers will say, and that is undoubtedly done whenever possible; but to examine sputum you have to get it first, and in many cases this is by no means easy to accomplish. The microscopic examination of the sputum, however, is really our one means of diagnosis in many cases, and an invaluable aid in all. The easy diagnosis of malaria in any case of fever, especially with a young, inexperienced sub-assistant surgeon, is often a cause of many early cases of phthisis being overlooked, and this disease should always be kept in mind in such cases, or where there is progressive failure in health and nutrition, and a thorough examination made, not only of the patient but also of the sputum and the blood.

As a rule such cases run a rapid course, and the prognosis is much less favourable than among the sane.

Pneumonia.—This is one of the most common causes of epidemic disease in Indian asylums, for its early diagnosis presents similar difficulties to those met with in tubercle—the patients expectorate on their blankets, which get mixed by careless attendants, and some other patient, wrapping himself up head and all in an infected blanket, contracts the infection.

Many and varied are its modes of onset and symptoms. In some cases consolidation of the lung suddenly appears without any fever, cough, or "rusty sputum"; some cases remain undiscovered till thrombosis of the pulmonary artery carries them off; while others, again, have a typical acute attack, pass through the crisis, and apparently are convalescent, with normal temperature, when death suddenly occurs from cardiac failure.

Extension to the pleura or pericardium has always to be looked for in these cases, as it is very liable to occur, and equally liable to be missed owing to the difficulty of auscultating such cases.

The remarks anent the diagnosis of phthisis apply equally to these cases.

Dysentery and Diarrhœa.—Except for malaria, these are by far the most common type of micro-organismal infections in asylums, as well as the most fatal. The dysentery, so far as my experience both at home and in India goes, is mainly of the bacillary type, but it is always a critical condition to deal with and very often terminates fatally. The incidence in Indian asylums, in my experience, is not nearly so great as is commonly supposed, many cases being diagnosed and treated as dysentery which are really suffering from colitis due to irritation from undigested food or some substance picked up and eaten by the patient when unobserved.

The difficulty in treating such cases is enormous, as it is much more common among the more degraded patients, who lie about naked, have no regard for cleanliness, but pass their motions anywhere, and probably soil themselves and their food. Such patients are too frequently addicted to eating anything they can lay hands on—excreta, mud, sticks, leaves, pebbles, are all one to them, and invariably find their way to their insatiable mouths, unless a constant watch is kept over them. The difficulty, therefore, in treating such cases can be well imagined, but it can to a certain extent be overcome.

All such cases should be at once isolated and placed under the supervision of the very best attendants available, their excreta should be promptly cleared up and burnt by a sweeper especially detailed for the purpose, and the strictest supervision exercised over personal cleanliness and what the patients eat. It sounds simple, but is really a most difficult task, though if it can be done the results of ordinary treatment are quite as satisfactory, on the whole, as among the rest of the population.

The number of cases of dysentery can be also enormously reduced if every latrine used by a dysenteric patient be burnt out with kerosene, and the barracks thoroughly disinfected with phenyl, while no one who has anything to do with such patients should have charge of anything connected with the feeding of the rest of the asylum.

Diarrhœa may be due to lack of proper secretion of the intestinal juices, causing an irritation of the intestinal tract by undigested food, or to irritation from some substance picked up and eaten during the day. Much the same remarks apply to it as to dysentery.

Malaria.—My experience among the insane in India has led me to regard them as no more liable to be attacked by malaria than are the rest of the community—in fact, I should say they were rather less so, for in asylums due attention is paid to drainage, standing water is sprinkled with kerosene, and a weekly issue of quinine during the malarial season is the rule.

The difficulty, however, is that, notwithstanding all one's efforts, a certain number of cases are bound to be overlooked at their commencement, and it is only when the patient is seriously affected and his constitution, at no time remarkedly strong, beginning to be undermined, that the illness is discovered.

Malaria seems also to take a firmer grip of the insane, and to have a more weakening effect on such patients, with the result that, though the percentage of deaths directly due to malaria may not be much larger than among the general population, yet indirectly it is the cause of a large number of deaths, patients, weakened by previous attacks of malaria, readily succumbing to other diseases, such as pneumonia and dysentery.

Under these circumstances, prophylaxis is our mainstay, and I would insist on the careful attention to efficient drainage, the application of kerosene to all stagnant pools around the house, and, above all, to the proper prophylactic use of quinine in every case of insanity, whether a private patient or in an asylum, as the baneful influence of malaria on such cases is very great indeed.

It must, however, be remembered that quinine is a powerful poison to the nervous elements, and that it must therefore be used with prudence and care, while the careless lavishness with which many people have recourse to it, especially in the East, cannot be too strongly condemned.

5. Menstrual Derangement.

One of the most common physical derangements among insane women in Europe is some alteration in the menstrual function—amenorrhœa and dysmenorrhœa being very common in all type of insanity. In India, however, such derangement is by no means common, and it is worth while, I think, spending a little space in describing the reasons for it.

Let us consider first the menstruation prevailing among women resident in India. Dr. Chunni Lal tells me that menstruation varies among healthy Indian women according to their mode of living. The peasant or village girl menstruates first as a rule between fourteen and sixteen years of age; her periods correspond closely to a four-weekly curve, and each period lasts about four days, rarely more; derangements of menstruation are rare in this class, and generally tend towards suppression. In the city or town bred female, on the other hand, especially among the richer classes, the girls menstruate much earlier—generally well before fourteen years of age; the periods are of longer duration (five to six days) and are menorrhagic in their tendency. Menorrhagia is a common condition among this class of female, and is probably due to their environment and mode of living: their leading a life of luxurious ease in hot, stuffy apartments; taking little, if any, exercise; eating plentifully of the richest of food, and allowing their minds to run mainly on one subject—their duty to their husbands and the procreation of children.

Among Europeans and Eurasians in India the climate and the mode of living seem to have a similar effect on the womenfolk as is seen in the city or town bred Indian women, and menorrhagia is a common complaint, while amenorrhœa or dysmenorrhœa is comparatively rare when we think of the frequency with which these last conditions are met with in England.

Having thus noted the conditions prevailing normally among women resident in India, let us now glance at the condition of things as they existed in 1912 in Agra Asylum, when this investigation was made.

Out of 48 Indian females under the age of forty, 12 suffered from disordered menstruation. Nine of these suffered from amenorrhœa—viz., 6 cases of mania, 1 case of melancholia, 1 epileptic, and 1 imbecile; of these 9, 2 cases are referable to childbirth—viz., 1 case of mania and 1 of epilepsy. Three cases of menorrhagia are also present—viz., 2 cases of excited melancholia and 1 of epilepsy.

Thus on the whole one cannot say there is much departure from the normal, though perhaps the incidence of amenorrhœa is somewhat increased. This, however, may be explained by the very much larger percentage of lower-class and peasant women in the asylum, among whom, as already shown, the tendency to amenorrhœa exists normally.

Out of nine European and Eurasian women under forty, seven suffer from menorrhagia, both as regards duration of flow and quantity of discharge, while two have normal menstruation. This result is very different from our experience in English and Scotch asylums, but is in all probability explicable by the very much larger percentage of chronic cases of insanity met with in Indian asylums, and also to the marked tendency to menorrhagia which normally exists among this class of the population in India.

If we may venture to generalise on such meagre figures, it would appear that menstruation in asylum cases in India, allowing for station of life and the results of climate, shows little, if any, departure from what might be expected among the sane population.

As a rule the appearance of a period tends to exaggerate the mental symptoms, and in cases of so-called recurrent mania menstruation seems at times to precipitate an attack, or if it occur during an exacerbation of the mental symptoms the flow is apt to be more profuse and of longer duration.

In one or two cases among Indian women I have elicited some history of deranged menstruation prior to the onset of the mental symptoms, but the reliability of such meagre information as one can gather on this point is always a matter for doubt.

CHAPTER XXVI

GENERAL TREATMENT

THE ideal treatment of insanity really lies in the early recognition of the physical symptoms which precede the mental manifestations in so many cases. At the present time, however, our knowledge in this direction is so meagre that until definite mental symptoms arise the condition is allowed, more often than not, to pass unnoticed, either through the patients, being ignorant of their danger, not seeking medical advice until too late, or when they do consult a doctor giving him a misleading account of their symptoms, which, in the absence of friends to reveal changes in habits, temperament, etc., are quite liable to lead to a mistaken diagnosis.

Prophylaxis.—As a rule every case of incipient insanity presents signs of nutritional failure. The patient looks ill; his skin is dry and unhealthy in appearance; he is losing weight, and troubled with dyspepsia, etc. Anæmia is usually present in such cases, and in certain of the toxic types a hyperleucocytosis with an increase in the polymorphonuclear elements precedes the onset of mental symptoms.

When in addition to the above symptoms the patient is nervous and irritable, troubled with insomnia, and has a high tension, rapid, irregular pulse, the possibility of an attack of insanity should always be kept in mind, especially where there is a neurotic taint in the family.

In such cases mental and physical rest are essential, and if the pulse be rapid and of high tension rest in bed is called for.

The diet should be liberal and nourishing, consisting mainly of milk and milk-puddings. Tea, coffee, alcohol, and butcher's meat should be strictly prohibited, while the patient should be encouraged to drink water freely between meals. Saline purges or enemata of normal saline solution should be regularly administered every third or fourth day. As a rule the symptoms subside rapidly under this treatment, but complete rest for at least two months should be insisted on.

Upbringing of Children.—In children of a neurotic heredity much depends on the method of their upbringing. Such children should be given a nourishing dietary, in which butcher's meat, tea, and coffee are reduced to a minimum. They should be encouraged to join in healthy outdoor games and sports, and their lives carefully regulated, any tendencies to loaf about in solitude or indulge in day-dreaming being firmly and promptly suppressed. Harshness is worse than useless in such cases, leading only to lying and cunning deception; the only chance ot guiding such frail craft through the perils of childhood and adolescence being the gaining of their affections and respect by kindness and tactful firmness. As such children approach the age of puberty their parents and guardians should be on guard for any signs of abnormal or undesirable sexual tendencies, should explain tactfully and by degrees the true relations of the sexes, and by encouraging frank and open enquiry lead to a proper understanding of life, and avoid that mock modesty and prudery which is so often the origin of a life of sexual perversion.

General Treatment.—Where the mental disease is fully developed the treatment practically resolves into the treatment of the physical symptoms, for, after all, mental diseases are in most instances an extension of physical disorders, and are best dealt with on the lines of common sense and general medicine.

In early acute insanities the *condition of the alimentary tract* calls urgently for treatment. Carious teeth are invariably a source of chronic toxæmia, and should be removed or stopped as soon as possible. Among Indian cases, too, a condition closely resembling pyorrhœa alveolaris is very commonly to be found, and in my experience seems often to be a factor in the production of the mental symptoms. Observation has led me to regard this more as a type of scurvy than as true pyorrhœa. It yields readily to treatment with tr. iodi—which should be applied to the bases of the teeth and well worked in between the teeth and the gums—and antiseptic mouth-washes; lime-juice is a powerful adjuvant in such cases, also tonics of iron and the phosphates.

Antiseptic mouth-washes and gargles, saline purges, etc., are also called for in cases of bacterial infection to remove the cause of the toxæmia as far as possible. In most early cases of insanity anorexia is a marked symptom, and in such cases food should not be forced upon the patient, as there is generally a marked deficiency in the secretion of the digestive juices, and if two or three pints of milk be taken in the twenty-four hours one should rest content. When artificial feeding is necessary the food should always be digested beforehand, whether it be given by the œsophageal or the nasal tube.

Tube Feeding.—For feeding with the *œsophageal tube* we require an œsophageal tube and funnel, which should have been previously thoroughly washed with warm water, and then coiled up carefully in a large, clean basin; a gag, with its levers covered with indiarubber or soft cloth, is also necessary; a small jug of cold water; a jug containing the food, which must be previously treated with pepsin; a small vessel of olive oil or glycerine; and a towel or waterproof sheet to prevent soiling the clothing. All these having been prepared, the patient is placed in a semi-recumbent position and the sheet carefully wrapped round him; the operator then takes the gag, and while an attendant steadies the head of the patient, gradually forces it between the teeth. Great care is needed during this part of the proceedings to keep the gag as nearly as possible at right angles to the plane of the teeth, for the least departure from this direction is apt to force a tooth out of the patient's jaw. The gag having been inserted, generally between the bicuspid or first molar teeth, the attendant in charge takes over the control of it, and is responsible for its being kept in position. The operator then, after lubricating the tube, passes it along the floor of the mouth and down the œsophagus for some 17 or 18 inches, when the escape of gas indicates the entry of the tube into the stomach. When this has occurred a small quantity of cold water is poured down the tube to ascertain if it be clear, and thereafter the liquid food should be given as quickly as possible. The food should be carefully examined before administration, and the operator must be certain that it is not too hot (about 70° to 80° F.). After the food has been administered the tube should again be flushed with cold water, and then rapidly and gently withdrawn, after which the patient should be placed in a recumbent position for about fifteen minutes to avoid the occurrence of vomiting.

The description sounds somewhat alarming, but in most cases it is a very simple matter, completed in less time than it takes to read the above details, and causing little, if any, discomfort to the patient.

When the *nasal tube* is resorted to practically the same appliances are required, except that a No. 12 or No. 13 nasal catheter with funnel replaces the œsophageal tube, and no mouth-gag is required. The patient should be in a sitting or semi-recumbent position, and his head steadied by an attendant. The nasal tube, having been lubricated, is then passed along the floor of one or other nostril—by no means always an easy matter, for a deflection of the nasal septum or an accumulation of dried mucus may completely obstruct the passage. During the passing of the tube the pharynx should be carefully watched for the reflex act of swallowing, when the tube can be passed into the œsophagus, otherwise the tube is liable to pass forward into the mouth, or curl up in the pharynx and cause choking. In the majority of cases choking occurs if the tube lodges in the pharynx, but in certain cases of stupor and G.P.I. the tube can be passed even into the trachea without causing any apparent inconvenience, and in such cases the only safeguard is to listen carefully to see that air does not pass through the tube during respiration. The rest of the operation is practically the same as with the œsophageal tube, except that during the act of withdrawal the tube must be firmly held between the finger and thumb of the right hand so that none of its contents can escape into the trachea.

Fever occurring in the insane is in India always a difficult problem to deal with, the question of malaria being an ever-present one, and having to be considered, as well as the possibility of the condition being purely a part of the insanity, as we have seen often happens in many types of mental disease. For this reason it is advisable, whenever possible, to make a blood examination of such cases, for though quinine is invaluable in its proper place, yet it is just as inadvisable to pile it unnecessarily into the insane as into the sane.

Hyperpyrexia as a purely mental manifestation rarely calls for treatment except in puerperal cases, and even there the condition is more probably due to physical than mental causes. When met with, the ordinary treatment for such a condition—cold baths, sponging, etc.—is alone required.

Subnormal temperatures are liable to occur in stuporose and exhaustion conditions, and require attention, calling for the application of hot bottles and extra blankets, and the administration of stimulants and hot milk, coffee, etc.

In acute toxic conditions, such as mania, acute melancholia, and katatonia, any sudden drop in the temperature of the patient is always suggestive of the onset of typhoid symptoms, and requires prompt attention and the administration of stimulants, the rectal injection of warm normal saline solution, and hot draughts of milk, etc.

Convalescence.—After the acute stage of any insanity is passed the patient should be encouraged to get outside, and endeavours made to stimulate his interest in his surroundings. Regular outdoor exercise should be arranged whenever possible, and regular work suited to his physical and mental capacity should be provided, as well as suitable amusements out of work hours. Walking exercise, tennis, football, hockey, cricket, are all possible even in an asylum, for such patients are as a whole imitative, and if one or two can be got to make a beginning others in time join in, and the exercise, both mental and physical, does incalculable good if it be properly supervised and the patients are not allowed to become over-fatigued. In epileptics especially, regular exercise, and fairly heavy exercise too, is of the utmost benefit, as in this way energy is worked off in its proper channels and the fits are less liable to occur.

Restraint.—In restless, violent cases we are often forced to adopt some one or other means of restraint. Various forms of appliances are in vogue, and each has some characteristic rendering it especially useful in a certain type of case. The forms most commonly in use are: (1) The padded room; (2) the sheet; (3) the strait-waistcoat; (4) the gloves or mittens; (5) Dr. Wolffe's "protective bed."

1. *The Padded Room.*—Although three or four of these are to be found in most asylums in Britain, I doubt if even one exists in India. Why this should be so was a constant puzzle to me on my first arriving in India, but I am bound to confess that I am now of opinion that they can be readily dispensed with out here. This sounds, perhaps, paradoxical after having stated that maniacal conditions are much more common in Indian than in British asylums; but the conditions are totally different in the two countries. In an Indian asylum if a patient shouts he is left alone—at most a sedative is given if he requires it—and allowed to shout to his heart's content, the other patients

apparently being in no way affected by the noise. In Britain such a patient seems to upset the whole place, and has to be shut up in the padded room, where he can shout certainly, but no one hears the music but himself. The padded room undoubtedly is useful in cases where patients go flinging themselves about reckless of the wounds and bruises thus caused, and also in cases of severe epilepsy; but I have found a thick layer of straw on the ground and a mattress on the top of that quite as serviceable.

The chief objection to such an appliance out here is primarily perhaps the initial cost, but mainly the extreme rapidity with which the climate acts upon rubber, which would necessitate its being renewed at least every two years, if not oftener. The climate, too, is a strong argument against it, as, even fitted with Tobyn's tubes and the most modern ventilators, such an apartment out here would be unbearably close and hot, unusable, indeed, for the greater part of the year.

Such a room is essentially a small cell, with floor, walls, and door completely cushioned with thick rubber pads, and lighted by small bull's-eyes, high up and quite beyond the patient's reach. A small trapped pipe leads off from the centre of the floor to carry off urine, etc., and ventilation is usually arranged for either by Sherringham's valves or Tobyn's tubes. The door is a double one, and the inner door is provided with a small flap shutter, fastening on the outside, for purposes of inspection.

A modification of the above, in use, I am told, in the asylum at Colombo, in Ceylon, consists of a room fitted—floor and walls—with movable panels of stout canvas tightly padded with oakum. This avoids the expense entailed by the rubber padding; but it seems to me more than likely that in a very short time the panels would become fouled and offensive, and, though their being movable undoubtedly permits of all possible airing and cleansing, a very suitable nidus for germs of all descriptions.

2. *The Sheet.*—This appliance is rarely, if ever, used now. It consists essentially of a stout canvas sheet, which is buckled to the bed over the patient. It has on its upper or outer surface two arrangements like pockets, into which the hands and arms of the patient are strapped. It is unnecessarily cumbersome, and too forcible in its action, and has practically dropped out of use now on this account.

3. *The Strait-waistcoat.*—This is an excellent means of restraint, especially in patients given to masturbation, to constantly

picking at their hair or skin, or assaulting other patients. It has, however, to be used with caution, as, though some cases never seem to mind it at all, others are liable to fret and worry about it, and often half an hour in it reduces such patients to a condition of extreme exhaustion. Even in this latter class its application is often of great use, for the moral effect is marvellous, and gives one a means of stimulating efforts at self-control. It must, however, be used with caution, and only as a last resource when all efforts at persuasion have failed.

It consists of a canvas body, fastening behind with three buckles, or else made in one piece like a jersey. From the body arms or sleeves come off, which continue beyond the hands and terminate in blind extremities, their ends being sewn up. From the end of the right sleeve a buckle, and from the left a strap, are led round the body and fastened behind the back, so that the arms are crossed on the chest. The special advantage of such an appliance is that the patient can get plenty of outdoor exercise even when under restraint.

4. *The Gloves, or Mittens.*—These are invaluable in cases given to masturbation or to picking or tearing their skin or hair. They consist of a pair of stout leather pockets, placed over the closed hand of the patient and fastened round the wrist with a buckle. As the hand is closed nothing can be grasped, and so our object is achieved quite simply in most cases, and, the patient's attention being distracted by the condition of his hands, it is often quite possible to remove the gloves after a week or so without the patient returning to his former habits. A rough-and-ready imitation of these can be carried out with a couple of bandages or dusters arranged over the closed hand and tied round the wrist.

5. *Dr. Wolffe's Protective Bed.*—This is a comparatively recent innovation, and has been much used in certain cases in the asylum at Basle. It is perhaps the best of all the methods at present in use, for instead of using forcible or mechanical restraint we are here employing what may be termed "psychical restraint."

It consists essentially of an ordinary Lawson Tait bedstead, with the sides raised up twenty inches and the ends fifty inches, so that it somewhat resembles a gigantic child's crib. Inside these iron bars is attached wire netting, and to the sides are hinged two frameworks of iron bars and netting which can be swung inwards and form a sloping roof over the patient. The lever mechanism controlling these flaps is, of course, outside the foot of the bed, and inaccessible to the patient. The side flaps can be worked independently of each other, and can be fixed in any position required. They can be turned right down outside the sides of the bed till they are in immediate contact with the legs of the bed, or raised till they meet and form an entire roof to the bed.

The bed, therefore, is intermediate between a padded room and a straight-waistcoat, and avoids most of the disadvantages of either. The patient remains in bed, in constant companionship and under constant supervision, and the disadvantages of the padded room are at once done away with. The patient enjoys the comparative use of all his limbs, can lie or sit at pleasure, and move his hands and arms freely, and hence we have a great advantage over the strait-waistcoat. Of course a certain number of cases cannot be allowed even this small amount of freedom, but such cases are rare indeed in India, and such beds, I hope, will soon find their way into our asylums here.

The effect of these beds on patients in Basle Asylum is said to be extraordinary, not only on restless, noisy cases, but in cases of delusional insanity and paranoia also; and in most, if not all, of the cases quoted the psychical effect was marked.

Before leaving the subject of restraint I would once more impress upon my readers the necessity of avoiding it whenever possible. It should only be used as a last resource, and even then should never be applied as a punishment, but only with a view of preventing harm accruing to the patient and others. A little tact and patience goes a long way in handling lunatics as in everything else, and where one man may be constantly resorting to some method of restraint, another man with a little tact and patience, a few chaffing remarks and kind interrogation or advice, may quiet some of the most turbulent patients and turn storm into calm, leaving the patient in entire possession of his liberty.

Hypnotism is, on the whole, best left alone in asylum practice and in our dealings with insane cases. It has been largely used in Europe, and occasionally good results have been obtained by it; but it tends to weaken volition and self-control still further, and I strongly warn the general practitioner against it, even though he may perhaps be an adept at it. In a certain few cases hypnotic suggestion may be at times employed with advantage, but such cases require to be selected with the greatest care, and I strongly advise my readers to leave hypnotism alone in this connection, or the probability is they will find they have done more harm than good by its use. The difficulty of hypnotising a lunatic is very great also, owing to the extreme difficulty there is in holding his attention, but it can be done if sufficient time and patience can be given to the task.

Serum-therapy.—Of late years the question of the bacteriological origin of many types of insanity has been a prominent one, and many authorities have been investigating it, with, on the whole, excellent results, and there can be no doubt that in the future serum-therapy will gain a wider scope in asylum practice.

As regards forms of insanity, such as mania and katatonia, in which at times a type of streptococcus has been found, polyvalent streptococcic vaccines have been used in such cases on one or two occasions, with, it must be confessed, no very definite or marked results; but as the early administration of the sera or vaccines is half the battle in physical diseases, such as diphtheria, and the injections have in most cases been tried only on patients of some months' standing, such reports are only to be expected, and judgment must be postponed till we hear the conclusions derived from further investigation.

Massage.—This, especially in the acute insanities and in conditions where exercise is contra-indicated and rest is essential, is a most useful auxiliary in our treatment of mental cases. It causes a muscular hyperæmia which suffices for the removal of waste products, and, at the same time, by withdrawing in this way blood from the cerebrum tends to quiet excitement and favour sleep. It must, however, be very carefully regulated, for if overdone or continued for too long a time it is apt to cause excitement. Gentle shampooing with the open hand over the whole surface of the body, working from the periphery upwards, is the best plan. The abdomen should always be carefully and thoroughly kneaded, and if it is found that the patient stands the shampooing well the muscles of the trunk and limbs may also be gently kneaded.

Massage should not be applied for more than five or ten minutes at first, but may be given three or four times daily. If the patient stands the treatment well the periods of application may be extended gradually up to half an hour.

In cases where there is much loss of weight and emaciation oil should be rubbed in by the masseur, and for this purpose I have found the crude cod-liver oil by far the most useful.

Massage is frequently useful also in constipated cases, kneading of the abdomen producing excellent results in most of such patients, and avoiding the constant recourse to purgatives which would otherwise be necessary.

Electrical Treatment.—Electricity may be employed frequently in mental and nervous cases, as well for the relief of special symptoms as for the general condition. Three methods of application are possible in such cases: (1) *The faradic current*; (2) *static electricity* (*high-frequency current*); (3) *galvanism*.

1. *The faradic current* is mainly used in cases of an hysterical type, and more for its stimulating moral effect than for any therapeutic action. I have used it frequently for hysterical paralyses and anæsthesia, and have invariably got good results from its use in such patients. For cases of insanity, however, it is to my mind worse than useless, as it merely tends to excite the patient without having any beneficial after-effect.

2. *Static Electricity*.—This method of electrical treatment is of great service in neurasthenic and hysterical cases, as well as in certain stuporose and melancholic cases. The patient is charged from one pole of the tertiary coil, and the charge may be allowed to dissipate itself gradually or may be taken off from any part of the body in the form of a spark, or, if a brusque effect be undesirable, the spark may be broken up by a suitable electrode and a milder stimulation obtained.

Besides the moral effect obtained by the withdrawal of the charge in the form of a spark, this method of treatment has a distinctly tonic and bracing effect, which is of great value in mental cases of the types mentioned above.

3. *Galvanism* is a form of electrical treatment which I am much given to using in all types of mental and nervous diseases. By my method of application moral effect is practically eliminated, but experience has given me an unshakable belief in its sedative and tonic effect in practically all types of mental and nervous diseases. I have used it in cases of hysteria, neurasthenia, mania, melancholia, delusional insanity, and certain stuporose cases, and in all instances have had marked improve-

ment to record, and in the majority of patients a perfect cure has resulted.

I administer it through a Schnee's four-cell bath, as by this means the dosage is more accurately estimated than is possible in a plunge-bath.

The dosage is as a rule 6 to 8 milliampères, and the length of each application from ten to fifteen minutes, and this is carried out three times a week except in very maniacal cases, when I give it daily at first in order to obtain the benefit of its sedative effect.

In excited, restless cases, and where the sedative effect is more urgently required, the anodes are attached to the arm-baths and the kathodes to the foot-baths, and the current is thus run through the body from the arms down to the feet. Where the tonic, bracing effect is required the above conditions are reversed, and, the anodes being attached to the foot-baths, the current traverses the body and emerges at the hands, which are immersed in the baths to which the kathodes are attached.

As already stated, no moral effect is desired from this method of treatment, and the current should be switched on and off very gradually and carefully, and no more should be given than suffices to give a tingling of the extremities immersed in the kathodal baths. Six to eight milliampères as a rule produce this effect, but in one case of mania I had at first to go up to 12 milliampères to get any result, though as the case improved I was able to reduce the dosage by degrees to the usual amount.

I would close this brief description by again emphasising my strong predilection for this form of electrical treatment in mental cases, and my conviction that its results in most cases are at least as good as, if not better than, those obtained by the use of static electricity, while the cost of the apparatus and upkeep are all in favour of galvanism.

Hydro-therapeutics.—Recourse may be had to these for two purposes—viz., (*a*) the sedative effect derivable from prolonged immersion in the hot plunge-bath; (*b*) the bracing effect obtained by the cold douche followed by a brisk rub down and a good reaction.

(*a*) *The Hot Bath.*—This is an excellent auxiliary in restless, excitable patients, or in those cases where insomnia is marked. It must, however, be used with caution, and only in cases where the physical condition is good, for if used in debilitated cases or in those where cardiac trouble exists dangerous collapses are liable to occur.

The method consists in the immersion of the patient in an ordinary plunge-bath at a temperature of 85° to 90° F. The immersion is continued for half an hour or even longer, the temperature of the water being kept at the same level throughout. Careful supervision of the pulse and condition of the patient is necessary, especially in the later periods of the immersion, to avoid any possibility of untoward occurrences. When the time of immersion has been sufficiently prolonged, the patient should be quickly dried with warm towels, clad in flannel bed apparel, and put to bed between blankets, the bed having been previously warmed with hot bottles. By these means everything possible is done to avoid the patient catching cold, and the sedative effects of the immersion are prolonged.

(*b*) *The Cold Douche.*—This consists of a douche of cold water, at a temperature of about 50° F., applied to the trunk and limbs for a period of fifteen to thirty seconds. Care must be taken to avoid the head, and, in hysterical patients, any hypersensitive zones, during the application of the douche. The douche should be followed by brisk friction with a rough towel.

In delicate or sensitive patients the douche may be begun with warm water which is rapidly cooled down. Other forms of cold bathing may be used to produce this effect, but reaction after the bath is essential, and if absent this form of hydro-therapy is contra-indicated.

The Weir Mitchell Treatment.—This method of treatment was introduced into this country by Playfair. It consists essentially in the removal of the patient from his home surroundings, from his family, his relatives and friends—from everything, in fact, which, by association, would stir up old worries and troubles —and placing him in the care of a suitable attendant in some home or some pleasant rooms in a quiet country or seaside village.

The choice of an attendant is of great importance. He must be kind, suitable, and firm, and in manners and education a suitable companion for the patient.

At first the patient is kept absolutely confined to bed and placed on a purely milk diet. Three ounces of fresh milk every three hours suffices for a beginning, but after two or three days this amount may gradually be increased up to ten or twelve ounces. Solid food is then gradually introduced into the dietary, till by degrees the full diet* is reached about the end of the second week. If any digestive troubles arise from the over-feeding, solid food must be stopped for twenty-four hours and then recommenced.

Massage is begun as a rule on the second or third day, and given twice daily. At first each sitting lasts for twenty to thirty minutes, but this is gradually increased till by the end of the second week, when the patient is on full diet, each sitting lasts for an hour to an hour and a half, the patient thus getting two to three hours' massage daily. After each sitting complete rest for an hour between blankets in a darkened room is advisable.

Electricity in the form of faradism to the larger muscles is sometimes used as an adjuvant to the massage, and may be begun about the end of the second week.

The surest test of progress is the weight of the patient. An emaciated patient may put on as much as five or six pounds a week in the beginning of the treatment, and later at least two and a half pounds; if two pounds, at least, are not gained during the week it may be assumed that things are not going well.

If the patient be abnormally fat it is necessary to reduce his bulk before starting the above treatment. Playfair recommends the following method: Confine the patient strictly to bed and place him on a diet of skim milk, at first two quarts per diem given in small quantities every two hours; but this amount should be gradually decreased till not more than a pint per diem is taken. When some fourteen to twenty pounds have thus been removed from the weight of the patient, pure milk may be substituted for the skimmed, and the treatment already described commenced.

In about six weeks the patient may begin to sit up and gradually return to normal conditions of life. When convalescence is well established a sea voyage or a trip to the Continent, with

* Dr. Playfair gives the following specimen of full diet:

Breakfast.—Plate of porridge with a gill of cream, fish or bacon, cocoa or café au lait.

At 11 *a.m.*—Cup of beef-tea, with two teaspoonfuls of beef peptonoids.

Luncheon at 1.30 *p.m.*—Soup or fish, joint or poultry, sweet.

At 5 *p.m.*—Beef tea and peptonoids as at 11 a.m.

Dinner at 7 *p.m.*—As for luncheon.

In addition it must be remembered that not less than 80 ounces of milk (10 ounces every three hours), sometimes 100 or 110 ounces, are being taken.

the attendant as companion, forms a good prelude to the return to home life and business routine.

This method of treatment is applicable to cases of hysteria and neurasthenia, and especially indicated in patients on the verge of a mental breakdown, but in whom no marked mental symptoms are yet apparent. It is on very similar lines also that we regulate the lives of our patients during the acute phases of all types of insanity, and it is particularly useful in melancholic cases, and those types of mental derangement met with at the climacteric, puberty, and old age.

Drugs.

From a perusal of the above pages it will be gathered that our treatment of mental cases is based mainly upon common sense and general medical principles. Even here, however, the knowledge of a bacterial toxæmia in many types of insanity is an excellent guide to the lines on which our treatment is to be based, and in all such cases purgation and disinfection of the alimentary tract, the mouth, nose, and naso-pharynx, are of great benefit. Calomel and salines are the best purges to use in such cases, and the occasional administration of large enemata is often of use in clearing the cæcum, especially if they be administered through the long rectal tube. Salol, in 5-grain doses, or liq. hydrarg. perchlor., ʒss., thrice daily, is as useful an intestinal disinfectant as any. During the administration of salol, however, the urine must be watched for symptoms of carboluria, and on its appearance the drug should be at once suspended. Medical izal is another drug which may prove serviceable in such conditions.

For disinfection of the mouth and naso-pharynx various gargles and nasal douches may be employed, those most commonly used being dilutions of hydrogen peroxide, cyllin, boracic acid, or potassium permanganate. The teeth should be carefully brushed after every meal, so as to keep the mouth as free from bacteria as possible.

Where the infection seems to be located in the lungs but little can be done. Inhalations of eucalyptus, creosote, etc., probably never reach the site of infection, or, if they do, are so diluted as to be of no effect, and the administration of creosote by the mouth is generally contra-indicated by the presence of gastric derangement and the probability of its exhibition causing nausea.

Hence, in these cases our attention must be mainly directed to building up the general health of the patient, strengthening his volition and self-control, and arousing an intelligent interest in his surroundings by means of suitable occupation and amusements. In puerperal conditions the uterus must be carefully examined and septic conditions treated.

Sedatives and Hypnotics.—Among a fair number of practitioners and students I fear the idea largely prevails that in sedatives and hypnotics lies the main treatment for maniacal conditions, and indeed for most forms of insanity. Nothing can be more erroneous, more harmful than such a belief, for though at times invaluable adjuvants in the treatment, no patient can or should be treated with them alone.

Before giving such a drug various questions have to be decided. Is the drug likely to disorder other functions while mitigating insomnia and restlessness? Is the drug tending to restore the natural sleep habit or is it forming a bad brain habit which it will be difficult to overcome—*i.e.*, is it setting up a drug habit? How does the patient look and feel in the morning after the drug sleep: is he refreshed or otherwise?

It must also be remembered that what is pleasant for the patient is not necessarily good for him, and that in many cases to effect a cure we require especially to strengthen the volition, and we rather delay than hasten this project by the administration of hypnotics.

Another question has also to be settled, and that is, What type of drug is required—whether a pure hypnotic, a general sedative, a motor depressant, or a combination of these? The reaction of patients to drugs varies widely, not only with the patient, but also at times in one and the same patient at different phases of his malady, and all this has to be carefully considered when we are going to order a sedative.

Roughly speaking, these drugs may be divided into four classes according to their mode of action: (*a*) *Pure hypnotics*, such as paraldehyde and chloral; (*b*) *hypnotic sedatives*—*e.g.*, sulphonal, trional, and veronal; (*c*) *sedatives, both cerebral and spinal*, such as the bromides and their combinations, with hyoscyamus and *Cannabis indica*; (*d*) *drugs which act by depressing the cortical motor centres*, such as hyoscine. We must therefore consider what class of drug is required before ordering blindly any sedative that comes into our mind, merely because we may have heard of its being useful in some other case of insanity, perhaps of a wholly different type from the one we ourselves are dealing with.

Opium and **chloral** are drugs I have little liking for in mental cases. In cases of brain exhaustion small doses of opium or morphia are strongly recommended by German and French authorities, and they undoubtedly have good results to show. The risk, however, of establishing a drug habit is very great in such cases, and I would recommend every possible means being tried to induce natural sleep in such cases before a drug is resorted to, and even then opium and chloral would be the last I should have recourse to, paraldehyde, in my opinion, being safer and better in every way. Opium, too, often seems to increase greatly the mental agitation of a patient, and this still further restricts its use. In fact, I limit its exhibition practically to cases of excited melancholia only, and in these I have often got wonderful results from a fairly small dose of some preparation of morphia.

Paraldehyde is one of the most valuable and reliable hypnotics at the disposal of the alienist, and very rarely indeed is its administration followed by any discomfort, or even the feeling of heaviness so common a sequel to the exhibition of other drugs of this class. One great feature in its action is that the drug sleep gradually passes into normal sleep, and in many cases there is a distinct tendency to restore the sleep habit.

Its use, however, has to be well considered, as even it will not suit all cases, and as a rule I make the pulse my guide under these circumstances. Thus in cases with high arterial tension and rapid pulse-rate, after all attempts at producing sleep by purgation, hot baths, etc., have failed, paraldehyde in large doses (2 to 3 drachms, or even more) is by far the best drug we have. Where the arterial tension is low, however, such a dose would be worse than useless, tending rather to exaggerate the condition, and in such cases 10 to 15 minim doses of paraldehyde, or sulphonal, grs. xx., or trional or veronal, grs. x., are rather indicated. In cases of extreme violence a cortical motor depressant is required, and here hyoscine is invaluable, $\frac{1}{200}$ to $\frac{1}{70}$ of a grain being injected subcutaneously. If, however, the violence be continuous then sulphonal, or a combination of it with the bromides, is indicated, being given frequently and in comparatively small doses.

Hyoscine and **hyoscyamine** must be given with care, and as a rule are best left alone, especially in acute cases, for there is always danger of their causing syncope. In such cases, too, especially in educated persons, I have seen vivid hallucinations of sight caused by these drugs. Consequently our administrations of these preparations should be mainly restricted to cases of chronic insanity accompanied by extreme violence.

The **bromides** are of great use, especially in those forms of insanity where there is marked depression and restlessness. In such cases the dose must be large (60 grains thrice daily), the patient practically being kept under the influence of the drug for some days and roused at periodic intervals to take food.

In epileptic cases bromides are our chief resource, and by their constant exhibition we can generally diminish both the number and severity of the fits.

Some years ago Richet and Toulouse pointed out that the absorption of bromides by the tissues was increased by the reduction of the chlorides present in food, etc. A special diet was drawn up by them whereby the chlorides, naturally present in the food, were reduced to a minimum, and the results are said to have been very successful. I have tried substituting bromide for the sodium chloride usually added to the diet to see if any increased effect would be obtained, and, as already stated (Chapter XX.), the results have been most satisfactory.

Sulphonal, trional, and **veronal** are very similar drugs.

Sulphonal is slow but cumulative in action, and should be given at least five hours before its effects are desired, or else should be combined with some other drug, such as potassium bromide. Owing to its cumulative action one dose often produces a good sleep on two consecutive nights, and this property also renders it an excellent auxiliary in cases of chronic excitement and restlessness. It is by no means a safe hypnotic, as so many of the laity fancy, for though some seem able to take it with impunity, others reveal a marked idiosyncrasy for it, and symptoms of poisoning occur. Muscular weakness, with incoordination of speech and action, vomiting, and other gastric disturbances are common in such cases, and hæmatoporphyrinuria practically invariably occurs, which is a serious condition, frequently terminating fatally in a few weeks. Sulphonal, therefore, must be administered with caution, and never continuously, and such patients should be carefully watched and the bowels opened daily by aperients if necessary.

Trional is more rapid in its action than sulphonal, and acts best in aged patients. Its bad effects are similar to those of sulphonal, but less common and milder as a rule.

Veronal is more uncertain, but acts well and rapidly in some cases. It is useless in insomnia due to pain. Its exhibition requires also the greatest care and supervision to prevent poisoning.

Antipyrin is a mild hypnotic which frequently proves valuable in cases of chronic restlessness and excitement due to a rapid, high-tension pulse. Its results are due almost wholly to its action on the bloodvessels, and hence to give it, for its hypnotic effect, combined with alcohol is absurd. It is a common belief that antipyrin is a dangerous drug, and very liable to cause syncope. Its action on the blood-pressure and pulse-rate has already been alluded to, and in cases where there is weakness of the heart as well as mental disorder one must naturally be careful and avoid this drug if possible. My experience of it, however, has led me to the conclusion that it is a very much safer drug than is commonly stated, and that it can be used freely if its action be remembered and due care and precaution taken in its use. Its bad reputation is due to the way in which, when first brought on the market, it was used lavishly by one and all, blindly, and in most cases with no knowledge of or thought for the proper dosage. Fatal results naturally ensued in many cases, and antipyrin had to bear the blame instead of those who used it foolishly and ignorantly.

Isopral is an hypnotic of more recent introduction. It belongs to the chloral group. It is taken readily by patients, and seems to produce a natural sleep without leaving any unpleasant after-symptoms. The dose is from 10 to 15 grains.

Dial is an hypnotic sedative closely allied to veronal. It is much more active than veronal, however, and is more rapidly absorbed and eliminated. It apparently is innocuous to the kidneys, and causes no irritation of the alimentary canal. The average dose is from 1½ to 3 grains, and its rapid disintegration and elimination prevent any cumulative effect; ¾-grain doses act well in cases of simple nervous agitation, and should be given thrice daily. For its hypnotic effect it should be given at bedtime in those patients whose insomnia is most marked in the early part of the night, but where the insomnia occurs in the small hours it should be taken on waking; 1½ grains is the usual dose in such cases, but in cases of extreme excitement it may be necessary to exhibit as much as 4½ to 6 grains. It appears to have a marked effect on epilepsy, either alone or in combination with such other drugs as the bromides, belladonna, or chloral.

Aponal is the popular term for amylene hydrate carbonate. It is an excellent hypnotic in insomnia of nervous origin, causing light sleep in about half an hour after administration, and having no bad after-effects. It is obtainable in tablets of 15 grains each, and the dose is 15 to 30 grains. It is readily soluble in alcohol or hot water, but almost insoluble in cold water and dilute acids and alkalis.

Monobromate of camphor is a substitution product of camphor, the hydrogen radicle being replaced by the halogen bromine. It is very volatile, and has to be kept in well-stoppered bottles. I have found it an excellent sedative in cases of hysteria and maniacal conditions where there is a strongly marked sexual element present. In stuporose conditions, associated in youths with masturbation, and in young women with disordered menstruation and sexual excitement, I have also had excellent results from the administration of this drug. It is my custom to dissolve the monobromate in almond or olive oil, emulsify this solution with mucilage and water, and prescribe it with extract. viburni prunifolii liq. This mixture requires to be dispensed daily, but in suitable cases its results are most satisfactory. I give as a rule 3 to 4 grains of the monobromate and ʒi. of extr. vib. liq. thrice daily, but I have given as much as 6 grains of the monobromate in a single dose.

Some writers consider monobromate of camphor liable to cause collapse, and recommend caution in its administration. I have never seen any such results myself.

Adalin is a very useful sedative in insomnia of nervous origin and in cardiac neuroses. As a sedative, 5 to 10 grains may be given three or four times daily. When its hypnotic result is desired, 10 to 15 grains, in a glass of hot milk, should be administered half an hour before bedtime.

Proponal is a somewhat dangerous drug, owing to the very small margin which exists between its therapeutic and toxic doses. The dose necessary to produce sleep is 5 to 6 grains, and a dose of 7 grains is liable to produce toxic symptoms.

Bromural is an excellent hypnotic in cases of neurasthenia, especially if marked excitability be present. It is a very safe drug to use, and its administration even in large doses is rarely, if ever, accompanied by toxic symptoms. The usual dose is 5 to 10 grains, but when necessary even 30 to 50 grains may be exhibited with safety.

A case is on record where a woman took 150 grains without any toxic symptoms, the only result being the production of a deep sleep for thirty-six hours.

Extractum piscidiæ liquidum (Jamaica dogwood) is at times a very useful sedative in cases of excitement with a markedly sexual trend. The dose in such cases should be a large one, ʒii. thrice daily, and I have seen excellent results from its administration in cases of the above-noted type.

Thyroid Treatment.

Thyroid treatment has of late come into prominence as a method of treating various forms of insanity, quite apart from those cases where the condition is due to disease or derangement of the functions of the thyroid gland.

It was first administered for the sake of the slight febrile attacks which result from its exhibition, for it was noticed that many insane patients began to improve mentally, and finally made good recoveries, after similar attacks arising naturally.

In such cases as a rule I confine the patient to bed, and give 30 grains of the extract daily for a week or ten days. After three or four days the patient's temperature becomes slightly febrile, rising to 99° to 100° F., and remaining so for nearly a week, when it returns to normal and remains there even if the drug be continued. Marked gastric derangement is caused by the drug, and nausea and vomiting occur readily during its administration. The pulse becomes rapid and irregular, and the arterial tension falls markedly, while there is a progressive fall in the leucocytosis, and the polymorphonuclear elements may fall below 40 per cent. Headaches, rheumatic pains, muscular tremors, profuse perspiration, and rapid loss of weight often accompany its administration, but as a rule can be alleviated by a mild purgative. It must be remembered that the administration of the drug tends to aggravate phthisical disease, and it is therefore contra-indicated in such cases.

Mentally its effects vary greatly in different cases, some becoming depressed, others maniacal, and others, again, emotional. Dr. Bruce explains this by the fact that a course of thyroid frequently reproduces for a short time the earlier acute symptoms of the mental disease from which the patient suffered. The question of thyroid extract being a direct cortical stimulant is still an open one. Undoubtedly in many cases of early secondary dementia, especially after acute mania, marked mental improvement has occurred during the administration of thyroid, but the condition is found on close examination to be as a rule more a state of subacute excitement than any mental improvement, and though possibly due to direct cortical stimulation by the thyroid, it is just as likely that the diminished leucocytosis may allow the persistent toxæmia, common in post-maniacal states, to gain the upper hand for the time being, and that the apparent improvement is really only a mild recurrence of the primary mania.

Thyroid should never be exhibited in the acute stages of mental disease, but only when these have subsided, and the case threatens to become chronic, and is in a subacute, perhaps stuporose condition. In acute cases, as I have already stated, the drug exaggerates the condition, either by acting as a direct cortical stimulant, or by allowing a greater degree of toxæmia from its effects on the leucocytosis.

When administered continuously, whether in large or small doses, much precaution is always necessary. Such patients should always be confined to bed, for the risk of heart failure is very great, and the diet must be carefully regulated and consist mainly of milk and farinaceous foods. Occasionally a toxic condition is noticed, with a rapid, thready pulse, dry, harsh skin, and subnormal temperature; but a hot drink and the application of hot bottles soon relieves this. In every case the lungs should be carefully examined before a course of the drug is commenced, for phthisical disease is invariably aggravated by its exhibition.

APPENDICES

APPENDIX I.

MODES OF PROCEDURE FOR DEALING WITH MILITARY INSANES.

A. European Soldiers domiciled in England or the Colonies.—These are brought before a Medical Board (A.F. B. 178) and then sent home by hospital ship. If a hospital ship be not immediately available they are detained either in the military hospital or sent to a specially detailed asylum (Yeravda), under Section 12 of Act IV., till such time as a hospital ship be available.

B. British Soldiers domiciled in India.—These are brought before a Medical Board (A.F. B. 178). The O.C. the hospital in which they are under treatment then discharges them in accordance with King's Regulations, para. 392, subpara. xvi., amended by Army Order (Home) No. 150 of 1918. They are then handed over to the civil authorities to be dealt with as civilians.

C. Indian Soldiers.—These are dealt with under para. 628, A.R.I., vol. ii. They are brought before a Medical Board, and if found to be insane are discharged from the Army in accordance with the terms of the Army Warrant. They are then handed over either to their relatives or to the civil authorities, according to the necessities of the case.

APPENDIX II.

SCHEDULE I., ACT IV. OF 1912.

FORMS.

(*See Section* 96.)

FORM 1.

APPLICATION FOR RECEPTION ORDER.

(*See Sections* 5 *and* 6.)

In the matter of A. B.,* residing , by occupation , son of ; a person alleged to be a lunatic.

To , Presidency Magistrate for (or District Magistrate of , or Sub-divisional Magistrate of , or Magistrate specially empowered under Act of 1912 for).

The petition of C. D.,* residing at , by occupation , son of , in the town of (or sub-division of , in the district of).

1. I am† years of age.

2. I desire to obtain an order for the reception of A. B. as a lunatic in the asylum of , situate at‡ .

3. I last saw the said A. B. at , on the§ day of .

4. I am the‖ of the said A. B. (or, if the petitioner is not a relative of the patient, state as follows):

* Full name, caste, and titles.

† Enter the number of completed years. The petitioner must be at least eighteen or twenty-one, whichever is the age of majority under the law to which the petitioner is subject.

‡ Insert full description of the name and locality of the asylum; of the name, address, and description of the person in charge of the asylum.

§ A day within fourteen days before the date of the presentation of the petition is requisite.

‖ Here state the relationship with the patient.

I am not a relative of the said A. B. The reasons why this petition is not presented by a relative are as follows: (*State them.*)

The circumstances under which this petition is presented by me are as follows: (*State them.*)

5. The persons signing the medical certificates which accompany the petition are*

6. A statement of particulars relating to the said A. B. accompanies this petition.

7. (If that is the fact) An application for an enquiry into the mental capacity of the said A. B. was made to the on the , and a certified copy of the order made on the said petition is annexed hereto. (Or if that is the fact)

No application for an enquiry into the mental capacity of the said A. B. has been made previous to this application.

The petitioner therefore prays that a reception order may be made in accordance with the foregoing statement.

Sd. C. D.

The statements contained or referred to in paragraphs are true to my knowledge; the other statements are true to my information and belief.

Sd. C. D.

Dated

Statement of Particulars.

(*If any of the particulars in this statement is not known the fact to be so stated.*)

The following is a statement of particulars relating to the said A. B.:

Name of patient at length.
Sex and age.
Married, single, or widowed.
Previous occupation.
Caste and religious belief, as far as known.
Residence at or immediately previous to the date hereof.
Names of any near relatives to the patient who are alive.
Whether this is first attack of lunacy.
Age (if known) on first attack.

* Here state whether either of the persons signing the medical certificates is a relative, partner, or assistant of the lunatic or of the petitioner, and, if a relative of either, the exact relationship.

When and where previously under care and treatment as a lunatic.

Duration of existing attack.

Supposed cause.

Whether the patient is subject to epilepsy.

Whether suicidal.

Whether the patient is known to be suffering from phthisis or any form of tubercular disease.

Whether dangerous to others, and in what way.

Whether any near relative (stating the relationship) has been afflicted with insanity.

Whether the patient is addicted to alcohol, or the use of opium, ganja, charas, bhang, cocaine, or other intoxicant.

(The statements contained or referred to in paras. are true to my knowledge. The other statements are true to my information and belief.)

(Signature by person making the statement.)

FORM 2.

RECEPTION ORDER ON PETITION.

(*See Sections* 7, 10.)

I, the undersigned E. F., being a Presidency Magistrate of (or the District Magistrate of , or the Sub-divisional Magistrate of , or a Magistrate of the first class specially empowered by Government to perform the functions of a Magistrate under Act IV. of 1912), upon the petition of C. D. of* , in the matter of A. B.,* , a lunatic, accompanied by the medical certificates of G. H., a medical officer, and of J. K., a medical practitioner (or medical officer), under the said Act, hereto annexed, hereby authorise you to receive the said A. B. into your asylum. And I declare that I have (or have not) personally seen the said A. B. before making this order.

Sd. E. F.
(Designation as above.)

To†

* Address and description.

† To be addressed to the officer or person in charge of the asylum.

Form 3.

MEDICAL CERTIFICATE.

(*See Sections* 18, 19.)

In the matter of A. B., of* , in the town of (or the sub-division of in the district of), an alleged lunatic.

I, the undersigned C. D., do hereby certify as follows:

1. I am a gazetted medical officer (or a medical practitioner
a holder of† (or declared by Local
declared by Government to be medical officer under Act IV. of
Government to be a medical practitioner under Act IV. of
1912) and I am in the actual practice of the medical profession.

2. On the day of , 19 , at‡ in the of (or the sub-division of , in the district of), (separately from any other practitioner,)§ I personally examined the said A. B., and came to the conclusion that the said A. B. is a lunatic, and a proper person to be taken charge of and detained under care and treatment.

3. I formed this conclusion on the following grounds—viz.:

(*a*) Facts indicating insanity observed by myself—viz.:

(*b*) Other facts (if any) indicating insanity communicated to me by others—viz.: (here state the information and from whom).

Sd. C. D.
(Designation as above.)

Form 4.

RECEPTION ORDER IN CASE OF LUNATIC SOLDIER.

(*See Section* 12.)

Whereas it appears to me that A. B., a European, subject to the Army Act, who has been declared a lunatic in accordance with the provisions of the military regulations, should be removed

* Insert residence of patient.

† Insert qualification to practise medicine and surgery registrable in the United Kingdom.

‡ Insert place of examination.

§ Omit this where only one certificate is required.

to an asylum, I do hereby authorise you to receive the sai A. B. into your asylum.

Sd. E.F.

(Administrative Medical Officer.)

To*

FORM 5.

RECEPTION ORDER IN CASE OF WANDERING OR DANGEROUS LUNATICS, OR LUNATICS NOT UNDER PROPER CONTROL OR CRUELLY TREATED (SENT TO AN ASYLUM ESTABLISHED BY GOVERNMENT).

(*See Sections* 14, 15, 17.)

I, C. D., Presidency Magistrate of (or Commissioner of Police for) (or the District Magistrate of , or the Sub-divisional Magistrate of , or a Magistrate specially empowered by Government under Act IV. of 1912), having caused A. B. to be examined by E. F., a medical officer under the Indian Lunacy Act, 1912, and being satisfied that A. B. (*describing him*) is a lunatic who was wandering at large (or is a person dangerous by reason of lunacy) (or is a lunatic not under proper care and control, or is cruelly treated or neglected by the person having the care or charge of him), and a proper person to be taken charge of and detained under care and treatment, hereby direct you to receive the said A. B. into your asylum.

Sd. C. D.

(Designation as above.)

Dated the

To the officer in charge of the asylum at

FORM 6.

RECEPTION ORDER IN CASE OF WANDERING OR DANGEROUS LUNATICS OR LUNATICS NOT UNDER PROPER CONTROL OR CRUELLY TREATED (SENT TO A LICENSED ASYLUM).

(*See Section* 14.)

I, C. D., Presidency Magistrate of (or Commissioner of Police for) (or the District Magistrate of , or the Sub-divisional Magistrate

* To be addressed to the person in charge of an asylum duly authorised by Government to receive lunatic Europeans subject to the Army Act.

of , or a Magistrate specially empowered by Government under Act IV. of 1912), having caused A. B. to be examined by E. F., a medical officer under the Indian Lunacy Act, 1912, and being satisfied that A. B. (*describing him*) is a lunatic who was wandering at large (or is a person dangerous by reason of lunacy) (or is a lunatic not under proper care and control, or is cruelly treated or neglected by the person having the care or charge of him), and a proper person to be taken charge of and detained under care and treatment, and being satisfied with the engagement entered into in writing by G. H., of (*here insert address and description*), who has desired that the said A. B. may be sent to the asylum at (*here insert description of asylum and name of the person in charge*), to pay the cost of maintenance of the said A. B. in the said asylum, hereby authorise you to receive the said A. B. into your asylum.

Sd. C. D.
(Designation as above.)

Dated the

To the person in charge of the asylum at

Form 7.

BOND ON THE MAKING OVER OF A LUNATIC TO THE CARE OF RELATIVE OR FRIEND.

(*See Sections* 14, 15, 17.)

Whereas A. B., son of , inhabitant of , has been brought up before C. D., a Presidency Magistrate for the town of (or Commissioner of Police for), (or the Magistrate of , or a Magistrate of the first class specially empowered under Act IV. of 1912). and is a lunatic who is believed to be dangerous (or deemed to be a lunatic who is not under proper care and control, or is cruelly treated or neglected by the person having the charge of him), and whereas I, E. F., son of , inhabitant of , have applied to the Magistrate (or Commissioner of Police) that the said A. B. may be delivered to my care:

I, E. F., above-named, hereby bind myself that on the said A. B. being made over to my care, I will have the said A. B. properly taken care of and prevented from doing injury to himself or to others; and in case of my making default therein,

I hereby bind myself to forfeit to His Majesty the King-Emperor of India, the sum of rupees

Dated this day of , 19

Sd. E. F.

(Where a bond with sureties is to be executed add):

We do hereby declare ourselves sureties for the above-named E. F., that he will, on the aforesaid A. B. being made over to his care, have the said A. B. properly taken care of and prevented from doing injury to himself or to others; and in case of the said E. F. making default therein, we bind ourselves, jointly and severally, to forfeit to His Majesty the King-Emperor of India the sum of rupees

Dated this day of , 19

(Signature.)

Form 8.

BOND ON THE DISCHARGE OF A LUNATIC FROM AN ASYLUM ON THE UNDERTAKING OF RELATIVE OR FRIEND TO TAKE DUE CARE.

(See Section 33.)

Whereas A. B., son of , inhabitant of is a lunatic who is now detained in the asylum at under an order made by C. D., a Presidency Magistrate for the town of (or Commissioner of Police for) (or the Magistrate of , or a Magistrate of the first class specially empowered under Act IV. of 1912), under Section 14 (or Section 15) of Act IV. of 1912, and whereas I, E. F., son of , inhabitant of , have applied to the said Magistrate (or Commissioner of Police) that the said A. B. may be delivered to my care and custody:

I hereby bind myself that on the said A. B. being made over to my care and custody, I will have him properly taken care of and prevented from doing injury to himself or to others; and in case of my making default therein, I hereby bind myself to forfeit to His Majesty the King-Emperor of India the sum of rupees .

Dated this day of , 19

Sd. E. F.

(*Where a bond with sureties is to be executed add*):

We do hereby declare ourselves sureties for the above-named E. F., that he will, on the aforesaid A. B. being delivered to his care and custody, have the said A. B. properly taken care of and prevented from doing injury to himself or to others; and in case of the said E. F. making default therein we bind ourselves, jointly and severally, to forfeit to His Majesty the King-Emperor of India the sum of rupees .

Dated this day of , 19 .

(*Signature.*)

APPENDIX III.

Form I.

FORMS OF ORDER AND WARRANT FOR REMOVAL OF EUROPEAN CRIMINAL LUNATICS TO ENGLAND.

V. Order of Removal of a Criminal Lunatic.

Colonial Prisoners Removal Act, 1884.

Whereas A. B. is in custody in the colony (or presidency, or) of , as a criminal lunatic, having been charged with the offence of , and found to have been insane at the time of such offence (or to be unfit on the ground of insanity to be tried for such offence), (or having been convicted of the offence of) and sentenced to penal servitude or imprisonment (or) for the term of years from the day of , 19 , (or for life), and afterwards certified (or lawfully proved) to be insane),

And whereas it is likely that the life (or health) of the said A. B. will be endangered (or permanently injured) by further detention in custody in the said colony (or presidency, or),

(Or the said A. B. belonged at the time of the said offence to the Royal Navy (or to His Majesty's regular military forces)),

(Or the said offence was committed wholly (or partly) beyond the limits of the said colony (or presidency, or)),

(Or by reason of there being no asylum in the said colony (or presidency, or) in which the said A. B. can be properly or conveniently detained and dealt with as a criminal lunatic, his removal to the United Kingdom (or to the colony (or presidency, or of .) is expedient),

(Or the said A. B. belongs to a class of persons who, under, the law of the said colony (or presidency, or), are subject to removal under the Colonial Prisoners Removal Acts 1884),

Now I do hereby, in pursuance of the Colonial Prisoners Removal Act, 1884, with the concurrence of the Government of the said colony (or presidency, or) (and the Government of the colony (or presidency, or) of), order that the said A. B. be removed to the United Kingdom (or to the colony (or presidency, or) of), there to be retained in custody as a criminal lunatic, and dealt with in the same manner as if he had there become a criminal lunatic.

Given under the hand of the undersigned, one of His Majesty's Principal Secretaries of State, this day of , 19 .

I, , the Governor (or Lieutenant-Governor, or officer administering the Government) of the colony (or presidency, or) of , with the advice of the Executive Council of the said colony (or presidency, or),

(And I, Governor, or Lieutenant-Governor, or officer administering the Government) of the colony (or presidency, or), of , with the advice of the Executive Council of the said colony (or presidency, or), hereby concur in the foregoing order of removal.

As witness my hand (our hands) this day of 19 .

Form 2.

WARRANT FOR REMOVAL OF A CRIMINAL LUNATIC.

Colonial Prisoners Removal Act, 1884.

To C. D., keeper of Lunatic Asylum, and to E. F. and G. H.

Whereas an order has been made, under the Colonial Prisoners Removal Act, 1884, by one of His Majesty's Principal Secretaries of State, with the concurrence of the Government of the colony (or presidency, or) of (and the Government of the colony (or presidency, or) of), for the removal of A. B., a criminal lunatic now in the custody of you, the said C. D., to the United Kingdom (or the said colony (or presidency, or) of), to be there dealt with in the same manner as if he had become a criminal lunatic in the United Kingdom (or the said colony (or presidency, or) of).

Now I do hereby, in pursuance of the said Act, order you, the said C. D., to deliver the body of the said A. B. into the custody of the said E. F. and G. H., or one of them; and I do hereby, in further pursuance of the said Act, authorise you, the said E. F. and G. H., or either of you, to receive the said A. B. into your custody, and to convey him to the United Kingdom (or to the colony (or presidency, or) of), and to deliver him to such person or persons as shall be empowered by one of His Majesty's Principal Secretaries of State (or the Governor of the said colony (or presidency, or)) to receive him for the purpose of giving effect to the said order of removal.

Given under the hand of the undersigned, one of His Majesty's Principal Secretaries of State (or the Governor of). this day of , 19

APPENDIX IV.

LIST OF ASYLUMS IN INDIA.

Assam : (1) Tezpur (Indians).

Bihar and Orissa : (1) Ranchi (Europeans) Central; (2) Patna (Indians).

Bengal : (1) Berhampur (Indians) Central; (2) Dacca (Indians).

Bombay : (1) Yeravda, Poona (Europeans and Indians) Central; (2) Naupada Thana (Indians); (3) Ahmedabad (Indians); (4) Dharwar (Indians); (5) Ratnagiri (Indians); (6) Hyderabad, Sind (Indians).

Burmah : (1) Rangoon (Europeans and Burmese) Central; (2) Minbu (Burmese Criminal Lunatics).

Central Provinces : (1) Nagpur (Indians).

Madras : (1) Madras Asylum (Europeans and Indians) Central; (2) Calicut (Indians); (3) Vizagapatam (Indians).

Punjab : (1) Lahore (Europeans and Indians) Central.

United Provinces : (1) Agra (Indians) Central; (2) Bareilly (Indians); (3) Benares (Indians).

Central Asylums under ordinary circumstances have mental experts as whole-time Superintendents; other asylums are collateral charges generally held by the Civil Surgeons.

APPENDIX V.

QUESTIONS THAT MAY BE PUT TO A MEDICAL WITNESS IN CASES OF SUSPECTED INSANITY.

1. Have you examined ?

2. Have you done so on several different occasions, so as to preclude the possibility of your examinations having been made during lucid intervals of insanity ?

3. Do you consider him to be capable of managing himself and his personal affairs ?

4. Do you consider him to be of unsound mind—in other words, intellectually insane ?

5. If so, do you consider his mental disorder to be complete or partial ?

6. Do you think he understands the obligation of an oath ?

7. Do you consider him, in his present condition, competent to give evidence in a Court of Law ?

8. Do you consider that he is capable of pleading to the offence of which he now stands accused ?

9. Do you happen to know how he was treated by his friends (whether as a lunatic, an imbecile, or otherwise) prior to the present investigation and the occurrences that have led to it ?

10. What, as far as you can ascertain, were the general characteristics of his previous disposition ?

11. Does he appear to have had any previous attacks of insanity ?

12. Is he subject to insane delusions ?

13. If so, what is the general character of these ? Are they harmless or dangerous ? How do they manifest themselves ?

14. Might such delusion or delusions have led to the criminal act of which he is accused ?

15. Can you discover the cause of his reason having become affected ? In your opinion, was it congenital or accidental ?

16. If the latter, does it appear to have come on suddenly or by slow degrees ?

17. Have you any reason for believing that his insanity is of hereditary origin? If so, please specify the grounds for such an opinion, and all the particulars bearing on it: as to the insane parents or relatives of the accused; the exciting cause of his attack; his age when it set in; and the type which it assumed.

18. Have you any reason to suspect that he is, in any degree, feigning insanity? If so, what are the grounds for this belief?

19. Is it possible, in your opinion, that his insanity may have followed the actual commission of his offence, or been caused by it?

20. Have you any reason to suppose that the offence could have been committed during a lucid interval, during which he could be held responsible for his act? If so, what appears to have been the duration of such lucid interval? Or, on the contrary, do you believe his condition to have been such as altogether to absolve him from legal responsibility?

21. Does he now display any signs of homicidal or of suicidal mania, or has he ever done so to your knowledge?

22. Do you consider it absolutely necessary, from his present condition, that he should be confined in a lunatic asylum? Or, again:

23. Do you think that judicious and unremitting supervision out of an asylum might be sufficient to prevent him from endangering his own life, or the lives or property of others?

APPENDIX VI.

LIST OF REFERENCES.

(*a*) **Statistical.**—(1) Provincial Asylum Returns for 1913. (2) Census Reports of India for 1901 and 1911.

(*b*) **Medico-Legal.**—(1) BROWNE: "Medical Jurisprudence of Insanity." (2) GUY: "Factors of Unsound Mind." (3) GUY and FERRIER: "Forensic Medicine." (4) LYONS: "Medical Jurisprudence." (5) MAUDSLEY: "Responsibility in Mental Disease." (6) OVERBECK-WRIGHT: "Mental Derangements in India." (7) TAYLOR: "Medical Jurisprudence." (8) WOODMAN and TIDY: "Forensic Medicine." (9) Indian Lunacy Act (Act IV. of 1912). (10) The Indian Penal Code. (11) Code of Criminal Procedure.

(*c*) **Psychological.** — (1) JUNG: "Analytical Psychology" (Chapter on the Contents of the Psychoses). (2) LOCKE: "Human Understanding." (3) STOUT: (i.) "Analytical Psychology"; (ii.) "Manual of Psychology."

(*d*) **Preventive Medicine.**—(1) CLIFFORD ALLBUTT: "A System of Medicine," vols. vii. and viii. (2) L. C. BRUCE: "Studies in Clinical Psychiatry." (3) OVERBECK-WRIGHT: "Mental Derangements in India." (4) WHITE and JELLIFFE: "The Modern Treatment of Mental and Nervous Diseases." (5) *Indian Medical Gazette*, October, 1914.

(*e*) **Anatomical and Pathological.**—(1) BEVAN LEWIS: "Textbook on Mental Diseases." (2) CRAIG: "Psychological Medicine." (3) BRUCE: "Studies in Clinical Psychiatry." (4) PURVES STEWART: "Diagnosis of Nervous Diseases." (5) H. CAMPBELL THOMSON: "Diseases of the Nervous System."

(*f*) **Psychiatrical.**—(1) BEVAN LEWIS: "Textbook on Mental Diseases." (2) BRUCE: "Studies in Clinical Psychiatry." (3) BUCKNILL and TUKE: "Manual of Psychological Medicine." (4) CLOUSTON: "Clinical Lectures on Mental Diseases."

(5) Craig : "Psychological Medicine." (6) Jung : "Analytical Psychology." (7) Kraepelin : "Psychiatrie." (8) Overbeck-Wright: "Mental Derangements in India." (9) Sajou : "Encyclopedia of Medicine." (10) Stoddart : "Mind and its Disorders." (11) Savage : "Insanity and Allied Neuroses." (12) Tredgold: "Mental Deficiency." (13) White and Jelliffe: "Modern Treatment of Mental and Nervous Diseases." (14) *Journal of Mental Science.* (15) *Indian Medical Gazette.*

INDEX